A

Peacekeeper

IN Africa

A project of the International Peace Institute

A Peacekeeper IN Africa

Learning from UN Interventions in Other People's Wars

Alan Doss

LYNNE
RIENNER
PUBLISHERS

BOULDER
LONDON

Published in the United States of America in 2020 by
Lynne Rienner Publishers, Inc.
1800 30th Street, Boulder, Colorado 80301
www.rienner.com

and in the United Kingdom by
Lynne Rienner Publishers, Inc.
Gray's Inn House, 127 Clerkenwell Road, London EC1 5DB

Library of Congress Cataloging-in-Publication Data
Names: Doss, Alan, author.
Title: A peacekeeper in Africa : learning from UN interventions in other
    people's wars / Alan Doss.
Description: Boulder : Lynne Rienner Publishers, Inc., 2020. | Includes
    bibliographical references and index. |
Identifiers: LCCN 2019035031 (print) | LCCN 2019035032 (ebook) | ISBN
    9781626378667 (hardcover) | ISBN 9781626378803 (pdf)
Subjects: LCSH: United Nations—Peacekeeping forces—Africa, Sub-Saharan. |
    Peacekeeping forces—Africa, Sub-Saharan. | Conflict management.
Classification: LCC JZ6374 .D67 2020 (print) | LCC JZ6374 (ebook) | DDC
    327.170967—dc23
LC record available at https://lccn.loc.gov/2019035031
LC ebook record available at https://lccn.loc.gov/2019035032

British Cataloguing in Publication Data
A Cataloguing in Publication record for this book
is available from the British Library.

Printed and bound in the United States of America

The paper used in this publication meets the requirements
of the American National Standard for Permanence of
Paper for Printed Library Materials Z39.48-1992.

5 4 3 2 1

For Soheir,
my wife, friend, and partner of more than four decades,
who in so many ways was with me on my journey in peacekeeping,
which would not have happened without her love,
encouragement, understanding, and fortitude.

And for our beloved children,
Carolyn, Rebecca, and Virginia,
together with Federico, David, and Francesco;
they have been our fixed pole in our very itinerant life.

In memory of my parents, Phoebe and Gerald Doss,
who made everything possible.

And to Kofi Annan,
whose humanity, wisdom, confidence, and generosity of spirit
inspired and guided me on my journey and beyond.

Contents

Foreword

Terje Rød-Larsen,
President, International Peace Institute

THE INTERNATIONAL PEACE INSTITUTE IS PROUD TO PRESENT Alan Doss's *A Peacekeeper in Africa: Learning from UN Interventions in Other People's Wars*. This volume reflects IPI's long-standing commitment to enhancing understanding of UN peacekeeping and peacebuilding.

For more than seven decades, UN peacekeeping operations have fulfilled an essential role in managing international crises. Since the first cease-fire monitoring mission in the Middle East, UN peacekeepers have become one of the most visible symbols of international cooperation. In response to the challenges of the time, they have continually evolved, taking on an ever-growing set of responsibilities—from disarming combatants and monitoring human rights to supporting elections and protecting civilians.

Alan Doss spent a decade at the highest levels of UN peacekeeping in Sierra Leone, Côte d'Ivoire, Liberia, and the Democratic Republic of the Congo—at the time, among the most vicious, intractable, and militarily robust operations in the world. Today, three of these missions—Sierra Leone, Côte d'Ivoire, and Liberia—are largely success stories, in which decade-long peacekeeping operations were able to close, leaving behind democratically elected governments and largely peaceful societies. And while the Democratic Republic of the Congo continues to face unacceptable levels of violence toward civilians and a worsening Ebola outbreak, the recent flawed but peaceful elections offer a glimmer of hope that the UN's role may yet evolve.

At a moment when peacekeeping faces enormous challenges, both politically in the Security Council and operationally on the ground, it is worth reflecting on the successes and failures of the past, and on the insights they may offer for UN operations under stress in Mali, Central African Republic, and elsewhere. Looking back on his years with the UN, Doss provides an unvarnished, firsthand account of the operations he led.

ix

The frustrations he recounts—with the Security Council, with UN headquarters in New York, with armed fighters and intransigent political leaders—are valuable both as history and for what they tell us about the limits of peacekeeping generally. The successes and satisfactions he relays—above all with the dedicated and courageous men and women with whom he served, as well as the countless individuals whose lives the UN has tried to make better—are valuable for their reminder of the UN's ability to rise above its limitations and the important contribution it makes to peace.

His perspectives on the future of peacekeeping are informed by its past—by its limitations and its ability to evolve. Alan Doss has done a remarkable job, not only in telling an extraordinary story on being a leader in the field, but also in having executed brilliant leadership under the most difficult of circumstances.

Acknowledgments

A BOOK, LIKE A LIFE, IS NOT ACCOMPLISHED ALONE. THERE ARE a number of people I must thank for their contributions and for ensuring that the final product is, I hope, reasonably readable.

First, I am deeply grateful to Lynne Rienner, my publisher, and to her team. She gave me great advice and warm encouragement. This book does not neatly fit into the roster of academic works and textbooks that her company publishes. So thank you Lynne for taking a chance with a new author and a personal story.

I am especially thankful to the International Peace Institute (IPI) in New York and its president, Terje Rød-Larsen, for sponsoring this book, which might not have seen the light of day without IPI's support. IPI's vice president, Adam Lupel, encouraged me to go ahead with the project, and both he and Jake Sherman, director of the Brian Urquhart Center for Peace Operations, reviewed the text and made excellent suggestions for its improvement, especially in the concluding chapter, where I peer into the future.

The IPI team was also most helpful with updates on recent policy and organizational changes at the United Nations of relevance to my narrative. Namie Di Razza, senior fellow at IPI, was particularly generous with her well-informed comments on the protection of civilians, one of the central themes of the book.

I have relied on the memories and suggestions of several former colleagues and associates from my peacekeeping days who graciously agreed to review the text. While any errors or heresies are mine, I do want to thank Lansana Gberie, Adrian Forster, Bert Coppens, Kevin Kennedy, Alexandra Novosseloff, Arslan Malik, and my wife, Soheir, who all waded through the manuscript. My thanks go as well to Hervé Le Coq, Herbert Loret, David Smith, and Ian Steele for comments and suggestions that have helped shape and enrich the book.

I consulted a number of friends and advisers from the academic and think-tank worlds. Let me acknowledge especially Mats Berdal, Department of War Studies, King's College London, and Thierry Tardy, head of the Research Division at the NATO Defense College, who read and commented on my first hesitant drafts. I also sought the advice of Ian Johnstone, dean ad interim, of the Fletcher School of Law and Diplomacy at Tufts University; Richard Caplan, Department of Politics and International Relations at Oxford University; Paul Williams of George Washington University; and the late Stephen Ellis of Leiden University. I am most grateful for their valuable insights and ideas.

Aliki Semertzi of the Graduate Institute in Geneva kindly assisted me with painstaking research and editing support that spared me many hours of homework, for which I owe her my deep appreciation.

I have also benefited from the youthful eagerness of a number of young colleagues who helped me with fact checking and digital editing at the Geneva Centre for Security Policy, where I was an associate fellow, and at the Kofi Annan Foundation. These include Andonis Marden, Emily Forster, Fukumi Orikasa, and Sulekha Agarwal; Michael Atkinson put some much needed order into my digital archive. I am particularly grateful to Chiara Cami at the Kofi Annan Foundation, who saved me from the tiresome but indispensable job of text formatting and the compiling of endnotes and bibliography while also aiding with research.

Though they may not be aware of it, my colleagues at the Kofi Annan Foundation have contributed to this book through the many debates we have had about peace and security in Africa and beyond. They are due my sincere thanks for their forbearance in enduring my frequent disquisitions as my writing progressed in fits and starts.

Finally, I want to express my indebtedness to the thousands upon thousands of people I worked with at the United Nations during my peacekeeping assignments. Some are mentioned in the chapters that follow; but whether they are named or not, they are part of my story. As I said, no life is accomplished alone—especially one lived in the maelstrom of peacekeeping operations.

—*Alan Doss*

1

A Journey in Peacekeeping

All wars are fought twice, the first time on the battlefield, the second time in memory.

—Viet Thanh Nguyen

My journey begins in the prosperous New York suburb of Westchester County, far from the hardscrabble battlefields of Africa, where the events I recount in this book unfolded. From there I commuted to United Nations headquarters in Manhattan and my job running the United Nations Development Group (UNDG), which had been set by the newly elected UN Secretary-General, Kofi Annan, as part of his reform program designed to enhance the impact of UN operations around the world.

One of my fellow commuters from Westchester was Hedi Annabi, assistant secretary-general in the Department of Peacekeeping Operations (DPKO) at UN headquarters. I first got to know Hedi (who was to die tragically some years later in the earthquake in Haiti, where he was heading up the UN peacekeeping mission) when I was leading the UN operation aiding Khmer refugees displaced into Thailand by the war in Cambodia. Hedi was working on the peace process that finally brought an end to that war (and the demise of the infamous Khmer Rouge), followed by the fielding of a UN peacekeeping mission to Cambodia.

Our professional paths crossed again in New York. In the late 1990s several new peacekeeping operations were established and Hedi was in charge of the planning for those missions, which he did with great professionalism, combining an eye for detail with a keen understanding of the political and organizational challenges inherent in a major peacekeeping deployment. One of those challenges was how to ensure cooperation between the peacekeeping mission and the UN development and humanitarian organizations already on

1

the ground (the so-called UN country team). Tensions between them bubbled to the surface, especially during times of crisis. Inevitably, those tensions were reported up the bureaucratic chain to UN headquarters, where I and Hedi tried to defuse or at least attenuate them, in line with the Secretary-General's call for a coherent "joined-up" approach to UN field operations.

On a December morning in late 2000, Hedi and I got off our train in Grand Central Station and headed toward the UN. Our conversation turned to Sierra Leone. Secretary-General Annan had recently visited the country following a major crisis that had almost derailed the United Nations Assistance Mission to Sierra Leone (UNAMSIL), the peacekeeping mission the UN had deployed to help end the bloody civil war. He had been dismayed by the poor state of relations between UNAMSIL and the UN country team (and more broadly the humanitarian community). Following this trip, the Secretary-General decided to reinforce the mission with the appointment of a deputy special representative of the Secretary-General (DSRSG) who would lead UNAMSIL's stabilization operations and head up the UN country team.

As we exited Grand Central, Hedi stopped, turned to me, and asked if I would be interested in the post. I said I would speak to my wife, Soheir, but my interest was certainly sparked. After nearly four years at headquarters, the opportunity of getting back to the field in a new and innovative post was a big pull.

After discussion with my wife, I let Hedi know that my name could go forward. A month later, my appointment was announced, and I was awarded the lofty title of the DSRSG for governance and stabilization. My journey in peacekeeping was about to begin.

Other People's Wars

In the long history of human warfare, UN peacekeeping operations are something of a novelty. Most people deployed in UN peacekeeping—soldiers and civilians alike—are not from countries that are seriously threatened or endangered by the conflict they are trying to contain or end. These are other people's wars.

UN peacekeepers are not sent forth with the usual aim of armies engaged in armed conflict: to impose their will on adversaries by force of arms. Peacekeeping demands a distinctive mindset and mode of engagement dissimilar from war fighting. Both employ armed soldiers, but with very different ends in mind. As one Indian commander who served with me in the Congo remarked, "You don't go to war in tanks painted white"—a reference to the UN practice of painting peacekeeping vehicles (military and civilian) white with distinctive black lettering (more on the UN "war of colors" later).

Peacekeeping operations are put in place at the request and with the consent of the so-called host government, however ineffectual, unrepresentative, or vile that government might be. UN forces are not armies of occupation (although some protagonists portray them as such). Nor do they normally exercise executive authority—they do not run the country where they are deployed.

These operations are something of a political conjuring trick. They are essentially a temporary convergence of concern that coalesces around a crisis—one usually characterized by a massive humanitarian disaster—rather than a stable alliance of national interests. They are put together as a desperate response to tragedies that the international community has failed to prevent. The UN departments responsible for mounting and managing these operations cannot count on a defined budget or call on armed forces that can be deployed at short notice. Every operation represents a new set of challenges, requiring intensive negotiation (particularly on their financing) among the member states of the United Nations.

All of these caveats have significant implications, which I explore, describe, and dissect in this book, for what peacekeepers can or cannot do.

A Peacekeeper's Journey

During my years as a UN peacekeeper, I was often invited to speak at conferences, symposia, and the like. I found that the remarks that really got the audience's attention were those where I recounted what I had learned in running large and complex peace operations. Several friends suggested that I should write about these experiences before they passed from memory. That is what I have now attempted to do.

My story focuses on the four African countries where I worked in UN peacekeeping operations. It encompasses a disparate cast of characters: warlords and warriors; politicians and prelates; advocates and activists; as well as ordinary people caught up in the bloody conflicts that progressively engulfed those countries. Some of those characters are still prominent; others are now forgotten or dead; a few languish in jail.

My account does not pretend or presume to tell the whole story of those conflicts or the ultimate impact that UN peacekeepers may have had on them. The origins of the conflicts that we were sent to contain or resolve were both proximate and profound, often reaching back to events, dramas, and tragedies that played out long before I, or any other peacekeeper, arrived on the scene. I throw only a passing light on some episodes in which I played a part.

UN peacekeepers have been deployed to deal with violent and protracted internal conflicts that have been years in the making. The troubles that overwhelmed countries like Sierra Leone were not temporary aberrations that suddenly emerged without warning. On the contrary: the past was never very far away and constantly intruded on the present. And because countries emerging from conflict appear to be especially vulnerable to a relapse into further conflict, peacekeeping mandates have become ever more complex and comprehensive as the international community has sought the ultimate fix for countries in deep trouble—peacebuilding.

Missions are now routinely tasked to go beyond the traditional confines of peacekeeping (providing inter-positional forces in support of peace agreements)[1] and expected to help resolve, or at least temper, the underlying drivers of conflict. So some understanding of the historical context that frames a peacekeeping mission is indispensable for understanding the complexities that such missions face. Consequently, in each of the country chapters, I give readers a glimpse of the past in order to better understand the present and the prospects for the future.

I have divided the story into four parts. In the first part, I delve into the peacekeeping operations in Sierra Leone, then Côte d'Ivoire, followed by Liberia, with a chapter on each country. The second part of the book covers my days as the special representative of the Secretary-General (SRSG) in the Democratic Republic of the Congo (DRC). That experience was especially intense and demanding, so much so that I have written four chapters on the DRC, reflecting the size, complexity, and significance of the United Nations Mission in the Congo (MONUC).

In the third part of the book I complement the mission-specific chapters with a few broader observations on the demands and constraints that peacekeeping missions face as they become entangled in other people's wars. I sketch some reflections about peace, politics, protection, and personalities and how they come together or don't. I ask whether leadership makes a difference, and if so, what kind of leadership works best, under what circumstances, and, by consequence, what are the limits of intervention by UN peacekeepers: In sum, where and under what circumstances can peacekeepers hope for success in their interventions?

In the fourth part I write about the challenges of running a large, multi-dimensional peacekeeping operation, and indulge in some speculation on the future of peacekeeping. I originally got involved in peacekeeping through my association with Kofi Annan's UN reform program. A quarter of a century later there are new reform efforts under way, and I ask if they will resolve, or mitigate, the complexities and contradictions that I encountered during my peacekeeping assignments.

Not long before I left New York for Sierra Leone and my first peacekeeping post, I met Secretary-General Annan on the margins of the Security Council, where he was attending a meeting on Africa. Hedi Annabi introduced me to him with some encouraging words. We then briefly discussed the situation in Sierra Leone and the need to get the UN country team and UNAMSIL working together. At the end of our conversation, he wished me well, saying "have fun" and adding that this would be a UN job unlike any other. How right he was.

Part 1

Things Fall Apart: West African Wars

A nation must believe in three things: It must believe in the past. It must believe in the future. It must above all believe in the capacity of its own people so to learn from the past that they gain in judgment in creating their own future.

—Franklin D. Roosevelt

Before I donned my (figurative) blue beret, I had headed up United Nations Development Programme (UNDP) offices in several African countries. So Africa was not new to me and I certainly did not think of or dismiss Africa as a homogeneous entity. In living, working, and moving around Africa, the ethnographic, cultural, political, and historical differences between and within regions and countries became very evident. It is a mistake to think of the many conflicts in Africa all emanating from a single source, even if the perpetrators, the forms, and the consequences of these conflicts—abusive security forces, marauding rebels, mass atrocities, child soldiers, rape, and refugees—bear some similarity from one country to the other.

In the decades following independence, several West African states descended into anarchy and violence. But their disintegration cannot be solely, or even largely, attributed to a single factor. The withdrawal of foreign patronage at the end of the Cold War did unsettle autocratic regimes that could no longer count on unquestioned political or security support of a major power. However, that realignment of international interests was not the principal cause of state failure. And while some countries were destabilized by, or were implicated in, the troubles of their neighbors, state collapse was not predestined in a West African version of the so-called domino effect.

So what caused these states to fail? They failed for a variety of reasons: domestic dissension stirred by ethnic rivalries, personal enmities, and

5

especially the competition for public largesse through the capture of state institutions all played their part in the spread of discord. As one disappointed politician in Liberia said to me after an election defeat, "If you are not in government, you are not in anything."

All of the contemporary states of West and Central Africa are the legacy of colonial enterprise of one kind or another; they are not nation-states that emerged from an incremental process of warfare, territorial expansion, and cultural assimilation. Africa's indigenous nation building was aborted by colonization, which either dismantled local centers of political power or absorbed them in larger administrative entities created by the colonial overlord. As a consequence, post-independence Africa is a continent of states that are building nations rather than nations building states. And as has been pointed out by Daron Acemoglu and James Robinson in their masterful survey of state failure,[1] nascent African polities and their economies were deeply impacted and adversely shaped by slavery and the pernicious slave trade, which was rampant in West and Central Africa.

The African Union (AU) (or more accurately its predecessor, the Organization of African Unity [OAU]) accepted the colonial boundaries even though it was evident that many of the states were constructed around an uncomfortable amalgam of disparate ethnic groups held together only by the power of the colonial presence. That OAU decision, which has never been seriously questioned by African states, has had two major consequences in the post-colonial era.

First, there have been almost no wars of territorial aggrandizement (unlike in Europe, where almost none of today's states have the same frontiers that they had a century ago). In the Horn of Africa, Ethiopia fought against its breakaway province of Eritrea while Somalia's attempts to create a greater Somalia provoked a military response from Ethiopia. Of course, several states intervened in the Congo wars and Tanzania invaded Uganda to oust Idi Amin, but these were not wars of premeditated conquest.

The second consequence of the decision to stick with the colonial demarcation is that multiethnic, multicultural, and multilingual states are the norm in Africa. So instead of wars between countries, many smaller wars have erupted within countries as various groups and leaders struggle to capture or resist the state, spawning abusive regimes and rapacious rule,[2] sometimes with the support or connivance of external powers.

Because much of my book dwells on the misfortunes of some African countries, I run the risk of conveying a very pessimistic impression of the continent as a whole. Although I write about what went badly wrong in some West and Central African countries, we should not fall into the trap of believing that everything is going wrong in Africa.

Despite setbacks and mistakes, there has been huge economic and social progress in Africa since the early years of independence. Africa is full of vibrant, diverse societies with rich cultural, linguistic, artistic, and religious traditions and values. Even in the countries that have needed a peacekeeping presence, common humanity has not disappeared. Far from it—on many occasions, I witnessed how individuals and communities stood up to the violence with enormous courage and determination. People suffered, survived, and have gone about rebuilding their lives and livelihoods with amazing resilience, showing that the past does not have to be the prologue for the future.

2

Sierra Leone:
The Search for Peace

The problem with leaderless uprisings taking over is that you don't always know what you get at the other end. If you are not careful, you could replace a bad government with one much worse!
                                                        —Chinua Achebe

When I first entered State House after my arrival in Freetown, the capital of Sierra Leone, I came across a forgotten but intriguing footnote to British colonial history. In the entranceway there was a plaque commemorating the founding of the Province of Freedom in 1787. That name, for what became the country of Sierra Leone, has an inspirational ring to it, implying liberation from oppression and the promise of opportunity.

Indeed, by the standards of the day, Sierra Leone was a place of progress. As Lansana Gberie, a Sierra Leonean writer told me, "Sierra Leone was the first modern entity where women had the right to vote." He added that "by the 1840s higher proportions of school age children attended school in the small colony enclave than in Britain."[1] Sadly, Sierra Leone could not sustain that progress. For a good part of the modern era, the country has suffered from social decay and economic decline.

This chapter first briefly charts the decline and fall of the state of Sierra Leone, which culminated in civil war and the rise of the notorious Revolutionary United Front (RUF), triggering in turn regional and UN military interventions. I then turn to the UN peacekeeping mission deployed to Sierra Leone, which was a central element of the international response to the crisis. I look at the role that I played in the mission following my appointment—in an institutional innovation—as the DSRSG for governance and stabilization, and as coordinator of UN operational activities; I conclude with some thoughts on that experiment and experience.

9

The Return

British abolitionists and philanthropists founded the Province of Freedom as a place of resettlement for former slaves who had fought with the British during the American Revolutionary War (1775–1783). In 1792, a second wave of African American refugees from that war joined them, under the auspices of the Sierra Leone Company, which established the settlement of Freetown.

The British government abolished the slave trade in 1807. Subsequently, the Royal Navy intercepted ships carrying slaves and landed them in Freetown, ironically a point of departure for the export of slaves in earlier times. Over time the initial immigrants and landed slaves coalesced into a group quite distinct from Sierra Leone's indigenous peoples; known as the Krio, they came to dominate local political and commercial life.

Freetown, and the peninsula where it is located, became a British crown colony in 1808. However, the people living in the hinterland, which constituted the great majority of the territory's population, remained under the rule of traditional chiefs. Several decades later, the chiefs entered into a formal relationship with the British crown after the interior became a British protectorate in 1896.

In 1957, following devolution of powers from London, parliamentary elections were held and won by Sir Milton Margai, the leader of the Sierra Leone People's Party (SLPP). Margai led the negotiations leading to Sierra Leone's independence in April 1961.

Margai died prematurely in 1964 with fateful consequences. Siaka Stevens, a trade union leader who split with the ruling party, won election as Margai's successor. His leadership was autocratic and deeply corrupt, provoking a procession of attempted coups that profoundly destabilized the country but did not dislodge Stevens.

Despite his disastrous rule, Stevens survived long enough to be able to stand down in 1987. He was succeeded by his designated successor, Joseph Momoh, an army commander later deposed in an army coup in April 1992 led by twenty-five-year-old Captain Valentine Strasser, who established the National Provisional Ruling Council (NPRC) and declared himself head of state (the youngest in the world at that time).

The Rise of the Revolutionary Front

Momoh's overthrow resulted in good part from his inability to halt the carnage unleashed by the Revolutionary United Front. Although the RUF was originally founded at Fourah Bay College in Freetown, it was not an organized movement based on a guiding ideology; it instead became a dystopian amalgam of the dispossessed, the discontented, and the defenseless. In some respects, the RUF was an "army" of the underclass, assembled without regard for religious affiliation or tribal origin. Lansana Gberie, in his pungent analysis of the RUF, colorfully described it as an "organized mass delinquency."[2]

Starting in Kailuhun district in southeastern Sierra Leone in 1991, the RUF pushed at an open door and quickly overran much of the eastern area of the country, including the diamond-rich district of Kono. The Sierra Leone Army (SLA), undermined by corruption and poor leadership, was unable to contain the RUF, making matters worse with its own brutal abuses of the civilian population. Even though the RUF was aided by weapons and fighters from Liberian warlord Charles Taylor (later to become the president of Liberia), the state of Sierra Leone crumbled from within, not from outside forces.

The RUF's foot soldiers were mostly young, poor, and uneducated. Many were child soldiers who had witnessed or participated in hideous atrocities. My meetings with the RUF were always unpredictable, and violence was never far from the surface. RUF commanders acquired fearsome reputations for their extreme and indiscriminate ferocity. "Sierra Leone" and "RUF" became bywords for "horror." The amputations, rapes, and other atrocities inflicted on the civilian population by the RUF attracted worldwide attention and condemnation.

The RUF derived much of its drive and notoriety from Foday Sankoh, who had been thrown out of the army for mutiny in 1971. By the time I arrived in Sierra Leone in early 2001, Sankoh was already in jail pending trial for war crimes before the Special Court for Sierra Leone (SCSL), so I never met him, although at one point I had to ask the government to allow UN doctors to examine him. Sankoh had suffered a stroke and was nonresponsive, but the prosecutor of the special court wanted to be sure that he was not malingering. Koka Rao, UNAMSIL's medical officer, assured me that he was not and then persuaded the Sierra Leone authorities that he should be hospitalized at a UN medical facility, where he died.

Sankoh was a product of his times. The economic decay, institutional collapse, and violent turmoil that overwhelmed much of West Africa in the decades following independence favored the emergence of charismatic, articulate, and ruthless figures like Foday Sankoh and Charles Taylor. Both of them received training and support from Colonel Muammar Qaddafi in Libya (along with the future leaders of Burkina Faso—Thomas Sankara and Blaise Compaoré), who was busily fomenting trouble in the region in an effort to extend his political influence and revolutionary zeal.

By many accounts,[3] Sankoh was a mix of populist agitator, shrewd negotiator, and remorseless thug. He was an instinctive demagogue capable of easily rousing a crowd. Recruited into the SLA before independence, he received training in the UK and Nigeria. The supreme irony is that he actually served in a UN peacekeeping force (with the Sierra Leone contingent) in the Congo at roughly the same time as Olusegun Obasanjo, who later, as president of Nigeria, helped put an end to the RUF.

A Democratic Interlude

As the war ebbed and flowed, the SLA gradually drove back the RUF with the help of an intervention force dispatched to Sierra Leone under the auspices of the Economic Community of West African States (ECOWAS).[4] But by 1995, the RUF was again able to gain control of the diamond-producing areas. Facing the complete collapse of his forces, Strasser resorted to hiring a consortium of mercenaries quixotically named Executive Outcomes. Largely of South African origin, with experience in counterinsurgency operations in Angola and Namibia, the Executive Outcomes mercenaries halted the RUF advance.

The mercenaries' success allowed the revival of democratic hopes. Pressed by the international community and Sierra Leonean activists, the NPRC agreed to elections. However, internal quarrels erupted in the NPRC, leading to Strasser's ouster in January 1996 in yet another coup; this one was led by Strasser's former comrade-in-arms and deputy, Brigadier Julius Maada Bio (who today, by an ironic turn of the wheel of fortune, is the elected president of Sierra Leone).

Mass demonstrations led by civil society activists forced Bio to allow the planned national elections to go forward in March 1996. These were won by Ahmed Tejan Kabbah of the SLPP, who had returned to Sierra Leone after retiring from a career at the UN.

The RUF still threatened much of the country and so the election could not be held everywhere because of inadequate security. Nevertheless, the result was widely accepted in Sierra Leone and the international community. A peace agreement[5] was negotiated with the RUF in Abidjan in November 1996. The agreement included a package of measures intended to disarm and demobilize the RUF and reform the SLA. But the OAU and UN also pressed Kabbah to terminate the contract with Executive Outcomes, which he reluctantly agreed to do (probably to his regret in light of what happened a few months later).

The Abidjan agreement did not stop the violence. An army rebellion in March 1997 freed Major Johnny Paul Koroma from prison (he had also been imprisoned for mutiny), who proceeded to set up the Armed Forces Revolutionary Council (AFRC). Koroma quickly enlisted the support of Sankoh (by then in exile in Nigeria) and other RUF commanders. A combined force of SLA elements loyal to Koroma and the RUF marched on Freetown, devastating the city and forcing President Kabbah into exile in Guinea.

This time there was a more vigorous response from the international community and regional powers in support of the popular discontent that erupted after the coup. The Abidjan agreement mandated ECOWAS Cease-fire Monitoring Group (ECOMOG) to bring back the constitutional order, by force if necessary. By March 1998, thanks to the ECOMOG intervention, the Kabbah government returned to Freetown.

However, despite its success in expelling rebel forces from Freetown, ECOMOG was not able to advance much beyond the capital and its immediate hinterland. In January 1999, the RUF, allied with remnants of the AFRC, again attacked Freetown, inflicting murderous reprisals on the civilian population in an operation terrifyingly but aptly labeled "No Living Thing."

The Price of Peace
Although ECOMOG repulsed the January attack, the security of the country remained extremely precarious. Encouraged by regional leaders, the Kabbah government agreed to reopen negotiations with the AFRC/RUF, resulting in a ceasefire and the convening of a peace conference in the Togolese capital, Lomé. The conference, which brought Foday Sankoh out of exile in Nigeria, culminated in the Lomé Peace Agreement, signed in July 1999.

The Lomé agreement[6] was highly controversial. Sankoh was granted an absolute and free pardon and awarded the chairmanship of a national commission established for the management of strategic resources, national reconstruction, and development,[7] with the status of a vice president, answerable only to the president. This commission was charged with securing and monitoring the exploitation of Sierra Leone's gold and diamonds.[8] The agreement also created a commission for the consolidation of peace,[9] later handed over to the direction of former mutineer Johnny Paul Koroma. For the Sierra Leoneans who had suffered at the hands of the RUF and AFRC, the agreement was tantamount to paying the arsonists to put out the fire.

Kabbah was harshly criticized in Sierra Leone for failing to stand up to the RUF. Some years later, he told me that while he did not trust Sankoh, he had no option but to sign the Lomé deal, claiming that he could not count on the loyalty or effectiveness of the Sierra Leone Army, and that the ECOMOG force had also shown its limitations. Moreover, Olusegun Obasanjo, who had just assumed office in Nigeria, was keen to reduce Nigeria's commitment to ECOMOG, which had proved costly in blood and treasure (Nigeria provided the bulk of the troops and most of the funding for its operations).

Enter the United Nations
In July 1998, the Security Council had authorized the small United Nations Observer Mission in Sierra Leone (UNOMSIL) "to monitor the military and security situation in the country as a whole, as security conditions permit."[10]

It was a very modest effort comprising at the outset only twenty-four military observers. Faced with burgeoning demands for missions in Kosovo, East Timor, and the Congo, the Security Council was not keen on creating another full-scale peacekeeping operation.[11]

The Council's reticence was challenged by the Lomé agreement, which called for a dramatic expansion of the UN role in Sierra Leone. The Council, under international and especially UK pressure, relented and in October 1999 agreed to establish a fully-fledged peacekeeping operation to work with other parties to implement the Lomé agreement. But the new operation—the United Nations Assistance Mission to Sierra Leone[12]—began life on shaky grounds. Secretary-General Annan had proposed to President Obasanjo to share the security responsibilities with ECOMOG. However, Obasanjo demurred and threatened to pull out if the ECOMOG force was not funded under international auspices.

Obasanjo's demand came as a surprise for the UN, which did not expect to take over sole responsibility for security. Nevertheless, the Security Council responded in a sanguine fashion to the Nigerian ultimatum. In February 2000 it authorized[13] a 6,000-person force with a Chapter VII mandate, subsequently raising the troop ceiling to 11,000 as ECOMOG forces began to leave Sierra Leone.

ECOMOG had held the line against the RUF and the AFRC and suffered heavy casualties in doing so. Despite criticisms of ECOMOG's tactics and behavior, ECOWAS did what no others had been willing to do. Now it was the UN's turn. Would it do any better?

UNAMSIL's responsibilities largely resembled those entrusted to ECOMOG in the Lomé agreement. However, it included an explicit provision for the protection of civilians—the first of its kind for a UN peacekeeping operation[14]—which has had huge significance for just about every UN peacekeeping operation since. UNAMSIL's mandate directed it to "afford protection to civilians under imminent threat of physical danger,"[15] reflecting Kofi Annan's "call to arms" made in his landmark report to the Security Council in 1999[16] on the protection of civilians in armed conflict.

A Mission in Trouble: The May Crisis

Not yet at full force level and still finding its feet, UNAMSIL quickly ran into trouble.[17] In May 2000, the mission and the government of Sierra Leone launched the program aimed at the disarmament, demobilization, and reintegration (DDR) of RUF combatants. These are tricky exercises at the best of times. This one went spectacularly wrong. The RUF commanders were not ready to disarm and they attacked UNAMSIL units, taking several hundred peacekeepers hostage. UNAMSIL commanders had not deployed their forces in concentrated, defensive positions, on the assumption that they were there to support the implementation of a peace agreement and to oversee the DDR program.

The RUF once again was on the verge of marching into Freetown and evacuations began. This was a crisis that threatened the credibility not only of UNAMSIL but also of UN peacekeeping more broadly—still recovering from the setbacks suffered in Somalia, Rwanda, and the Balkans—as a viable instrument of international security cooperation. Indeed, as Bernard Miyet, then head of UN peacekeeping, told me, there was even talk in the UN of pulling UNAMSIL out, which he refused to accept. The UNAMSIL crisis seemed to underscore systemic failings of peacekeeping and undoubtedly influenced the thinking of Lakhdar Brahimi in his seminal report on peacekeeping operations published a few months later, in August 2000.[18]

At the request of Secretary-General Annan, the United Kingdom fielded a mechanized brigade to bolster the Freetown defenses and to secure the airport; the immediate crisis was contained. Led by Brigadier David Richards (who subsequently went on to become chief of the UK defense staff), Operation Palliser prevented the advance of the RUF forces and provided a vital breathing space for UNAMSIL to regroup and for the UN to secure the release of the hostages with help from an unlikely source—Charles Taylor. He was prevailed upon to exert his influence with the RUF to secure their release, which he did, hoping perhaps that this intervention would gain him some support to deal with an increasingly violent insurgency challenging his rule in Liberia (if this indeed was his calculation, he was mistaken—the insurgency eventually forced him out of office).

The Fall of Sankoh

The reaction in Freetown to these events was dramatic. Outraged by the attacks and already unhappy with the Lomé agreement, the people of Freetown went into the streets to protest. These protests culminated in a massive demonstration outside the residence of Sankoh, who had returned to the capital following the signing of the accord in Lomé. His bodyguards fired on the crowd, killing several protestors and further enraging public opinion. The government moved to arrest him. After initially fleeing his house, Sankoh returned and was captured. It was never clear why he went back, but one senior member of the police told me that he did so to recover his rainy-day fund—a cache of rough diamonds hidden in the house.

Sankoh was not the only casualty of the RUF attack. Popular opinion turned against UNAMSIL. Media and advocacy groups denounced the mission as ineffectual and incompetent. SRSG Olu Adeniji, a senior diplomat from Nigeria (and subsequently Nigerian foreign minister under Olusegun Obasanjo), and the UN force commander, Lieutenant-General Vijay Jetley of India, were both roundly criticized amid calls for their removal. The deputy force commander, General Mohammed Garba of Nigeria, clashed with Jetley, who had accused him of covering up wrongdoing by the Nigerian contingent in UNAMSIL; Garba in turn blamed Jetley for failing to share vital intelligence and relying on a coterie of Indian officers.[19]

As I learned later from my own experience, relations within a mission's leadership can easily go off the rails in times of crisis. While there may be genuine differences of opinion on questions of policy, the interplay of personalities looms large, magnified by the exhaustion and exasperation that happens when people are operating in the hothouse of a mission under extreme stress.

The Fallout

The upshot of this imbroglio was the removal of both Jetley and Garba. Lieutenant-General Daniel Opande, a Kenyan veteran of earlier peacekeeping operations, was named UN force commander, and Major-General Martin Agwai of Nigeria replaced Garba. However, India took offense and decided to withdraw its contingent. While Adeniji stayed put despite the pressures to remove him (Nigeria threatened to quit the mission if he was fired), UN headquarters decided to reinforce the mission with the assignment of Behrooz Sadry, another veteran of peacekeeping operations, as the DSRSG responsible for management and planning.

The May events also amplified the distrust between the mission, the UN country team, and the many international nongovernmental organizations (NGOs) that were dealing with the humanitarian crisis in Sierra Leone. There was a cascade of criticism, brought on by the breakdown of communications among the mission and the humanitarian community at the height of the crisis.

In the aftermath of the crisis, as I mentioned earlier, the UN Secretary-General visited Sierra Leone in December 2000 to assess the situation. He was surprised, a colleague present at the time told me, by the absence at the airport of any senior member of the UN country team to greet him on arrival. Perhaps this was simple oversight, but it seemed to signal that not all was well in the UN house. Subsequently, in his remarks to UN staff and the media, Annan was at pains to emphasize the need for close collaboration, stating that "it is vitally important that you pull together as one—as a single United Nations."[20]

Another source of disquiet that emerged during the visit was the apparent reluctance of the Sierra Leone government to actively restore its authority in areas not controlled by the RUF. This complaint was voiced not only by the UN but also by donor partners, the NGOs, and civil society, which blamed the government for a lethargic unwillingness to start rebuilding the presence of the state in the areas under its control.

Following his visit, Annan decided to appoint a second DSRSG who would focus on the restoration of state authority while also promoting greater operational cohesion among the peacekeeping mission, the UN country team, and the humanitarian community.

This then was the train of events that led to my early-morning conversation with Hedi Annabi in the Grand Central concourse and my subsequent appointment to the Sierra Leone mission.

First Steps

Institutional innovation does not come easily to the UN. My appointment to UNAMSIL, and with it the integration of several functions assigned to a single individual rather than dispersed among several officials, was a contentious innovation. Yet despite the novelty of my appointment, which conferred on me multiple "hats"—DSRSG, UN resident coordinator, UNDP resident representative, and UN humanitarian coordinator—I was appointed with remarkable celerity.

Jordan Ryan, the highly able chief of staff of the UNDP administrator Mark Malloch Brown (and later on my deputy in Liberia), drew up the terms of reference. The Secretary-General's office and DPKO quickly approved the draft, which then circulated for interagency review. We completed the whole process in a week or two—the speed of light by UN procedural standards. No doubt Mark's own close relationship with the Secretary-General helped, but he also anticipated possible objections from the humanitarian agencies and took the precaution, as the chairman of the UN Development Group, of calling key players like Carol Bellamy of the United Nations Children's Fund (UNICEF) and Catherine Bertini of the World Food Programme (WFP) to assure them that humanitarian concerns would not be marginalized or subordinated to political expediency (true, as I relate further on).

Arrival in Salone

Due to the war, no international airlines flew into Lungi, the airport that serves Sierra Leone (*Salone* in the patois, Krio). So my first port of call was Conakry, in the neighboring Republic of Conakry. From there, UNAMSIL helicopters shuttled incoming passengers to Lungi and then flew them over to the mission headquarters in Freetown (to get to Freetown by road required a lengthy journey over broken roads plus an intermittent and uncertain ferry crossing).

As the helicopter descended into Lungi, I caught first sight of the massive UN presence. The airstrip was rimmed by an impressive flotilla of passenger and military helicopters (including the lethal M24 gunships) along with a fleet of cargo and passenger aircraft. A container city, workplace and home to UNAMSIL civilian and military staff, sprawled around the runway. A fleet of armored personnel carriers and SUVs completed this prodigious display of UN might, all of which seemed to confirm that peacekeeping is a very expensive response to failed government.

My awe grew on arrival at UNAMSIL headquarters, which was installed in a former Sofitel hotel—the Mamy Yoko. There I discovered that UN peacekeeping operations love abandoned hotels: they have lots of bedrooms for offices and officers; restaurants that become canteens; and conference facilities that convert into situation rooms. The Mamy Yoko still bore the bullet marks of rebel attacks. None of the elevators worked and the plumbing gave off a distinctive odor of raw sewage. To my pleasant surprise, however, I was awarded an office overlooking the magnificent sweep of Lumley Bay. From up there, one could appreciate why—in better times—the Freetown peninsula had been a tourist destination.

While I had a "room with a view," I did not have a ready-made staff, but there were a number of vacancies that I could use to recruit for my office. At that time, it was surprisingly easy to hire (or transfer) people in contrast to later years when recruitment became increasingly bureaucratic. I was able to bring in some colleagues who had worked with me in the UNDG and UNDP. Hervé Lecoq, Carole Joseph, Jessica Eliasson, and I became the nucleus of a highly capable team who provided the energy and imagination for much of my work as the newly minted DSRSG.

A Man of Many Hats

My terms of reference were expansive. As the DSRSG, I was tasked to "assist the Government of Sierra Leone in extending its authority and institutions throughout the country; stabilizing areas under its control; rehabilitating national institutions; and, in due course, planning and organizing elections." I was also expected "to plan and supervise the implementation of reintegration projects and peace-building initiatives."[21] At the same time, as the UN resident coordinator, I had to coordinate the UN's operational activities, essentially focusing on development cooperation. As the humanitarian coordinator, my job was to encourage and build coordination among the UN, bilateral agencies, and NGOs to ensure that victims of the war got the support they so desperately needed.

Given the scope of my responsibilities, I realized that I would need to navigate the institutional cross-currents carefully and build relationships within and outside the mission. That started with the SRSG. I had not been chosen by him. There was another complication too. In the aftermath of the crisis of May 2000, Adeniji's relations with the UK had turned quite frosty. It was rumored that I (a Brit) had been selected in a British maneuver to keep a close eye on him. The contrary was true. The British high commissioner to Sierra Leone, Alan Jones, a good friend and steadfast supporter of UNAMSIL, later confided to me that he had actually advised against my appointment, fearing that Adeniji would indeed see it that way.

Aware of these sensitivities, I took care to build a solid rapport with Adeniji and to avoid giving any impression that I might be surreptitiously reporting on him. Despite the initial coolness, I developed a respectful and constructive relationship with Adeniji. I can honestly say he never interfered with any of my decisions in the humanitarian or development areas. Once he concluded that I was not there to undermine him, he was open to my advice.

I also made sure to build close relations with the incoming UN force commander, General Daniel Opande, and his deputy, General Martin Agwai. Both were highly professional soldiers and definitely not gung-ho types. Their caution earned UNAMSIL public criticism from Sierra Leonean politicians and the media (blue helmets taking a break on Lumley Beach always attracted derisory commentary) as well as some elements of the UK military mission. Nevertheless, Opande and Agwai quickly gained the respect of the military units within the mission and, indeed, the RUF.

My other day job was to oversee the operational activities of the UN in Sierra Leone wearing my UN coordination hats as well as representing the UNDP. The humanitarian responsibility was especially sensitive, as I soon learned at my first meeting with representatives of the humanitarian community when it was suggested that I should set up my principal office outside of UNAMSIL in order to safeguard humanitarian neutrality. Right up front, I decided not to take that route, as I was sure that it would greatly reduce the effectiveness of the novel arrangements that the Secretary-General had put in place with my appointment. Quite the opposite, I felt I could best improve relations between UNAMSIL and the humanitarian community by working from within the mission.

Besides, the UN Office for the Coordination of Humanitarian Assistance (OCHA), which backstopped me in my role as the UN humanitarian coordinator, was not part of the peacekeeping structure. Led by an experienced American colleague, Dennis Johnston, who had a delightful penchant for colorful Hawaiian-style shirts and large cigars, the OCHA office worked well. I decided to spend my energies on improving relations between UNAMSIL and the humanitarian community rather than forcing further institutional integration, which was sure to unleash a turf fight.

I did decide, however, to keep an office in the UNDP to support my resident coordinator and UNDP roles. Bert Coppens, a seasoned and steady UNDP hand (who years before had been posted in Freetown during the Siaka Stevens despotism), joined me along with a genial and perceptive Ghanaian economist, Eugene Owusu, to handle day-to-day operations. I mandated weekly meetings with the UNDP staff and every fortnight with the heads of UN agencies so as to keep key colleagues aware of what I was doing and why.

As part of a "big tent" strategy, I reached out to civil society and the NGO community (national and international). While embassies scale back or close in times of violent conflict, NGOs expand. Many of the large international NGOs (INGOs) were present in Freetown as well as dozens of local NGOs (there was some rivalry between two groups) together with an assortment of civil society organizations.

Collectively, they constituted not only a huge operational capacity in the humanitarian sector but also an invaluable source of information about what was going on around the country. I was cautious, however, in trying to tap into this reservoir of information. NGOs and civil society actors were skeptical of UNAMSIL and concerned about getting too close to the mission for fear that they would compromise their neutrality. Nevertheless, some, like the Campaign for Good Governance, headed by activist Zainab Bangura, offered sound advice and balanced opinion, even though she was not uncritical of the mission.

A Special Relationship

Although I had never worked in Sierra Leone before, I did have one personal association with the country. Many years before, President Tejan Kabbah and I had worked together as colleagues in the UNDP's Africa Bureau in New York. Nevertheless, I was anxious to avoid creating any friction with the SRSG, who might have resented my using a back channel to the president. So I worked closely with the minister in the president's office, Momodo Koroma, and the secretary to the president, Sheka Mansaray, both of whom were close to the president.

The government of Sierra Leone was of course not just the president. With my several hats, I soon met with most departmental ministers and their senior officials. I had an easy rapport with them; being a Brit probably helped (we were generally well regarded locally as a consequence of the military intervention). But my association with the president may have given me some clout too—ministers occasionally asked me to put in a good word with "His Excellency."

Actually, my first meeting with a departmental minister, the minister of planning, Kadie Sesay, turned out to be quite a testy surprise. I called on her in my capacity as UN resident coordinator and UNDP representitive to talk about planning for postconflict recovery. Having struggled up to her seventh-floor office (the elevators in the ministry's building having long given up), I was out of breath and ill-prepared for the sharp criticism the minister launched at me over UNDP's failings, which included an insinuation of corruption arising from contract awards. This took me aback but I promised to look into the matter and take action if required (which I did). That meeting was a salutary and worthwhile reminder that although the country was on life support from the UN and other international partners, it still had strong-minded ministers willing to ask hard questions.

Meetings and More

My "big tent" approach made for many meetings with much of my time spent shuttling from office to office across Freetown. Years of neglect had turned the roads into a jarring tangle of chassis-fracturing potholes linked by sparse stretches of tarmac that quickly turned into rivers of brown slurry during the rainy season. These daily excursions across the city required a tortuous navigation around the cavalcade of decrepit, fume-dispensing, overloaded mini-buses and cars that crowded the streets of Freetown. This, I soon realized, was where many of the trade-in vehicles from Europe went to die—on the thoroughfares of African cities. In Sierra Leone, however, they displayed bold declarations of faith that told us, "With God, all things are possible"; we should "Try Islam!"; "God answers prayers"; and that "Allah's justice is best."

During these forays, I also started keeping an inventory of the extraordinary array of Christian sects that had sprouted all over the capital (and indeed throughout West Africa). They too conveyed an imaginative roster of inspirational themes: Wonder Church International, Faith Assembly of God, Word of Faith Ministries, and Central Christian in Action Church, to name but a few. The churches were sometimes no more than an open-air meeting place with a few ragged banners where the pastor would rev up the faithful with fiery and lengthy sermons that evoked God's wrath and mercy, delivered via ear-splitting acoustics.

These churches—largely funded from the pockets of their congregations—reminded me of the many chapels that once dotted the towns and valleys of South Wales, where I grew up. Those chapels had thrived in hard times, providing spiritual fellowship and comfort to the working poor. So too in West Africa, where the proliferation of denominations reflects the same search for solace and support by people who live uncertain and precarious lives; they were also a reminder that private thrift is possible even in the midst of penury.

People and Priorities

I have dwelt on the importance of relationships because I knew they would have a profound impact on the integration initiative that we were trying out in Sierra Leone. I understood that I would have to manage ("juggle" might be a better word) my institutional relationships with some dexterity if I was to get close to fulfilling the large ambitions set out in my terms of reference. However, I was less certain of how I should prioritize the multiple tasks that the terms of reference sketched out. Priorities imply choice: So how would I manage the competing demands on my time and energies?

In reality, events dictated my priorities. Three emerged as the top of the do-now list: support for the disarmament process; stabilization and the restoration of state authority in "liberated" areas; and expanding humanitarian access to vulnerable populations.

Getting to Peace

Despite the May 2000 debacle, the government, encouraged by hardline Deputy Minister of Defense Samuel Hinga Norman, demanded UNAMSIL to recover RUF-controlled areas, by force if need be. The Freetown press was having a field day, energetically denouncing the mission for its perceived sloth and spinelessness. Activist organizations like Human Rights Watch had taken to criticizing UNAMSIL for its lack of "robustness." The successful rescue operation mounted in September 2000 by UK special forces to rescue British servicemen taken hostage by the West Side Boys (essentially remnants of the ex-AFRC) left UNAMSIL looking passive by comparison.

An Opening to the RUF

Despite the pressures, Adeniji remained reluctant to seek an armed confrontation with the RUF, preferring to open a dialogue. To do so, he brought the weight of Nigeria to bear and arranged for Obasanjo to bring together representatives of the government, the RUF, ECOWAS, and UNAMSIL in Abuja in November 2000. The RUF agreed to a ceasefire and to resume the DDR program as well as allow unimpeded UN access to RUF-controlled areas.

This success, however, did not translate into movement on the ground. Despite the entreaties of the UN and ECOWAS, RUF leader Issa Sesay, who had taken over as interim leader in the absence of the imprisoned Sankoh, stalled, claiming that he had to consult his field commanders before the RUF could implement the agreement. He also demanded the release of Sankoh as a precondition for further progress in the peace process; he then added additional conditions, including the establishment of a government of national unity pending new general elections.

The Choirboy

Issa Sesay was about thirty years old but still looked like a choirboy. Despite his boyish looks, Sesay had gained a fearsome reputation for violence, which eventually earned him a life sentence from the Special Court for Sierra Leone. But Sesay had none of Sankoh's charisma, eloquence, or political cunning and he was clearly not comfortable in the presence of senior UN officials (except for the force commander, General Opande, with whom he developed an almost paternal relationship).

I met Sesay for the first time in Makeni in early 2001, where the RUF had set up a makeshift headquarters. I had gone there as the UN humanitarian coordinator with Carolyn McAskie, acting head of the UN's Office for the Coordination of Humanitarian Assistance in New York. We wanted to persuade the RUF to release child soldiers as had been promised in the Abuja ceasefire agreement. It was a bizarre meeting. Sesay arrived with his bodyguards, mostly teenagers wearing Bob Marley T-shirts (but one also emblazoned with an unforgettable line: "I've used all my sick leave, so I'm calling in dead"), together with the mandatory aviator sunglasses. They were adorned with heavy gold chains and amulets (a treasured item among West African fighters due to their supposed power to ward off bullets); and like teenagers everywhere (at the time), they were equipped with a couple of boom boxes. More worrying, they casually sported an assortment of lethal weaponry including a couple of RPGs (how they might have been used in the confines of the small house where we were meeting was, to say the least, a troubling thought).

Although a diplomat by profession, Carolyn did not engage in diplomatic chitchat. She bluntly told Sesay that he needed to release the children or face the consequences. Sesay made some perfunctory remarks about the peace process and why the RUF was refusing to move ahead with the Abuja agreement. Mostly, he remained taciturn and seemed a bit overawed by Carolyn. Nevertheless, he did commit to release some children provided they would be taken into care by the UN and not the government services, which he refused to recognize unless there was a government of national unity. We left the meeting unsure whether we had made any impact, but to our pleasant surprise, dozens of children were released a few days later.

My next meeting with Sesay, some weeks later, was less composed. I met him to discuss the deployment of the Sierra Leone Police (SLP) to Makeni. Sesay turned up high and drunk. His bloodshot eyes flaring, he launched into an angry and not very lucid tirade against UNAMSIL. Obviously, we were not getting very far and my close-protection team was becoming increasingly nervous about Sesay's erratic behavior in front of his teenage bodyguards, so I suggested a break. We went outside for a breather and I noticed an SUV painted in a vivid canary yellow parked close by. The SUV, it turned out, was Sesay's newly acquired pride and joy, which he was delighted to show off to me. We kicked the tires and the mood turned more cordial. He calmed down and we parted on reasonably good terms. Nevertheless, after that encounter, I understood better why the rank and file of the RUF, and indeed his fellow commanders, were very apprehensive of Sesay and his volatile moods.

Over the following months, I met other RUF military commanders as well as foot soldiers from the rank and file. Conversation was difficult and could quickly deteriorate into confrontation. Very few of them had held any office, military or civilian. One who had (until he as was dismissed for misconduct from the police) was Augustine Gbao, the RUF security chief. When I met him to talk about police deployment, he railed at the injustices of life in Sierra Leone, but this flowed more from his own personal resentments than any reasoned ideological conviction. As Lansana Gberie and others have noted, the RUF was not an organization with defined political goals and a structured agenda (different from the rebellion that I was to encounter later in Côte d'Ivoire).

Impatience Grows

In the absence of any tangible signs of progress in the peace process, the government and the public became increasingly impatient with the RUF and, by extension, UNAMSIL. The mission was publicly chastised for its apparent lack of aggression. Among the sternest of our critics was the UK minister for international development, Clare Short. I was present at one particularly heated encounter during which, in so many words, she accused Adeniji and UNAMSIL of cowardice. How much of her broadside was UK policy as opposed to vintage Clare was not entirely clear, but given the critical military and financial support that the UK was providing to Sierra Leone, her words carried weight, especially in Freetown.

To his credit, Adeniji did not rise to the bait; nor did Martin Agwai, representing the military. They kept their cool, responding with a clearheaded explanation of why they believed that the gradual buildup and forward deployment of UN forces allied to a regional political strategy to pressure the RUF was the best way forward.

Adeniji delegated me to accompany Short as UNAMSIL ferried her around the country. She was not shy about expressing her opinions. Among the places we visited was the town of Bo, Samuel Hinga Norman's fief and the base of the Civil Defense Forces (CDF), a militia commanded by him. On that occasion (and indeed others), she displayed her oratorical skills to great effect. In a public speech at the Bo town hall, she launched into a blistering attack on the RUF and called for their "extermination." That line brought the crowd to its feet in thunderous applause. It was a popular message that certainly went down a lot better than talk of national reconciliation.

Adeniji continued to oppose any intervention by the Sierra Leone Army (by now renamed Republic of Sierra Leone Armed Forces [RSLAF]), which he believed would doom the ceasefire. He had an unannounced ally in his position—the British-seconded inspector-general of Police, Keith Biddle. Contrary to the advice the president was receiving from his senior British military adviser, Keith was convinced that the RSLAF intervention would not work and that there was a real danger that the newly trained units (by the UK-led International Military Advisory and Training Team [IMATT]), whose loyalties and steadfastness were uncertain, might disintegrate under fire.

Tensions came to a head at a meeting that President Kabbah convened to review the implementation (or more accurately the nonimplementation) of the Abuja ceasefire accord. The president and his key advisers (including the combustible Samuel Hinga Norman) attended, as did the SRSG, the UN force commander, myself, and other senior UNAMSIL staff.

At the meeting, the UNAMSIL military presented a rolling concept of operations for the progressive forward deployment of UNAMSIL units into RUF-controlled areas, starting with the town of Lunsar, some 120 kilometers from Freetown. The deployment would be accomplished in phases ending in the eastern, diamond-producing districts of Kono and Kenema.

In response, Norman was voluble, demanding loudly that UNAMSIL must move immediately to recover the country's sovereign wealth, by which he meant throwing the RUF out of the diamond-producing areas. Even though he understood the constraints on UNAMSIL, the president did not want Norman and the other hawks in the government to outmaneuver him. So he joined the chorus and insisted that UNAMSIL should take action on both the military and diplomatic fronts.

The discussion then turned to disarmament. For the government, this meant disarming the RUF, forcibly if need be, and certainly not the national army, as demanded by the RUF. As I was later to find in both Côte d'Ivoire and the DRC, governments assume that the deployment of UN peacekeepers means that they are there to disarm rebels and put the government back in the driver's seat. Although the relevant UN resolutions refer to "voluntary" disarmament, that word tends to get lost in the invective. There was little mention from the government side of the CDF, which had fought the RUF but had also committed gruesome atrocities in doing so.

Trying to lower the temperature, Adeniji announced that I would work out a plan with the government to accelerate the DDR process. This came as a surprise to me. While the DDR portfolio was part of my mandate, I had not spent a great deal of time on it pending progress on the political-military front, which was a prerequisite for the revival of the DDR program abandoned in May 2000.

Finding the Key

I was not at all sure what to do, but despite my uncertainty I immediately met with Francis Kai Kai, the executive director of the National Commission on

Disarmament, Demobilization, and Reintegration (NCDDR), to explore how we might restart the DDR program. Finding the right incentives to bring the RUF back into the DDR process was the key challenge. UNAMSIL did not have a mandate to force disarmament, and I doubted that the mission was willing to do so.

The DDR debacle of May 2000 had shown that while the foot soldiers of the RUF might be ready to turn up for DDR, their commanders were not. For them, DDR meant the end of their power and their source of income (a recurring obstacle to DDR that I was to encounter in other missions). The RUF business model was a brutally simple but effective one: grab what you can. So, commanders were not ready to see their "paycheck" walk away. However, there was also a genuine fear that by disarming unilaterally, they would open themselves to violent retaliation either from local people whom had harmed, or else the RSLAF or the CDF, both of which could be as vicious as the RUF.

After much debate on how we could tackle the conundrum, I suggested that we should explore some form of disarmament equivalence. There was never any question of the RSLAF disarming, as the RUF had demanded. However, most of the effective offense against the RUF was coming from not the RSLAF but the CDF and the traditional hunters known as the Kamajors. Between them, the RUF and the CDF controlled much of the country, dominating adjacent districts. We developed the idea of a parallel disarmament and demobilization campaign with each side agreeing to disarm simultaneously in designated districts, moving from west to east, starting in Kambia while the RSLAF remained in barracks for training. No doubt, Samuel Hinga Norman would have preferred that we start with Kono, but the RUF leadership was still very hesitant about disarmament and UNAMSIL was not ready to fight its way into the district.

We recognized that the RUF had not been defeated on the battlefield. It had suffered serious losses and the UK intervention had pushed the front line back from the Freetown peninsula and Lungi. Nevertheless, large areas of the country were still under RUF sway. I agreed with Francis, therefore, that we should avoid any triumphalism or talk of surrender even though Norman and some RSLAF officers were still in that frame of mind.

At the same time, we looked again at the material incentives that we could offer the RUF and CDF combatants. As a part of that review, we also decided to move away from a purely cash-based disarmament incentive. We agreed to redesign the program and find alternative reintegration incentives, including training for employment and educational opportunities.

More controversial, the program offered demobilized RUF combatants the opportunity, after screening, to join the army or police force. Actually, relatively few of the ex-RUF combatants got that far, but the prospect that they might was an attractive enticement for some. Fortunately, unlike what

I found in the DRC some years later, there was no wholesale recruitment of ex-combatants into the security forces.

The Breakthrough

While the initiative to revive and restructure the DDR program was taking shape, there was an intriguing development in the RUF camp. A Peace and Security Council was set up and led by Omrie Gollie, a London-trained barrister and relative of President Kabbah who had recently returned from the UK. Kabbah did not trust Gollie; he considered him an opportunist (and later imprisoned him, unjustly in my view). Nevertheless, Gollie brought to the table the political sophistication and lucidity that the RUF lacked. Although never fully trusted by the RUF leadership, Gollie could hold his own in negotiations with the government and the UN, whereas Sesay and other commanders often seemed tongue-tied.

Adeniji continued with his strategy of mobilizing regional support for the peace process. At a meeting in Abuja on May 2, 2001, the government and the RUF met again under the joint auspices of UNAMSIL and ECOWAS. Critically, they agreed to the parallel-disarmament plan. The RUF dropped its demand for the RSLAF to be part of DDR, while the government gave some ground by agreeing to the release of RUF political prisoners and a pledge to bring the CDF fully under its control.

The big breakthrough came, however, when the RUF announced it was ready to disarm and evacuate its fighters from Kambia. For its part, the government agreed to assist the RUF to transform itself into a political entity. The deal set up a joint oversight committee for the DDR program with the RUF, the CDF, and government representatives, chaired by UNAMSIL.

The committee held its first meeting in Freetown on May 15 at UNAMSIL headquarters. SRSG Adeniji chaired the meeting, flanked by the force commander and myself; Solomon Berewa, the attorney general, led the government team; Omrie Gollie headed the RUF delegation. The first hour or so was predictably tense as Berewa and Gollie, using their legal wits to good effect, sparred over the agenda and other details. Gollie was a match for the shrewd and patient Berewa.

However, there was little progress and Adeniji, anxious to avoid any bust-ups that might derail the meeting, called a tea break. Both delegations got up and then something quite unexpected happened. As cups were being filled, good-natured banter broke out between the two delegations. It turned out that a member of the RUF delegation was a cousin of Attorney General Berewa whom he had not seen for years. There was an air of a family reunion, making it hard to believe that they had been at daggers drawn barely minutes before. Everyone seemed to know everyone else. This unexpected reunion reminded me that Sierra Leone was a small country and the leadership class even smaller. I also learned that as outsiders we would never fully comprehend, or even be aware, of the contours of family and personal relations that so often play a crucial role in conflicts and how they are eventually settled (or not).

After the tea break, progress was more rapid, and during the course of the day we agreed on a timetable for the initial phase of the DDR program based on the plan developed on the reciprocity principle starting on May 18 with the Kambia and Port Loko districts respectively. We also agreed that following the disengagement of the RUF, the RSLAF would deploy into Kambia district.

This was a personal triumph for Adeniji. Despite the May 2000 debacle, he hit a home run with the Kambia agreement.

Hope Flourishes: DDR Begins

On May 18, 2001, we flew down to Rokupr in Kambia to witness the start of DDR. It was a momentous and emotional day, which we hoped marked the beginning of the end of a terrible conflict that had cost the lives of more than 70,000 people,[22] inflicted grisly amputations, employed rape as a weapon of war, forced child soldiers to commit barbarous acts (often against their own families), while addicting many of them to drugs and alcohol. The conflict had landed half of the population into squalid camps for internally displaced persons (IDPs) and refugees. The filmmaker Sorious Samura graphically captured the horror of what happened in his wrenching documentary on Sierra Leone, *Cry Freetown*.

That day in Rokupr, hope flourished. Hundreds of combatants turned up, mostly young men and boys. UNAMSIL tasked its military observers to screen those coming forward with some simple tests to check if they were indeed combatants. One of those tests required the applicant to strip and reassemble an AK-47. I was amazed to see boys—some not older than eleven to twelve years—do so with extraordinary dexterity.

AK-47s and RPGs were not the only weapons handed in by the assembled combatants. They showed up with heavy mortars, recoilless rifles, and even a surface-to-air missile, although the latter piece of hardware looked as if it would be more harmful to the person who fired it than the intended target. We mentioned this item in our report to headquarters, indicating that we had recovered a Stinger missile. A few days later, we received a polite note from the US embassy, informing us that this was an error; the weapon in question was a Russian-made surface-to-air missile, not a US Stinger. However, this haul of weapons (even though we suspected that some had been shipped elsewhere) was a timely reminder that if the RSLAF had attacked in Kambia, the RUF fighters still had ample means to defend their positions.

There were young girls present in the queues. On what was otherwise an exuberant occasion, their presence was a grim reminder of the human impact of the war, which would long outlast the completion of the DDR process. In the registration line, I spoke (through an interpreter) to a girl who was no more than fourteen years old. She was carrying a baby on her back and was clutching a mortar bomb. Since we had insisted that anyone trying to qualify for the DDR must turn in weapons and ammunition, someone had given her the mortar so that she could claim a reintegration benefit. Almost certainly she was a "bush wife," an ugly and demeaning phrase applied to any girl who had been abducted and then grievously abused by rebels for sex and manual labor.

In the years since, I have often wondered what happened to that girl and her child. Ostracized from their communities and families, and left to fend for themselves, many of these girls ended up on the streets. One lesson I took away from the Sierra Leone DDR exercise was that we needed to do much more for the women and girls abducted or coerced by fighters and then abandoned. Sad to say, I was to see similar outrages again in other war zones, notably in the eastern DRC.

At the end of the day, SRSG Adeniji addressed the assembled and now former combatants. Speaking in English, he promised them a better future. He then switched to Krio and mentioned my name; the combatants clapped enthusiastically. Not speaking Krio, I could not figure out what he was saying. After the ceremony concluded, Adeniji cheerfully told me what he had said. He had assured the ex-combatants that they would receive their benefits because he had brought with him a white man who worked for the UNDP and who had lots of money—hence the applause! He added that when it came to money, they would have far more confidence in me than the NCDDR, which they were convinced would rip them off (after all, in their experience, that was what officialdom always did, even though NCDDR leadership did not behave in that fashion).

In the months that followed and as DDR went ahead, I realized that Adeniji was not too far off the mark. Repeatedly, rumors would circulate that NCDRR officials had absconded with money owed to ex-combatants and a riot would ensue. Even though the rumors were patently false, UNAMSIL often had to intervene to calm potentially explosive situations. I met with many ex-combatants and these could be tricky encounters; I kept the meetings short and insisted that the ex-combatants designate a small group with a spokesperson whom they trusted. When large numbers of ex-combatants gathered, they could become volatile—especially when money was involved—and then anything could happen.

Hope Confirmed: DDR Moves to Kono District

On June 2 a second meeting of the joint committee was held in Magburaka in the northern district of Tonkolili. This was an open-air encounter held under a spreading mango tree. There was some nervousness all around: this was the first time government and CDF representatives were holding a meeting in an area still dominated by the RUF. There was progress; we agreed on the next phase of the DDR to cover Bonthe and Kono districts (the latter was the leading "diamond district" in Sierra Leone). For the first time, however, the RUF representatives began to express unease about the establishment of the Special Court for Sierra Leone with a mandate to try perpetrators of war crimes and crimes against humanity.

Despite the progress in the joint committee, clashes between the CDF and the RUF continued, especially in Kono district, where the CDF was try-ing to gain access to the diamond areas. Generals Opande and Agwai man-aged to keep the lid on, traveling frequently into the contested areas and calling the CDF out when they were clearly the instigators of an incident. These interventions helped to reassure the RUF that UNAMSIL was acting impartially, making them amenable to UNAMSIL's patrols and presence in its areas of control.

A key step forward was accomplished with the initial deployment of a Bangladeshi unit into Kono in May; this was followed by a full Pakistani brigade in August (in effect, the replacement of the Indian brigade that had left in 2000) in time for the completion of the RUF and CDF disarmament in Kono district in late August. The unopposed move into Kono was a major boost for UNAMSIL. In early September, President Kabbah met with Issa Sesay, for the first time, in the presence of President Obasanjo and President Konaré of Mali. Significantly, Obasanjo promised that Nigeria would make scholarships available to the RUF for study in Nigeria.

Further meetings of the joint committee to map out the next stages of the disarmament campaign followed around the country. These joint meet-ings became more than DDR oversight, as they touched on the political future of the RUF, the impending national elections, national recovery, as well as developments relating to the Special Court and the Truth and Rec-onciliation Commission. I attended all of these meetings, which were a fas-cinating and formative experience in peacemaking and peacebuilding.

Despite occasional flare-ups, the NCDDR and UNAMSIL completed the disarmament at the beginning of 2002, ending the program in Kailuhun district (where the war had begun a decade before). Altogether, 72,500 combatants were disarmed; the reintegration program continued after the disarmament phase until February 2004, when it was wound up.[23]

The DDR program in Sierra Leone was the subject of numerous assess-ments with mixed findings. Some observers believed that a substantial num-ber of weapons remained hidden; others pointed to the shortcomings in the reintegration component and labeled it as only a short-term palliative. It's true that UNAMSIL could not certify that all weapons had been handed in, nor could we say that the reintegration program had put every ex-combatant to work or into training; there was fraud in the program (training given on cardboard computers was one of the more flagrant wheezes). Nevertheless, the DDR program made the reunification of the country possible, permitting the gradual return of the state (a very weak one, though), thereby creating a momentum of confidence that peace was possible.

The War Ends and Tony Blair Arrives

The formal end of the war was marked by a ceremony held near Lungi airport in late January 2002. Kabbah, Sesay, SRSG Adeniji, and John Kufuor, the Ghanaian president, lit a huge bonfire of 3,000 weapons. All of us then threw in our own firebrands and joined hands for the Sierra Leone national anthem. More than a decade of terrible warfare had ended.

One month after the Lungi bonfire, Tony Blair came to Sierra Leone for three hours to celebrate the end of the war. For security reasons, he did not go to Freetown and the government organized his welcome ceremony close by Lungi airport. He had sustained Sierra Leone through some dark moments, and his government urged the Security Council to take action, so it was right that he too should savor the moment of success.

SRSG Olu Adeniji, Behrooz Sadry, the force commander, and I were invited to a private meeting with the prime minister at Lungi. Clare Short was present at the encounter, which took place almost a year after our earlier, fractious confrontation with her. This time around, the encounter was far more convivial. Graciously, she conceded that she had underestimated UNAMSIL and praised the conduct of the mission. Blair smiled and noted that we were not the only ones who had been "hand-bagged" by the tempestuous Short.

Protectors or Predators?

As the meeting with Tony Blair attested, by early 2002 the public perception of UNAMSIL had improved dramatically. But that more positive outlook took another nosedive in February 2002 with the publication of a report alleging peacekeepers' involvement in sexual abuse and exploitation. The United Nations High Commissioner for Refugees (UNHCR) and the UK charity Save the Children had commissioned a consultant to look into claims that aid workers had sexually abused the beneficiaries of humanitarian aid in Liberia. The enquiry probed further and alleged that UN peacekeepers and humanitarian workers in Sierra Leone were also culpable.

Inevitably, the report was leaked (these sorts of reports often are). Mark Doyle of the BBC reported on the allegations under the sensational and devastating headline "Food for Sex." An international outcry quickly erupted. The enquiries that followed did not substantiate all of the allegations. Nevertheless, there was evidence enough to show that humanitarian workers and peacekeepers alike had committed abuses. This finding produced a tsunami of soul-searching at the UN and among aid agencies. It also resulted in an unprecedented level of institutional cooperation. I invoked my mandate as UN resident and humanitarian coordinator to get most of the humanitarian agencies in Sierra Leone—UN and non-UN—together quickly to sign onto a joint code of conduct that explicitly prohibited and sanctioned any use of aid for sexual or other purposes. DPKO instructed UNAMSIL to prepare and publish its own code of conduct that mirrored the interagency one.

That experience in Sierra Leone was my first exposure to a recurring crisis—sexual abuse and exploitation. I shall come back to this deeply troubling failing later on because it was a constant source of anxiety in all of the peacekeeping missions of which I was a part. For UNAMSIL it tarnished our success in the peace process. But the opprobrium was not evenly shared; the mission took the hit while the countries of the troops involved were not ready to acknowledge their responsibility.

War Don-Don

So after many failed attempts, why did the war finally end? There is no single answer. There were many contributing factors—political, diplomatic, military, and personal—but several stand out. First, with the capture and imprisonment of Foday Sankoh, the RUF lost its voice. There was no binding ideology to keep the group together; Sankoh was the adhesive. Issa Sesay could not match the charisma of Sankoh nor could he provide political direction. Omrie Gollie tried but the RUF commanders did not trust him and he was always nervous of outbursts that could turn deadly. In fact, a couple of times he called me from Makeni in a high state of anxiety, fearing for his life.

Second, I am sure that the RUF's leaders believed that they were immune to any prosecution at war's end. Indeed, they may have received some discreet assurances to that effect from regional leaders, without which I am not sure that they would have gone along with the DDR.

A third element was the RUF's intervention as Taylor's proxy in neighboring Guinea. Guinea fought back and the RUF lost men and weapons. In the end, however, faced with an insurgency backed by Guinea (and to a lesser extent by Côte d'Ivoire) and UN-mandated sanctions, Taylor was forced to reduce his support to the RUF in a vain effort to save his own regime. Although the RUF was at base a homegrown rebellion, the Liberia connection was a vital conduit for weapons and the smuggling of diamonds.

A fourth factor was undoubtedly the UK's political and military interventions. The military action in May 2000 gave UNAMSIL the breathing space to reorganize and reshape its political-military strategy, but also demonstrated that the UK could and would use force to prevent the RUF from taking over. UK forces did not pacify the country but the continuing commitment as an over-the-horizon standby force together with the presence of the UK-led IMATT boosted confidence. In the Security Council, the UK's permanent representative, Jeremy Greenstock, successfully rallied support for continued UN engagement in Sierra Leone.

A fifth conclusion I draw is that the UN and Adeniji largely got the political strategy right despite the May 2000 calamity. Bringing the region on board, especially Nigeria, to pressure both the RUF and Charles Taylor, was a crucial step, as was Adeniji's intervention to forestall government forces from confronting the RUF in Kambia, which would have torpedoed the ceasefire. At the same time, the joint coordinating committee, skillfully chaired by Adeniji, provided the government and the RUF with a workable mechanism for direct negotiation.

A sixth point I would emphasize was President Kabbah's willingness to accept political compromise, despite the domestic pressures on him to do otherwise. He cut a sympathetic figure in the international community, which earned him substantial support, especially from the UK. By contrast, the RUF was toxic, depriving it of any help in or outside of Africa (except from Charles Taylor, who was rapidly becoming an international pariah).

Finally, the UN Security Council, the Secretary-General, and DPKO stood firm. After the UN disasters in Somalia, Srebrenica, and Rwanda, many wondered if another UN withdrawal and humiliation was in the making. Thankfully, the UN did not abandon Sierra Leone; it soldiered on and UNAMSIL rose from the ashes. Most important, the Council remained largely of one mind and avoided the divisiveness that has paralyzed other missions caught up in crisis.

Bringing Back the State

Following his visit to Sierra Leone in late 2000, Secretary-General Annan had noted that the "challenges confronting the country remain daunting. There is an urgent need to stabilize the areas of the country under government control and to address the roots of the conflict. In addition, social and economic reconstruction, the forthcoming elections and the long-standing need to revitalize State institutions will require an inclusive and comprehensive strategy, with the active support of the international community. With that in mind, I am considering . . . the appointment of a second Deputy Special Representative for Sierra Leone who would closely work with the Government to address these crucial matters."[24]

This was my second key priority: assisting the government of Sierra Leone to put in place this "inclusive and comprehensive" strategy for recovery and renewal that Kofi Annan had outlined, employing my various UN hats to do so.

That strategy had to respond to three principal challenges. First, stabilization could not happen if there was not some clear direction for the physical recovery of the country, its infrastructure, and its economy. Second, any semblance of good governance required the restoration of the rule-of-law institutions, notably the judiciary and security services, throughout the country. And finally, governmental authority had to be legitimized through free, fair, and transparent elections.

I cannot claim we were able to develop a master strategy as a single, coordinated whole that provided a comprehensive blueprint for rebuilding the state. Much of what follows probably appears more logical and straightforward than it really was. Like the peace process itself, we sometimes took a leap of faith or simply improvised on the fly. There were mistakes and course corrections along the way. Luck, too, played its part.

Goods and Services

As the DDR process advanced, the planning for postwar recovery began to take hesitant shape. A Sierra Leone NGO invited me to a workshop to talk about what the UN might do to help the recovery process. Ceremonies and public events in Sierra Leone, even minor ones, are rather heavy on protocol. The chair dutifully acknowledges all the dignitaries present (and even those who are absent) and there is an elaborate introduction of the guest of honor, including a detailed rendition of his or her curriculum vitae. For the sake of brevity on such occasions, I had shortened my own title from "deputy special representative of the secretary general for governance and stabilization" to "DSRSG (G&S)."

When it came my turn to speak, the chair began to introduce me to the audience with a rendering of my curriculum vitae. However, when he got to my abbreviated title, he hesitated and then announced me as the deputy special representative of the Secretary-General for "goods and services"! On reflection, I thought this was not such a bad description. After all, the people of Sierra Leone were expecting that the end of the war would lead to an early, material improvement in their daily lives.

The Road to Recovery

The attacks of the RUF and the AFRC, and the ECOMOG counteroffensives, had devastated much of Freetown. The rural areas were in even worse shape. The war had destroyed or badly damaged much of the basic infrastructure—schools, district offices, clinics, courts, prisons, police stations, and water supply. Looting was commonplace; everything that could be physically removed, including choice items such as tin roofs, toilets, doors, window frames, and washbasins, was hauled off (some of it ending up in the markets of neighboring countries).

Regrettably, marauding armed groups were not the only culprits; local people got involved too, taking the opportunity to make away with whatever was left over even though they were demolishing infrastructure like school buildings that they would need when peace returned. The conflict had gravely weakened the sense of community and created a dystopian free-for-all.

During the war, the RUF had targeted and killed many local officials, including traditional chiefs. Displaced officials (including chiefs) sheltering in Freetown and other reasonably safe locations were in no hurry to return to the countryside. The gradual forward deployment of UNAMSIL units into RUF-held areas and the resumption of the DDR program in May 2001 opened up an opportunity to reenergize the campaign to get government services back into areas abandoned under the onslaught of the RUF.

In an effort to jumpstart the recovery process (and to respond to the mounting criticism for its perceived inactivity), the government created a task force on the restoration of state authority, chaired by the vice president, Joe Demby; he invited me to join the task force along with an assortment of ministers, UN staff, and donor agencies. The vice president presided over the task force meetings from an oversized executive desk with the participants aligned in rows in front of him like pupils in class. A single, languid fan, turning reluctantly, barely disturbed the stifling atmosphere while the meetings meandered on interminably. Demby seemed content to denounce the RUF for all of Sierra Leone's ills or to berate UNAMSIL for not bringing the rebels to heel. There was no agenda, minutes, or agreed conclusions.

After one particularly dreary session of the task force, the newly arrived commander of the UK military mission and adviser to the president, Brigadier Nick Parker, and I met to air our mutual frustrations. We agreed that the task force was a directionless talking shop. He suggested that I might raise the issue discreetly with the president and seek his agreement to convert the task force into a more structured, forward-looking entity that could plan rather than simply complain.

Getting to Grips

From these conversations emerged the National Recovery Committee (NRC), still headed by the vice president but now backed up by the dynamic Kadie Sesay (minister of planning), assisted by a small secretariat to service the NRC. Donning my UNDP hat, I was able to steer some support into the NRC to give it the means to act as more than a talking shop.

As peace returned, foreign aid increased exponentially, resulting in the duplication of programs in some localities but the neglect of others. The government complained, with reason, that it had no idea of who was doing what and where; for their part, donors expressed irritation about bureaucratic delays. The NGOs voiced their worries about government efforts to control their activities; conversely, government ministers denounced what they claimed were commercial NGOs set up as tax-avoidance schemes. I envisioned the NRC as an expedient venue to review and resolve those problems and thereby hasten recovery.

The NRC was not a mechanism designed to lead the structural reforms that Sierra Leone desperately needed in order to achieve a more stable and prosperous future. The World Bank and the International Monetary Fund (IMF) had already started consultations and preparations of an interim poverty reduction strategy paper, the sine qua non for Sierra Leone's access to debt reduction through the Heavily Indebted Poor Countries Initiative (HIPC).

From prior experience, I knew that preparing the strategy paper would be a complex and time-consuming process. I doubted that Sierra Leone could quickly meet all the requirements for such a paper. In the meantime, the government needed to bolster its credibility and show some change for the better, especially in those districts faced with a cascade of returning IDPs and refugees.

In May 2002, a new vice president assumed office—Solomon Berewa, the former attorney general and the government's chief negotiator with the RUF. Although he projected an air of unhurried deliberation, Berewa's impact on the NRC was immediate; he was intellectually engaged and politically committed and probably hoped that the NRC might enhance his own political prospects when it came time for Kabbah to step down.

With Berewa's arrival, I counseled that the NRC should start to set priorities and channel resources to areas in greatest need. The NRC commissioned a series of district assessments led by joint teams drawn from the government services, donor agencies, UNAMSIL, UN agencies, and NGOs. The teams visited every district in the country, several of which had been largely isolated during the war years.

In consultation with local leaders and communities, these assessments focused on immediate recovery needs, identifying priorities and gaps. Subsequently, the vice president convened a series of town hall meetings in each district to present and review the findings of the assessments. At the end of the exercise, a joint team from the government and donors pulled together the individual assessments into a national recovery plan as the framework for prioritizing the immediate needs of the country.

The national recovery exercise was not a panacea. It did not produce instant recovery or overcome local bureaucratic obstacles, nor did it dispense with the plethora of bureaucratic demands from the aid agencies, which placed a heavy administrative burden on a very weak administration. One criticism that frequently surfaced, including from UNAMSIL colleagues, was that we were creating a dependency syndrome by taking over responsibility from a government that was too pliant and amenable to donor demands. Other critics argued that we were creating a model that was not viable in the long run. But I kept reminding colleagues and critics alike of Lord Keynes's famous aphorism that "in the long run, we are all dead."

The NRC's national recovery program was an initial but vital step in the process of stabilization. Through the NRC, the government and donors could direct resources toward the country's most battered and deprived areas. But above all, the program was intended to demonstrate to the people of Sierra Leone that their government was gradually—if somewhat hesitatingly—reestablishing some semblance of state presence, weak though it was. This, to my mind, was the real importance of the NRC.

Back to Makeni

The first goal of the national recovery program—reestablishing basic state services and structures in newly accessible areas—aimed to show the population that the war was ending and the state of Sierra Leone was coming back to life. The return of the Sierra Leone Police to rural areas was a critical benchmark of progress in this effort. Keith Biddle, the forceful inspector-general of police, who was leading the reform and retraining of the SLP with the aid of a Commonwealth team, was keen to get the police back into "liberated areas." We also made this a top priority for the UNAMSIL civilian police advisers who were assigned to work with the newly deployed SLP units. But the police could not be deployed without some basic logistics and shelter. Here again my access to resources from the UNDP and UNAMSIL (through its quick-impact funding) was a godsend, enabling us to move quite rapidly to rebuild police stations and magistrate courts at low cost, employing local labor.

The RUF remained reluctant to accept the SLP in areas it dominated. The presence of UNAMSIL was acceptable because it implied the internationalization of the conflict, but the restored and visible presence of the SLP was a different matter; it implied defeat (and reduced scope for rackets). Makeni, the erstwhile headquarters of the RUF, was the test case. We had negotiated with the RUF the staged deployment of the SLP into the town, or so I believed. I was keen to show off this event as evidence of our success in restoring state authority. We invited Mark Doyle of the BBC to witness the event. With Inspector-General Keith Biddle and the top brass of the SLP on board, we took off in a UNAMSIL helicopter to monitor the progress of the police column (and get some good footage) as it made its way to Makeni.

A couple of miles from Makeni, when all seemed to going well, the column ran into a RUF roadblock, which was not supposed to be there. The column halted and we encountered a dilemma that I was to face at other times, in other places: Do we force the issue? The police column was only lightly armed but a strong UNAMSIL (Nigerian) unit was already in the town. Did we want to risk a violent confrontation that could result in SLP casualties?

Keith decided he did not want to take that risk. I agreed with his caution. Even light casualties would have proved deeply discouraging to the

SLP; if UNAMSIL military units had intervened to lift the blockade forcibly, the wider peace process might have taken a serious hit. Embarrassed, we headed back to Freetown without the headline. It was a setback but not the end of the story.

After further negotiations, the SLP returned to Makeni a month later— this time without the BBC but to the applause of the local population. Within a matter of weeks, the ghost town came back to life. I was astonished and deeply heartened to see how quickly people began to resume their lives and livelihoods. There was no master plan for return and reintegration. Once people felt reasonably secure, they simply returned.

The gradual return of the police force to areas under RUF control was a step toward the reassertion of state authority. However, the deployment of the SLP was only a part of the answer. The judicial system was in ruins both institutionally and materially. Sierra Leone's jurisprudence was founded on the British system of case law (rather quaintly, Sierra Leonean lawyers still appeared in the High Court wearing wigs like their peers in London); unfortunately, many of the legal archives had gone up in smoke, leaving judges to apply case law without case records.

The UK's Department for International Development (DFID) made a major investment in renovating the High Court in Freetown, badly damaged during one of the spasms of violence that had engulfed the city. I encouraged donors, including UNAMSIL through its quick-impact program, to follow suit and rehabilitate the judicial infrastructure in smaller towns and rural areas.

In this effort, I had an amiable ally in the chief justice of Sierra Leone, Abdulai Timbo. In a refreshing break with protocol, he took to dropping by my office in search of UNAMSIL's help for redeploying magistrates to the interior or for rebuilding courts in areas that had not known any judicial presence for a decade or more. Several times I had the pleasure of joining him on these excursions, which to me were tangible if modest demonstrations of the return of state authority.

Leading by Example

The reestablishment of state presence was of course much more than the return of the SLP and the courts. District administrators, health workers, teachers, and other functionaries needed to go back to their places of assignment. Many were reluctant to do so, understandably fearing the residual RUF presence. The return of the SLP and the expanding presence of UNAMSIL would, I hoped, gradually attenuate those fears. For some functionaries, however, life in Freetown was comfortable, as they were still being paid (not much, true) and the absence of schools, clinics, and phone lines meant life in the rural areas was tough. There were no banks operating outside of Freetown, and so civil servants could only draw their salaries in person, which meant a trip (sometimes an arduous one) to Freetown to get money for family expenses.

We had to find a way to encourage the return of officials. I believed that UNAMSIL should set an example by deploying its own staff to the districts as quickly as possible. Initially, these staff deployments were from the mission's civil affairs and human rights sections but other units followed. There was some grumbling. Facilities in war-torn Freetown were limited, but compared to those in towns like Koidu and Kailuhun, which had been totally ruined during the years of conflict, it was quite comfortable, with a scattering of restaurants, bars (including the notorious Paddy's, a rather *louche* establishment conveniently situated down the road from UNAMSIL headquarters), and beaches for those so inclined.

I wanted the UNAMSIL staff recently deployed in areas formerly under rebel control, along with UN agency staff, to identify and develop projects for priority rehabilitation. I was convinced that visible signs of the state would not only encourage the return of traditional chiefs, civil servants, and teachers but also trigger the gradual revival of the rural economy.

Blood, Sweat, and Diamonds

A key marker for the restoration of state authority was control over the diamond-rich Kono district. The popular (foreign) perception about the war in Sierra Leone was that it was all about diamonds, an impression graphically reinforced by films like *Blood Diamond* and *Lord of War.* Diamonds certainly helped to fuel the war but they were not the primary cause. In fact, the industrial mining of diamonds ended in 1984 when a subsidiary of De Beers, the South African diamond company, pulled out of the country, fed up with Siaka Stevens's predatory habits of stealing and smuggling diamonds. Nevertheless, artisanal mining continued, producing a limited but lucrative supply of high-quality stones that were the source of the infamous blood diamonds.

By world standards, Sierra Leone was (and remains) a relatively small producer of gemstones. Nevertheless, the profits were large enough to attract the attention of Charles Taylor and his RUF associates, who benefited from them to buy arms, drugs, and favors. The people of Sierra Leone saw no benefit from the diamonds. Quite the opposite; while the warlords profited, those who did the job—working day after day in waist-deep, disease-ridden waters sluicing the diamond-bearing gravel—gained a pittance.

I first visited Koidu, the capital of the diamond-producing district of Kono, while it was still under RUF control. It was a rather startling scene. Seen from the air, the terrain around Koidu appeared pitted by bomb craters. This reminded me of a flight I had made into Hanoi not long after the Vietnam War had ended. Approaching Hanoi airport, I noticed that the countryside was pockmarked by what I took to be fishponds. Closer to the ground, however, I realized that the fish ponds were in fact craters left by US bombers.

The craters around Koidu were not made by bombs; they were diamond pits that had gradually crept uncontrolled into and literally under the town. After the disarmament of the RUF, artisanal diamond mining intensified, bringing a new wave of diggers and community tensions that threatened renewed violence. The government needed to regulate mining activities. However, I strongly discouraged the deployment of UN peacekeepers or the SLP into the diamond fields for that purpose. Chasing poverty-stricken miners around diamond pits was likely to be a vexing and fruitless exercise (even the ruthless RUF had not been able to stop all smuggling) and there was significant reputational risk. The international media had frequently accused ECOMOG forces of diamond trafficking.

Closing down the artisanal mining was not an option. The miners' earnings were meager but there were no alternatives, pending the return of industrial-scale mining or other employment (later I encountered a similar dilemma in eastern Congo with cobalt diggers). When the RUF was present, concealing stones was dangerous: miners found with them risked summary execution. Now chaos threatened, with young people flooding in from other parts of the country hoping to strike it rich.

At the national level, we set up a high-level steering committee with the aim of bringing together the main players to establish and manage a development policy for the diamond industry. Contrary to popular opinion, Sierra Leone's diamonds could not generate enough revenues to keep the government afloat. If anything, the opposite was true: to keep the trade honest, the government had to set export and other taxes at a modest level. The problem with diamonds was not so much the good they could do but the harm they might cause should they once again get into the wrong hands.

US ambassador Pete Chaveas and the US Agency for International Development (USAID) came up with an interesting and practical idea: the diamond-tier Star Alliance. This initiative aimed to get local communities engaged in the orderly management of the diamond fields by returning a portion of the revenues directly to them. To make the scheme more attractive, I proposed that as an additional incentive, donors like the UNDP should add a matching contribution for community-based projects.

Shadows of the Past

Justice Calls: The Special Court for Sierra Leone

While the efforts of UNAMSIL, the DFID, and others to rebuild the Sierra Leone judicial system inched forward, international attention increasingly shifted to the Special Court for Sierra Leone. The court was established to "prosecute persons who bear the greatest responsibility for serious violations of international humanitarian law and Sierra Leonean law committed in the territory of Sierra Leone since 30 November 1996."[25] The Sierra Leone judicial system was not considered strong or objective enough to mount credible prosecutions, and the jurisdiction of the International Criminal Court (ICC), of which Sierra Leone was a member, became effective only in 2002, after the war was over.

The UN Secretary-General instructed UNAMSIL to provide initial logistical and security assistance for the SCSL, which was set up in Freetown. However, Adeniji was not an enthusiastic supporter, believing that the court might disrupt the peace process and undermine the prospects for national reconciliation. He was not alone in that view. Some leaders in the region were also opposed to the court (this was long before the current debate about the ICC and Africa erupted). Indeed, if the RUF had not attacked UNAMSIL in May 2000, the SCSL might not have been established.

The prosecutor of the court, David Crane, and his deputy, Desmond de Silva, were something of an odd couple. David was quite abstemious and intense; Desmond came across as a charming and gregarious bon vivant. Both, however, were determined to get convictions, and not only of former RUF leaders. They were prepared to cast their prosecutorial net widely.

On March 7, 2003, the prosecutor unsealed the first batch of thirteen indictments. The indictments included several RUF commanders (among them, Sankoh, Sam Bockarie, and Issa Sesay) but also some senior members of the CDF; Johnny Paul Koroma, the former leader of the AFRC, was on the list and, most surprising, so was Samuel Hinga Norman.

Norman's indictment and arrest made waves. His many supporters expressed outright dismay, denouncing President Kabbah for betraying the person who had done more than anyone else to keep him in office. The president simply responded that the court was not under his control and the indictments were not his doing (although he was not displeased to see Norman neutralized, at least temporarily).

The court informed UNAMSIL the day before of the impending announcement and arrests. We went on full alert without revealing the reason for doing so. Amazingly, there were no leaks and the Sierra Leone Police were able to complete all of the arrests without incident. Norman was arrested in his ministerial office by one of his subordinates (a senior SLP officer, Francis Munu, later to become inspector-general of the SLP).

Sankoh was already in jail. The SLP arrested all of the other RUF indictees (except for Bockarie, later confirmed dead in Liberia) without incident. They clearly did not expect arrests so soon after the DDR was completed. As I mentioned earlier, I am sure that the indictees believed they would get some kind of amnesty deal as a recompense for their cooperation on DDR, likely recalling that past peace deals had granted amnesty.

By coincidence, the evening before the arrests I was at a charity event to raise money for Bo School, an old and prestigious Sierra Leone educational establishment. As a prominent personality from Bo, Norman was there along with another Bo luminary, Attorney General Berewa. I was aware of the imminent arrests, as no doubt Berewa was. I sat at the same table as Norman, who was his usual voluble self. Perhaps he had some inkling of what was coming, as he spent a good part of the evening stating for all to hear that he was not afraid to appear before the court; all he had done was to defend his people and his country. I remained tactfully silent.

The prosecutor had one more surprise up his sleeve. Three months later, on June 4, 2003, another indictment was unsealed, this one for Charles Taylor. He was attending peace talks in Ghana. In my time with Adeniji, we had never had any kind of blowup. That morning was different. He stormed into my office claiming that I had colluded with the prosecutor and failed to keep him informed. In fact, Crane informed me of the indictment precisely one hour before he went public, a few moments after he advised the SRSG. The unsealing of the indictment while regional heads of state, including Obasanjo, were meeting to deal with the Liberian crisis embarrassed Adeniji even though he was not implicated in that decision. Later in the day, however, he apologized to me, having realized that I was not privy to the prosecutor's decision.

Apparently, Crane and de Silva had hoped to get hold off Taylor while he was in a country where they could serve an international arrest warrant. If that was indeed the tactic, it backfired. The announcement did not go down well with the regional leaders attending the peace talks. President Kufuor, the host of the talks (and in many ways an exemplary head of state), refused to honor the arrest warrants.

Fourteen years later, the ICC tried the same maneuver when President Bashir of Sudan attended an AU summit in South Africa. That attempt failed too; African leaders do not like to arrest each other at summit meetings.

Almost all of the prosecutions ended in convictions, although Sankoh and Norman died of natural causes before the ICC could hand down verdicts. The ICC repatriated the body of Bockarie from Liberia, where he had died under mysterious circumstances. Johnny Koroma escaped from police custody and is presumed to have also met his end in Liberia, which was not a very safe place for former Sierra Leone warlords. I shall return to Taylor's fate as part of my story on Liberia.

There has been abundant commentary on the value and impact of the Special Court for Sierra Leone. The court was expensive, costing (in infrastructure and proceedings) upward of $300 million[26] (not including the security expenses incurred by UNAMSIL), against an initial estimate of $75 million.

Can one put a price on justice? I recall discussing this issue with Chief of Justice Timbo, who told me rather ruefully that the annual budget for the judiciary for the entire country was $2 million. There was no money for legal aid to indigent defendants (or for much else), and so by default the prisons had become the poorhouses of Sierra Leone.

Despite the runaway costs of the SCSL, Sierra Leoneans generally supported the indictments issued by the court. Most did not see the court as a front for victors' justice, although there was a muted opposition to the indictment of Samuel Hinga Norman from those who believed he had defended the state against the RUF.

The court enjoyed political support in the United States and in Europe but in Africa opinion was divided. Human rights and civil society activists strongly supported the indictments. However, political and diplomatic circles echoed Adeniji's concerns about the impact the court might have on future peace negotiations, a view that incidentally was shared by some UNAMSIL colleagues as well.

It is difficult to assess how the outcome of the Sierra Leone trials may have contributed to the ending of impunity, an aspiration that is frequently voiced in UN resolutions dealing with conflict and violence. Perhaps we should simply judge such trials on their own merits. As Peter Maguire has said, "There is no empirical evidence to support the idea that trials lead to truth, reconciliation and healing. In the end, the most anyone can expect from a war crimes trial is the guilty will be punished and the innocent exonerated."[27]

The Far Side of Revenge

The Special Court for Sierra Leone tried only those perpetrators held "most responsible" for crimes; this was a tiny fraction of the individuals, many of whom were young people, who participated in atrocities, often under life-or-death compulsion. The Lomé peace agreement tried to cope with that appalling legacy by mandating the formation of a truth and reconciliation commission. The apparent success of the South African Truth and Reconciliation Commission, under the leadership of Archbishop Desmond Tutu, created an almost mystical belief in the redemptive powers of such commissions (although nowadays, revisionist commentary is challenging the positive impact of the South African commission).

Despite its lofty mandate, petty problems dogged the commission from the outset. Ironically, the reconciliation commission could not always reconcile its own members (I encountered the same problem later on with the Liberian commission). There were tensions between the national and international members, with the latter complaining of exclusion. The donors (including the UNDP) questioned the administration of the commission and insisted on the appointment of an outside manager. I spent a lot of time trying to sort out these problems, not always successfully.

The commission's relationship with the Special Court for Sierra Leone raised a raft of sensitive issues. The court insisted that it had primacy and therefore could subpoena witnesses and documents in respect of any cases within its jurisdiction. The commission objected, claiming that testimony submitted confidentially and in good faith to the commission should not then be used in evidence in trial proceedings because that might discourage witnesses from testifying to the commission. The commission asked me to intercede and we eventually agreed on an informal "don't ask, don't refuse" arrangement, with the court informally conceding that it would not use evidence gathered by the commission.

Norman was keen to testify to the commission, pointing out that President Kabbah had done so. The SCSL prosecutor objected and the court denied him permission (unfairly in my view) to testify publicly. However, he did file a written brief with the commission in which he argued that he had acted to save his community from a ruthless and brutal enemy (even though the CDF, under his command, committed horrific acts of violence).

The commission published its report in 2004, shortly after I left Sierra Leone. The report echoed Samuel Hinga Norman's protest that the SCSL should also have called President Kabbah to account, as the head of state, for ignoring Norman's warnings that the 1997 coup attempt was in the making. Setting aside that controversy, however, did the commission pave the way for or help the country to achieve some measure of reconciliation?

That is hard to judge, but the report did provide catharsis to those who suffered terribly and had no other form of redress. The report is a record of what happened to ordinary people caught up in extraordinary circumstances. It is a historical record of remembrance, a solemn reminder for future generations. One can only hope that Franklin Roosevelt was right when he observed that people have to "learn from the past that they gain in judgment in creating their own future."

Restoring Legitimacy

President Kabbah's term of office expired in September 2001. The Sierra Leone constitution allowed parliament to grant a six-month extension to the presidential term under the state-of-emergency provisions, which meant that elections were due by March 2002. With the DDR largely completed, the demand for elections began to acquire momentum. IDPs and refugees were returning and, with the deployment of UNAMSIL and the SLP across the country, the security situation was far better than during the previous presidential election in 1996, when a large part of the country was not accessible.

ECOWAS, the AU, and Nigeria did not seem particularly worried about the legitimacy issue. For them the stability of the country came first. However, the Western powers (essentially the UK, the EU, and the United States) pressed for a mandate renewal, believing that this would complete the political transition and put the country on a firm footing to undertake the reforms needed to consolidate stabilization and gradually rebuild the economy.

I was also convinced that we needed to seize the moment and move forward with the elections before the euphoria of peace began to dissipate. Olu Adeniji was more cautious. He was concerned that the election might be premature, fearing that a successful election would encourage the UN Security Council to declare victory and order an accelerated drawdown of UNAMSIL. Prior to his UNAMSIL assignment, Adeniji had been the SRSG in the Central African Republic (CAR), where a UN peacekeeping mission was precipitously withdrawn after a general election despite his warning that the security situation was still very unstable. His caution was right in that case; soon after the mission's withdrawal, a fresh cycle of violence erupted; ever since, the CAR has been plagued by recurring bouts of warfare that have led to new peacekeeping deployments.

President Kabbah decided to go ahead with the elections. The government lifted the state of emergency and scheduled the elections for May 2002. Kabbah also probably calculated that after ending the war he was in a strong position to win the election and, in doing so, sustain international support.

Although the RUF was now disarmed (and Issa Sesay and company were in jail awaiting trial by the Special Court for Sierra Leone), we still worried that disaffected elements might disrupt the electoral proceedings. In fact, the RUF registered itself as a political party and began campaigning. It quickly found out that the power of arms does not translate into political power after disarmament. Far from gaining any political traction, it languished and was itself the victim of violence when political hooligans attacked and burned down its Freetown office in the only serious preelection incident of violence.

My mission portfolio included oversight of UNAMSIL's assistance to the national electoral commission. The commission had to do a credible job—politically and organizationally—to ensure the legitimacy of the election outcome. But many of the problems were about basics—electoral logistics—such as the printing of ballot papers. One of the biggest problems, however, was the payment of temporary electoral staff (polling officers, etc.). The donors didn't want to fund local salaries and so the government agreed to make a special contribution to cover these expenses.

Perversely the government's offer created a problem. There were no banks operating outside Freetown, so how, we wondered, could we arrange cash payments in the hundreds of locations where the temporary electoral staff would be posted? I suggested that we use UNAMSIL transport (helicopters and vehicles). That, I was firmly told by the administration, would not be possible. UN rules prevented us from employing UN transport for the physical transport of cash that did not belong to the UN.

Among the many things that my years in UNDP field operations had taught me was the value of improvisation. The UNDP is a decentralized organization and the staffs of the country offices are given considerable latitude to find local solutions to local problems. We set about "laundering" government funds into UN money—all in a good cause, of course. Fortunately, the UNDP had a well-established financial mechanism known as government cost-sharing. This allowed countries to contribute their own funding for local projects cofunded by the UNDP. One of my former bosses in the UNDP, Nessim Shallon, had invented this ingenious scheme when he was the representative in Iran. He had persuaded the Shah's government to recycle funds generated by the huge surge in oil revenues to expand the UNDP's technical assistance programs in the country.

President Kabbah, as a former UNDP director of administration, was comfortable with this arrangement and authorized the transfer into the UNDP bank account. The bank transfer took place almost on the eve of the elections. Then, of course, we had to find a way to get the money to election supervisors at dozens of locations, while avoiding the risk of loss, diversion, or skimming. We had to do this in very short order; otherwise there would be no polling staff on polling day.

We decided that the only way to make the deadline was to withdraw the money in cash and start stuffing envelopes. The UNDP's country director, Bert Coppens, and the senior governance adviser, Sylvia Fletcher, spent most of the night getting the envelopes, payment lists, and receipt forms, now suitably labeled as UNDP property, ready for takeoff at first light. I made sure we had a company of Ghanaian soldiers patrolling the grounds of the Mamy Yoko just in case. Early the next morning, we all breathed a huge sigh of relief when the money was on its way, leaving me to reflect whimsically that for once cash stuffed in envelopes was not a means to perpetrate electoral fraud.

Election day went off remarkably well with few incidents. The president returned to office with a decisive majority on the first round. However, the opposition candidate, Ernest Bai Koroma, a successful business executive turned politician, came to see me to protest. I was able to tell Koroma in good conscience that UNAMSIL had monitored the elections very carefully and that while there were some dubious returns, overall we—and independent observer groups—were sure that Kabbah had won.

While the All People's Congress (APC) (the party of Siaka Stevens), led by Koroma, did not win the presidential race, it did quite well in the legislative contests, especially in Freetown. I thought this was a good outcome, as it meant that presidential power would not be absolute. I sounded this positive tone to Koroma. I added that he needed to rebuild the APC's electoral base and not wait until the eve of the next elections. I do not know if my words had any effect, but five years later Bai Koroma won the presidency, defeating the incumbent, my old friend, Vice President Solomon Berewa.

Finding Humanitarian Space

The collapse of the peace process in May 2000 was a grave setback not only for the political process but also for the international humanitarian intervention in Sierra Leone. It set off a wave of displacement as well as the evacuation of humanitarian agencies from some of the most deprived areas of the country. At the same time, the increasing violence in Liberia and Guinea was producing yet another exodus, leading Ruud Lubbers, then the UN High Commissioner for Refugees, to describe West Africa as the worst humanitarian situation in the world.

The RUF attacks against the humanitarians were not aimed at achieving a political objective; they were more an opportunity for looting. However, relations between the mission and the humanitarian community, already quite shaky, worsened because of the confusion and poor communication during the crisis.

I had to take on three key problems. The first was to repair relations between UNAMSIL and the humanitarian community and allay the concerns arising from my dual role as the DSRSG and humanitarian coordinator. The second, and in a way the most urgent, was to gain access to areas controlled by the RUF in order to deliver humanitarian assistance. The third was to start preparing for the return of IDPs and refugees, even though peace was still far from ensured.

Switching Hats: Humanitarian Coordination in Practice

As I mentioned at the beginning of this chapter, the humanitarian community did not universally welcome my appointment as the humanitarian coordinator. I had to convince humanitarian partners that I was not putting political considerations ahead of humanitarian principles. I thought that the best way to do that was to be open and available. I attended and briefed the humanitarian coordination meetings, visited IDP and refugee camps and made a point of meeting visitors from humanitarian agencies. But I encouraged other members of the mission, especially the military, to do the same.

I also offered access to UNAMSIL facilities, including transportation. This was not a popular move with UNAMSIL administration, which (reflecting UN policy) took a rather narrow accounting approach to such matters. This institutional parochialism was not confined to the UN. Several leading international NGOs were at pains to keep their distance from UNAMSIL; under no circumstances would they make use of any UNAMSIL facilities, for fear of tarnishing their self-declared policy of strict neutrality (although this policy did not prevent attacks and looting of their premises and vehicles by the RUF, the AFRC, and other rebel groups). There was even a quarrel about the colors of the insignia on UN vehicles; UN blue, it was decreed, could be used only for UN vehicles that were not from UNAMSIL, which would stick with black lettering.

Fortunately, in the two biggest UN humanitarian agencies operating in Sierra Leone—the World Food Programme (WFP), led by Louis Imbleau, and the UNHCR, led by Arnauld Akodjenou—displayed more pragmatic attitudes. The WFP was especially helpful in supplying and managing the food component of the DDR program. When the UNHCR needed UNAMSIL assistance for protecting and moving refugees or IDPs away from dangerous areas, they asked for it. UNICEF also chose to work closely with UNAMSIL to manage (with the mission's child protection unit) the release of child soldiers. By contrast, one leading NGO actually withdrew its team from an operation to move refugees from the border to safety when it realized that UNAMSIL would do so in trucks under armed guard.

My policy was a simple one: We would not force UNAMSIL's assistance on any agency nor shun those who chose not to use it. Nor would we seek any intelligence from humanitarian organizations (in or outside the UN). If some chose to share information with us, this was their choice, but we would not insist that they do so.

In practice, even some of the most outspoken NGO critics of UNAMSIL would discreetly turn to the mission for assistance—even the military—in times of emergency. I encouraged UNAMSIL staff to respond positively and not publicize our support, which might cause embarrassment even though some of those organizations that asked for help were not above upbraiding us publicly.

To its credit, in Sierra Leone as elsewhere, I found the International Committee of the Red Cross (ICRC) very constructive in the way it managed to uphold fundamental humanitarian principles while acting in a pragmatic manner. ICRC staff would quietly seek our cooperation to resolve issues instead of resorting to "ambush" press releases that created ill-will and mistrust.

Reaching the Vulnerable: Extending Humanitarian Space

By the time I arrived in Sierra Leone, the horrors of the conflict—characterized by amputations and AK-47-toting child soldiers—was widely known. Behind those realities, however, lay a multitude of other, unseen calamities. Healthcare in areas outside of government control (not that it was great in the government-held areas) had completely collapsed. After the events of May 2000, the NGOs had largely pulled out of the areas overrun by the RUF. Infant and maternal mortality as well as malnutrition increased dramatically as a result. Cholera and other treatable diseases broke out in areas we could not access.

Following UNAMSIL's first forward deployment to Lunsar in early 2001, humanitarian agencies also began to return. This pattern of UNAMSIL forward deployment (military, police, and civilians), shadowed by the gradual expansion of the humanitarian presence, was replicated in other areas. The districts dominated by the RUF were in desperate shape. So the expansion of humanitarian access was literally life or death for many people; but as so often happens, solving one problem raises another—in this case the vexed debate over humanitarian space.

When UNAMSIL military units deployed in newly accessible areas or towns, we found widespread sickness and untreated injuries. One of those areas was Koidu, to which a Bangladeshi unit was sent to secure the town. I visited what remained of the local hospital. The RUF and other intruders had looted the building, and all of the equipment had been torn out (even the operating table); there were no medical supplies. There were a few patients, including a couple of heavily pregnant women together with some injured RUF combatants whose wounds appeared (and smelled) as if they were suppurating. An RUF "doctor"—in fact a medical orderly—was trying to make the best of a bad situation.

Bangladeshi medics began to treat patients. Word spread and more patients, some in a terrible state, began to arrive. The unit quickly ran out of medical supplies and called for more. However, the administration informed me that the peacekeeping budget paid for the supplies and that the supplies could be used only for the unit's own needs. The rules did not permit the mission to provide medical supplies to civilians except in dire emergencies (which I thought was the case). Fortunately, we were able to get supplies from UNICEF and the World Health Organization (WHO) as well as the Ministry of Health. These were mainly simple and cheap items like rehydration salts and common antiseptics, but the impact was felt immediately. I encouraged other units that were moving into newly accessible areas to be equally forthcoming; this earned a great deal of goodwill for the mission, even if we were bending the rules.

Naively, I assumed that through this medical outreach we were providing a much needed and valued humanitarian service; however, I was quickly taken to task for invading humanitarian space. Several NGOs complained that we were doing their job, creating dependency (a familiar argument by now) and linking assistance to cooperation on security. I was lectured that our job was to create, not fill, humanitarian space.

I responded that UNAMSIL would furnish humanitarian aid on a strictly impartial basis. I emphasized also that we would not trade medical (or any other) aid for information; nor would we intervene if others were already providing emergency health services in the area. I also cautioned UNAMSIL military units not to build facilities (clinics, schools, etc.) that the local community could not maintain after their departure. However, I absolutely refused to discourage UNAMSIL's military units from providing emergency humanitarian aid. To my mind, such demands were unreasonable; I had no doubt that the people who benefited from UNAMSIL's aid agreed with me.

Going Home: The Reality of Reintegration

The war had uprooted a large proportion of the Sierra Leone population. As the peace process took hold, reintegration of displaced populations loomed large as a crucial element in the stabilization of the country. This included ex-combatants. However, many people deeply resented the assistance provided to the ex-combatants, which they denounced as a reward to those responsible for bloodshed and mayhem. I found it very hard to explain to people who had lost so much that the future stability of the country depended in good measure on the successful reintegration of the ex-combatants.

The war had touched everyone, irrespective of class and ethnicity. A relative of Vice President Berewa told me how RUF fighters had herded members of her family into a building, which they then set on fire. They all burned to death. I could not find the words to console her much less defend without qualm the reintegration support for the ex-combatants. But amazingly, as the reintegration program moved ahead, there very few reports of reprisals against ex-combatants, possibly due to the fact that the majority of the ex-combatants associated with the RUF did not return home out of shame or fear of reprisals.[28]

Because of their numbers, the return of refugees and the IDPs posed far greater problems if fewer dangers than the return of ex-combatants. The number of ex-combatants were relatively small (all told about 76,000)[29] compared to the hundreds of thousands of civilians seeking to return home. However, from my experience managing the UN's relief operations on the Thai-Cambodia border years before, I knew that once people heard through the grapevine that their areas of origin were safe, whether formally declared or not, they would vote with their feet and start moving home. So we had to prepare for spontaneous as well as organized return.

The government agency responsible for the resettlement and reintegration was the National Commission for Reconstruction, Resettlement, and Rehabilitation (NCRRR), headed by an articulate and politically astute official, Kanja Sesay (no relation to the minister of development, Kadie Sesay). Like Francis Kai Kai, who headed up the sister commission, the NCDDR, Kanja had worked for an international NGO and so was well versed in the susceptibilities of the international aid community. The NCRRR had a wide remit, which inevitably created tensions with the government's line departments—health, education, agriculture, etcetera. As a commission, the NCRRR could operate less bureaucratically than those departments, which made it attractive to donors, especially the World Bank, which was anxious to get reintegration programs moving and show some tangible results.

The OCHA team in Freetown, which was leading the planning and coordination of the return exercise, did an extraordinary job getting the many players involved to work around a common plan with the national commission. Wearing my UNAMSIL and UN coordinator hats, I backed up OCHA's efforts by mobilizing support from UNAMSIL, but mostly by deflecting the pressure from politicians to accelerate returns even when few if any amenities for the returning populations were available.

The challenge of reintegrating populations was immense. But the return also created some extraordinary opportunities. One of the areas badly affected by the war was the western district of Kambia. Before the war, the number of girls in school in Kambia was low, even by Sierra Leone's standards. During the war, much of the population ended up in IDP or refugee camps. They were not pleasant places. Nevertheless, there were some benefits, including free primary education, for both girls and boys. As a result, the number of girls in primary education rose dramatically, creating a huge demand on the schools as people returned home and wanted their children to continue learning. So in effect, a humanitarian intervention had created a development demand—education—that we had not anticipated.

To get a firsthand impression of the situation, I went to Kambia with other members of the National Recovery Committee. Almost all of the schools had been destroyed or severely damaged. We stopped at one of the few secondary schools in the district. The school had been stripped bare; windows, doors, furniture, even the roofing were gone. And yet in the assembly hall, inexplicably, a lectern remained standing, a solitary sentinel of hope, a rebuke to the nihilism that had smashed up everything, signaling perhaps that learning and pupils would someday return to the building, including girls who had started their education in the IDP camps.

Despite the intermittent squabbles over humanitarian space, the overall humanitarian intervention in Sierra Leone was remarkably successful. During the war, 2.6 million people were displaced—almost half of the country's population of 4.5 million.[30] Within a year of the war ending, most people were either home or on their way back.

Combining the DSRSG and humanitarian roles was a debatable step; it still is, and the argument rumbles on. Did the "many-hat model" make sense? Others will judge but I believe that I was far more effective in articulating and advocating the worries and ideas of the humanitarian community from inside rather than outside of UNAMSIL. Moreover, as an integral part of the mission, I was uniquely placed to keep humanitarian actors advised of political and security developments from the UNAMSIL perspective.

Moving On

By the end of 2002, UNAMSIL turned the corner in local and international opinion. The gradual extension of the state presence, the completion of disarmament, the return of populations, the successful elections, and the transitional justice initiatives opened up the optimistic prospect that Sierra Leone was moving into the postconflict column.

Strategies to Exit

Despite Olu Adeniji's earlier apprehensions, there was no rush to the exit. The UN Security Council was willing to stay the course, although it wanted progress on the rebuilding of state institutions and the government's progressive assumption of UNAMSIL's security responsibilities.

The government was in no hurry to see UNAMSIL leave. There was lingering concern about the ex-combatants and the possible repercussions of the impending SCSL trials. Also the collapse of neighboring Liberia and the implosion in Côte d'Ivoire raised fears that Sierra Leone might be caught up in a backwash of arms and combatants said to be moving around West Africa (in reality far fewer than assumed). In addition, of course, UNAMSIL brought money into the country and employed a large number of local people.

As the threat of renewed armed conflict gradually receded and confidence grew, the mission and the UN country team began to shift to transition planning. Back in 2001, as the DDR progressed, the UN country team already took the first step, drawing up a joint strategy to guide UN support for national recovery. UNAMSIL also signed on to that strategy.

With the success of the elections, the UN could contemplate a broader platform for peacebuilding. My versatile special assistant, Hervé Lecoq, developed a matrix with some basic benchmarks for assessing progress on governance and stabilization. The matrix had the singular virtue of simplicity. We could see where we should be going without getting too caught up in myriad details that could obscure rather than enlighten the assessments made in Freetown and New York.

In his September 2002 report, the Secretary-General presented to the Security Council the main elements of a broader mission transition strategy that encompassed the governance and stabilization dimensions. The core of the strategy was the progressive transfer of UNAMSIL's security tasks to the Sierra Leone security services and in particular to the police. We wanted to ensure that the SLP would take over UNAMSIL's internal security responsibilities; the newly trained RSLAF would be deployed for territorial security but not internal policing. The army had not regained public confidence, and its presence on the streets would have created popular disaffection.

The mission's military planners developed an adjustment, drawdown, and withdrawal plan as part of the transition strategy. The plan envisaged a four-stage exercise that would progressively draw down UNAMSIL forces with concomitant handover of security responsibilities to the national government by the end of 2004. Following the approach taken in the national recovery strategy, the government and UNAMSIL made joint district security reviews to assess the feasibility of transferring security responsibilities from UNAMSIL to the Sierra Leone security services.

There was no overarching, single peacebuilding strategy embracing all of Sierra Leone's partners. UNAMSIL developed a mission transition strategy and the adjustment, drawdown, and withdrawal plan; the UN country team helped develop the national recovery strategy and an embryonic UN development assistance framework; the humanitarian community relied on the humanitarian funding appeal; the instrument of choice for the World Bank (and for some of the major donors too) was the interim poverty reduction strategy. So there was no shortage of strategies, but the sum of the parts did not add up to a coherent and navigable roadmap. This would have required a strong lead from the government, which at that point did not have the political weight or management capacity to impose its priorities and process on the international community.

Adeniji Exits

In June 2002, Soheir and I were on a break in Europe. We were relaxing far from the intensities of mission life, or so I thought. I should have known better. With a week still to go, I received a message from Hervé that I should urgently call the SRSG, which I did, wondering what new disaster might have befallen UNAMSIL (missions with active operations live with a constant sense of foreboding).

When I spoke to Olu, he announced that he had been appointed by President Obasanjo as the foreign minister of Nigeria and that he would be leaving the mission within a couple of weeks. Behrooz Sadry, the senior DSRSG, had already left the mission some months before on transfer to the Congo, and so by default I was named as the officer-in-charge of the mission pending the designation of a new SRSG, and I returned immediately to Freetown.

Adeniji left with his reputation bruised but intact. He survived the May 2000 meltdown and, as I have already described, managed to get the mission back on track. He was able to overcome the crisis and eventually restore confidence in the mission, skillfully managing his Nigerian and regional connections. He left on a high note with plentiful plaudits from the local media, which barely two years earlier had loudly called for his head.

In Charge

Following SRSG Adeniji's departure, I acted as the officer-in-charge of the mission for six months. My time in charge was much longer than expected because the government did not agree immediately to the candidates proposed by the Secretary-General to replace Adeniji. The designation of a SRSG is the prerogative of the Secretary-General, who makes the appointment after consultation with the Security Council. There is no formal process of diplomatic *agrément,* as the accreditation of an ambassador requires. That said, the Secretary-General invariably conducts informal consultations with the host authorities as well as the Council to ensure that the candidate will be broadly acceptable.

In many respects a mission runs itself, irrespective of who is in charge. The administration chugged along under the stern eye of an experienced mission manager, Steiner Bjornson. The military under General Opande focused on preparing for the mission drawdown. In contrast, UNAMSIL's civilian police (CIVPOL) component ramped up its training support for the SLP in conjunction with the Commonwealth police team (a good example of interagency cooperation that bears emulation) under the auspices of a joint SLP/Commonwealth/UNAMSIL steering group.

I did not have to face any major security crisis during my tenure as the officer-in-charge of the mission. A couple of weeks after I took charge, however, Foday Sankoh died and as a precaution the mission went on alert but there were no incidents. Most of Sankoh's erstwhile commanders were in jail or dead and he passed from the scene almost without notice.

Nevertheless, the citizenry remained deeply nervous. The trauma of the war years was not far beneath the surface, as I found out when UNAMSIL set out to destroy (just outside of Freetown) some unstable explosives and ammunition recovered during the DDR exercise. Unfortunately, we neglected to inform the good people of Freetown of what we were intending. With the first explosions, panic immediately set in; the business district closed, schools emptied; the prisoners in Pedemba Road prison thought that liberation was at hand; and I received a flurry of agitated calls from the presidency.

We remained wary of ex-combatants. At the time, it was widely believed that Sierra Leonean fighters would return from the fighting in Liberia. The anticipated opening of the SCSL trials added to that apprehension. In January 2003, a group of disgruntled soldiers attacked an RSLAF munitions depot in an abortive attempt to steal weapons. The culprits were probably linked to Johnny Paul Koroma, who may have been seeking to derail the special court. Samuel Hinga Norman's partisans also took to the streets. Nevertheless, the overall security situation within the country remained relatively benign.

By contrast, security in Liberia was worsening by the day. UNAMSIL dispatched the initial wave of peacekeeping troops for Liberia. By a nice irony, these troops came from the Nigerian unit, which had led the first forward deployment into RUF-controlled territory in 2001. General Opande (later appointed as the force commander in Liberia) and I attended the sendoff as the troops, all in full battle gear, boarded the helicopters to take them to Monrovia. It was all very stirring as the general and I pumped them up, urging the troops to make Nigeria and the UN proud.

As agreed by the Security Council, the UNMASIL drawdown proceeded apace. The first two phases were completed by December 2003 without any resurgence of major violence in the areas UNAMSIL vacated.

The Prospect of Peacebuilding

In November 2003, for the first time in many years, the World Bank convened a meeting of the donor consultative group for Sierra Leone. Although chaired by the World Bank, this meeting (held in Paris) recognized the leading role that the UN was playing in Sierra Leone and it was agreed that I would cochair in my resident coordinator and UNDP capacity.

I am rather allergic to big, hyped-up donor conferences. They promise a great deal and deliver much less. While such conferences come up with impressive headline numbers, the disbursement of the pledged funds is often much lower (and slower) than anticipated; donors have even been known to recycle previously approved contributions as new ones.

So, going into the Sierra Leone consultative group, I was at pains to emphasize that the main aim was not so much to mobilize a vast amount of new funding as to agree with development partners on priorities and conditions to ensure that funding would continue to flow and be utilized well. Given Sierra Leone's extremely limited institutional capacity, we had to moderate ambitions of both the government and donors. I was especially concerned that even though new donors would help diversify funding, if they all came with their own priorities and conditionality, the administrative burden would overwhelm the government, resulting in mutual disappointment.

Of course, such events have to be seen to produce results and the conference duly announced some major funding commitments. But more important, in my view, was the agreement on a common framework for peace, recovery, and development building, which identified a number of benchmarks drawing on the work already done through the recovery and transition strategies. A joint government/donor mechanism chaired by the vice president was set up to regularly review progress against the agreed benchmarks.

By the end of 2003, the building blocks of the transition were largely in place. Peacebuilding, at least in terms of democratic representation, reintegration, judicial and security sector reform (SSR), and national recovery, was under way. Economic growth had resumed for the first time in many years. Coordination mechanisms led by the government with donor, NGO, and civil society participation had been established in key policy areas. All of this was a considerable achievement in a country that had gone through more than a decade of hideous conflict and decades of dreadful governance. Despite these undoubted accomplishments, in which UNAMSIL and the UN system had played a central role, there was no shortage of problems in waiting, not least the restoration of public confidence in state institutions, the unfinished reform of the security services, the campaign against corruption, and above all the fissures in society that reached back to the founding of Sierra Leone. In short, there was no room for complacency; peacebuilding was still very much a work in progress.

Farewell Salone

In January 2004, a new SRSG, Daudi Mwakawago, finally arrived in Freetown. A former minister and Tanzania's ambassador to the UN in New York, he was more outgoing than Adeniji. But he had not worked in West Africa before, nor was he familiar with peacekeeping operations. However, I felt that he, as a former politician and minister, would understand the constraints and hard choices that even the most well-intentioned political leaders face in a country recovering from a prolonged conflict.

As Ambassador Mwakawago assumed full management of the mission, my role changed. But I had more than enough on my plate. We were winding down the OCHA-led humanitarian operation and I was keen to move forward from crisis mode toward a developmental focus. I was able to spend more time on the governance dimension of my mandate; I was especially concerned about the lamentable condition of the public service, which had largely collapsed during the war years. So I was not seeking a new job—but one came looking for me.

In February 2004 the United Nations Operation in Côte d'Ivoire (ONUCI) was established. ONUCI followed a small political and military observer mission, the United Nations Mission in Côte d'Ivoire (MINUCI), which had been set up to monitor and facilitate implementation of the Linas-Marcoussis peace agreement. The government of Laurent Gbagbo had signed the agreement with Ivorian political leaders in January 2004 in a bid to end the conflict that had erupted in Côte d'Ivoire a couple of years before.

The mission was already struggling, for reasons I shall explain in my chapter on Côte d'Ivoire. The deputy SRSG post was vacant. Hedi Annabi called and asked if I would help out. Jean-Marie Guéhenno, head of DPKO, felt that my experience in Sierra Leone, especially in the area of DDR and transition, would be valuable. After a quick reconnaissance mission to Abidjan, I accepted the appointment.

So I left Sierra Leone with a sense of accomplishment. Of course, I was only a part of a far greater effort that involved thousands of people. But as a newcomer to peacekeeping, Sierra Leone was a powerful learning experience that afforded me several valuable insights. The first insight is what I call the imponderables of peace. The war in Sierra Leone was not ended by a single diplomatic master stroke or military intervention, but rather by an accumulation of decisions, events, and incidents. Some were fortuitous but nevertheless profoundly affected the course of the war and the search for peace. I wonder, for example, what might have happened if a Conservative rather than a Labour government had won office in the UK in June 1997. Without Prime Minister Tony Blair's personal connection to Sierra Leone (his father had been a visiting lecturer at Fourah Bay College), would the UK's commitment have been as strong and determined as it was? For a country in trouble, it helps to have a committed champion in the Security Council, especially if a peacekeeping intervention is being considered. Fortunately for Sierra Leone, the UK was ready and able to take on that role.

Moreover, as Adrian Foster, a colleague and former military chief of staff of UNAMSIL and later a deputy military adviser to the UN Secretary-General, has pointed out: "The fact that Sierra Leone government's interests were well aligned with those of the Mission and the international community (and that the personalities gelled) had a fundamentally positive effect on peacebuilding and drawdown. This is seldom seen."[31]

The way the war ended does illustrate that the pursuit of peace is not a linear process that moves forward step by irreversible step. Trial, error, and try again were integral parts of the process that brought peace back to Sierra Leone. This required patience and perseverance from the Security Council, the regional institutions, and the UN Secretariat, and it took ten years. The arc of conflict can be long, and while outsiders may try to prolong or shorten it, they ultimately cannot define it.

A second insight, one related more directly to the postconflict transition, was the need to move quickly to shore up the peace process with tangible actions that address the welfare and well-being of the population. During peace negotiations, there is always easy talk of a peace dividend, which is held out as an incentive for peace. In reality, these good intentions often become bogged down in donor procedures or government incapacities.

I spent a lot of my time in Sierra Leone attempting to break through logjams of one kind or another to get services back to the population. I recognized that there was a danger of overreach, doing what the government should have been doing for its own people. Nevertheless, I strongly believed that we had to demonstrate that change was possible in order to create the space and time required to rebuild the country's capacities and to allow longer-term reforms to come online. These early initiatives were a down payment on the future.

My third insight was the need to sidestep the energy-sapping "strategy syndrome." We spent a lot of time thinking, talking, and writing strategies of one kind or another on recovery, transition, humanitarian, drawdown, peacebuilding, and so on. The strategy factory, of which I was the general manager, worked overtime and produced many good ideas. Nevertheless, we also imposed an unnecessary burden on the national authorities (and ourselves), struggling to cope with the daily round of crises of one kind or another.

A sense of national direction and clearly set priorities is of course vital to guide a postwar transition. However, given the many political uncertainties, the weak national capacities (aggravated by the demands of donors and democracy alike), and the absence of reliable (or any) data, we should have focused from the outset on a limited set of goals and easily measurable indicators, at least for a couple of years after the war formally ended. We eventually came around to that approach in the framework presented to the donor consultative group in October 2003.

Another lesson relates to the UN integration agenda. Kofi Annan and the Security Council wanted the UN and its constituent parts to work more cohesively or, at the very least, not at cross purposes. A worthwhile goal, but did it work? I cannot say that my opinion is totally objective, but I do believe the integration initiative paid off. I was empowered to steer resources and capacities to key priorities, which would have proved far more difficult without my multiple institutional links. For example, without those links, I could not have mobilized the funding for the elections nor rallied the resources of the mission for the reintegration programs—a key dimension of the stabilization agenda.

With some variations, the model of integration we tried out in Sierra Leone has been applied in almost all of the multidimensional peacekeeping operations fielded since, which means, I suppose, that it worked. Nevertheless, an integration project that cuts across institutional lines is not easily or quickly achieved. The initial impetus from New York was crucial: without the commitment of the top tier of headquarters management, this effort might have been stillborn.

I took away a final, lasting lesson from Sierra Leone. Throughout my time there, I made a point of getting out of my office and Freetown as much as possible to meet people and see at firsthand conditions on the ground. I visited many villages; paid calls on dozens of chiefs and elders; opened schools, community centers, and courts; bumped over many kilometers of broken roads; talked to countless community groups; and met with hundreds of ex-combatants. Nevertheless, I felt that I was only just touching the surface of life in Sierra Leone and that my understanding of the deeper forces at work in the society was quite superficial (as I had discovered during that first meeting of the DDR joint committee). That sense of inadequacy—of not really understanding the societies that I was expected to assist—challenged me in all the missions that followed.

3

Côte d'Ivoire:
The War of Succession

Happy are those few nations that have not waited till the slow succession of human vicissitudes should, from the extremity of evil, produce a transition to good; but by prudent laws have facilitated the progress from one to the other!

—Cesare Beccaria

The title of this chapter derives from a late evening conversation with President Laurent Gbagbo (he liked night meetings) not long before I left Côte d'Ivoire. During the conversation, he remarked that the troubles that had overtaken the country and led to the deployment of UN peacekeepers were really about the succession to the long-serving President Félix Houphouët-Boigny, who had died in 1993. The title of this chapter is inspired by that comment because it explains in part why an apparently stable country, often touted as an African success story, fell into violent disarray.

The succession, as I discuss further on, was highly disputed from the outset. Personal ambitions certainly played a part in the struggle to inherit Houphouët-Boigny's mantle. But behind those ambitions lay an array of other factors that aggravated and intensified the struggle for the succession. Some reached back to colonial times and earlier; others, more recent, were the direct consequence of policies that Houphouët-Boigny had himself pursued. I explore them briefly in order to set the context for the UN peacekeeping intervention that followed ten years after Houphouët-Boigny's death.

A Colony Becomes a Country

European inroads along the West African coast from the Atlantic seaboard began with the arrival of Portuguese mariners in the fifteenth century. Those initial forays were expanded over the next three centuries by trading companies, among them the French Company of Senegal. In 1843–1844, the company set up a trading post in Assinie on the Ivorian coast and concluded treaties with local chiefs in Assinie and Grand Bassam.

In 1885, the Conference of Berlin recognized European spheres of influence in Africa and as a result Côte d'Ivoire became a French colony in 1893. Subsequent French efforts to penetrate the interior areas of Côte d'Ivoire provoked a series of wars with the indigenous Mandingo people led by Samory Touré and culminated in Samory's defeat, capture, and exile in 1898.

Unlike Sierra Leone, which comprised a small crown colony at the coast and a much larger protectorate in the hinterland where traditional rulers retained authority under British tutelage, French rule in Côte d'Ivoire was far more centralized (as was the case throughout French West Africa). Appointments to all levels of government from the district up were made by the French authorities. Local chiefdoms were subject to French control.

World War II weakened colonial rule and encouraged the aspirations of local political leaders throughout the colonial world. The "winds of change" were stirring in Africa as in other regions under colonial rule. In Côte d'Ivoire, African plantation owners joined together to demand recognition of their rights, creating the African Agricultural Union (Syndicat Agricole Africain), led by Félix Houphouët-Boigny, the scion of a family of traditional chiefs of the Baoulé ethnic group. He was active in local politics before World War II, organizing African planters (commercial farmers) to protect their rights under the colonial administration.

In contrast to UK colonial rule, which favored decentralization but not representation in Westminster, the French system allowed for colonial representatives to sit in parliamentary institutions in Paris. In 1945 Houphouët-Boigny was elected to represent African interests in the first postwar French constituent assembly, where he militated for changes to colonial policy and founded the African Democratic Rally (RDA). Local parties were established in individual countries in support of the RDA (in Côte d'Ivoire it was the Democratic Party of Côte d'Ivoire [PDCI], led by Houphouët-Boigny).

Following the collapse of France's Fourth Republic in 1958 and Charles de Gaulle's return to power, Houphouët-Boigny was appointed as a minister in the French government and charged with developing the specific laws for the new constitution that would govern the colonies. In the referendums that followed to decide on the new order, Côte d'Ivoire voted to become an autonomous republic within the French community.

Two years later, on August 7, 1960, Côte d'Ivoire became a fully independent nation, with Houphouët-Boigny as its first president. He remained in office until his death in 1993.

Toward the Abyss

Côte d'Ivoire under Houphouët-Boigny's rule avoided the serial coups that badly damaged Sierra Leone. But his style of government was decidedly authoritarian. Even before independence, he had exiled opponents within the PDCI who opposed the policy of close ties with France. Until the last years of his administration, Houphouët-Boigny kept a tight rein on the country, combining selective repression with generous patronage.

The close rapport with France, which had long been a cornerstone of Houphouët-Boigny's policy, stood in stark contrast with Sierra Leone's relationship with the UK during the rule of Siaka Stevens. For most of his time in office, Houphouët-Boigny was well regarded in France (and indeed by the West) and lauded as a pillar of political and economic stability in an increasingly unstable and violent West Africa.

This foreign perception of Côte d'Ivoire as an African success story masked, however, deep disaffection that would eventually come back to haunt the country when the powers of the president began to wane before he eventually left the stage. Houphouët-Boigny stymied political expression and activism until almost the very end of his "reign," leaving a legacy of resentment among groups who felt excluded and marginalized.

Already in 1970, a violent confrontation with the Bété community from the center-west part of the country resulted in several hundred deaths and the Bété's permanent estrangement from the PDCI.[1] That enmity was clearly present decades later when Laurent Gbagbo, a Bété who had been arrested and imprisoned in 1972, competed fiercely with the PDCI.

An equally fundamental challenge arose from the migrant-dependent growth of the Ivorian economy. At the time of independence, the population was only 3 million. The economic "miracle" that came about after independence was in good measure founded on plantation agriculture manned by immigrant labor from neighboring countries. By 1990, in some regions of the country, 40 percent of the population was of non-Ivorian origin.[2] Houphouët-Boigny encouraged this migration for economic reasons but also because of his long-standing belief in the value of regional integration. This policy worked well but stored up trouble for the future as economic growth began to slow and the competition for arable land increased.

Houphouët-Boigny's heavy dependence on French advisers and security apparatus was another source of lingering resentment. He relied on French forces stationed in Côte d'Ivoire under treaty arrangements to help him maintain order. There was an assumption that French support for the security of the Ivorian state would remain an unqualified constant, an assumption that did not hold up in later years.

A House Divided

President Houphouët-Boigny died in December 1993. He had decreed that on his death, he would be succeeded by the president of the National Assembly. The president of the assembly was Henri Konan Bédié, rumored to be Houphouët-Boigny's natural son. His appointment ushered in almost two decades of fierce personal rivalry, a de facto partition of the country, and armed conflict.

From the outset, Bédié's claim on the presidency was contested. Alassane Ouattara, a former senior official of the IMF and governor of the West African Central Bank, who had been made prime minister in 1990 with a mandate to reform and redress the Ivorian economy after a severe downturn, together with the army chief of staff, Robert Guei, opposed his assumption of the presidency. The courts sided with Bédié, and Ouattara resigned and returned to a senior post at the IMF in Washington, D.C.

In the run-up to the 1995 elections, Bédié set about reinforcing his electoral prospects by modifying the electoral code to exclude candidates whose parents (both) had not been born in Côte d'Ivoire or who had not lived in the country for the preceding five years. He termed this requirement *Ivoirité*. The measure was clearly intended to exclude Ouattara, whom Bedié considered an electoral threat. The issue of *Ivoirité* became a central element in the political crisis that progressively enveloped and profoundly destabilized Côte d'Ivoire.

Laurent Gbagbo and his party (the Ivorian Popular Front [FPI]) actually sided with Ouattara on this issue and opposed the *Ivoirité* requirement. Later he reversed his position and adamantly refused to modify the provision (Article 35 of the constitution adopted in 2000). On the occasion of another late evening meeting, I asked Gbagbo, by then president, why he had initially opposed the *Ivoirité* provision but was now firmly insisting that it be maintained. His response was disarmingly simple and cynical: "I didn't want to give Bedié a political boost."

Bedié won the 1995 election in a landslide made possible by the exclusion of Ouattara and by Gbagbo's boycott of the polls. It was a pyrrhic victory; discontent burgeoned, culminating in an army coup in December 1999, ostensibly with the objective of restoring democracy. Bédié fled the country and General Robert Guei, a popular and retired former army chief of staff, was named the head of a government of national unity that was formed but then subsequently dissolved as Guei declared that he would run for the presidency, reneging on his earlier promise not to do so, and then arranging for the Supreme Court to disqualify Ouattara.

The subsequent presidential election in October 2000 proved to be a fiasco. Gbagbo claimed victory but Guei initially refused to cede power, triggering demonstrations by Gbagbo and Ouattara supporters against him but also against each other. Gbagbo was able to assume office but the legitimacy of his electoral victory was disputed from the start because of Ouattara's exclusion.

So like his predecessor, Gbagbo became president under a cloud. An attempted coup in early 2001 signaled continuing disaffection. In an effort to quell the violence and opposition to his regime, Gbagbo convened a forum for national unity in October 2001 and then, in July 2002, formed a national unity government. Later that month a court delivered a nationality certificate to Ouattara, thereby settling, it seemed, a major source of grievance and dissention.

It was too late. On September 12, 2002, there was another uprising, this time led by soldiers recruited during General Guei's regime slated for demobilization. Despite counterattacks by loyalist forces, the rebels consolidated their hold in the northern half of the country and put forward a political program under the banner of the Patriotic Movement of Côte d'Ivoire (MPCI); a few weeks later the MPCI was joined by two armed groups from the western part of the country demanding revenge for the death of Guei, who had been killed in the early hours of the attempted takeover of Abidjan.

French forces helped to hold back the rebel forces but they did not act to defeat and disarm them. France's reluctance to defeat the rebellion became a permanent bone of contention, exacerbated by the personal antipathy between French president Jacques Chirac and his Ivorian counterpart. While the French government did not want the rebellion to take over the country, it did not display much enthusiasm for Gbagbo either, as I found out from my own interactions with senior French diplomats and officials.

On October 17, 2002, a ceasefire (called Accra I) was concluded under ECOWAS auspices at a meeting of the government and armed groups in the Ghanaian capital.[3] In late October, ECOWAS proposed an intervention force, known as the ECOWAS Mission in Côte d'Ivoire (ECOMICI), with a mandate to monitor the cessation of hostilities, facilitate the return of public administrative services, contribute to the implementation of the peace agreement, and guarantee the safety of the rebels and humanitarian workers. However, ECOWAS struggled to find enough troops for ECOMICI. By February 2003, there were approximately 3,000 French soldiers but only 500 ECOWAS troops on the ground.

The Search for Solutions: From Lomé to Linas-Marcoussis

Negotiations on a political agreement began in Lomé in late October 2002. Despite some initial progress, the talks stalled as the MPCI insisted on Gbagbo's resignation, a new constitution, and fresh elections.[4] Meanwhile the Gbagbo government insisted that the rebels should first demobilize and disarm. This remained the sticking point in all the subsequent negotiations.

At the beginning of 2003 the French government, despite the tense relations with Gbagbo, convened a roundtable of the Ivorian political groups at the Chateau of Linas-Marcoussis, outside Paris. The conference, chaired by Pierre Mazeaud of the French Constitutional Court, included all the Ivorian protagonists.

The conference produced the Linas-Marcoussis Agreement,[5] signed by the parties on January 23, 2003. Considering it was drafted and approved in less than two weeks, the agreement was detailed and ambitious. It was anchored on three main points: the need to maintain the territorial integrity of Côte d'Ivoire; the creation of a government of national reconciliation, with a new prime minister, who would hold office until elections scheduled for late 2005; and the conduct of transparent and free elections that would not exclude candidates based on *Ivoirité*. Other points covered land tenure rights, army reform, amnesty for mutineers and insurgent forces, and, more far-reaching, the issue of identity or nationality with new legislation that would integrate and protect the millions of immigrants residing in the country.[6] The prime minister would receive delegated powers from the president. The agreement also established an international monitoring committee chaired by the UN with representatives of the major foreign players. The Linas-Marcoussis Agreement also assigned the UN a role in guaranteeing the reform and restructuring of the defense forces.

Linas-Marcoussis was a model agreement in the sense that it covered all the bases. It was a well-reasoned and well-structured document. But it was essentially a legal agreement rather than a political settlement. With the benefit of hindsight, that outcome was hardly surprising given the brief period of the negotiations and the pressures put on the protagonists to reach a deal.

Gbagbo did not sign the agreement personally and agreed very reluctantly to the designation of Seydou Diarra, a well-regarded former minister and ambassador, as prime minister. Even before the parties left Paris, Linas-Marcoussis began to unravel. Violent protests against the agreement broke out in Abidjan and elsewhere, which prevented Diarra's return to Abidjan. This was a tactic that the Gbagbo camp devised on later occasions to derail agreements he or his delegates signed without conviction.

After I took up my post in Abidjan, I met with Pascal Affi Nguessan, the president of the FPI (and a former prime minister under Gbagbo), to discuss various points, including the reform of the electoral commission, which the FPI was blocking. When I pointed out that the reform was mandated by Linas-Marcoussis, which he had signed on behalf of the government, he brushed my argument aside, saying that they had no choice but to sign. In other words, Linas-Marcoussis was a tactical maneuver, not an act of settlement.

The security situation calmed down but as the weeks passed it became abundantly clear that Gbagbo would not implement Linas-Marcoussis as originally envisaged. There was constant wrangling among the president, the prime minister, the political parties, and the armed groups over the application of the agreement both in letter and in spirit. The prime minister and opposition complained vehemently that the delegation of authority—a key provision of the agreement—was not being respected.

The UN Intervenes: From Observation to Operations

Despite the Linas-Marcoussis Agreement, by March 2003 the peace process had been bogged down again in boycotts and bickering. In an effort to get the process back on track, President Kufuor of Ghana, in his capacity as chairman of ECOWAS, brokered another agreement (Accra II) with the Linas-Marcoussis signatories. This allowed the government to go forward with the selection of the ministers of defense and interior (a make-or-break point for both sides) and the president formally delegated authority to the prime minister to implement the Linas-Marcoussis work program, but only for six months.

Despite this apparent breakthrough, there was growing apprehension that the peace process was floundering and hostilities might resume. The ECOWAS force was underresourced and struggling to field and equip enough troops. Sitting nearby in Sierra Leone, we were hearing the rumors that the UN might have to take on a larger role. However, there was some reluctance in the Security Council to see another major peacekeeping operation launched in West Africa (the Liberia mission was already in the works).

The response, in the best of UN traditions, was to send an assessment mission. The mission, led by Hedi Annabi, was duly dispatched in March to assess "the situation on the ground, including the prospects for the implementation of the Linas-Marcoussis agreement and the role that the United Nations could play in supporting its implementation."[7]

Based on findings of the assessment mission, the Secretary-General concluded that "the Linas-Marcoussis Agreement offers the best chance for the Ivorian people to peacefully resolve the conflict that threatens to plunge their country into a crisis of the proportions that have devastated neighboring Liberia and Sierra Leone."[8] So despite the unpropitious start to its implementation, the Security Council and Secretary-General decided to bet on the Linas-Marcoussis Agreement as the framework for resolving the conflict.

The reference to Sierra Leone and Liberia in the Secretary-General's report was instructive. It reflected a domino theory of security in West Africa. There was a fear that the subregion was threatened by a wave of violent uprisings, with armed groups migrating from one country to another, and with Côte d'Ivoire seen as the next tile to fall. I was in Sierra Leone and attended regional meetings where this thesis was expounded. West African fighters did cross borders, but the failure of the Ivorian polity was the fundamental reason for the crisis, not Liberian or Sierra Leone mercenaries, just as state failure was at the origin of the Sierra Leone conflict.

A general ceasefire was agreed on in early May 2003 and with it the creation of a weapons-free zone of confidence between the opposing forces that would be monitored by French and ECOWAS forces. This was tantamount to a de facto partition of the country. The Forces Nouvelles, the armed wing of the MPCI, with its headquarters in the northern city of Bouaké, began to "administer" the territory under its control. Their areas of control were divided up and put under the control of zone commanders from the Forces Nouvelles, who quickly transformed themselves into local warlords pledging ostensible allegiance to Forces Nouvelles leader Guillaume Soro (more on him later).

Later that month, the Security Council, buoyed by the ceasefire announcement, authorized a limited UN peacekeeping operation in support of Linas-Marcoussis—notwithstanding the doubts about its viability as a solution to the Ivorian crisis. The UN Mission in Côte d'Ivoire was established essentially as a military observer and liaison mission. The mission was expected to advise and assist the SRSG in his role as chair of the monitoring committee and help "build confidence and trust"[9] between the National Armed Forces of Côte d'Ivoire (FANCI) and the armed groups.

For a while there seemed to be genuine progress. FANCI and the Forces Nouvelles declared an end to the war in July; a DDR program was developed by the World Bank and the UNDP; and trade and communication links between the north and south were restored. Nevertheless, despite this progress, the political tug-of-war continued. In September, the Forces Nouvelles pulled out of the government, claiming that the president was not respecting the provisions of Linas-Marcoussis.

The political and security situation again began to deteriorate, aggravated by incidents caused by FANCI and the pro-Gbagbo Young Patriots (Jeunes Patriotes) militants, who attempted incursions across the ceasefire lines. ECOWAS turned to the UN in November and requested that the Security Council transform the ECOWAS Mission in Côte d'Ivoire into a peacekeeping operation. Ironically, considering what was to come a few months later, President Gbagbo strongly supported this demarche and wrote to the Council, pointing out the weakness of the ECOWAS deployment as a deterrent force, and adding that as the United Nations Mission in Côte d'Ivoire (MINUCI) "has no direct mandate to intervene in order to maintain the peace, it complements the operations carried out by the French and ECOWAS forces which themselves are limited by their mandate." In his letter, he went on to urge the Council to help put an end to the "conflict–coup d'état spiral that is preventing the sub-region from devoting its resources and energies to the only worthwhile struggle, namely, the struggle for development."[10]

Obviously, Gbagbo was endorsing the idea of a fully fledged peacekeeping operation in the expectation that it would help him to deal robustly with the rebellion, which neither the French nor ECOWAS seemed willing or able to do. As we saw in Sierra Leone (and as I point out later in the chapter on MONUC), there was an assumption (a mistaken one) that the deployment of armed UN peacekeepers would automatically aid the regime in place. Disappointment lay in wait.

Another UN assessment mission was dispatched in December. There had been some movement in the weeks prior to the assessment, including the decision of the Forces Nouvelles to reintegrate the cabinet and the joint withdrawal of heavy weapons from the zone of confidence. This was enough for Secretary-General Annan to refer to "significant steps" that would allow the UN to deploy a mission, which he believed would "show that the international community is determined to support this progress and to ensure that there is no turning back." He recommended a peacekeeping operation, but on the understanding that the parties would "engage in a viable peace process that the [UN] could support."[11] Further on in his report, Annan stated that "there should be no illusions" and that the Ivorian leaders must show good faith and make sufficient progress before the expiry date of the MINUCI mandate (February 4, 2004), to ensure that a peacekeeping operation would go ahead.[12] Unfortunately, experience had shown that a peacekeeping operation deployed on the assumption of good faith is a mission that will almost certainly run into trouble. ONUCI was established on April 4, 2004, with a Chapter VII mandate and a wide span of tasks ranging from political mediation to the protection of civilians.

These were the circumstances that brought me to Abidjan and another war. This one, however, had not yet wrecked the entire country or driven a vast number of its people into refugee and IDP camps. But the demons had been let loose and the dangers of a protracted and nasty conflict were all too present.

A City Redefined

I had known Abidjan in its "glory days" in the 1970s and 1980s. I visited from Niger and Benin, where I was representing the UNDP. Abidjan was the big, bustling metropolis, the "Paris of West Africa," which left other capitals in the shade with its fine boulevards, upmarket restaurants, and the luxurious Hotel Ivoire, which even boasted, incongruously, an ice-skating rink. Of course, the country was not Abidjan and the conspicuous wealth on display in those years bypassed much of the population.

But after spending three and a half years in Freetown, which had been ruined by armed incursions and deeply impoverished by the war, I expected Abidjan to present a more pleasant prospect. And indeed, unlike Freetown, the lights were still on, the water and sanitation services were functioning, and the phones worked. Traffic was as congested as ever, with the ambulatory supermarkets—iterant hawkers selling everything from toilet paper to oriental carpets—crowding the approaches to the bridges crossing the Abidjan lagoons. And despite the crisis, Abidjan still hosted some excellent if very pricey restaurants.

I soon discovered, however, that the earlier glitter of Abidjan had been dimmed by the years of strife, even though there had not been any significant armed violence in the city up to that point. The capital no longer enjoyed the ease and affluence of its best days; the city's infrastructure was deteriorating and the influx of people displaced from the northern and western areas of the country was overwhelming the health and educational services. Businesses were closing down as the political crisis eroded confidence in the economy. Blocks of office towers still dominated the skyline but were half-empty, immobilized by elevators that no longer worked.

The decay of the Hotel Ivoire, a showpiece from the Houphouët-Boigny days, told a depressing if elitist tale of the times. The hotel was decidedly run down and no longer the plush palace of privilege of its earlier years. The lobby was full of sullen young men, said to be Jeunes Patriotes who were camping out in the hotel. The staff, in their shabby uniforms, shuffled around with a rather downcast demeanor, regretting, I sensed, the loss of the hotel's former splendor.

The heavy and oppressive presence of the security forces was palpable across the city. Units of the security services positioned themselves at strategic points, ostensibly to conduct security checks but actually to extort payment from any unlucky drivers and passengers who ventured onto their terrain. The soldiers, gendarmes, and police manning these checkpoints (dubbed by Abidjan residents as the *barrages sauvages*) could be very unpredictable and nasty, especially at night, when they were often high on alcohol, drugs, or both (shades of the RUF). UN vehicles were not spared these alarming encounters. In areas of the city thought to be opposition strongholds, the security presence was even more intense, with militias targeting suspected opposition sympathizers.

Getting Started

In February 2003, the Secretary-General appointed Albert Tévoédjré as his special representative for Côte d'Ivoire. A former minister and legislator from Benin, Tévoédjré was well known and respected in West African academic and political circles. Rather saturnine in character, he was much more at home dealing with diplomatic and political issues than the day-to-day management of a multidimensional peacekeeping operation. However, given the nature of the Ivorian crisis, and its regional implications, Tévoédjré was a logical choice to head up of the mission. His principal task was to chair the monitoring committee for Linas-Marcoussis, which was expected to ensure that the agreement's signatories respected their commitments. This quickly proved to be a thankless task, as the parties continued to contest almost every aspect of the agreement.

I am not sure how pleased Tévoédjré was by my appointment. He had other candidates in mind but headquarters insisted that my Sierra Leone experience would be of value to the operation, especially for what was assumed would be a transition from war to peace. So again, I had to take care to build a good relationship with the SRSG and avoid the debilitating intramural squabbles that had proved so damaging in the early days of UNAMSIL.

As in UNAMSIL, I sought to build a good relationship with both the force commander and the UN police commissioner. The force commander, Lieutenant-General Abdoulaye Fall from Senegal, and the police commissioner, Yves Bouchard from Canada, were highly professional officers with whom I developed close and warm relationships, ones that served me well during the days of duress to come.

Completing the senior management team was Abdoulaye Mar Dieye from Senegal. Earlier we had worked together in the UNDP. Mar was already the UN resident coordinator based in Abidjan and was then rehatted as DSRSG with a portfolio similar to the one I had carried in Sierra Leone. Mar had an office and a small staff in ONUCI but decided to keep the UNDP office in Abidjan as his primary base. Mar was already resident and humanitarian coordinator before ONUCI arrived and felt that he could discharge those functions more effectively without integrating physically with the mission. He closely engaged with the mission, attending key events and meetings. So I have to say that his alternative office accommodation was not a grave impediment to the functioning of the mission. However, I still believe that proximity does help to facilitate day-to-day interaction, which makes a mission more manageable and cohesive.

As it happened, while the force commander had an office at the Cocody headquarters, his military staff could not be accommodated there and were installed in the Pergola Hotel in another part of the city reached by crossing a strategic and vulnerable bridge. As we found to our cost later in the year when fighting flared in Abidjan, the old maxim of the real estate business—location, location, location—holds true for peacekeeping missions too.

A Deputy by Any Other Name

My terms of reference awarded me a rather lofty title: principal deputy special representative of the Secretary-General. The "principal" designation was added, I was told by Hedi Annabi, as recognition of services rendered in Sierra Leone. In practice, it didn't make much difference.

I did insist on one perquisite, however: the transfer of some colleagues from UNAMSIL with whom I had worked closely during my years in Freetown. Despite the fact that the staff members in question were all a known quantity with excellent records, it still took months to get my team together. Transferring Bert Coppens from the UNDP, Sierra Leone, as my chief of staff (later ONUCI chief of staff), who was fluent in French, was especially difficult, as was transfer for staff already with DPKO. I asked for Carol Joseph, my invaluable assistant in UNAMSIL, to join me, and for Arslan Malik, who had worked as a civilian assistant to the head of the United Nations Police (UNPOL) in UNAMSIL. A lawyer by training, Arslan replaced Hervé, who moved on to DPKO, New York; Arslan in ONUCI (as well as in later missions), along with Bert, helped me keep my finger on the mission pulse—not so easy to do from the higher reaches of the hierarchy.

My title was quite grand but my responsibilities in ONUCI were narrower than those I had exercised in UNAMSIL. I was no longer the DSRSG, resident coordinator, nor humanitarian coordinator, and had to be careful not to wander into areas that were now part of Mar's portfolio. Although my area of responsibility was smaller, it did include a number of strategic issues that became mission-critical as the peace process began to fall apart.

Part of my job was to exercise general oversight of the administration and staff. As the SRSG had not managed a peacekeeping operation, DPKO believed that my experience in Sierra Leone would be helpful for mission management and the expected postconflict transition in Côte d'Ivoire. The daily administrative management was in the hands of Hugh Price, an experienced and long-serving UN staffer who didn't need any guidance from me. I decided that I would be more productive if I concentrated on issues of cross-mission coordination. This was a lesson I gained from UNAMSIL, where weak internal coordination had impaired its effectiveness.

The mission had not set up any internal coordination mechanisms. As I talked to mission colleagues, I heard complaints about not knowing what was happening. I developed some procedures to promote stronger internal cohesion and to ensure a better flow of information. The senior management began to meet on a regular basis. Not rocket science but helpful nonetheless. A separate arrangement was put in place to coordinate staff security, which proved to be an important but imperfect innovation when violence exploded in Abidjan later in the year.

All of this may seem somewhat inconsequential and hardly a career highlight. But as I had found in UNAMSIL, and found again in subsequent missions, the flow of information is critical for team building. The hard part, however, is finding the right formula that brings all mission components together in a manner that doesn't overload everyone with endless, unproductive meetings that serve only as a mechanism for the passive exchange of information (or the meanderings of the chairman). I don't think I ever came up with the perfect formula in ONUCI or elsewhere—there were always grumbles from one quarter or other—but it's a critical dimension of peacekeeping management that often goes unnoticed.

Chimera: Reform and the Rule of Law

Management oversight was only one part of my job description. I was given the portfolio of the rule of law and the elections. Rule of law included the human rights component of the mission and the police. In contrast to Sierra Leone, where the worst of the human rights violations had passed by the time I left, Côte d'Ivoire was descending into the inferno, with daily reports of mistreatment of civilians both by government and rebel forces. On paper the institutions of justice were in place, but in reality the rule of law had been largely eroded as a functioning institutional system.

The police and the gendarmerie were not receptive to advice and assistance from UNPOL, despite the efforts of Yves Bouchard and his team. While some training continued, the results were desultory. Only later, after a military escalation (the crisis of November 2004, which I describe further on), did the government turn to ONUCI for assistance with the police.

Our rule-of-law team encountered similar frustrations. But whereas the leadership of the Ivorian police refused to cooperate, the minister of justice in the coalition government, a thoughtful and gracious lawyer, Henrietta Diabété, was very open to advice and dialogue whenever I met with her. She was a member of Ouattara's Rally of the Republicans (RDR) party and as such subjected to constant harassment from the media friendly to Gbagbo as well as obstruction from the security services and the presidency. Although nominally the minister, she had little authority and certainly could not launch any meaningful reforms. So our efforts on law reform and institutional development really got nowhere. The courts were increasingly politicized, especially at the highest level, with the Constitutional Court becoming an adjunct of the presidency.

The UN force commander and I also tried, unsuccessfully, to encourage a dialogue on security sector reform as called for in the mission mandate. At a couple of desultory meetings with the defense staff (together with French advisers), we got nowhere. Given the increasingly tense relationship between ONUCI and the government, our ability to achieve any kind of reform dropped close to zero notwithstanding the admonitions of the Security Council.[13]

The Struggle for Human Rights

With the increasing violence against civilians, this area of my responsibility gained importance. Both government and rebel forces committed abuses against civilians. They also fell out violently among themselves (rebel leader Guillaume Soro escaped several assassination attempts, while his principal rival in the Forces Nouvelles was killed in unexplained circumstances). This made the task of recording, investigating, and reporting on the multiple violations a demanding and dangerous task for field officers;

neither the government nor the Forces Nouvelles were willing to cooperate with these investigations.

Given the alarming deterioration into insecurity, the Security Council called for internationally led investigations into human rights violations,[14] including the deadly attacks on opposition supporters by the security forces and the Jeunes Patriotes during a protest demonstration in Abidjan. Although the UN urged the authorities to take action against the perpetrators, the unwillingness of state institutions to impose an objective judicial process meant that there was no effective follow-up. All this did was to fuel the government's anti-UN and anti-ONUCI rhetoric.

Fortunately, ONUCI had a strong human rights team, headed up by Simon Munzu from Cameroon. We were aware that it was not only government-related security forces that were committing egregious human rights violations. The staff started to investigate allegations that Forces Nouvelles commanders in the north of the country had also committed massacres. Led by a courageous young Congolese staffer, Guillaume N'Guefa, a field team began to investigate a suspected atrocity committed by the Forces Nouvelles. As the site was in an area of northern Côte d'Ivoire controlled by a notorious Forces Nouvelles commander and local warlord, this was a hazardous undertaking and I hesitated to authorize the mission. I was persuaded to do so only after the force commander assured me that the ONUCI military would provide protective security.

The investigation found mass graves in the Korogho area in the far north of the country. Word got out about the investigation and I started to receive calls from some Western embassies urging me to publish the results, even though the work was not fully completed. We were certainly not intending to suppress the report, but I was concerned about leaks; the investigating team was still in the area and there was a risk that the local Forces Nouvelles commander would disrupt the investigation, possibly violently. In addition to safety concerns for our team, I wanted the Office of the High Commissioner of Human Rights to sign off on the report before we went public, as I knew that it would become a political football. Having been accused of committing grave violations itself, the government would undoubtedly seize on the opportunity to paint the Forces Nouvelles in the same colors.

The report was published and of course the Forces Nouvelles denied the charges, while the government jumped on to brand the Forces Nouvelles as mass killers. The report contained documented evidence that could validate UN sanctions against Forces Nouvelles commanders implicated in the killings. I thought the case was a good one. Unfortunately, sanctions were not imposed; the Security Council, acting on the recommendation of President Thabo Mbeki of South Africa, the AU mediator for Côte d'Ivoire, decided to postpone a decision while his Ivorian mediation was under way, which I thought was a mistake. Both sides needed to know that the Council would hold them to account.

Despite the commitment and diligence of the UN human rights staff in Côte d'Ivoire, they could not substitute for the police and the courts or overcome the unwillingness of both the government and the Forces Nouvelles to denounce human rights crimes committed by their own people. The staff working on these investigations, seeing no tangible action against perpetrators, became rather despondent. I tried to rally morale, contending that despite the lack of evident progress, it was still vitally important that the state authorities, the Forces Nouvelles, and victims knew that grave violations did not go unnoticed.

The Electoral Conundrum

The Linas-Marcoussis Agreement stipulated several electoral reforms. By the time of my arrival in Abidjan, these reforms were already the subject of intense debate and dispute. With a presidential election due in October 2005, the reforms moved to the center of the political stage. The disputes centered on three interrelated points: the membership and mandate of the Independent Electoral Commission (IEC); the voter eligibility requirements; and the presidential exclusion clause in the constitution (the infamous Article 35). Each of these issues became a *cause célèbre* that periodically threatened to derail the whole peace process.

On the first point, the IEC was mandated to play a central role in managing what was likely to be a highly contentious and quite possibly violent presidential election. The commission was responsible for the compilation and verification of the voter roll as well as the organization of the balloting (location and supervision of voting stations, etc.). Even though it was supposed to be bipartisan body, control of the commission was a huge prize in such a polarized political atmosphere. The opposition parties were deeply suspicious of the chairman (and sought to replace him) and alarmed by what they believed was a government effort to buy off its own nominated members.

The second and most controversial point centered on Ouattara's eligibility for office. Article 35 of the constitution was in essence a legal device to preclude Ouattara from running for the presidency. The Linas-Marcoussis Agreement called for the article to be amended. But the government deployed one delaying tactic after another to prevent the required constitutional change from being implemented. Even after Gbagbo seemed to have reluctantly agreed to the amendment, the National Assembly, controlled by a close ally, Mamadou Koulibaly, delayed a decision.

The third point revolved around the registration of voters. *Ivoirité* was not limited to barring Ouattara from the presidency; it applied equally to as many as a million[15] people living in Côte d'Ivoire who did not have documented proof of their Ivorian citizenship. Many were of Burkina Faso or Malian descent and had lived in the Côte d'Ivoire for decades.

Ivoirité was a form of voter suppression motivated essentially by political calculation. Most of the disenfranchised were expected to vote for the RDR and Ouattara. Although there were important pockets of support for the RDR in areas of the south including Abidjan, there was no doubt that Bédié and the PDCI, and then Gbagbo and the FPI, were fearful that the full emancipation of northern voters would damage their electoral prospects.

West Africa is a mosaic of peoples fostered by multiple migrations over many generations. In the 1980s, Nigeria attempted to forcefully expel West African migrants, detonating political and economic shock waves throughout the region. I witnessed this mass expulsion firsthand when I was the UNDP resident representative in neighboring Benin and had to hastily arrange humanitarian relief on the border. I still remember the tide of desperate people flooding across the border into Benin, carrying whatever they could: on their heads, on their backs, on bikes, in wheelbarrows, in perilously overloaded buses, and even in leaky barges dragged along the coast from Lagos.

With the staff from the mission's electoral and political sections, I spent countless hours working on these issues in a vain effort to find compromises that would move the electoral process forward. We worked intensively with the government, the National Assembly, the political parties, the Forces Nouvelles, and the IEC, but to no avail. The depth of distrust was so great that we could not find acceptable compromises to untie the electoral knot.

All the political protagonists shared some of the blame for the impasse. The refusal of the Forces Nouvelles (backed by Ouattara's RDR party) to go ahead with disarmament and demobilization was mirrored by Gbagbo's unwillingness to push ahead with all the reforms promised by Linas-Marcoussis until the Forces Nouvelles began disarming. Actually, the Forces Nouvelles was not in any great hurry to move ahead; its so-called zone commanders were doing well from the lucrative rackets they controlled in the northern part of the country.

Managing Mediation:
The Linas-Marcoussis Monitoring Committee

The Linas-Marcoussis Agreement set up a committee "in charge of ensuring compliance with commitments made" and mandated to report to "national, regional and international authorities all cases of obstruction of the Agreements and failure to apply them, to ensure that appropriate remedies are implemented."[16] SRSG Tévoédjré chaired this committee, known as the Comité de Suivi (Monitoring Committee); ONUCI provided the secretariat. The members included regional entities (AU, ECOWAS); international organizations like the UN, the EU, the Francophonie, and the World Bank and IMF; as well as France and a Group of Eight (G8) representative (the US ambassador).

Although the role of the committee was to monitor the Linas-Marcoussis Agreement, almost inevitably it was pulled into partisan politics. Within the committee, we attempted to monitor but also to mediate, a role for which the committee was ill-suited. The committee was too large and disparate, making it difficult to reach consensus. Some members, France in particular, pushed for more assertive action against the Gbagbo government, while others, notably the African institutions, were more cautious. The committee was also quite porous, with leaks to the presidency and the media.

Interaction between the SRSG, as the bearer of sometimes unpalatable messages from the committee, and the president and his party-faithful became ever more fraught, with Gbagbo refusing to receive him at one point. The encounters with the prime minister were much less fraught, since he viewed the committee and ONUCI as allies in the struggle to secure his authority as agreed by Linas-Marcoussis. The leadership of the RDR, PDCI, and Forces Nouvelles were only too happy to let Tévoédjré do the heavy lifting and butt heads with the president even though the Forces Nouvelles dragged their feet when this suited their purpose.

The role of the Monitoring Committee—and the SRSG as its chair—became increasingly untenable. The French ambassador, Gildas Le Lidec, told me on one occasion that the committee should act as the referee, pulling out a red card when needed. The idea was an intriguing one, but I pointed out that neither the committee nor the SRSG had the power to send players off the field for bad fouls. MINUCI had been set up to assist with the implementation of Linas-Marcoussis—not to enforce it. When the successor operation—ONUCI—was established, it was mandated to take military action, but only in support of the protection of civilians and UN personnel, equipment, and installations.[17]

The Security Council Takes a Turn

Shortly after I arrived in Abidjan, a Security Council delegation arrived to give added impetus to the peace process. On arrival, the Council delegation, led by the British ambassador to the UN, Sir Emyr Jones Parry, immediately ran into barricades and protests by young patriots who "spontaneously" turned up outside the venues where we had scheduled meetings with civil society.

Most of the civil society groups actually turned out to be fronts for the political factions. Their meetings with the Security Council were quite boisterous but they gave the delegation a taste of the virulence that had invaded Ivorian politics. I should have known better after my Sierra

Leone experience and had the groups vetted more carefully before the invitations were sent out. An innocuous-sounding name doesn't mean an innocuous group. But this encounter was a sharp reminder that far from the measured statements and earnest calls for national reconciliation issued in New York, we were faced with an increasingly polarized society where compromise for the greater national good did not feature on the political agenda.

The antics of the pro-Gbagbo militants, and a very unhelpful encounter with the National Assembly, led by Speaker Mamadou Koulibaly (an unyielding supporter of the president), left the delegation with an even more unfavorable impression of the president and his party than the one before they arrived. It is not advisable to antagonize a visiting Security Council delegation if you hope to mobilize international sympathy and support for your cause; following the Abidjan visit, the Council signaled that sanctions against individuals who obstructed implementation of the Linas-Marcoussis Agreement would be considered.[18]

Back to Accra

As security deteriorated in and around the zone of confidence, which was rapidly becoming a zone of no confidence, and with the Monitoring Committee seemingly unable to halt the slide, there was a rush of UN and regionally brokered mediation meetings. In July 2004, Secretary-General Annan called for a high-level meeting of the parties in Ghana (so-called Accra III). In preparation for the meeting, my office drew up a detailed matrix of actions and actors required to move the peace process forward. I was somewhat inspired by the work we had done in Sierra Leone, where our matrix had become a template for the transition. But despite my enthusiasm, we were out of step with reality; the time was not right. Côte d'Ivoire was moving in the opposite direction, away from and not toward peace. Linas-Marcoussis had postponed and not resolved the problems at the heart of the Ivorian crisis.

The meeting in Accra, chaired by Secretary-General Annan, attempted to breathe new life into the Linas-Marcoussis process. At the end of the meeting another agreement was signed, one that provided "a framework for the reactivation of the peace process."[19] It was agreed, among other points, that President Gbagbo would use his constitutional powers to amend Article 35, that the National Assembly would adopt by the end of August all legal reforms envisaged under the Linas-Marcoussis Agreement, and that the DDR program would begin by October 15. In addition, a tripartite monitoring group consisting of ECOWAS, the AU, and the UN, chaired by ECOWAS, would be set up and submit fortnightly reports on the implementation of the Accra III accord. This new arrangement seemed to confirm that the monitoring arrangements decreed by Linas-Marcoussis had not worked.

Complicated before Accra, the monitoring/mediation now became even more convoluted. The Linas-Marcoussis Monitoring Committee was still expected to "follow progress in the overall peace process"[20] while the Accra monitoring group, which excluded key players like France, was expected to take a more hands-on approach to getting the parties to move forward. This new arrangement seemed to confirm a typical response when peace processes get stuck—find alternative mechanisms and mediators. But as subsequent developments were to show, this kind of "forum hopping" encouraged rather than moderated intransigency; the peace process did not advance because neither side was ready to fulfill the bargain struck in Paris. A change of the monitoring arrangements could not bridge that gulf.

Peace Fails: The November Crisis

On the political front, the initial response to Accra III was promising. Ministers from the opposition were readmitted to the government; powers were delegated to the prime minister as originally envisaged by the Linas-Marcoussis accord; and an extraordinary session of the National Assembly was called to consider draft legislation required to implement the provisions of Linas-Marcoussis. Unhappily, this interlude of optimism soon ended.

The National Assembly did not pass the legislation and Article 35 was not amended as promised. Although FANCI and the Forces Nouvelles reaffirmed in early October 2004 their earlier agreement not to resume armed hostilities, tensions continued to mount. Mutual suspicions resurfaced, accompanied by demonstrations in the north and south of the country. On October 9, Forces Nouvelles leader Soro announced that DDR would not begin as envisaged on October 15 because the reforms had not been enacted. On October 12, Gbagbo countered, announcing that Article 35 would not be amended until DDR had started.

At the end of October, I left Abidjan for a few days' leave in Europe. I had originally intended to go earlier but had delayed because of the mounting tensions, which we thought might be aggravated by the publication of the draft report of the international commission of inquiry into the human rights violations. In the event, there were no serious incidents and I decided to leave.

Before I left, I submitted a memo on October 25 to the SRSG in which I warned that the peace process was stalling, carrying with it the risk of renewed violence and events spinning out of control. I suggested that the Security Council should signal its intention to draw up targeted sanctions for noncompliance with its demands. I would like to think that my memo was an act of singular prescience. It wasn't. I had no direct inkling of what was to come.

A couple of days after my departure, I received a call from Simon Munzu, our human rights chief, who told me that he was picking up rumors of

FANCI troop movements in the direction of the zone of confidence. I asked him to report this information to the SRSG and the force commander.

On November 4, FANCI attacked Forces Nouvelles positions from the air. Chaos followed in Abidjan as Young Patriots tried to invade the Golfe Hotel on the outskirts of the city, where Forces Nouvelles ministers were housed. They were repelled by ONUCI and French (Operation Licorne) forces. The premises of the prime minister and the opposition political parties were ransacked and newspapers favoring the opposition torched.

The air assault continued the following day and FANCI units began to cross the zone of confidence to attack Bouaké. ONUCI forces intervened to block the FANCI movement but they simply took another route and bypassed the small blocking force. Worse was to come. In the early afternoon another air strike by FANCI aircraft hit a French military base in Bouaké, killing and wounding a number of French soldiers from the Licorne force as well as an American civilian.

The Sukhoi-25 fighter-bombers were likely flown by Belorussian pilots[21] who may have misunderstood or misread their targets. But the French response was immediate and draconian. Orders, apparently issued directly from the Elysée Palace (i.e., the French president), instructed France's commander, General Henri Poncet, to disable or destroy the Ivorian aircraft. A Licorne unit based at the airport in Yamoussoukro hit the Sukhoi aircraft on the ground and then destroyed three military helicopters near the presidential compound.

The French attack triggered a series of violent confrontations between enraged Young Patriots and French troops as they moved to control strategic points in Abidjan, including the airport and key bridges. Mobs attacked French civilians and looted properties. The French school was burned down. Within a matter of hours, thousands of French and other nationals flooded into ONUCI premises in search of safety.

I immediately called the SRSG and told him that I would be heading back to Abidjan, which was not so easily done as all commercial flights had been suspended and the airport closed by French troops. The solution came via a flight to Freetown, where I was picked up by an ONUCI aircraft and then ferried into Abidjan's airport, where the mission maintained its own air service facility. The airport terminals were closed and the runways ringed by French armor. My plane was the only one allowed in, apart from French military aircraft.

We then drove into the city with my close-protection team, by this time well into the evening of November 6. The streets were absolutely deserted, with only French and UN military vehicles visible. It was a haunting experience to witness a vibrant city go silent. We crossed the main bridge on the lagoon, where the night before there had been violent clashes between French troops and the militants.

I was staying at the Novotel Hotel in downtown Abidjan, where we had rented a small apartment. Normally a thriving and popular hotel, it was deserted when I arrived. The French manager had already been evacuated along with his senior expatriate staff. I was almost alone in the hotel and the Ivorian staff were extremely pleased to see me, as they had practically no other customers and my presence somehow carried some assurance.

From there I went straight to ONUCI headquarters, which had become a refuge not only for UN staff but also for expatriates who feared attacks. Conditions inside the compound deteriorated rapidly with the overflow of people fleeing the chaos outside. Fortunately, we had on hand a stock of ready-to-eat meals from the military, not *haute cuisine* but enough to keep everyone more or less fed. The toilets did not hold up so well.

The following morning, while the SRSG worked on the diplomatic fallout, I went back across the lagoon to our military headquarters at the Pergola Hotel and then on to our logistics base in the Kumasi neighborhood. Both were packed with people in distress and fearful. With the force commander and the police commissioner, I tried to reassure them (and our own staff) of ONUCI's support and protection.

But beyond the concern for the (mainly) Western expatriates sheltering at ONUCI facilities, we had a larger worry: that the militants and militias would turn their anger on the communities of West Africans and the northerners living in the city. If that happened, and notwithstanding our protection-of-civilians mandate, we would have been hard-pressed to prevent massacres. The mandate would have outrun the means. We avoided that tragedy; Gbagbo, by now aware of the chaos that he had unleashed, called for calm and for the militants to get off the streets (which they did).

While ONUCI was not the immediate target for FANCI and the militants, there were frequent incidents, especially after ONUCI and Licorne prevented attacks on Forces Nouvelles ministers lodged at the Golfe Hotel. In the north, ONUCI was blamed for allowing FANCI to get into the zone of confidence and there were rowdy demonstrations outside of UN premises orchestrated by the Forces Nouvelles, although they did not turn deadly.

In Abidjan, the situation remained chaotic and highly precarious. ONUCI facilities were spread around the town and staff members were living in localities scattered around the city, some of which were very vulnerable to attack or looting. Several embassies announced that they would close and asked for UN help to evacuate staff and dependents. Special flights were arranged and evacuees went to the airport under UN convoy to avoid possible attacks on French escorts.

Both the French embassy and residence were surrounded by militants and FANCI armed units. The French residence was particularly vulnerable because of its location right next door to the presidential residence, a legacy of the close relations that prevailed during days of Houphouët-Boigny. The ambassador's wife could not leave the residence and was protected by a small detachment of French troops while the ambassador was trapped in the embassy downtown. It was a nervous time and we were all on edge.

On the morning of Wednesday, November 8, tensions were still running very high. A French unit had taken up positions at the Hotel Ivoire to protect expatriates sheltering in the hotel and also because of its commanding position overlooking the Cocody district. A large and angry crowd, including Young Patriots, had gathered outside the hotel and seemed set to force its way in, which could have triggered a bloodbath. Already the pro-Gbagbo media and the national radio and television stations were claiming that French snipers had fired on the crowd. The situation was explosive.

At that point I received a call from General Poncet asking if we could open a channel of communication with the Gbagbo entourage in order to help defuse the situation. I couldn't call Gbagbo directly but I was able to get hold of Mamadou Koulibaly, who had some influence with the Young Patriots. The force commander, Lieutenant-General Fall, and I agreed to meet at Koulibaly's official residence, close to the Hotel Ivoire. We set off in a couple of UN SUVs but didn't get too far. About 300 meters from the Ivoire, we were engulfed by the militants and could not move forward without running over people. We decided that discretion would definitely be the better part of valor and turned around. After a few anxious moments, we extricated our vehicles from the crowd and headed back to UNOCI headquarters.

There I called Koulibaly and informed him that we could not get to his residence. He offered to come over to UNOCI with a delegation. I had met with him several times over the course of the months since I arrived in Abidjan. He was articulate and willing to engage but still a hardliner and adamant that the constitution could not be changed to accommodate Ouattara. But that morning, as the crisis threatened to literally set Abidjan aflame, he was willing to help.

We met in my office because Koulibaly and the SRSG were not speaking. As we discussed what we could do, another urgent call came in from General Poncet, who was in direct contact, on another line, with the unit commander at the Hotel Ivoire. He warned me that the situation was quickly becoming uncontrollable. As he did, we suddenly heard the sound of gunfire on the incoming call, which was being relayed via the general's phone. I put Poncet's call on speaker so that Koulibaly and company could hear what was happening. He then got up and announced that he would go to the Ivoire and calm things down, which to his credit he did.

After further negotiations, the French command agreed to evacuate the Ivoire and a convoy left the hotel under the hostile glare of the irate crowd. But the drama was not yet over. Leaving the hotel, the convoy turned in the wrong direction and ended up next to the presidential and French residences. Fortunately, the sudden arrival of an armed convoy did not lead to a shootout and after a tense standoff the unit was able to leave without further hostilities. Later in the day, the force commander together with the FANCI chief of staff and Licorne commander announced that they would start joint patrols to help restore calm.

The following day I went to see the embattled French ambassador at his embassy in central Abidjan. In marked UN vehicles, we were much less of a target than any Licorne vehicles, and the streets were empty. The ambassador, unable to leave the embassy compound since the crisis erupted, was looking the worse for wear. There were large demonstrations outside the building, but the demonstrators did not attempt to break into the fortified compound; if they had, there would have been serious casualties with disastrous consequences for French civilians elsewhere in the city.

Counting the Cost

The dance of damage control began immediately. The UN Security Council, the AU, ECOWAS, the EU, and the United States all launched appeals for the cessation of hostilities and an immediate return to the peace negotiations. President Thabo Mbeki was named as the AU mediator (more on the Mbeki mediation, in which I played a small and rather awkward role, further on).

The Security Council reacted, as it usually does following a disaster, by recalling its previous resolutions (even though they had been willfully ignored by the Gbagbo government). This time, however, it also imposed an arms embargo and authorized targeted sanctions against individuals who "constitute a threat to the peace and national reconciliation process in Côte d'Ivoire, in particular those who block the implementation of the *Linas-Marcoussis* and *Accra III* Agreements."[22] But it still took several months for the Council to approve the military reinforcements for ONUCI that Secretary-General Annan had called for at the time of the crisis.

Sanctions were not imposed. The Council heeded President Mbeki's advice that they would complicate his search for a settlement. I was disappointed. We had already gathered and submitted enough information— even before the crisis began—to warrant sanctions against some individuals associated with the Forces Nouvelles; so the imposition of sanctions against the Gbagbo regime would not have been lopsided, which was Mbeki's concern.

Gbagbo was heavily criticized in the international community for the resort to force but less so in Africa (except in West Africa), where the reaction to French intervention stirred up ghosts of the colonial past. Predictably, commentary within Côte d'Ivoire split along partisan lines.

ONUCI did not escape criticism. The mission was charged with passivity and poor intelligence. Why, we were asked, did we not know that an attack was about to be launched despite the presence of UN military observers on the ground? Why had ONUCI forces not prevented FANCI from moving into the zone of confidence? And why had ONUCI not blocked FANCI when it became evident that it was launching an offensive?

No one seemed to have predicted an attack, with the exception of the Forces Nouvelles, not even French diplomats (if they had some inkling of an impending offensive, they did not share it, as far as I know, with ONUCI). But that was cold comfort and we had to accept our share of the fallout of the November debacle. There were three immediate consequences for ONUCI.

The first was the loss of confidence in ONUCI's preventive presence—military and political. We had been blindsided by the attacks. We were worried about the general security situation but I don't think any of us had considered that Gbagbo would authorize a full-scale attack (as opposed to the recurring skirmishes in and around the zone of confidence), especially as the two military commands had just reaffirmed a cessation of hostilities.

Clearly our "intelligence" had failed. On the political front we had no intimation that Gbagbo had decided, in effect, to jettison Linas-Marcoussis. Nor did we pick up, until too late, that FANCI was on the move in strength. The dearth of actionable intelligence—tactical as well as political—was a damaging failure. Part of the problem was technical: we didn't possess signals-intercept equipment, much less drones to monitor troop movements. But there was also an analytical failing. We wrote and sent to headquarters reams of reports to meet the daily, weekly, and monthly appetite for information but little of it was of real-time intelligence value. The tripartite monitoring mechanism set up in the wake of Accra III did not help either.

The second and predictable consequence was the hostile reaction of the Forces Nouvelles, which publicly turned against the mission even though ONUCI (with Licorne) had protected Forces Nouvelles ministers sheltering at the Golfe Hotel.

The reaction of the Forces Nouvelles was harsh, essentially reproving the mission for dereliction of duty. Soro asked for an African Union force, which he claimed would do a better job. Part of the reason for this hard line was that the SRSG had been in Bouaké on October 30 to meet with Forces Nouvelles leadership in an effort to reduce tensions. Soro had told him that an attack was being prepared. He felt that the SRSG had ignored his warning. In fairness to Tévoédjré, the Forces Nouvelles was quite paranoid about FANCI, and earlier doomsday warnings had to be proved wrong.

A short while after the attacks, I was back in Bouaké and met the commander of Forces Nouvelles forces, gendarmerie general Soumaila Bakayoko. He insisted on giving me a personal tour of bomb-damaged buildings. Actually, the damage was not extensive but the bomb or bombs were powerful enough to demolish buildings close by the hotel where the Forces Nouvelles held meetings and press conferences. He and other Forces Nouvelles leaders believed that they were the real targets of the air attacks. Concluding the tour, General Bakayoko implied that ONUCI had not deterred the attacks, so what was its value?

The third consequence was an internal crisis of confidence (amplified by the customary second-guessing when things go wrong). Within the mission, staff criticized the leadership (civilian and military)[23] and the way it had responded to the crisis. Some thought ONUCI should have confronted FANCI more forcefully even though ONUCI units had obstructed the first advance. Given the modest size and state of readiness of the ONUCI units concerned, I am not sure they could have stopped FANCI in full battle mode. Moreover, an all-out shooting match with FANCI would certainly have created divisions within the Security Council and with the troop-contributing countries.

To make matters worse, the staff security arrangements within the mission did not work out well. The staff were widely dispersed around the city, a logistical problem that was compounded by the quick onset of the crisis. We lost contact with a number of the staff in Abidjan, some of whom were threatened and assaulted. Then when staff evacuations began, our adoption of the standard UN term "nonessential" to designate staff members for evacuation created further friction, with the colleagues so-designated resenting the implication that they were redundant (after the crisis, we looked for a better euphemism).

Staff opinions on the French intervention were sharply divided. Some felt that the intervention was excessive and unwarranted and smacked of neocolonialism; others, especially those who had been harassed by militants or were from West Africa, felt that Gbagbo and his partisans had got their comeuppance, an opinion I shared. However, I had to maintain a stance of impartiality publicly in order to keep the door open to the Gbagbo camp.

Amid the welter of recrimination, I am not sure that we ever really asked and answered the most fundamental question: Why did Gbagbo authorize the attacks? I believe that the bombardment of the French camp really was a pilot error; otherwise, what possible interest could he or the FANCI command have had in taking such a risk? Conversely, the overall assault on the north was evidently not an unplanned mistake. Speaking to Secretary-General Annan during the crisis, Gbagbo told him that the military operations "were limited and targeted at the recapture of specific towns,"[24] after which the UN would be asked to ensure the security of the towns.

What then was the stratagem behind the attacks? In FPI circles at the time, there was growing criticism that Gbagbo had conceded too much at the Accra III negotiations. On return to Abidjan, he had quickly pulled back on some key provisions of that accord, which the Forces Nouvelles in turn used to withdraw from their DDR commitment. This stalemate could have continued, but I speculate that Gbagbo was drawn to the idea that if he could inflict a rapid knockout blow on the Forces Nouvelles by recapturing Bouaké (a commercial and strategic prize), he would then sue for peace from a position of strength and the world would reluctantly accept a fait accompli.

Later I wondered if President Gbagbo's willingness to launch military operations may have been encouraged by discussions we held in the Monitoring Committee about the limits of ONUCI's mandate. Those discussions centered on the extent to which the mandate required the mission to intervene to prevent an act of aggression by either FANCI or the Forces Nouvelles. The resolution establishing ONUCI authorized French forces to "use all necessary means in order to support UNOCI" and to "intervene against belligerent actions, if the security conditions so require, outside the areas directly controlled by UNOCI."[25] This provision was understood as authorizing Licorne to act as a kind of rapid-reaction force for ONUCI in case it came under threat, not as a call to arms should FANCI and Forces Nouvelles attack each other.

In the event, after French forces were pinned down dealing with the security threats to the French community, ONUCI was pretty much on its own trying to protect UN installations and the multitude of terrified people who had sought refuge in them. If the attack on the French base in Bouaké had not happened, it's quite possible that Gbagbo's presumed strategy might have worked. I doubt that the Security Council would have authorized ONUCI forces to take action to dislodge FANCI if it had captured Bouaké; I suspect that the Council would have grudgingly accepted a fait accompli.

Another Departure

At the end of January 2005, Albert Tévoédjré resigned as SRSG. He carried the proverbial can for the November events even though ONUCI's shortcomings were not his responsibility alone. By then, however, Albert was persona non grata with the president and his entourage (as well as the Forces Nouvelles), which made it impossible for him to operate effectively despite public support from Kofi Annan. To function in a political role, you need access. When that access is denied, however unfair or unwarranted that may be, your utility is significantly impaired.

There was no love lost between the president and the SRSG, but whoever had headed the mission would have likely encountered the same difficulties. Gbagbo wanted a UN (and French) intervention to support his regime against the rebellion of the Forces Nouvelles. Leaders don't request outside intervention by armed peacekeepers in the expectation of even-handed restraint, much less to receive advice on their human rights records or their failures in governance.

Pending the designation and arrival of a new SRSG, I found myself again holding down the fort—this time, however, only for a couple of months until the new SRSG, Pierre Schori from Sweden, took over. Pierre was Sweden's ambassador at the UN in New York and veteran of Swedish politics. A former minister of development cooperation and member of the Swedish and European parliaments, he knew Gbagbo personally from their days as members of Socialist International. He knew President Mbeki from the apartheid era, when Sweden strongly supported the South African liberation movement. So even though he had not served in Africa before, Pierre did have a personal connection to a number of the leading players in the Ivorian drama.

War by Other Means

ECOWAS, as the regional body most directly concerned by the Ivorian crisis, should have assumed the role of mediator in the November 2004 crisis. However, Gbagbo did not elicit much sympathy from his peers in the subregion (unlike Kabbah in Sierra Leone). This was partly because of his divisive rhetoric that appeared to threaten migrants from other West African countries but also because President Obasanjo, the chair of ECOWAS, did not have much time or sympathy for Gbagbo, who had generally ignored his and ECOWAS's advice. So despite political proximity, ECOWAS was not well placed to mediate. The ball passed to the African Union, which, as I mentioned earlier, designated Thabo Mbeki as the mediator.

Mbeki's Moment

Mbeki had succeeded Nelson Mandela as the president of South Africa, and his designation was generally applauded, not least because South Africa was still basking in the glow of Mandela's immense prestige. Mbeki flew into Abidjan on November 9, 2004, and in the days that followed he met with all the main national and international interlocutors, including the SRSG, before leaving to meet with regional leaders.

In early December, President Mbeki returned to Abidjan and convened an international support group to assist his mediation effort. I was designated to represent the UN. Mbeki was willing to patiently hear out all sides, sometimes at great length. The support group joined most of his meetings except his tête-à-tête meetings with President Gbagbo, who went out of his way to welcome Mbeki as a fellow head of state. However, Mbeki's rapport with Prime Minister Diarra, who complained bitterly about Gbagbo, was less convivial. Although he did not share confidences, I got the impression that Mbeki had concluded that Diarra was not the man for the job.

As part of the consultations, the mediation group visited Bouaké to meet Soro and the Forces Nouvelles leadership. As I expected, during the discussion Soro roundly denounced ONUCI, although he did not attack me personally. President Mbeki then called on me to speak for ONUCI. It was an awkward moment. I didn't want to launch into a blow-by-blow defense of ONUCI, which would have distracted from the intended purpose of the meeting, but I felt I had to stand up for the mission of which I was the deputy head. So I tried to explain in an even tone what ONUCI had done to hinder the movement of FANCI and the protection offered to the Forces Nouvelles in Abidjan.

To no surprise, I did not convince Soro (nor, I believe, Mbeki). To the contrary: he pleaded for an AU force to replace ONUCI. The president was cautious but did promise to look into the possibility of South African training support for the close-protection team of the Forces Nouvelles.

Over the next two months, President Mbeki developed a series of proposals for ending the conflict based on the main tenets of the Linas-Marcoussis Agreement. Although the support group continued to function and there were several rounds of consultation with the Linas-Marcoussis Monitoring Committee, the president relied heavily on his own South African team of advisers, who worked in a close and closed circle around him to produce his AU action plan. I had no doubt about the good faith of the South African team, but given the complexities of the Ivorian crisis, it might have been better for President Mbeki to have enlarged the circle and consulted more widely before making proposals, especially in the legislative arena. It didn't take long for the opposition to start casting doubts—unfairly—about the impartiality of the Mbeki mediation. But Gbagbo shrewdly played to Mbeki's visceral antipathy toward colonialism, which France may have aroused by its armed intervention.

Despite the initial optimism, President Mbeki's mediation ran into difficulties fairly quickly. I sat in on meetings during which he expressed mounting irritation with the Forces Nouvelles; he began to privately castigate the Forces Nouvelles as capricious. But he was also unhappy with Prime Minister Diarra, whom he felt should grumble less and do more to move the peace agenda forward. For its part, the Forces Nouvelles began to intimate that the president was too partial to the Gbagbo camp.

An upshot of this cooling of relations was the request by the Forces Nouvelles that ONUCI should be integrated into all its meetings with the mediation's military team. Considering the cold shoulder that I had received in Bouaké only a couple of months before, this was quite a turnaround, reflecting once again the shifting parameters of the peace process in Côte d'Ivoire.

In March 2005, I was asked, in the absence of a SRSG, to brief the Security Council on the crisis. At the Council meeting, I emphasized the ambiguous position of the mission, which was constantly obstructed and even denied access to port facilities for resupply.

But the issue that preoccupied me most was the stalemate blocking the presidential election, nominally scheduled for October 2005. I saw the election as the lynchpin of the peace process, and in my remarks to the Security Council, I emphasized that the election was at the heart of all political calculation. Gbagbo and the FPI as well as the opposition wanted elections, but neither side was willing to concede any ground that would make them possible. The opposition members of the electoral commission were refusing to attend its meetings, claiming that the proposed reforms of the commission before the National Assembly were not compatible with the spirit of the Linas-Marcoussis Agreement. They defended their boycott in a letter to Secretary-General Annan in which they also requested that the UN organize the elections.

The Mbeki mediation had picked up on that point and asked me if the UN could take on a supervisory role despite the habitual UN preference for leaving the organization of elections to national authorities. I thought that this was an idea worth pursuing. I reasoned that if the UN took a leading role, it might be possible to overcome some of the suspicions that were blocking the election; the UN's direct engagement would give the elections a higher degree of legitimacy.

After the Council meeting in New York, I worked with Hervé Lecoq, by then on the Côte d'Ivoire desk in DPKO in New York, to develop the idea of appointing an UN elections commissioner to the national elections commission. We developed terms of reference for the post, which were expanded to become a post of UN high representative for the elections. I suggested that the post should be separated from ONUCI. I did so because I could see that every time the mission took a position on the election that President Gbagbo or his party did not like, we risked retaliation of one kind or another. The high representative, on the other hand, would have UN authority but would be unencumbered by ONUCI's operational obligations.

The Council reacted favorably to the idea. Some months later, in June 2005, with the encouragement of President Mbeki, it endorsed the Secretary-General's proposal for the designation of high representative and authorized the creation of the post.[26]

The Pretoria Procession

In the meantime, in early April 2005, President Mbeki convened the key Ivorian players to a roundtable in Pretoria to review the AU action plan that he had formulated based on his visits and consultations. Pierre Schori, who had just joined the mission, attended the conference on behalf of the UN, which resulted in yet another peace agreement—Pretoria I.[27] The agreement prescribed a set of measures intended to put the peace process back on track. It opened with a joint declaration of the end of the war.

The most significant point of the agreement concerned the presidential eligibility clause. Referring to the controversial Article 35 and "having listened to the views of the Ivorian leaders, the President Mbeki undertook to make a determination on this matter"[28] following consultation with the chair of the AU and the UN Secretary-General. Shortly after the Pretoria meeting, Mbeki determined that President Gbagbo, after consulting with the president of the National Assembly and the Constitutional Council, could use the emergency powers granted under Article 48 of the constitution to accept the eligibility of candidates presented by political parties that were signatories to the Linas-Marcoussis Agreement. President Gbagbo duly obliged, announcing on April 26 that he would use the special powers as recommended by President Mbeki. We all rejoiced, forgetting perhaps the caveat about the concurrence of the National Assembly and the Constitutional Court, both of which Gbagbo had manipulated to delay or block earlier reform measures.

Yet another oversight mechanism—a troika—was set up in Abidjan under the prime minister's authority. It was intended to map out and oversee the steps needed to secure implementation of the Pretoria agreement. To keep the group tightly focused, its membership was limited to the prime minister's office, the South African mediation, and ONUCI, in which, at Pierre Schori's request, I represented ONUCI along with the UNPOL commissioner, Yves Bouchard. The force commander was engaged in a parallel process on the military side with FANCI, the Forces Nouvelles, and South African military advisers.

In the prime minister's group, we developed detailed plans under each of the headings of the Pretoria agreement. We spent many hours producing impressive, well-reasoned timelines that spelled out what had to be done, by when, and by whom. We put the priority on the return of state authority, DDR, and preparations for the elections. There was some progress. The Forces Nouvelles accepted the DDR plan and there was agreement in the State Council on electoral reforms.

In reality, however, we were spinning our wheels. Our many meetings with the prime minister were always very constructive, but the troika did not have much impact simply because the prime minister did not have the power to implement his own decisions. Ministers implemented the decisions according to their political loyalties or not at all if the state apparatus refused to respect their instructions.

The National Assembly under Mamadou Koulibaly remained obdurate, continuing to balk at the amendment of Article 35, the reconstitution of the Independent Electoral Commission, and other Pretoria-prescribed measures. Despite our cooperation at the time of the November 2004 crisis, my efforts to keep a dialogue going with Koulibaly went steadily downhill, especially after I wrote to him on behalf of the Linas-Marcoussis Monitoring Committee, raising concerns about the National Assembly staying in power beyond its mandated term of office, which was coming to an end. The day after I sent him the private letter, I was at the receiving end of a broadside in the pro-Gbagbo press, which blasted me for all kinds of misdeeds including the closing of the British embassy in Abidjan, which was rather ironic as I had pleaded with the UK—without success—for it to be kept open.

Koulibaly had the strong backing of Simone Gbagbo, the wife of the president but a power in her own right, who led the FPI faction in the National Assembly. Madame Gbagbo was a formidable force, a veritable *dame de fer,* and, if anything, even more truculent than her husband. My few encounters with her were stiff, with no casual conversation and certainly no humor (unlike Gbagbo himself).

The ink was barely dry when the first cracks in the Pretoria agreement appeared. In late April, Gbagbo informed the country that he would activate the same Article 48 to overcome other obstacles to the peace process and would do so to authorize the National Institute of Statistics to produce voter lists and voter cards. Designed to mollify the critics in his own party, Gbagbo's statement set off another storm of protest; the opposition immediately claimed that he intended to use Article 48 to make decisions that went beyond Mbeki's ruling.

The impasse continued despite President Mbeki's efforts to find solutions. In mid-May 2005, the Forces Nouvelles used the impasse to once again announce that it would not go ahead with the DDR until all the provisions of Pretoria had been implemented to its satisfaction. Further meetings in Pretoria failed to move the process forward. On August 30, Deputy Foreign Minister Aziz Pahad made a public statement announcing the end of South Africa's mediation efforts while condemning the opposition's objections as "legalistic gymnastics."[29] Although the South African Ministry of Foreign Affairs subsequently attempted to row back from Pahad's statement by "clarifying" his remarks, the damage was done. On August 31 the Forces Nouvelles spokesman declared: "Starting today, the New Forces completely reject the South African mediation in the Ivory Coast."[30]

As the political crisis was building, the security situation was also becoming increasingly tense. ONUCI forces were continually obstructed by FANCI units and local militia. Pierre Schori's vehicle was attacked by stone-throwing Young Patriots. There were violent incidents in the central/western areas of the country (always the most volatile region) as well as attacks in the Abidjan suburbs against alleged opposition supporters. I went on a tour of the central-west region and met intense hostility from local politicians and community leaders who were claiming that ONUCI was aiding the Forces Nouvelles (a similar experience awaited me some years later in eastern Congo).

One suburb of Abidjan in particular—Agboville—was targeted by a pro-Gbagbo militia and in late July there were rumors of massacres. ONUCI sent a reinforced patrol to investigate, which was blocked on the road into Agboville by civilians manning a makeshift barricade. Given the worries about the alleged massacres, we had to decide (Pierre was traveling outside the country) whether to force the barricade with the risk of civilian casualties, or else be blamed for failing to protect civilians. General Fall and I decided that at all costs we had to avoid any impression that ONUCI was attacking civilians (the French confrontation with civilians in Abidjan was still fresh in everyone's mind). Nevertheless, we still had to quickly confirm or discount the allegations. The general ordered an airborne patrol to leapfrog the barrier and get into Agboville. The patrol landed in Agboville without incident and we were relieved to learn that there had been no massacres and the situation was calm.

I cite this particular incident (there were plenty of others as well) because some mission staff felt strongly that once again ONUCI had not stood up to FANCI. They argued that we should have made a determined and public effort to remove the barricade, by force if needed, in order to make the point that ONUCI forces would not accept constraints on their freedom of movement.

My view was that it was not worth the risk of civilian casualties. I was convinced that the pro-Gbagbo groups were trying to provoke incidents like the one we had encountered on the road to Agboville. This was a way of discrediting ONUCI, thereby providing a pretext to call for the removal of UN forces, no longer considered by the Gbagbo partisans as impartial.

The Illusion of Peace

By early September 2005 the Mbeki mediation had essentially ended. The Secretary-General informed the Security Council that once again Côte d'Ivoire was at a crossroads and that the African Union had "entrusted ECOWAS with the responsibility of determining how to overcome the current impasse in the peace process in Côte d'Ivoire."[31] And so after eighteen months of constant and intensive negotiations, punctuated by the violence of November 2004 and many other deadly incidents, the peace process had come full circle, with the war of succession not yet ended.

But my part in the Ivorian drama was finished. In July, I received a call from the office of the Secretary-General asking if I would be willing to be interviewed for the vacant post of SRSG in Liberia. I was indeed willing, although I had not asked to leave Abidjan. I had developed an excellent rapport with Pierre Schori, who was keen that I stay on but generously did not want to stand in the way of a possible step up.

I did the interview and was informed a few days later that I would be proposed as the next SRSG for Liberia. I left Abidjan for Monrovia in late August 2005.

As part of the round of farewells, I flew up to Bouaké for a final meeting with Guillaume Soro. The meeting was cordial and he expressed regrets that I was leaving. Again, I could only marvel at the turnaround in our relations with the Forces Nouvelles, even though, as far as I was concerned, Soro had not personalized the November crisis. At the conclusion of our meeting, we had a short one-on-one during which I expressed my hope that Forces Nouvelles would come back to the negotiating table. As we concluded the meeting, he smiled broadly and said that what had happened could have been avoided if he had been made prime minister at Linas-Marcoussis.

My farewell call on President Gbagbo was, as usual, a late-evening encounter and a very relaxed one. We spoke about another civil war with which he seemed quite familiar—the English civil war. He called for a bottle of champagne and he went on to tell me how British seafarers had recruited (or probably pressed) Africans from along the coast as crew, from which was derived the name used for peoples in those areas, the Kru. That evening he was very urbane and pleasant and I had to remind myself that notwithstanding this bonhomie, the president had constantly thwarted the peace process and, when it suited his purpose, turned on ONUCI.

Onward to Ouagadougou

As I expected, the elections could not be held in October 2005. The AU Peace and Security Council (PSC) recognized this reality and decided that Gbagbo could remain in office for another year in order to give time for elections to be organized. The Security Council endorsed this position.[32] At the same time, it authorized an international working group and a mediation group cochaired by the SRSG with a mandate to draw up a roadmap for the elections.

The Council also endorsed in the same resolution[33] significantly broader powers for the new prime minister, but to little avail. Seydou Diarra could not impose his will on a fractured administration that was a government only in name. He finally resigned in frustration in December 2005. I had worked closely with him; he was a man of reason and dialogue, but those qualities were not the ones that prevailed in the Ivorian conflict.

Over the next year, the familiar pattern of commitments made and broken continued. It proved impossible to secure the essential tradeoff between disarmament and electoral reform. The UN and other interlocutors could not overcome the political obduracy, try as they did. In a repeat of the 2005 experience, the AU and the UN agreed in November 2006 that President Gbagbo could remain in office for a further final year of transition. Gbagbo then proceeded to pull another conjuring trick from up his sleeve, and opened direct talks in January 2007 with the Forces Nouvelles facilitated by his erstwhile nemesis, President Blaise Compaoré of Burkina Faso. As with his earlier, casual abandonment of Article 35, what had seemed impossible now became permissible. An agreement was signed on March 4, 2007, in Ouagadougou. In another extraordinary twist to the tale, Guillaume Soro became Gbagbo's prime minister, an ambition he had confided to me almost two years before.

But the tale did not have a happy ending, at least not for President Gbagbo. After another three years of maneuvering and delays, the elections were finally held in November 2010 (five years later than initially foreseen—the equivalent of a regular term of presidential office); Gbagbo probably agreed to the elections because he thought he would win.[34] He did not, although the result of a second-round runoff was close.

At that moment, the electoral certification mechanism that I had helped devise several years before assumed critical importance. We had originally vested that responsibility in the high representative but it reverted to the SRSG following a standoff between the then High Representative Gerard Stoudmann and Gbagbo. Based on the results provided by the Independent Electoral Commission, the SRSG, Choi Young-jin, declared Ouattara the winner, a decision endorsed by ECOWAS and then by the AU and the UN.

This was the turning point. At Gbagbo's behest, the Constitutional Court declared him president. But the certification of the SRSG provided the legitimacy that made it possible for the regional organizations as well as the UN and international powers to reject his claim and to recognize Ouattara as the duly elected head of state. But there was intense debate within the UN Security Council, with some members (the "sovereigntists") questioning the certification and opposing the view of other members (the "legalists") who argued that it afforded the UN the right to intervene even though some troop contributors were averse to direct military action by ONUCI.[35]

Unwisely, Gbagbo decided to rebuff the certified result and to spurn the prospect of a comfortable and respectable life as an African elder statesman. Subsequently, fighting erupted between Gbagbo supporters, along with elements of FANCI, and the Forces Nouvelles moving down from the north. Pro-Gbagbo's forces launched attacks against civilians they claimed were in league with Ouattara.

On March 30, 2011, the UN Security Council adopted a resolution[36] that authorized the UN (and Licorne forces backing it) to "use all necessary means to carry out its mandate to protect civilians under imminent threat of physical violence." Following further incidents in early April during which UN troops were killed, the UN Secretary-General requested French support for military operations to be conducted by UNOCI to neutralize heavy weapons used against civilians and UN personnel. The joint UN-French military action, conducted in the name of civilian protection, led to the capture, on April 11, 2011, of Gbagbo, his wife, and some close associates by pro-Ouattara forces; it was, in effect, regime change by another name, but not, in my view, an illegitimate one given the election outcome and the Security Council's authorization for the use of force (admittedly to protect civilians). But the manner in which the Gbagbo regime came to an end was far from ideal and has left an abiding legacy of rancor and mistrust.

The Ivorian Puzzle

My peacekeeping sojourn in Côte d'Ivoire was relatively short but discouraging. Unlike my departure from Freetown, I left Abidjan with a sense of unfinished business. I could report little or no progress in the areas under my direct responsibility: human rights were still being flouted with impunity throughout the country; the rule of law had completely broken down; there was no progress on either security sector reform or DDR; and the election conundrum remained unresolved.

Why did the peace process in Côte d'Ivoire take a different trajectory from the one that unfolded in Sierra Leone? Admittedly, at the outset, Sierra Leone was not a success story, but the war there did end peacefully and not with a final, violent showdown as was the case in Côte d'Ivoire. I came to three conclusions.

The first was that we—the external actors—failed to fully grasp the multidimensional nature of the Ivorian crisis, which was rooted in an intricate mix of politics and personalities. This was a conflict of layered complexity and not simply a repeat of the "good versus evil" struggle that characterized the war in Sierra Leone. I don't think we understood that we were grappling with the reordering of a patronage state, which was no longer a viable construct after the demise of Houphouët-Boigny.

My second conclusion was that we became too heavily vested in the Linas-Marcoussis Agreement as the only pathway to peace. As is so often the case, peace agreements do not make peace. Linas-Marcoussis was essentially a legalistic response to a struggle for political power. The Security Council, regional organizations, and the mission continued to cite Linas-Marcoussis as the frame of reference for peace even though it was in trouble right from the start. We remained committed to a strategy that was not working but one that we could not (or would not) change, although several fixes were attempted through the Accra, Pretoria, and Ouagadougou agreements.

The Linas-Marcoussis Monitoring Committee, established as the platform for overseeing implementation of the agreement, became a talking shop rather than a creative tool for mediation. From my own (brief) experience chairing the Monitoring Committee, I came to the opinion that the peace process would have been better served by a more informal consultative arrangement. This would have allowed the SRSG the freedom to mediate directly as the UN representative rather than on behalf of a group representing sundry and sometimes contradictory interests and loyalties.

The reciprocal concession approach that had succeeded in Sierra Leone and which I pushed in Côte d'Ivoire never got much traction. The troika adopted a revised version of that approach in the chronograms we elaborated to implement the Pretoria agreements, but that did not work either. The reason was that our well-crafted plans and projects could not overcome the lethal lack of trust that poisoned the political well.

In fact, neither side was ready—nor exhausted enough—to make the necessary compromises. The political opposition was more flexible than the Forces Nouvelles, but the Forces Nouvelles held the military card and were not prepared to give it up until they were certain that elections—to their liking—would happen. But we underestimated too the tenacity of President Gbagbo, who was highly adept at political gymnastics and seemed to bounce back after every setback.

My third and final conclusion was that ONUCI—unlike UNAMSIL in Sierra Leone or UNMIL in Liberia—did not enjoy a preponderance of presence that would have enabled it to influence the political process in a more decisive manner. Its force level and capabilities were more appropriate for a peace-monitoring mission than a robust peacekeeping operation. It depended, for example, on Operation Licorne for rapid-reaction support. While cooperation with Licorne was generally good, the instructions came from Paris, not New York. This was abundantly clear during the November 2004 crisis when ONUCI was not informed in advance of the French retaliatory action even though the French intervention had immediate and unpredictable consequences for the UN mission. The deployment of "parallel forces" is always susceptible to operational contradictions arising from the duality of command in a single theater of operations.

The Line of Succession

The war of succession continues to cast a long shadow. During the early months of 2017, mutinies broke out involving soldiers and gendarmes protesting the government's failure to pay arrears and war bonuses. The mutineers, who were recruits from the rebel forces who helped Ouattara to power, were protesting that they had not benefited sufficiently from the new dispensation (unlike their former commanders—ex-warlords—who had acquired influence and wealth since the end of the war). Well-informed commentators make the point that postwar reintegration and reconciliation in Côte d'Ivoire is unfinished business.[37]

There is a pervasive belief in some communities that victors' justice has prevailed. To date, not a single major figure from the Forces Nouvelles/ Ouattara side has gone on trial for participating in wartime crimes. A truth and reconciliation commission in September 2011 (as originally prescribed in the Linas-Marcoussis Agreement) was established under the leadership of Charles Konan Banny, a former prime minister (under Laurent Gbagbo). The commission has been derided as ineffectual and expensive and it has certainly not healed the wounds of war. On a visit to Côte d'Ivoire in 2014 with Kofi Annan, I met Banny and members of the truth and reconciliation commission. They described their elaborate plans for extensive public engagement, but we wondered what, if any, tangible impact the commission would have in reconciling a still highly divided country.

In the meantime, Laurent Gbagbo stood trial before the ICC for crimes against humanity and other counts (along with his acolytes Blé Goudé and Lida Kouassi). Although initially convicted by the Court, Gbagbo's conviction was subsequently set aside in early 2019 by the ICC's Court of Appeal; pending the outcome of an appeal by the ICC prosecutor, he remains in Europe. Madame Gbagbo was also indicted by the ICC but she was tried and convicted by an Ivorian court and then pardoned by President Ouattara as an "act of reconciliation."

Because of term limits, President Ouattara is scheduled to step down from office in 2020 (although as I write, this remains to be confirmed). The contenders for the succession are already positioning themselves. Allegiances are once again in flux. The language of *Ivoirité* has resurfaced in political discourse.[38] I earnestly hope, nevertheless, that the political class has taken to heart the hard lessons afforded by the two decades of disruption and devastation that followed Houphouët-Boigny's death. The competition for power must be tempered by the compromises of peace. The last thing that Côte d'Ivoire needs is another war of succession.

4

Liberia:
From War to Peace

The old is dying and the new cannot be born. In this interregnum there arises a great diversity of morbid symptoms.
—Antonio Gramsci

Liberia's official coat of arms depicts a ship sailing close to land, a pictorial representation of the arrival of the first settlers in Liberia, who landed in the early nineteenth century. It bears the motto: "The love of liberty brought us here." Those early settlers, former slaves or free blacks from the United States, were seeking, like the settlers in Sierra Leone, a new life and the promise of liberty. And yet since those first settlers arrived, liberty has often proved to be an elusive ambition, especially for the great majority of indigenous Liberians, who were neither settlers nor descended from them.

The Americo-Liberian Ascendancy
The settlers came to Liberia thanks to the American Colonization Society (ACS), which founded settlements in a unique process of reverse colonization. The ACS was created in 1816 to advocate for the manumission of slaves and the return of free blacks to Africa. It was supported by a coalition of interests, including abolitionists who believed that freed blacks could not be integrated into American society as well as slave owners who feared that the presence of free blacks would encourage others to militate for their freedom.[1] The ACS, which arranged passage for approximately 10,000 settlers[2] over several decades, received the support of some very prominent Americans, including Abraham Lincoln, Henry Clay, and James Monroe. This population—the Americo-Liberians—were joined by immigrants from the West Indies as well as Africans who were liberated on the

97

high seas by British and US warships and then landed in Liberia (or Sierra Leone). As in Sierra Leone, this group was labeled the "Congos."

The original American settlers established their colony in 1822; the colony declared itself independent of the ACS in 1847, becoming the first independent African republic. In fact, several settler colonies were established along the coast. They gradually coalesced, with the principal settlement in Montserrado, where the capital, Monrovia—named after James Monroe, the fourth US president—is located.

The ACS settlers did not install themselves in an empty land. Indigenous peoples were present in all parts of the country, usually living in small communities under the authority of traditional chiefs or clan leaders. From the outset, these peoples were treated with a mixture of fear, hostility, and disdain by the settlers. Over the course of the decades, the descendants of the original Americo-Liberian settlers created a highly segmented and discriminatory society, not unlike the one they had left behind.

The native population was excluded from the voting franchise. By contrast, the Americo-Liberian elite, representing at most 5 percent of the country's total population, controlled all of the key institutions of the nascent state.

As Arthur Barclay, an early-twentieth-century president of Liberia, stated in his 1904 inaugural address: "We made a great initial mistake in the beginning of our national career. We sought to obtain, and did succeed in grasping an enormous mass of territory, but we neglected to conciliate and attach the resident populations to our interest."[3] Liberia developed into something of a caste society, with a small minority constituting an aristocratic ruling class over a suppressed majority. The country still struggles to overcome that legacy.

The Monrovia government exercised little control over the rural areas, most of which were not easily accessible due to the absence of roads, hostile societies who resisted settler encroachment, and the dense rain forests. As Stephen Ellis has pointed out in his landmark study on Liberia, *The Mask of Anarchy,* only toward the end of the century did the Monrovia government begin to establish a formal system of governance by appointing district commissioners to work alongside local chiefs. This action was partly due to pressure from the UK and France, which did not want the laissez-faire governance prevailing in Liberia to spread to their neighboring colonies. The governance of Liberia was a patchwork of administrative contrivances developed according to the region and locality and run with a mix of coercion, control, and patronage.[4]

Liberia, the League of Nations, and Globalization

In 1908 a national army, misleadingly named the Liberian Frontier Force, was established, replacing the self-defense militias created in the early days of settlement. Ostensibly, the force was there to protect the nation from armed incursions by its neighbors. In fact, the Frontier Force, created with the assistance of the British in neighboring Sierra Leone, became an instrument of repression. The US government even offered a loan to the Liberian government if it would accept an early version of what today we might call security sector reform—US officers to improve the discipline and efficiency of the Frontier Force.[5]

Despite the draconian effort to raise revenue through oppressive tactics (or perhaps because of it), successive Liberian governments faced chronic deficits. So much so that in 1912 the United States offered another large loan conditional on the oversight of government finances by a group of Western countries. Another forerunner of a reform initiative—the Governance and Economic Assistance Programme (GEMAP)—was set up almost a century later to tackle the recurring problem of state finances.

Nevertheless, the coercion continued and eventually attracted the attention of the League of Nations (of which Liberia was a founding member). The League dispatched a commission of inquiry and in 1930 accused the government of "systematically and for years fostering and encouraging a policy of gross intimidation and suppression."[6] The commission's report pointed out that Liberia "represents the paradox of being a Republic of 12,000 citizens with 1,000,000 subjects."[7] The commission also found "conditions of criminal compulsion scarcely distinguishable from slave raiding and slave trade."[8]

Globalization came to Liberia's economic rescue. In 1926, Harvey Firestone established the first rubber plantation in Liberia; other companies followed in Firestone's footsteps. These companies were awarded long-term concessions, and when required, native populations were evicted to make way for the plantations. In a quid pro quo, Firestone arranged loans for the Liberian government.

In 1943, William Tubman was elected president. He promised change but reinforced his rule by dispensing favors and political support through a network of traditional chiefs and concessions to Mandingo and Lebanese traders.[9] The commodities boom Liberia enjoyed during World War II continued after the war ended. The country registered one of the highest levels of gross domestic product (GDP) in Africa, with the fastest rate of growth in the world after Japan.[10] The country also received significant injections of foreign aid from the United States. Nevertheless, the gap between the Americo-Liberian elite and Liberians of local origin remained as great as ever.

Fin de Regime

Tubman ruled until 1971. He was succeeded by his vice president, William R. Tolbert Jr. Although a scion of the Americo-Liberian elite, Tolbert was something of a reformer. He attempted to liberalize Liberian politics, allowing an opposition party to form (which subsequently played a major role in his downfall). This seemingly progressive policy earned Liberia a US presidential visit by Jimmy Carter in April 1978.

But reform was abruptly halted in 1979 when the government announced a hike in the price of rice (the basic staple of urban Liberians), which was a political windfall for the opposition. Strikes and demonstrations organized in Monrovia in April 1979 ended in violence and bloodshed. The reform was caught between the pressures of the street and the old guard of the Americo-Liberian elite, fearful for their status and privilege.

The crisis culminated in a coup in April 1980 mounted by a small group of young soldiers led by Master Sergeants Samuel Doe and Thomas Quiwonkpa. They set up the National Redemption Council, which announced that it would end the dominance of the Americo-Liberia elite. Tolbert was killed in the early hours of the coup. Government ministers were rounded up and summarily executed on a beach near the Executive Mansion, the official residence of the president of the republic.

One minister was spared—the minister of finance, Ellen Johnson Sirleaf. Appointed by Tolbert only eight months before the coup, she was allowed to go into exile. This was thanks to the vigorous intervention of Howard Wolpe, then chair of the US House of Representatives' Foreign Affairs Subcommittee on Africa, and his chief of staff, Anne Forrester (later a US ambassador to Mali and then a senior colleague in the UNDP). In her exile Ellen attended Harvard and then joined the World Bank, later becoming head of the UNDP's Africa Bureau.

Apocalypse Now

With the seizure of power by Doe, Liberia plunged into a quarter-century of extreme brutality, social disorder, and economic collapse. The violence and its consequences (including starvation among the civilian population) probably killed at least 250,000 people[11] and displaced many more.

Liberia's progressive descent into chaos was marked by three phases. First was the ascension of Samuel Doe after the 1980 coup, which ended with his gruesome death a decade later. Doe's death ignited a second phase of conflict marked by internecine warfare that eventually brought Charles Taylor to power in 1997. The third phase began in 1999 and ended in 2003 with Taylor exiled in Nigeria and the establishment of the United Nations Mission in Liberia (UNMIL) as a peacekeeping force.

The Gathering Storm

Doe rapidly consolidated his authority, exiling or executing opponents, including some of his former comrades-in-arms. He held on to power for another decade, building a power base around his own Krahn group, winning a rigged election in 1985, and surviving coup and assassination attempts, all while launching murderous campaigns against other ethnic groups, notably the Gio and Mano in central Liberia. Despite his awful human rights record and extensive corruption, Doe was a convenient—if embarrassing—Cold War ally in Africa.

Notwithstanding the initial patronage of the United States, Doe's foes gained strength. Many were living in exile, having escaped palace purges or the ethnic pogroms he launched against other ethnic communities. An unlikely alliance among Côte d'Ivoire, Burkina Faso, and Libya emerged to provide training and funding to back Liberian dissidents. Houphouët-Boigny had never forgiven Doe for executing the husband of his goddaughter, despite his appeal for clemency; Blaise Compaoré had enlisted Liberian exiles linked to Charles Taylor in his overthrow of Thomas Sankara, then president of Burkina Faso; and the messianic Muammar Qaddafi disliked Doe intensely for his pro-American and Israeli sympathies.

On December 24, 1989, a small group of fighters moved across the border from Côte d'Ivoire into Nimba County under the banner of the National Patriotic Front of Liberia (NPFL). The NPFL, although founded by Thomas Quiwonkpa, was taken over by Charles Taylor after Quiwonkpa was killed in a failed coup attempt. Taylor, having escaped custody in the United States, was to become a central figure in the life and times of Liberia for more than two decades before he was eventually forced into exile in 2003.

Anarchy and Accords

The incursion launched on Christmas Eve in 1989 was the start of the first Liberian civil war, which lasted until 1997. The war was marked by extreme violence and serial peace agreements that fell apart almost as soon as they were signed.

Taylor's NPFL pushed forward to Monrovia with the aid of another warlord, Prince Johnson. Although Johnson later split with Taylor to create his own armed group (the Independent NPFL), they succeeded in reaching Monrovia within a few months, creating panic among residents, especially those from the Krahn and Mandingo groups.

Alarmed by Taylor's success, Nigeria mobilized ECOWAS to create an ECOMOG force (not to be confused with the ECOMOG force later deployed to Sierra Leone in 1997), which debarked in Monrovia in August 1990. The ECOMOG force soon ran into trouble. Samuel Doe was taken prisoner in September by Prince Johnson when he went to meet with the ECOMOG commander at the Port of Monrovia. He was tortured and then murdered by Johnson's fighters, who filmed the grisly atrocity.

Over the next three years, several peace agreements[12] were signed to halt the fighting and set the stage for national elections. None of them succeeded.

They included the 1993 Cotonou Agreement, which established a transitional government and called for UN observers to monitor the ceasefire, the disarmament of the factions, and national elections. In response the Security Council established the United Nations Observer Mission in Liberia (UNOMIL) in September 1993.[13] The operation was unarmed and consequently had to depend on the protection of ECOMOG,[14] largely nullifying its credibility as an independent agent. When fighting again engulfed Monrovia in April 1996, UNOMIL was evacuated.

In September 1996, yet another agreement was signed in Abuja, Nigeria, known as the Abuja II accord, which set a date for elections and the start of a DDR process. An interim president, Ruth Perry, was appointed. The DDR program was started but only partially completed. Taylor (whose faction remained well armed) announced his intention to run for the presidency in the elections scheduled for mid-1997.

A few months before the election date, I was temporarily assigned to New York as deputy director of the UNDP's Regional Bureau for Africa, which Ellen Johnson Sirleaf was running. Not long after my arrival, she left on holiday to West Africa, leaving me as officer-in-charge. A week later, I picked up a barely audible phone call from Monrovia. Ellen was on the line; she told me that she had been trying to connect with Gus Speth, head of the UNDP, to tell him that she was resigning her post in order to run in the Liberian elections. Her decision was a brave one. She was obliged to sever her links with the UN while risking the wrath of a vengeful Taylor.

The elections were held in July 1997. Taylor was elected president by a wide margin in an election deemed acceptable by international observers. The result was not entirely surprising. Johnson Sirleaf had been absent from Liberia for the better part of two decades, and the climate of apprehension over what might happen if Taylor did not win undoubtedly weighed in his favor. Ellen did not return to the UN after the election. She remained in West Africa and began to quietly build a wider political base within the country and the region.

Following the election, UNOMIL was closed and replaced by a small UN peacebuilding support office, the first of its kind, with the mandate to assist the government to consolidate peace.[15] The office didn't have much impact; Liberia with Charles Taylor in charge was not an easy sell to international donors who wanted to see progress on human rights and reconciliation before making any substantial aid commitments to the country.

The Downfall

The past came back to haunt President Taylor very quickly. A Mandingo-backed group called Liberians United for Reconciliation and Democracy (LURD) soon emerged from Guinea to the north, while from the southeast a Krahn faction calling itself the Movement for Democracy in Liberia (MODEL) began hostilities.

Despite his electoral victory, Taylor remained a pariah in the international community. Although Qaddafi was still willing to lend support, Taylor could no longer count on Côte d'Ivoire or Burkina Faso, which were enmeshed in internal discord. Sanctions were imposed by the Security Council as a riposte to Taylor's support to the RUF (which he was using to counter the pressure from LURD, based in Guinea). By early 2002, LURD had got close enough to Monrovia to shell the city.

As the situation deteriorated and the risk of a bloodbath in Monrovia loomed, President John Kufuor of Ghana, chairman of ECOWAS, called for urgent peace talks in Accra. The Accra talks opened on June 4, 2003, with the participation of LURD and MODEL as well as Taylor. Then a bombshell hit the conference. As I mentioned in my chapter on Sierra Leone, David Crane, the prosecutor at the Special Court for Sierra Leone, released the court's indictment of Taylor and asked the Ghana government to arrest him. President Kufuor of Ghana, angered by what he considered an unwarranted intrusion into the peace talks, sent Taylor back to Monrovia in his presidential jet. On his return, Taylor warned menacingly that there would be no peace in Liberia unless the indictment was dropped.[16]

Years later I asked (by then) President Johnson Sirleaf about the impact of the indictment on the peace talks in Accra, where she was leading a delegation from civil society. I assumed that the indictment had complicated the talks by provoking Taylor's abrupt withdrawal and return to Monrovia. To my surprise, she told me that the opposite was true; despite the official annoyance by the heads of state present, the indictment had actually facilitated the talks because Taylor was now no longer a player; he was yesterday's man, having lost what little legitimacy he could still claim.

Ever the political chameleon, Taylor declared on his return to Monrovia that he would resign provided troops from a US amphibious group stationed offshore intervened. President George W. Bush would have none of it and insisted that Taylor must resign and leave the country. Taylor reluctantly agreed to go into exile in Nigeria. He did so on August 11, declaring with a MacArthuresque flourish[17] that "God willing, I will be back."

Shortly afterward, a Nigerian unit from UNAMSIL was transferred to Monrovia as a vanguard of a peacekeeping force. Just after the unit arrived, a cargo plane landed unannounced at Monrovia's airport; the Nigerians surrounded the plane and ordered the crew to open the hold, revealing a shipment of arms and ammunition. The flight had originated in Libya but it arrived too late to help Charles Taylor.

A week after Taylor left Liberia the Liberia Comprehensive Peace Agreement (CPA)[18] was signed on August 18, 2003, in Accra by the armed groups. It formally declared an end to the armed conflict and requested the

United Nations to deploy a force to Liberia to support a national transitional government and to assist in the implementation of the agreement. Given past experience, however, the question remained: Would the ceasefire hold? Or would the CPA be added to the long list of failed Liberia peace agreements?

Resurrection

In anticipation of progress on the peace process, Secretary-General Annan announced in July 2003 the appointment of Jacques Paul Klein from the United States as his special representative for Liberia. Jacques, a former diplomat, US Air Force general, and UN envoy in the Balkans, was mandated with "coordinating the activities of the United Nations agencies in Liberia and supporting the emerging transitional arrangements."[19]

On September 19, the Security Council formally approved the establishment of UNMIL, which was to become operational on October 1, 2003.[20] The main elements of the mission's mandate followed the integrated model, with a wide array of responsibilities including civilian protection, DDR, support for national elections, security sector reform, and sanctions monitoring. UNMIL was to be a "stabilization force" with a Chapter VII mandate, with an initially limited timeframe of (optimistically) twelve months.

Shortly afterward, in accordance with the Accra peace agreement, the National Transitional Government of Liberia (NTGL) was inaugurated. The NTGL was headed by Gyude Bryant, a prominent Liberian businessman who had somehow managed to maintain a reputation for independence and was therefore acceptable to all factions.

Return of the Peacekeepers

In contrast to other startup missions, UNMIL was generously resourced. The initial troop level was set at 15,000, with 1,115 UN police officers, including formed units to assist in the maintenance of law and order throughout Liberia. As usual, however, the buildup of troops and equipment was slow.

Jacques Klein took office in Monrovia in October. On the way, he stopped by Freetown for a briefing on UNAMSIL's experiences with DDR and postconflict stabilization. At the time, I was officer-in-charge of the mission and I invited him to lunch before the formal briefing. I had not met Jacques before, so I wasn't quite sure what to expect. He walked into the restaurant wearing aviator sunglasses and a US Air Force flight jacket replete with service patches and a fur collar; outside the temperature must have registered at least 30 degrees Celsius. As prelude to lunch he handed me a cigar with his own brand label. As first encounters go, Jacques made quite an impression.

We talked about DDR and I outlined the difficulties UNAMSIL had experienced with DDR, including the RUF attacks on DDR sites in 2000. I also explained how we had managed to relaunch the program, emphasizing the importance of disarming units together and then aiding individual ex-combatants to go back to their areas of origin to prevent units from reforming.

Jacques wasn't persuaded and countered with his own UN experience from the Balkans, where he had launched a weapons buyback program. He saw this as the quickest way of achieving disarmament and putting the armed groups out of business. I wasn't so sure and advised caution, arguing that the cash approach might short-circuit reintegration, as ex-combatants would opt for an immediate cash payment (and spend it quickly) rather than the promise of training or other reintegration opportunities. There was also a considerable risk that a cash-for-weapons plan would create an inflow of arms from neighboring countries.

The DDR program in Liberia was launched on December 7, 2003, and ran into serious trouble. Both the numbers of registered combatants (almost three times the initial estimate) and their expectations quickly outpaced the cash flow. In December, when payments could not be made, violent riots broke out, which spilled over into Monrovia. The DDR program had to be suspended "in order to redesign the process, organize more cantonment camps, and await the deployment of more peacekeepers."[21]

The Government of No Return

The transitional government installed after Taylor's departure was essentially a division of the spoils. The Accra peace agreement allotted—"awarded" might be a more accurate word—positions in the executive branch, the legislature, state enterprises, and other national institutions to the various groups who signed the accord. The lion's share of the big (and most lucrative) posts went to the armed groups, with LURD, MODEL, and the rump government, headed by Taylor's former vice president, Moses Blah, receiving the bulk. But under the terms of the agreement, the chairman of the interim government still had to approve individual names for ministerial positions and send them on to the Transitional Assembly for endorsement. This led to intense and prolonged wrangling between the chairman, the parties, and the legislature, which delayed the full startup of the government and the state apparatus.

The CPA also contained another critical stipulation: the chairman and vice chairman as well as all cabinet members "shall not contest for any elective office during the 2005 elections to be held in Liberia."[22] This provision created a term limit for the NTGL in a (successful) effort to preempt any attempts by the transitional government to prolong its stay in office. Similar term limits were mandated for the legislature and the judiciary. The constitution was suspended pending the restoration of an elected government. Of equal significance, the CPA mandated security sector reform (military, police, and justice). Article VII of the CPA called for the disbandment of irregular forces and the reformation and restructuring of the Liberian armed forces. This directive was quite prescriptive and included a specific provision that the United States play a lead role in organizing the restructuring program. This provision, as I mention later on, greatly aided UNMIL in its task of restoring and maintaining stability.

The CPA created a raft of supporting institutional measures to tackle the baleful legacy of the Taylor years. These included a truth and reconciliation commission and a monopolies commission (which was expected unwind some highly dubious deals concluded by the Taylor administration).

These measures were accompanied by a monitoring and coordinating framework for the implementation of the Accra arrangements. This framework comprised a joint ceasefire monitoring committee chaired by the UNMIL force commander; an implementation monitoring committee chaired by ECOWAS and tasked with overseeing the execution of the CPA; and an international contact group chaired by Sweden and Ghana.

In addition, the CPA included provision for a (nonresident) chief mediator to be appointed by ECOWAS who could mediate and rule on disputes arising from the CPA. General Abdulsalami Abubakar, a redoubtable former head of state of Nigeria, assumed the position. By virtue of his personal prestige and with Nigeria's powerful backing, the general played, in effect, the referee role that the French ambassador in Côte d'Ivoire posited as a solution to the interminable disputes that bedeviled the Linas-Marcoussis Agreement. I benefited from his interventions on several occasions when he weighed in at my request to resolve disputes that threatened to disrupt the electoral calendar.

This coordination structure set up by the CPA was quite complicated. But it did not suffer the same fate as the Linas-Marcoussis oversight mechanisms, which gradually lost relevance. Why? In good measure the CPA was the outcome of an ECOWAS-brokered peace agreement, and the key committee—the one for implementation—was chaired by ECOWAS. The region and its major players like Nigeria and Ghana had a direct stake in making the CPA a success and were in a position to influence the direction of events in a way that was never possible in Côte d'Ivoire due to the mutual antipathy between Gbagbo and regional leaders and the country's still significant economic weight in the West African monetary zone.

In addition to the locally based mechanisms, I was a member of the International Contact Group on Liberia (ICGL), led by a top Swedish diplomat, Hans Dahlgren, and the foreign minister of Niger, Aïchatou Mindaoudou (later to become the SRSG). The ICGL brought together regional and international players and took on the job of messaging the NTGL rather than leaving that to the Security Council and the African Union, which might have been more reluctant to challenge the prerogatives of national sovereignty.

Recovery Gets Started

During more than two decades of warfare, Liberia had gone from a relatively prosperous state (by African standards of the day) to a totally impoverished one. Admittedly, that earlier prosperity was not well shared. By the end of the conflict, however, the country had lost about 80–90 percent of its GDP according to one study by the IMF.[23] Even at a steady growth rate of 8 percent per annum (very high by historical standards), it would still take the country twenty-five years to get back to where it was in 1979. So the sooner some measure of stability was achieved, the sooner some semblance of economic revival could begin. This was a massive task for a country devastated by years of warlord economics and the exodus of Liberia's professional class.

With the gradual deployment of UNMIL throughout the national territory, UN agencies, NGOs, and civil society began to move out from Monrovia into the interior. With the improved security situation, they were able to access areas of the country that had been deprived of any aid for many years. As in Sierra Leone, however, they found the population in desperate need and the social infrastructure demolished. Far more than in Sierra Leone, the restoration of "state authority" (perhaps not the most apt term given the absence of such authority for much of the country's history) was a slow-moving and laborious process. As Lansana Gberie remarked to me, despite the ferocious war in Sierra Leone, its basic institutions survived (in a much-weakened state, true), whereas in Liberia they had largely disappeared.

The General Calls It a Day

In April 2005, Jacques Klein departed Monrovia. He left behind a controversial legacy. He made no secret of his "irritation" (my euphemism—Jacques used less diplomatic language) with NGOs, UN agencies, regional organizations, and even his force commander. By the end of his time in Monrovia, that exasperation was widely reciprocated. But while I heard plenty of criticism of him in the international community, I heard little from Liberians. They rather liked his tough talk and flamboyant style (he once rode through town on a tank); they saw in him someone who would stand up to the warlords, a military man who was not afraid to crack heads if needed. In the months after the Accra agreement, when confidence in the peace process was still shaky, many Liberians found reassurance in Jacques's rambunctious presence. Nevertheless, when I took over from him,

I was advised by New York to lower the temperature and build a more serene relationship with the assorted actors in the Liberian peace process.

From War to Peace

Pomp and Ceremonies

With the announcement of Jacques's impending departure, I was asked to interview for the Liberia post. It was my first formal interview for a UN post since the one I had done when I originally applied to be a UK-sponsored volunteer at the UNDP back in 1966, almost forty years before. But I must have said something right, because Jean-Marie Guéhenno called me a few days later to say that I was the panel's choice, which the Secretary-General had approved. I was surprised by the quick decision; it seemed easier to appoint an under-secretary-general than a junior staff member.

So off we went to Monrovia. Again, I asked for a small group of staff from Côte d'Ivoire to work with me in this third peacekeeping mission. These included Arslan Malik, my versatile and always well-informed special assistant, and Carole Joseph, my highly competent personal assistant. Bert Coppens eventually joined me as the chief of staff. This time, however, unlike in UNAMSIL and ONUCI, which were relatively new missions, I did not need to build a staff from scratch. On arrival, I was impressed by the SRSG's office, which was led by Karen Tchalian, an immensely hardworking Russian colleague (he read absolutely everything) with a dry sense of humor.

I made the short air journey from Abidjan assuming that I would be met on arrival by the DSRSG, Abou Moussa (who had previously been running the UN peacebuilding office in Liberia) and possibly one or two other senior UN colleagues. Abou was indeed there, but so was a pageant of UNMIL's military and police, smartly turned out on the tarmac with flags flying while a Nigerian military band played an exuberant rendition of the UN anthem (yes, there is one). Somewhat overwhelmed, I proceeded to inspect the massed ranks, trying to assume a suitably martial posture for the occasion, and glad that I had worn a tie that morning.

After I completed the tarmac formalities, I was mobbed by local journalists. I mumbled a few words to say how pleased I was to be in Liberia and that I was looking forward to helping the country in its progress toward peace. Before I could escape, one of the journalists shoved a microphone in front of me and said that on his arrival my predecessor had promised that he would get the electricity back on in three months, and then asked what I was promising. Two years had elapsed since Jacques was alleged to have made that commitment and still no electricity (it had been off for more than a decade since the power station had been blown up in 1990). I scrambled for a response but then an old rule in politics came to my rescue: if you give a date, don't give a number (and vice versa). So I responded saying that we would indeed be working to get the lights on in Monrovia and left it at that.

From the airport, we were escorted to the residence of the SRSG. This turned out to be a large, isolated villa outside of town, guarded day and night by a platoon of special forces from the Philippines. The house was a rather bizarre construction; it included a master bedroom with a mirrored ceiling and a king-size Jacuzzi for which there was no water supply. In fact, water for the house had to be trucked in every few days. Only later did I discover that the house was owned by Charles Taylor's brother.

Because the house was out of town, I had to battle the morning traffic into Monrovia. When war-scarred cities like Monrovia become clogged up by vehicles, it's actually a good sign. It shows that confidence is returning. But in the case of Monrovia (like Freetown), the traffic returned to roads that had not seen any maintenance for many years. Huge potholes scarred the main highway into the city and the traffic detoured around them, creating new potholes and mud traps in the rainy season.

Fortunately, a solution was in the works. The mission management, led by Ronnie Stokes, a former US marine turned peacekeeper, had located a building downtown suitable for mission premises that was close to the government offices. At the time, we were renting the German embassy compound, but it could not accommodate all of the mission headquarters, which was spread around the city.

Part office complex, part shopping mall, and part private apartments, the building stood empty and forlorn after being looted several times during the war years. It was located right on the seafront, a few hundred meters from the Executive Mansion (the presidential palace) and the Ministry of Foreign Affairs. The building was actually owned by a state company that had been set up with Libyan funding.

I discovered at the top of the building an apartment that could be renovated as a part of the overall rehabilitation of the structure. This meant living over the store, but the compensation was the convenience and a magnificent panorama stretching over the ocean, the beaches, the wetlands, and the inland waterways that encircle Monrovia—south Florida without the condos and congestion. I persuaded myself, of course, that there would be cost savings too as we would no longer need a residential guard unit nor the expense and bother of trucking in water every day or so. Moreover, I reasoned, given the dearth of decent hotel accommodation in Monrovia, the apartment would also serve as a convenient guest house for visiting UN dignitaries. I was relieved as well that the rent I paid for the apartment (SRSGs do not get rent-free accommodations) would go to the UN and not end up somehow with the Taylor family.

That wonderful vista, however, could not obscure the scars of war. Monrovia was coming back to life, but the extensive battle damage was still very visible. Just about all major public buildings had been wrecked; many had been taken over by squatters who subsisted in burned-out or half-finished buildings. Municipal services had collapsed and whole sections of the city survived without any sanitation or clean water. Like in Freetown, two decades of warfare had greatly impoverished the capital and its people.

Nevertheless, as in Freetown, the people of Monrovia found solace in their places of worship. One of those sprang up right next door to the UN compound just after we moved in. Actually it was an improvised tent church made of salvaged canvas patches (complete with the UNHCR's logo). Starting bright and early every Sunday morning, we were awakened by the faithful and their pastor conducting a very animated and lengthy prayer meeting amplified by several loudspeakers. The congregants may have been extremely poor but their spirit was undiminished.

Peace, Piece by Piece

I had experienced the challenges of war and peace in Sierra Leone and Côte d'Ivoire from two different perspectives. In Sierra Leone, the critical challenge was to find a way to turn the tenuous military stalemate into a peace deal before hostilities exploded again; in Côte d'Ivoire, the challenge was to stop the country from sliding into hostilities. By the time of my arrival, Liberia was somewhere in between; armed violence had largely subsided but the fear of renewed violence hovered over the country and the transition to an elected government was still to be achieved.

It seemed to me that we had to achieve three principal goals in Liberia. The first and most immediate was to secure peaceful, free, and fair national elections followed by a smooth transition to a new administration. The second was to consolidate the gains on the security side while pushing forward with security sector reform. Finally, we needed to move ahead with the monumental task of national reconstruction and prepare the way for institutional reforms.

UNMIL could not (and was not mandated) to take on these challenges alone. My experience in Sierra Leone had shown me the vital importance of building good working relations with a wide range of local and international allies and associates in order to push ahead with an ambitious peace-building agenda.

General Abdulsalami, the ECOWAS mediator, proved to be an indispensable ally. His interventions were exceptionally helpful, particularly in the run-up to the elections when fractious Liberian politicians were threatening to derail the process through spurious legal maneuvers. The ECOWAS representative based in Liberia was equally helpful. He chaired the in-country coordination mechanism but called on me and the force commander to lead on security-related issues.

Getting the UN country team on board was relatively straightforward. I knew that the relations between my predecessor and the UN agency heads were fraught, so with the help of DSRSG Abou Moussa I set out to repair them. This included a more liberal policy on the use of mission assets (including access to UNMIL's post exchange shop).

Unlike in the other missions in which I had served, the UN humanitarian office was integrated into the UNMIL structure. OCHA and the NGOs were not overjoyed with this arrangement, so I was at pains to reassure them that the humanitarian office would not be subjected to any political interference from the mission. Quite the opposite; resettling and reintegrating hundreds of thousands of refugees and IDPs was a massive job and I could offer UNMIL support for both tasks. Fortunately, Dennis Johnston, who had worked with me previously in Sierra Leone, headed up the humanitarian office and was well-versed in my ways of working.

I counted on the DSRSG, initially Abou Moussa and then Jordan Ryan, to move forward with the recovery effort wearing the humanitarian and development hats. Abou had worked for the UNHCR for many years and grasped the advantages that a close relationship with the mission could bring from an operational perspective. Jordan had developed the agreement between the UNDP and DPKO that had introduced the integrated-mission concept with my multihatted appointment in Sierra Leone. So he was well placed to understand the challenges (and pitfalls) of mission integration and how to manage them.

The top team was rounded out by Luiz Carlos da Costa from Brazil as the DSRSG brought in to focus on mission management together with the police and rule-of-law components (somewhat similar my role in ONUCI). Luiz was another veteran of peacekeeping operations and knew how to navigate the shoals of the UN bureaucracy, especially in the areas of budget, finance, and administration, which was not my strong suit.

The Economic Consequences of Peace

While I moved quickly to build a constructive relationship with the regional partners, the UN country team, and the humanitarian organizations, the national administration was an altogether different proposition. The transitional administration, headed by Gyude Bryant, had been in office for about twenty months by the time I arrived in Liberia. Among the donors, the NTGL was written off as a disaster. ECOWAS was less disparaging in public of the NTGL's performance but equally despairing in private.

The NTGL was a government that functioned on patronage and pillage. Bryant had little to no control on the individual ministers and their ministries. Corruption was rife and ministerial coordination nonexistent. One of the first meetings I attended with the "government" was convened by Bryant to discuss the economic reform package. All the members of the ECOWAS coordination group were there, as was Chairman Bryant, who sat at the head of the imposing conference table in the cabinet room. We all sat on one side of the table facing what we thought would be the government, except no one was there. Bryant had sent out an invitation but ministers simply didn't show up.

I did the round of some of the more critical ministries but I met hardly anyone with whom I could have a serious and substantive discussion. Because they knew their time in office was limited, most of the ministers and their aides seemed to care little about the future.

With the end of the war, the donors had returned to Liberia with generous offers of development aid as well as humanitarian assistance. But within a few months, disappointment set in as the struggle to get projects off the ground ran into indifference or ill-disguised attempts to extort financial incentives (bribes). President Kabbah confided in me his exasperation about this state of affairs, having seen a huge bill for expenses from the Liberian government for a short visit to Freetown funded by the Sierra Leone government. The European Union and the United States were especially frustrated as they struggled to get the rehabilitation of the power grid and other infrastructure projects under way. The Chinese ambassador too privately expressed to me his intense frustration with the way China's aid was being handled.

Matters came to a head when the EU, United States, and World Bank threatened to cut off aid if reforms were not put in place. Bryant pleaded impotence. By this time, he had taken to inviting Don Booth, the US ambassador, and me to long Sunday lunches at his private residence in an effort to get our help in dealing with the crisis. We used these occasions, however, to press him to lead rather than resist the reform initiative. Reluctantly he agreed to do so.

The core of the reform program was GEMAP.[24] It included a number of quite intrusive measures such as the appointment of non-Liberians to work at the central bank with executive authority, and a monopolies commission that could review and cancel dubious government contracts. Other provisions called for the designation of an independent auditor-general and so on. Not surprisingly, the NTGL and the Legislative Assembly were opposed to GEMAP, and so the negotiations dragged on.

The World Bank asked me to intervene to see if there was a way of overcoming this resistance. I felt that the best way to do so would be to get regional players on board, particularly if GEMAP was to be endorsed by the Security Council (as suggested by the World Bank). To do that, I proposed that Nigeria and Ghana should be invited to join the GEMAP steering committee even though they would not be directly funding GEMAP. Despite their hesitations over the intrusive nature of the proposed agreement, both countries agreed to join the committee.

Notwithstanding the pressures, Chairman Bryant continued to hold out. His reluctance gave rise to speculation that an independent auditor might turn up some awkward findings. In the end he did sign, although only a short time before he handed over the reins of government following the elections. In fact, after President Johnson Sirleaf took office, Bryant was detained on corruption charges. He pleaded with me to intercede with the president on his behalf. As one of the international partners who had pushed her to go along with GEMAP and its aim of cleaning up government finances, I felt I could not do so.

The NTGL was an economic disaster for the country. And yet paradoxically it was a political success. By bringing the factions into government, it gave them an incentive to abide by the terms of the Accra agreement, which afforded the UN time and space that was needed to organize the DDR, elections, and other key provisions stipulated by the accord. And while GEMAP came too late to save the reputation of the NTGL (and the economy), it did have an important impact on the government and governance after the elections.

The Electoral Imperative

The Accra peace agreement had mandated that the national elections take place no later than October 2005. It was an uphill struggle to meet that deadline. The electoral commission was woefully underequipped, with relatively few trained staff. Hundreds of thousands of refugees and IDPs remained in camps or in host communities, which made it difficult to register them. In anticipation of the elections, however, the UN had positioned an electoral support team in the mission. Headed up by Ray Kennedy, a very experienced and diligent elections adviser, UNMIL's electoral team provided extensive support for the registration exercise and for the organization of the polls. Remarkably, more women than men registered to vote.

More than a dozen candidates entered the presidential race, although several were vanity candidacies, enjoying no popular support. There were persistent rumors that armed groups and political parties were mobilizing to manipulate or disrupt the elections, possibly with the encouragement of Charles Taylor in exile. I decided that I would get out in front and make it clear that UNMIL would not tolerate any disruption of the elections. I convened all the presidential candidates and emphasized that UNMIL would act decisively to defeat any effort to upset the elections. As the mission was now operating at full strength and deployed across the country, I was fairly confident that we had the means to back up our mandate.

Two leading candidates emerged from the scrum: Ellen Johnson Sirleaf and George Weah, a former football star. Johnson Sirleaf was by then a well-known political figure. Weah, a hero among the young because of his highly successful football career (he was one of the first Africans to enjoy a highly lucrative career playing in Europe), grew up in the West Point slum of Monrovia, which was devastated by the Ebola epidemic a decade later. But he was a political neophyte and relied heavily on political advisers who had survived the Doe/Taylor years.

In the run-up to the first round of the elections, both Weah and Johnson Sirleaf toured the country and relied heavily on public rallies and traditional rulers to galvanize support. This was an old-style election; the influence of modern media (of any kind) was minimal. Weah seemed the most popular, judging by the massive turnout for his public appearances. On one occasion, I was returning to mission headquarters from a meeting in another part of Monrovia and got caught up in a huge crowd following the Weah motorcade, which he led in his colorful campaign Humvee. It reminded me of my encounter outside the Hotel Ivoire, except this time the youthful crowds were very cheerful and the organizers escorted me through the throng with singing and dancing. The force commander, General Moses Bisong Obi of Nigeria, was in the car with me. I remarked to him that Weah appeared to be gaining support; Obi was not convinced and wryly observed that this was a "T-shirt crowd"—there for fun and freebies, which would not necessarily translate into votes on election day.

Given my past UN relationship with Johnson Sirleaf, I was worried that the mission might be accused of favoritism. As it happened, Ellen was not in the country when I had convened the presidential candidates to caution them about the conduct of the campaign. However, as soon as she returned, she immediately came to see me and I repeated the same remarks that I had made to the other candidates, even though I found it rather ironic that I was laying down the law with my former boss. But she assured me of her full support. At the same time, and to my surprise, she expressed some doubts about her chances, believing that she was the underdog in the contest with Weah.

The first round of the elections took place on October 11, 2005. The mission was on full alert. Journalists arrived in busloads, including Mark Doyle from the BBC, who had covered some of the worst periods of the Liberian civil wars. There were plenty of observers too, including President Jimmy Carter, who came to my preelection briefings. Led by my deputy, Luiz Carlos da Costa, the senior staff fanned out across the country. I toured some polling stations in Monrovia and was truly moved by how the voters (which included as many women as men) calmly waited for hours in the heat and humidity to cast their ballots.

The day proceeded without any significant violence or evidence of electoral fraud. We all breathed several sighs of relief. The results, announced by

Frances Morris Johnson, the feisty chair of the electoral commission, gave George Weah 28.3 percent of the vote; Ellen Johnson Sirleaf received 19.8 percent. As the threshold for a win on the first round was 50 percent plus one, Weah and Johnson Sirleaf went on to a runoff that was scheduled for November 8, 2005.

None of the candidates associated with major armed factions made any significant inroads in the presidential elections. This was not the case, however, with the legislative elections, where several notorious figures like Prince Yomi Johnson (more on him to come) were elected by substantial margins in their home areas.

The runoff was held on November 8 as scheduled. We sensed a rise in tensions; the generally relaxed atmosphere that had characterized the first round of voting began to wear thin. It was essentially a contest of personalities and generations. Weah emphasized his own personal success and decried the elite and their education, which he claimed had brought the country to ruin. Johnson Sirleaf, by contrast, emphasized health and education while again rejecting GEMAP as an infringement of state sovereignty.

Polling day was again relatively peaceful but tensions mounted with the results announced on November 23, 2005. Ellen Johnson Sirleaf won by a wide margin of 18.8 points. Weah and his party—the Congress for Democratic Change (CDC)—immediately denounced the results and claimed that he had been cheated. He clearly believed that having won the first round, he should have won the second ballot as well. His entourage, led by Gabriel Baccus Matthews (a seasoned activist who had figured prominently in the rice riots in 1979 that led to the demise of the Tolbert government), egged him on and he refused to accept the result. I was able to confirm that UNMIL was satisfied that Johnson Sirleaf had won; I advised the UN Secretary-General accordingly.

Unknown to me, however, someone had slipped a spoke into the electoral wheels. A French diplomat had sent a message to Paris questioning the validity of the results. When a permanent member of the Security Council raises an issue, it tends to get a high level of attention in the UN Secretariat. Almost immediately, I received a cable from DPKO expressing concern and even suggesting that an international commission of inquiry should be set up to look into the election results so as to forestall a possible outbreak of violence.

I was appalled and annoyed. I called in Ray Kennedy and asked him to check again to see if there were any reasonable grounds to justify such a move. He meticulously went over all the returns and the reports received from observers and our own staff on the ground. Their view was unanimous: Ellen Johnson Sirleaf had won fair and square. I strongly advised UN headquarters against any action that might throw the election results into doubt. To my relief, the idea of an inquiry was quickly dropped.

Weah did not give up. He publicly declared that he had won and called on his supporters to protest. US ambassador Don Booth and I met with him to try to persuade him that he had not been cheated out of victory. Secretary-General Annan called him, as did other prominent personalities, including Silvio Berlusconi, his former employer at the Italian football club AC Milan. All to no avail; he was totally convinced that he had won.

A CDC protest outside UNMIL's office turned ugly and had to be dispersed by force. Another demonstration outside the US embassy was also quite violent. The situation was becoming tense and we had to act to avoid a breakdown of confidence and back up what I had said before the election: UNMIL would not allow the election to be thwarted by violence. So we mounted a strong show of force with our armored units rumbling through the streets of Monrovia. Actually, the most effective response came from UNMIL's formed police units, who were well trained in crowd management and riot control. The Liberian National Police (LNP) were in the first line but the formed police units provided a stiffener without resort to the use of the military. This was a tactic that we used several times in the following months when the fledgling government was faced with violent demonstrations by one or another group of protestors.

I had spoken out to declare UN confidence in the election results. What was far more important, however, was that the people of Liberia accepted the results as a reflection of their collective will; they did not want to see any return of violence. As a diplomat from Sierra Leone said to me: "George misjudged the voters. Ellen's message of education, health and hope was much more in touch with the public mood of the day, especially among women. People did not reject education; they wanted more of it." She also made some shrewd strategic choices, making alliances with influential chiefs and leaders in populous "swing" counties like Nimba even if this meant doing deals with unsavory characters.

The election appeal went through due process and was rejected: Ellen Johnson Sirleaf was formally declared the winner. Weah eventually came around, albeit grudgingly. A number of regional leaders weighed in to convince him that he must accept the result; among them was President Obasanjo, who enjoyed great influence throughout West Africa and was not shy about using it. The last thing Nigeria and ECOWAS wanted was a standoff that threatened to unravel the still fragile peace of Liberia.

Madame President

The inauguration of Africa's first elected female head of state and government was expected to draw quite a crowd. A number of African presidents declared that they would attend. The United States announced that the wife of its president, Laura Bush, accompanied by one of her daughters, and the secretary of state, Condoleezza Rice, would represent the US government.

The presence of such a roll call of prominent dignitaries required a formidable capacity for event management. In principle this was the responsibility of the outgoing government, but the NTGL had no idea how this could be done, nor the capacity to do so.

Matters came to head a couple of days before the inauguration. The US Secret Service, together with staff from the White House, was in town to check out the arrangements for the first lady. They quickly discovered the disarray. A lot of the important details, like where Mrs. Bush would sit during the ceremony, had not been worked out. I got a rather panicked call from Gyude Bryant asking if we could somehow help out. I went over to the venue for the inauguration with a team from UNMIL.

After some back-and-forth, it was finally agreed where the podium with the VIPs would be located. Then another problem emerged. About a dozen heads of state were expected to attend. But as Laura Bush did not rank at that level, where should she sit? It would need to be somewhere both visible and secure. Finally, after various configurations were tried out, a young protocol officer from UNMIL, Vedran Pataki, came up with a clever solution. The heads of states would sit on a first row of chairs facing the audience. A second row of chairs was placed immediately behind the first row, largely obscuring those seated in that row except for a chair or two that would extend beyond the first VIP row and were thus fully visible to the audience in front. That is where Laura Bush and party would be seated; not quite with the heads of state but close and visible enough to ensure that the presence of the US guests was prominent. With such flashes of ingenuity are diplomatic dilemmas resolved.

With those arrangements in hand, I was able to adjourn to UNMIL headquarters and prepare for the arrival of the UN guest of honor, Deputy Secretary-General Louise Frechette, representing Secretary-General Kofi Annan. I had arranged a reception for her to meet the senior UN staff at our rooftop residence, where she was going to stay during her visit. We gathered for pre-inaugural drinks and it was a pleasant evening, with Louise emphasizing the contribution that the UN had collectively made in making the transition a peaceful reality.

After the guests left, we sat down for a nightcap. A few minutes later, Gerry Brasselle, from my close-protection team, came in looking rather nervous. He had spotted smoke billowing out of the ventilation ducts in the corridor leading to the apartment. He suggested that we move to my office on the floor below while he checked out the problem. At that moment, thick black fumes began pouring into the apartment, so we hurried downstairs. Another half hour was enough to force the evacuation of the entire building. UNMIL fire crews struggled up to the top floor to find the source of the smoke, which turned out to be an electrical fire. Providentially, the fire itself was contained by the fire doors of the computer room where it had ignited, but the smoke rendered the apartment uninhabitable.

We were lucky to find a room for Louise at a nearby hotel, and I decamped to Luiz Carlos da Costa's house to catch some sleep. Fortunately, Pierre Yelcouni, a delightful Burkinabe whom I knew from my Abidjan days, braved the smoke and managed to salvage a suit for me. Luiz lent me a shirt and tie for the inauguration ceremonies. As he was much taller than me, the shirt and tie were several sizes too big.

My somewhat ill-fitting appearance at the inauguration ceremony (and the whiff of barbecue from my suit) was the least of my concerns. My main worry was the possibility that the ceremony might be disrupted by dissident elements (Taylor supporters figured high on the list). We put UNMIL into a security overdrive for the inauguration, deploying our military and police on high alert throughout Monrovia. The United States also was not taking any chances; Laura Bush was on the ground for only a few hours. And just in case, a couple of US naval vessels were visibly patrolling the waters off Monrovia.

Despite the earlier scramble to get the venue sorted out and security worries, the inauguration passed off flawlessly. There were no serious problems of protocol, although the ceremony started with a delay because of the jam at the airport caused by so many presidential jets arriving at more or less the same time. But on the podium the VIP guests found their seats and the "Pataki plan" worked perfectly.

President Johnson Sirleaf dressed in a splendid inaugural robe and a spectacular traditional headdress, looking and playing her part to perfection. She took the oath of office in a confident voice. Her inaugural speech hit all the right notes, even extending an olive branch to "Ambassador Weah," who was accorded a seat of prominence in the audience.

After so many years of horror, something had finally gone right for Liberia and the country rejoiced.

Peacebuilding, Personalities, and Persuasion

The transitional arrangements decreed by the Accra agreement came to an end with Ellen Johnson Sirleaf's inauguration; national sovereignty was restored. And yet the incoming president faced immense impediments to the exercise of that sovereignty. Liberian society was deeply traumatized by the years of civil war; the economy was devastated and encumbered by a massive debt burden; the security forces were widely feared as the forces of insecurity; and a debilitated public administration was further corroded by pervasive corruption. And just to add to these complexities, the elections had not produced a presidential majority in the legislature. This meant that the president's freedom of political action would be constrained from the outset.

Nevertheless, President Johnson Sirleaf's election enhanced the prospects for peacebuilding immeasurably. Despite the Weah fracas, the Liberian people and the international community endorsed her election with enthusiasm.

She brought with her not only the invaluable asset of legitimacy but also a very solid professional reputation from her days at the World Bank and UNDP. Donors quickly began to queue up with promises of aid.

Brave New World

President Johnson Sirleaf took office with a wealth of goodwill but also an abundance of expectations. I had seen in Sierra Leone how hard it was to live up to those expectations; the euphoria of peace could easily give way to the disenchantment of disappointment. Memories are short. Not long before, people could not walk down the streets of Monrovia without fearing for their lives. But now, electricity, education, health, and jobs were the demands of the day. It seemed to me that the new government and its well-wishers would need to temper public expectations while also showing some early progress that would help to persuade the Liberian public that the future could be better than the past.

The president-elect set up a transition team and began to appoint ministers and advisers with solid professional qualifications and experience (although some were to disappoint later on). The ministers included people such as Antoinette Sayeh from the World Bank as minister of finance, and Togah Macintosh, a former UN official, as minister of planning. Johnson Sirleaf also reached out to some trusted expatriates like Steve Radelet, an accomplished American economist (later chief economist at USAID), for economic advice. These appointments were a hallmark of her extraordinary willingness and ability to pull in all kinds of talents and resources.

While such appointments brought competence, they also provoked strong criticism. Some of the appointees were expatriate Liberians who had not lived in Liberia for much of the war; others were spurned as part of the old Americo-Liberian elite; some appointments were derided as patronage and rewards for loyal service.

Several weeks later, I got another telling insight into the meaning of peacebuilding in an impoverished postwar country like Liberia. At his request, I met George Weah's election adviser, Gabriel Baccus Matthews. He remained skeptical about the election outcome, but this was not the real purpose of the visit. He went on to explain that "if you are not in government, you are not in anything." In other words, not winning the election meant no government job, and there were no other comparable jobs available. He asked me if I could have a word with the president to see if she might consider him for a post (I did not).

Afterward I discussed my conversation with Matthews with Femi Babatunde, the mission's political director from Nigeria. He pointed out that one of the flaws of peacebuilding was the failure to find what he called "social space" for those who, like Matthews, had lost out. In more advanced economies, the private sector could offer opportunities or possibly civil society (think tanks, NGOs, and the like). In Liberia at the time, there were very few such openings, especially for a man with a reputation as a political troublemaker. I didn't have an answer to that dilemma—the government simply could not go around bestowing largesse on all its former opponents. One thing President Johnson did wisely, however, was to reach out to Weah to avoid his defeat becoming a personal humiliation, publicly referring to him as "Ambassador Weah" (he had been a goodwill ambassador for UNICEF).

Managing Expectations

Because I was worried that popular expectations would run far ahead of reality, I proposed that the UN and the members of the International Contact Group on Liberia should open a discreet dialogue with the president-elect to help get her off to a fast start. In anticipation of that discussion, we agreed to submit to the president a joint memorandum on the looming challenges and how they might be managed with the support of the international community.

I prepared the draft of the paper. Shamelessly cribbing from the title of a 1960s policy document of the UK Labour government, I called the paper "In Place of Strife." I was perhaps tempting fate, as the Labour government did not manage to overcome industrial strife, which was a major reason for its eventual loss of office to another iconic female leader, Margaret Thatcher.

In discussion with Mats Karlsson, the World Bank director for Liberia (with whom I had worked very closely on the economic revival of postwar Sierra Leone), I also prepared a separate, private paper outlining some specific actions that the president could take early on in her administration. That paper ("Hope Renewed") included a proposal for a hundred-day post-inaugural program of priority actions together with some "quick wins." This was not meant to be a catchy gimmick; it was about demonstrating to the Liberian people some early progress that would boost the president's credibility and gain her some time to develop the far-reaching reforms that the country clearly needed.

I suggested that the incoming government could build confidence through a judicious mix of action initiatives, policy announcements, and public appointments. I also proposed arrangements for government/donor engagement and coordination, suggesting a nationally led mechanism that subsequently became the Liberia Reconstruction and Development Committee (LRDC). To avoid any claim that this was a donor-run group and to emphasize national ownership, I recommended that the committee should be chaired by the president. I again insisted that ECOWAS, Nigeria, and Ghana, even though they were not donors, should be full members as well.

I was convinced that their membership would help to make the decisions of the LRDC more acceptable within the region, which, after all, had shouldered a great part of the burden in resolving the Liberia conflict.

We met with the president-elect before her inauguration and discussed these ideas in some detail. She liked the idea of the priority action program but suggested that 100 days was too short to achieve significant results and suggested 150 days instead. She also wanted to broaden the scope of the program and include a wider range of priority actions. I had some doubts about the wisdom of doing so, knowing how difficult it would be to achieve even a limited number of priority objectives. Nevertheless, we agreed that if we wanted to put "national ownership" into practice, the final word on the scope and duration of the action program must lie with the president. And so it was. The president launched the action program in February 2006.

Let There Be Light

The LRDC (and thematic subgroups) started work on some of the action priorities almost immediately. The restoration of electricity in Monrovia was the top priority for the president. This time around, she had made the promise and she was determined to keep it, making it abundantly clear to government agencies and donor partners alike that she would not accept any excuses for delay. But it was a complicated project; generators had to be imported, the distribution system replaced, and a proper management structure put in place. All of this was done, and finally, in a joyful ceremony, jointly led by the president and her counterpart from Ghana, John Kufuor (Ghana had supplied equipment funded by the EU), the lights came back on in central Monrovia for the first time in a generation.

A couple of days later, however, I received an agitated call from the president. She wanted UNMIL to step up patrols around central Monrovia. The request, it turned out, was not because the president was expecting (at that moment) violent demonstrations. Instead, she had discovered that the recently installed electricity cables and wires were being vandalized and sold off for scrap. She was exasperated. After all her efforts, this was a dispiriting commentary on national reconstruction.

This incident was also a reminder that peacebuilding had to become a national project in which leaders and the led would need to play their part. Peacebuilding is a fine but theoretical concept that has to be translated into reality by persuading people—those in positions of national and local influence but also the populace—of the value of peace and how it can be achieved and sustained. So like in Sierra Leone, I saw the importance of reaching out and talking to a wide array of institutions and individuals about peace, security, and the rebuilding of the country.

Peacebuilding in Practice

At the top of the list was the president herself. I was knocking at an open door. She was acutely aware that she needed to show results and turn the country in the direction of peace and development. But she was also aware of the promise and pitfalls of peacebuilding and very willing to use her own voice, energy, and political capital to push ahead with the reform agenda. She readily accepted to chair both the LRDC and the committee set up to manage GEMAP.

At a more personal level, we agreed to meet privately on a weekly basis. This was a handy arrangement because it afforded me the opportunity to touch on some very sensitive questions that I could not raise publicly. Similarly, my chief of staff, Bert Coppens, met regularly with the president's affable chief of staff, Edward Mclean, a Liberian psychiatrist educated in France, to sort out issues that we might need to bring to the president's attention. Again, as I had found previously in Sierra Leone with President Kabbah (and indeed in Côte d'Ivoire with Seydou Diarra), this informal approach was very productive, allowing me to head off or deal with problems before they assumed public proportions.

The legislature was next on my persuasion list. The president did not command a majority in the legislature and so the adoption of key pieces of legislation was not ensured, however critical they were to the good of the country. Many of the newly elected were novices and had no conception of parliamentary procedure. The minister of finance, Antoinette Sayeh, had a hard time convincing them that the treasury was not their personal piggybank. The UNDP and other organizations organized special training programs for the members, so I focused on the parliamentary leadership. In this I was greatly aided by UNMIL's legislative liaison officer, Deborah Schein, who somehow managed to divine the political allegiances, ambitions, and peccadilloes of key members of the legislature.

I soon developed a cordial relationship with the president of the Senate, Isaac Niemba. He was very amenable to suggestions and ideas and occasionally asked me to pass along a message to the president that he didn't want to send directly. This behind-the-scenes diplomacy was an important part of the relationship building that is so essential to building peace.

The Speaker of the House of Representatives (the lower chamber per the US model) was an altogether different proposition. An erstwhile ally of Charles Taylor, Edwin Snowe had run the Liberia National Oil Company during the NTGL transition and was rumored to be quite wealthy as a consequence. Driving around town in a late-model Porsche Cayenne did not help him to dispel those rumors. He made no secret of his higher political ambitions, and with his control of the House he was well placed to thwart the president's legislative program. I made a point of meeting him soon after the inauguration, both to brief him on UNMIL's security posture but also to persuade him of the importance of working for peace. Knowing that he was on the UN sanctions list, I conveyed a thinly veiled warning that if he wanted to get off the list he could not play spoiler. Whether or not my intervention changed his attitude, I cannot say. In the end it didn't matter. Several months later, Snowe lost the support of his parliamentary faction and stepped down from the speakership (to the relief of the president, I am sure).

Another influential personality from the newly installed legislature called me early on for an appointment. This was Prince Johnson, recently elected as the senior senator for Nimba County following his return from a lengthy exile in Nigeria. He won a Senate seat with a handsome plurality (along with Adolphus Dolo, another former warlord from Nimba with a checkered past). I hesitated about meeting with him given his history and his role in the death of Samuel Doe. However, he was not under any criminal indictment and I knew that his support for the peace process was important, whatever we thought about his violent past.

I agreed to receive him as the chair of the Senate Standing Committee on National Security and Intelligence. He arrived in my office and I had time only to make a brief remark before he stood up and asked us all to join hands in a prayer. During his exile in Nigeria, he told me, he had found Jesus Christ (at the Synagogue Church of All Nations) and was an ordained Evangelist at the Christ Deliverance Ministries in Lagos. We prayed for peace and then sat down and moved from the spiritual to the temporal. He assured me of his commitment to peace and that he would support the president now that she had won office. He added that I could call on him at any time for his assistance (no mean offer considering the popular support he enjoyed in Nimba County).

As he was leaving, after insisting again that he was a firm supporter of peace, the senator handed me a gift—a book, *The Rise and Fall of President Samuel K. Doe: A Time to Heal and Rebuild Liberia.*[25] This turned out to be his semi-autobiographical account of his role in the civil war and the events leading up to the death of Doe. Bizarrely, he also handed me a copy of a videotape taken at the Monrovia Freeport, where Doe was captured and tortured before being executed later by Johnson's men.

I wasn't sure what to make of the whole episode. Was this an effort by Johnson to gain some goodwill and head off any possibility of a criminal prosecution for past crimes? Or was it a genuine demonstration on his part of repentance and willingness to work for the good of the country?

Perhaps there was a clue on the inside cover of his book. There the senator had added a personal inscription in which he stated that it was "the author's hope and prayer that the past will be forgotten and Liberians will forge ahead through National Reconciliation and Healing." But a footnote was appended that read: "noticeable errors will be corrected in subsequent publications." For as long as I was in Liberia, there were no noticeable errors. Johnson kept his word and did not pose any security threats; in fact he helped to resolve ethnic conflicts that threatened stability in his senatorial constituency. He is still the senior senator for Nimba County.

Of course, the country was more than the president and the legislature. I traveled out of Monrovia at least a couple of times a month to visit our troops, police, and civilian staff and to meet and talk with local officials, community and religious leaders, NGOs, and ex-combatants. Liberia is a small country, so it was possible for me to visit every county and most districts several times. I spent a lot of time in helicopters and then SUVs churning through dust and mud. But the time I spent on the road was invaluable.

Both in and out of the capital I tried to put a public face on UNMIL so that we were perceived as something more than a horde of well-paid foreigners driving around in expensive vehicles. It helped, of course, to inaugurate a school, a community center, or police station that had been built with funding from the mission's quick-impact fund or a UN agency budget. On these trips, I usually took along one or more of my colleagues from the UN country team to share the limelight. We usually received a warm welcome. UNMIL and the UN were viewed as a force for good, which helped us during those times when our reputation was tarnished by incidents that did not reflect well on the mission.

Securing the State

The Accra peace agreement mandated a series of reforms for what is now generically called the security sector. Security is more than the absence of egregious violence; it is about the capacity of the state to identify, isolate, and deal with the causes of violence. UNMIL was mandated to work within this larger frame of reference—preserving peace while rebuilding the institutions of state authority. To do this, the mission had to balance its day-to-day responsibilities for security of the state and its people with the longer-term challenge of structural reform, which would put the state on a surer footing and allow for a managed drawdown of UNMIL forces.

This meant the mission had to simultaneously deal with a whole range of real and perceived security threats while also assisting and encouraging the larger effort to promote security sector reform.

Rumors and Reality

The mission faced three immediate and interlinked challenges to national security: the threat of armed uprisings by disaffected groups who had not yet accepted, or did not feel any allegiance to, the peace process; wayward ex-combatants; and demobilized security personnel.

In the early months of the new presidency, UNMIL received frequent warnings that one group or another was plotting to overthrow the government. Sometimes these claims originated from the government's own security services. A lot of them were spurious and made up, I suspected, to show the president how diligent some officials were in seeking out personal threats to her and to justify why they needed money to pay informers.

Many of these claims related to Charles Taylor. Taylor was in exile but he still cast an ominous shadow over Liberia. After all, he had said that he would return. The Nigerian security services were supposedly keeping a close eye on him, but nevertheless there was a constant fear that somehow he might escape (subsequent events showed that fear to be well-founded) and return to reignite conflict.

UNMIL took all of these rumors and claims seriously. Time and again we sent teams to check out tips about the location of arms caches or stories of ex-combatants gathering in remote areas for training and indoctrination. None of them proved valid, although occasionally we turned up a few unserviceable weapons. At one point, I quietly cautioned the president that we needed to filter these allegations more carefully. But she was not persuaded; she was not taking any chances. UNMIL could not afford to take risks either; an attempt on the life of the president would have been immensely damaging to public confidence.

Part of this disquiet was inadvertently fueled by the UN itself. After the completion of DDR exercises, UN teams are regularly dispatched to evaluate the exercises. Understandably, they tend to hedge their bets and caution that they cannot be certain that all weapons and ammunition have been surrendered. Such findings give some credence to the fear that there are caches of hidden weapons that will be used by ex-combatants or other disaffected groups.

A Fiery Celebration

The pervasive fear about national security took on an incendiary dimension in July 2006. On the occasion of the national independence day, the first since the elections, the government organized a major celebration and invited heads of state from the region to attend. Regional leaders delivered fulsome speeches of congratulations, including one by Laurent Gbagbo, who spoke without notes in French and yet somehow still managed to get an enthusiastic response from the audience.

After the speeches, we all trooped off to a celebratory luncheon in the Executive Mansion. As we arrived in the state dining room, smoke began to seep into the room. Panic followed. The guests of honor were hastily evacuated (they never did get lunch) and the rest of us headed downstairs to the lawns outside the mansion. Only then did we realize that there was a serious fire in the building. There was no firefighting equipment at hand. In fact, only UNMIL had any equipment nearby, which we quickly mobilized to help to put out the fire before the whole mansion was engulfed. During the conflagration, I found myself playing the role of fire marshal along with the minister of defense, Brownie Samukai, who had proudly retrieved the national flag from the presidential office before it too went up in flames.

The fire provoked a surge of conspiracy theories. Given the disputed election, fingers were pointed at the Weah camp; others saw darker forces at work, orchestrated by Taylor and his cohorts. Given the state of maintenance of the Executive Mansion, I wondered if something more prosaic might be the reason. I asked a US police officer assigned to UNPOL with some professional training in arson investigation to take a look. He came back with a report indicating that the cause of the fire was an overload on the air-conditioning wiring that had ignited close to the cabinet room where the walls were lined by wood panels. In other words, it was an accident.

I sent the report to the president, who remained skeptical. In West Africa, accidents are not accidental. She asked the South African government to send a team, which it did. I was quietly gratified to later learn that the South Africans had arrived at the same conclusion.

Conflict Rubber

Our concerns about weapons, ex-combatants, and disaffected groups coalesced around the rubber plantations. Liberia's economy depended to a significant extent on rubber exports. But the years of warfare had devastated the plantations; there was little or no replanting of trees and the infrastructure in the plantations had suffered from a lack of maintenance.

While some of the plantations, like the Firestone plantation, were still producing, others were more or less abandoned or had been expropriated during the Taylor years and sold, creating conflicting ownership claims and litigation. In this chaos and uncertainty, local chiefs had asserted their control over some plantations while in others ex-combatants were in control and extorting the rubber tappers.

One of the biggest plantations was the Guthrie plantation, nominally owned by a Malaysian company but abandoned during the war years. A group of ex-combatants had installed themselves in the plantation with the connivance of the local authorities. The plantation was still producing raw rubber and the ex-combatants were making money from the illicit export of this rubber (we dubbed it "conflict rubber"). A number of other plantations had also been taken over unlawfully by various interests as well as ex-combatants.

The rubber industry in Liberia was founded on expropriation and exploitation. But for postwar Liberia, the revival of the industry offered the prospect of jobs and foreign exchange, both in short supply. However, the plantations needed substantial investment and assurances of security to make them fully productive again.

The president was keen to get control over Guthrie and to make the point that Liberia was open for investment. Guthrie was something of a test case. While I did not want UNMIL to become embroiled in a clash over restoring foreign ownership of a plantation, we could not leave the plantation in the hands of ex-combatants. If we did, there was always a risk that they might use the money they extorted to buy weapons to protect or even extend their fiefdom. Rubber was not as lucrative as diamonds, but weapons could be bought at discount prices throughout the region.

Led by Andrea Tamagnini, a gentle and wily Italian who had run reintegration operations for the UNDP in Central America, UNMIL and the Ministry of Agriculture developed a plan to progressively exfiltrate the ex-combatants while also refurbishing the social infrastructure (schools and the like) to attract civilian managers and workers back to the plantation. At the same time, Andrea opened a dialogue with the ex-combatants. He explained to them what was going to happen and offered them incentives to leave the plantation while making it clear that UNMIL would steadily increase its forces in the area.

Along with the incoming force commander, Lieutenant-General Chikadibia Obiakor, I visited the Guthrie plantation (and others) on several occasions to see how the preparations for the repossession of the plantation were proceeding. The sheer vastness of the plantations, running to hundreds of thousands of hectares, was truly amazing. In their heyday, the plantations operated like separate provinces, largely left to their own devices. I knew that President Johnson Sirleaf would not allow such a derogation of central authority under her administration. Nevertheless, as part of the operation we insisted that the government should set up an interim operating authority so that there would be no management vacuum while the legal process of repossession took its course.

These careful preparations paid off. While there were protests from the ex-combatants (and some local politicians), the repossession was carried out without bloodshed. Of course, the massive UNMIL military and police presence helped, but we were relieved that we did not have to use force. This was a model that we adopted for the repossessions of other plantations.

In total, the rubber plantations covered more than 1 million hectares of Liberian land. They represented a huge economic asset, but many Liberians were doubtful about the justice and wisdom of returning the plantations, in some cases, to foreign ownership. By assisting in this restitution process— and I didn't see any viable economic alternative—we were accused by some Liberian civil society organizations of helping to restore the old exploitative model of landownership. Although the president clearly did not want to be accused of reviving neocolonial enterprises, she knew the plantations represented a source of employment and income for which there was no immediate replacement.

Victims of Peace

Another security challenge arose as an unintended consequence of peace. A crime wave hit Monrovia and other urban centers. Armed groups were no longer a potent threat but the end of the war put a lot of young men (including former child soldiers) on the streets, most without an economic lifeline. Armed robberies (sometimes with an AK-47, more often with machetes and knives) increased dramatically, creating public discontent and demands for action.

This quickly became a political problem for the president (opposition politicians took this as an opportunity to discredit her). It also became an UNMIL problem. Questions were tabled in parliament and the press took up the chase. I was asked: What was UNMIL doing to stop the explosion in crime? When I pointed out that most of our forces were military and not police and that the Liberian National Police had the primary operational responsibility for dealing with criminal activity, I was given short shrift. The politicians and the public were not interested in this distinction; they wanted action by UNMIL, which was perceived as the ultimate guarantor of national security.

I agreed with our UN police commissioner, Mohammed Alhassan, a very experienced commander from Ghana, that we would mount a special operation with the LNP in an effort to reassure the population of Monrovia (and the president and parliament). With a combination of UNPOL advisers, formed police units, and the LNP, and with the military on standby in the event of any serious trouble, UNPOL organized nighttime sweeps in the most crime-affected areas of the city.

To underline that UNMIL was giving public safety foremost priority, I joined some of the night patrols. By then, thanks to President Johnson Sirleaf's action plan, public lighting had been installed in some central parts of the city. But most areas (especially those vulnerable to crime) were not yet connected to the grid. Walking and driving around with the patrols, I realized how dark (and scary) the city was at night. The street signage had long since disappeared and there was a lot of improvised construction; urban planning was not a wartime priority. This made the job of policing far more difficult. If a household got in touch with the police (we had set up a hotline for emergency calls) to report a crime in progress, finding the exact location in the absence of any up-to-date cadastral references was more luck than locational exactitude.

We debated whether these operations actually reduced crime. But the sweeps did have a positive effect on public morale, and the criticism in the media and the parliament abated. Our focus on crime prevention, however, showed up another and far more disturbing fact. UNPOL's detailed analysis of crime patterns revealed that the most common serious crime was not armed robbery or murder but rape (and was almost certainly underreported).

Rape used as a weapon of war had already attracted widespread international condemnation. Liberia was no longer a zone of violent conflict, but the incidence of rape remained extremely high, involving perpetrators from all parts of society, not only ex-combatants. Women and girls, too often the first victims of war, were now the victims of peace as well. The president was horrified by these findings. She decided to mount a national campaign and asked for UN support, to which we readily agreed.

The campaign was duly launched. I spoke at several public events. One of them was at a congregation of leading churchmen and churchwomen. In my remarks, I was fairly graphic and I could tell by the averted glances and steady silence (Liberian congregations are usually very demonstrative) that my comments were causing uneasiness and some embarrassment. Rape was not normally a subject for public conversation, partly because the crime (assuming that the perpetrator was known) was often handled as a domestic matter, with reparations made to the family of the victim. But the president had no inhibitions about speaking out forcefully to make the fight against rape a central issue of her administration.

My message on rape was gravely compromised, however, by the assault on a child by an UNMIL soldier. This happened close to mission headquarters and not in some far-off, isolated hamlet. Despite the mission policy that civilians should not frequent military facilities, a family living close to an UNMIL unit did some chores in return for a small payment and food (again forbidden by UNMIL). The young girl was washing dishes when she was attacked. The family came to UNMIL after they found her bleeding. We immediately ordered an investigation and arranged for a local childcare organization to provide medical and counseling support. I also quickly informed President Johnson Sirleaf, who was appalled by the assault.

Knowing that the investigation would take time and would necessarily involve a lengthy process of review, I suggested to DPKO that we should make an ex-gratia payment to the family to cover immediate medical and associated expenses while we awaited the outcome of the investigation. This proposal ran into the habitual concern that we might be prematurely conceding liability before the investigation was completed. But I persisted and a payment was arranged.

Later when the assault was indeed confirmed, we agreed that the UN should make a compensation payment to the girl. On the advice of the president, we sent up a trust fund in the name of the child to cover future medical expenses and educational support. Interestingly, the president insisted that the trust fund should be administered independently of the family by a well-respected trustee. She was afraid that the money might otherwise disappear quickly.

Securing the Future

After more than two decades of endemic violence, Liberians had no confidence in the country's security services. People were targeted because of their ethnicity or simply because they were in the wrong place at the wrong time. The progressive collapse of any semblance of the rule of law left them without protection or redress.

The Accra agreement opened up the opportunity to build accountable and better security and judicial services. The security reform agenda focused around four core elements: the army; the police; the judicial and penal services; and the national security architecture. For the armed forces and the LNP, the policy parameters had been laid down by the Accra agreement, but in outline only. The assumption was that the new and popularly elected government should draw up detailed plans for both the army and the police.

In reality, the reforms were enacted on a piecemeal basis. There was no overall doctrine that spelled out and assessed the threats to law and order and territorial integrity and how the security forces and judicial authority would be prepared, deployed, and funded to confront them. This was to come later but by then the building blocks of the new security order were already in place.

The New Model Army

The Accra agreement called for the restructuring of the army and the police. Urged on by the United States, the army was not simply recast but disbanded by the NTGL. There was even some discussion on whether Liberia might adopt the Costa Rica model and dispense with an army altogether. ECOWAS was not in favor of that option, which might have created an uncomfortable precedent. The more palatable alternative was to reconstitute the army.

Based on assessments made by the United States and the EU, the government set the army force level at 2,500 soldiers (all ranks). This modest force level was privately derided by regional institutions. Certainly compared with most military establishments in Africa, the planned force size was very small. But I argued (along with the United States and the EU) that creating a military establishment without the means to maintain it was asking for trouble. I made some projections of the costs of the security services at "steady state" consequent on UNMIL's departure. From these projections, it was clear that even with an expanding economy and a rising budget, the government would struggle to cover those costs without substantial and sustained donor support, which was not a given.

Fortunately, the president had already declared that she wanted to see more state money spent on education and health than the military. She was also wary of a military establishment that might overshadow the civil authority.

All officers and other ranks were demobilized. They were pensioned off or given lump-sum payments (funded by donor contributions) depending on their grade and length of service (a general was discovered who had been on the payroll since World War II). This was a drastic approach to reform but one that enjoyed wide public support. The government appointed a senior Nigerian officer as the interim commanding officer (one who had previously served with UNMIL) of the new army.

The CPA stated the United States would be the lead partner on the reform of the military. Perhaps taking a cue from the UK effort in Sierra Leone, the US government committed to a long-term plan that included reshaping of the Ministry of Defense as well as training, equipping, and housing the new force. Unlike the UK initiative, however, the funding was dependent on annual congressional appropriations, which were by no means automatic. At one point the relevant appropriations bill was held up for months as Congress quarreled over amendments that had nothing whatsoever to do with Liberia. According to information released by the US government in February 2015, it had invested over $411 million in security sector assistance to Liberia, most of that (about $300 million) toward the Armed Forces of Liberia (AFL) and $108 million toward the development of the justice sector and the Liberian National Police.[26]

I left Liberia well before I could have an informed opinion on this investment in rebuilding a national army. The real test of the effectiveness of the reforms will come in the years ahead. It will be a test not only of the new army and its leaders but also of the civilian leadership, which will have to ensure that the soldiers are paid and housed and the military is neither politicized nor tribalized.

A Tall Order: Reforming the Police

Under the Accra accord, UNMIL was tasked with leading the reform of the Liberian National Police. However, the UN made no financial provision for police reform beyond the resources allocated to the UNPOL component of the mission (largely personnel but no cash). As a result, like in Sierra Leone, I spent time running around trying to raise funds, which made it difficult to plan and implement a cohesive program of reform.

Although there was broad public support for the principle of police primacy in handling domestic security, there was little public confidence in the police, which were widely accused of preying on the people they were supposed to protect. As a means of restoring confidence in the police, UNMIL set up a vetting process aimed at weeding out the worst elements and improving the professionalism of the police force.

We encountered numerous difficulties with this exercise, as police and government officials sought to influence the decisions on who stayed or left. Nevertheless, after the vetting more than half of the serving officers were let go. UNPOL organized training courses for those who were retained plus the new recruits. In an effort to increase female participation in the police force, UNPOL and the LNP set up a special recruitment and training program to encourage more women to join up. This affirmative action met a lot of resistance within the LNP (a largely male force). Fortuitously, the arrival in UNMIL of a female formed police unit from India gave a timely and visible boost to this initiative, especially when the unit was assigned protection duties at one of the most sensitive locations—the president's office.

However, the most telling example of the president's efforts to get women into positions of authority was her appointment of a female head inspector-general of the LNP, Beatrice Muna Sieh-Browne, one of the few long-serving female officers in the LNP. This was one of the toughest of all the jobs in the Liberian public administration, made more difficult by the rampant misogyny in the police force. I thought this was a bold and progressive appointment, even though later on Muna ran into some serious difficulties (of her own making) that eventually cut short her tenure as the inspector-general.

The LNP, despite the vetting and retraining of staff, continued to prove the adage about old habits dying hard; a decade later, a UN report still voiced serious complaints about the LNP.[27] Absentee rates were unacceptably high and allegations of petty corruption resurfaced. Admittedly for police officers with families,· especially those posted outside their home areas, it was hard for them to make ends meet, so I understood the temptations. However, this "survival" corruption—petty bribes paid at traffic stops and police barriers—had a pernicious and contagious effect, because any public servant who had something useful to sell (for example, school exam questions) or withhold (such as building permits) could do the same. In any event, the government simply did not have the means to increase salaries in the public sector.

The Price of Reform

The police and army reforms, although much needed and welcomed by most Liberians, put more men on the streets with few—if any—job prospects. Some of the demobilized soldiers and policemen received compensation but others had not, including those who claimed to be former soldiers or policemen forced to flee during the war. Predictably, those who had been rejected in the vetting process, or who thought they could extort more money than was offered, took to the streets.

These demonstrations turned violent and UNMIL had to intervene to keep the peace. During one particularly aggressive demonstration, UNMIL military fired into the air to prevent the demonstrators from overrunning police positions. There were civilian casualties from stray bullets and UNMIL was accused of deliberately targeting civilians. I responded that UNMIL troops had not targeted anyone, but I also promptly announced that we would meet with the families of victims to examine their claims.

There was some concern in-house that I was opening the mission to spurious claims. On that occasion, as with other personal injury cases, I argued that UNMIL had a larger interest in hearing out the claimants even if the claims were bogus. Retreating behind the defensive wall of UN immunity struck me as self-defeating; it would likely tarnish our reputation locally and risk perpetuating rather than resolving the problem.

These demonstrations were better organized and more belligerent than those that had erupted following the elections, probably because former military and police were involved. But the president stood firm and went on the air to say that the demands by people who had inflicted so much harm were not acceptable. She took a considerable risk but remained obdurate. After some further payments were made to genuine cases, the demonstrations gradually wound down as it became clear that the government was not going to backtrack and that UNMIL was capable of containing the demonstrations.

Guarding Ellen

The presidential security service was at the apex of the security pyramid. Before her inauguration the president selected a new set of bodyguards whom she felt she could trust. They received some crash training from the US Secret Service; a handful of US advisers remained to continue the monitoring and training. However, it soon became apparent that the performance of the close-protection team left much to be desired. Perhaps its members had watched too many action movies featuring the heroics of the US presidential detail. On one occasion, I witnessed the presidential motorcade roaring off leaving half the guards behind. On another, a guard fell off the president's SUV and in doing so dropped his gun, which skittered across the street, thankfully without discharging into the crowd.

Worse was to come. After the president appointed a new head of the Special Security Service (SSS)—the presidential guard—quarrels erupted among the senior staff of the unit. These quarrels came to an ugly conclusion in a shooting incident at the residence of the newly appointed head of the SSS; the culprit was another senior SSS officer who had not obtained the coveted appointment. These appointments had all been made outside the formal system of police vetting, and UNMIL was not consulted. In a meeting with a team sent from Washington, D.C., at the request of President Johnson Sirleaf to assess the situation, the force commander, the UNPOL commissioner, and I expressed our dismay at the turn of events. Although UNMIL had deployed a Nigerian unit to provide perimeter security for presidential events, the president would still be very vulnerable to any disaffected element in the SSS. Moreover, the Security Council had agreed on a waiver to the UN sanctions to allow the United States to import weapons for the SSS, but with the proviso that the weapons would be under strict control. Obviously, that was not the case.

The upshot of this affair was the president's decision to restructure the SSS and to bring in outside expertise to manage the service until it was fully trained and properly managed. This was a decision I heartily welcomed. The realization that the president's personal security was so poorly run was the stuff of nightmares.

A State of Security

During the SSS crisis I got to know the newly appointed national security adviser, Henry Boima Fahnbulleh, a veteran politician and activist. He had actually worked for Doe at the outset of the master sergeant's regime but left after a couple of years and went into exile. I found Fanbulleh to be refreshingly frank and open and not too worried about political correctness. He warned me that much of the information on security threats was no more than a parade of rumors that needed careful scrutiny.

The recurring problem of faulty intelligence and personal rivalries spoke to a more fundamental problem. The Accra agreement had stipulated some immediate reforms but had not recommended any kind of national security structure or policy. This was left, understandably, to the incoming government. But the government security machinery was so preoccupied in responding to day-to-day security scares that it had little time for deeper, more analytical thinking about national security policy.

I was a member of the LRDC security group chaired by the minister of defense. But here again we tended to focus on the specifics of individual reform measures such as logistics for the army and police rather than on fundamental issues that had remained unresolved for decades. How, for example, should the respective roles and relationship between the military and the police be defined? Which institution or entity would provide overall policy guidance and coordination to the security and intelligence services? And how should the accountability of the security services to elected civilian authority be defined and safeguarded?

The government invited the RAND Corporation to undertake a study on the national security architecture. UNMIL submitted a paper[28] to the

RAND team in which we outlined a range of threats and risks to state security and the security of the individual. We emphasized that these threats and risks could emanate not only from ill-disciplined or abusive security agencies but also from poor governance and corruption that undermined the rule of law and public faith in national institutions. We stressed the importance of democratic, civilian oversight of the security forces and the need to consult civil society as the national security policy was being developed.

The RAND study traced the way toward a well-reasoned national security strategy. I was concerned, however, that the report and its recommendations would languish without a push from the top. Both the US ambassador and I pressed for the creation of a special interagency working group that could take the recommendations forward and ensure that there would be a forceful follow-up, including, as needed, appropriate legislation. The group was set up and I encouraged the members to get specific measures onto the president's desk as soon as possible before the enthusiasm for security sector reform began to wane under the weight of vested interests that were happy with the old ways of doing business. Frustratingly, the process still took longer than I expected and I was able to see a only first draft of the proposed strategy before I left Liberia. This was another file that I had to leave to my successor to guide toward fruition.

Preparing for Steady-State

As in other peacekeeping missions, security sector reform was one of the key benchmarks for assessing postconflict progress and by extension the prospects for drawing down UN forces. While the Security Council was not rushing to the exit, the mission was nevertheless instructed by headquarters to prepare plans for an eventual departure.

Already in late 2005, I had asked Adrian Foster, who had worked on drawdown planning in UNAMSIL, to undertake an assessment of the security prospects and risks for Liberia and the implications for UNMIL's consolidation, drawdown, and withdrawal. Working with a broad range of actors, national and expatriate, engaged in security sector reform, humanitarian aid, and economic development, Adrian developed a comprehensive approach that linked the consolidation, drawdown, and withdrawal to a number of benchmarks and indicators that could inform and determine the pace and depth of the process.

Two bright special assistants in my office—Fred Wooldridge and Comfort Ero—developed a "traffic lights" set of benchmarks, which they grouped as core (essential) or context (desirable). With this simple system we could quickly see where problems were arising that could impede the overall progress of the peacebuilding effort and the possible consequences for the plan for consolidation, drawdown, and withdrawal.

The president was particularly taken by the "traffic lights." The information we provided didn't always coincide or confirm the internal information that she was receiving through bureaucratic channels. So it was a useful crosscheck for her, although it probably annoyed departmental officials who may have been reporting otherwise. Of course, this system had its shortcomings. It tended to emphasize quantitative measures over the qualitative. This was a problem particularly in areas like the rule of law, where the quality of justice could not be measured by the number of arrests made or judgments issued. But on the whole the system was helpful; it was one of the first to anchor a plan for consolidation, drawdown, and withdrawal in a framework of national benchmarks and indicators that could be regularly monitored.

In a further effort to anchor national security planning and the consolidation, drawdown, and withdrawal in local realities, I encouraged the mission and the UN country team, together with national and local authorities, to undertake visits to the individual counties across the country to assess security risks and threats. Under the leadership of Jordan Ryan, the teams fanned out across the country and returned with a trove of information.

The local appreciation of risks and threats obviously varied from county to county. Maritime counties worried about piracy and fishing rights; counties bordering Côte d'Ivoire and Guinea were concerned about cross-border attacks; those with large rubber plantations faced violent disputes over ownership and exploitation; others flagged their apprehension about the return of the internally displaced and refugees and the property disputes that might follow; alarm over ritual killings surfaced in a couple of the southeastern counties. All of this information was fed into a county template that gave us and the Liberian authorities a much clearer picture of the potential threats that would have to be managed as part of the consolidation, drawdown, and withdrawal.

One general refrain echoed across all the assessments: an appeal to UNMIL not to leave too soon. The mission was still widely perceived as vital to the security and stability of the state.

Rules and Rights

The Legacy of Lawlessness

During the war years, the rule of law became the rule of warlords. Many rural communities maintained their traditional means of arbitrating and settling disputes (some of them, such as trial by ordeal, not very compatible with modern approaches to human rights), but the institutional framework that underpins the rule of law essentially collapsed. Courts ceased to function or functioned under duress; lawyers and judges were targeted and many left the country; and prisons became notorious as places of abuse and execution.

Clearly the needs far outweighed UNMIL's capacities. Nevertheless, I felt strongly that we could not hope to stabilize the country if we did not make a serious effort, working with the UN country team and donors, to rebuild the capacity of the justice system.

This was a formidable agenda. Qualified counsel, magistrates, and justices were in very short supply. As in Sierra Leone, the prisons were full of minor offenders who could not meet bail requirements. Court buildings, prisons, and police stations had been looted and often burned down. Whole areas of the country were devoid of any judicial access. The Ministry of Justice struggled to handle its prosecutorial responsibilities.

Fortunately, the mission had strong and capable rule-of-law and human rights teams to take this agenda forward. We were not helped, however, by the chief justice, Johnnie Lewis. Appointed by President Johnson Sirleaf shortly after her inauguration, he was an experienced lawyer and had done a stint with the UN in the Balkans. In the name of judicial independence, the chief justice refused to allow court officials to participate in the working group set up by Luiz da Costa to help the Ministry of Justice to coordinate and rationalize the multiple interventions by donors on rule-of-law issues. He argued that all branches of the government (executive, legislature, and judiciary) were equal and that the invitation was therefore not receivable because it had not come personally from the president. This attitude contrasted sharply with that of the chief justice in Sierra Leone, who had gone out of his way to work with UNAMSIL (and other partners) to resuscitate the judicial system.

Luiz was later succeeded as the DRSG by Henrietta Mensa-Bonsu, an imposing lawyer from Ghana with experience in government and academia. She set about improving relations with the chief justice, whom she knew before her UNMIL appointment. I hoped that she could make progress where I had obviously failed. And indeed she did make some, leading to the establishment in 2008 of a special jurisdiction to deal with cases of sexual violence.[29]

During the years of conflict, the Liberian judicial system had been decimated, none more so than the Department of Corrections. Prisons are not institutions that enjoy much public sympathy in war-torn countries; prisoners are there either for political affiliation or because they are very poor. The conditions in the Liberian prisons were absolutely dreadful. Overcrowding and severe malnutrition were rife; women and children and hardened criminals were all mixed in together.

Given the scale of the problem, I agreed that we should set up a dedicated corrections unit in the mission. We also decided to put quick-impact money into prison refurbishment and pressed for the reform of the bail laws so that the indigent would not be incarcerated without recourse. Perversely, our construction projects had an unintended consequence: we found prison officers sleeping in the newly constructed cells, which were better than their own accommodations at home.

One of our strongest supporters on corrections reform was the president. On the first Easter weekend following her inauguration, she visited the Monrovia central prison. A former prisoner herself, she took small gifts for the prisoners. I went with her to show her the work that UNMIL was undertaking to improve prison conditions and staff training. It was a poignant moment. I wonder if any heads of state ever visit prisons unless, of course, they are prisoners themselves.

Truth or Reconciliation

The Accra agreement recognized that the judicial system would never be able to deal with all—if any—of the injustices meted out during the warlord years. It stipulated, therefore, the establishment of a truth and reconciliation commission both as a partial response to that dilemma and also as a step toward building a more peaceful future. The Liberia commission was launched by President Johnson Sirleaf and included, like the Sierra Leone commission, a mix of national and international commissioners. And like its counterpart in Freetown, it too ran into strong headwinds.

Quarrels broke out among its members, and donors threatened to cut funding because of lax management. There were serious delays in holding hearings. At one point, the president and I met jointly with the chair of the commission, Jerome Verdier, to express our concerns about the seeming lack of progress. Frankly, I was glad to unload the day-to-day responsibility for UNMIL's relations with the truth and reconciliation commission on Jordan. Mirroring my experience in Sierra Leone, he too had to spend many hours trying to keep the commission on track.

The final report of the Liberia commission was published after I left Monrovia. In another parallel with its counterpart in Sierra Leone, the Liberia report was controversial, probably even more so because it recommended that Ellen Johnson Sirleaf should be barred from running again for presidential office, claiming that she had supported Charles Taylor in an earlier phase of her political career. Unlike the Sierra Leone commission, however, its Liberian counterpart did not have to contend with an international court looking over its shoulder.

Charles Taylor's government signed the Rome Statute, which created the ICC, in July 1998. However, Liberia ratified the statute only in September 2004 (after Taylor's departure from the country) and the ICC could not exercise retroactive jurisdiction to cover Taylor's time in office. In the absence of an ICC jurisdiction, human rights activists pressed for a special court. Certainly the crimes committed in Liberia were just as bad as those perpetrated in Sierra Leone. But neither the government nor major bilateral partners pushed for a Liberia special court.

Why was a special court not created for Liberia? By 2006, when Ellen Johnson Sirleaf took office, the appetite in the international community for special courts was diminishing. More important, the war in Liberia was over. The Sierra Leone court was created when the RUF broke with the Lomé peace agreement and attacked UN peacekeepers. By contrast, in Liberia a tenuous peace was taking hold. Various Liberian leaders told me that a special court might unravel the peace, as it would surely indict several figures who were by then part of the political establishment.

The president did not take sides on this argument. She expressed her support for a truth and reconciliation commission and essentially deferred to its judgment, which was a convenient way to avoid any pronouncement on criminal trials. Although I have no doubt that several individuals in Liberia deserved to be prosecuted, criminal proceedings would have created political waves and possibly violence. UNMIL was there in force and could have contained any violent reaction, but nevertheless confidence in the peace process might have suffered. Pragmatism prevailed—much to the dismay of human rights activists, it has to be said.

The Reckoning

While Liberia was deciding not to create a special court, the Sierra Leone special court ploughed on. I have written already about the announcement of Charles Taylor's indictment while he was attending the 2003 peace talks in Accra. Shortly afterward, Taylor went into exile in Nigeria, but he remained a central figure in the Liberian political landscape. Before and after Ellen Johnson Sirleaf's election, there were constant rumors of his impending return. Some of his former commanders remained in the country while others were said to be holed up in neighboring countries biding their time.

The prosecutor of the Special Court for Sierra Leone (by now Desmond da Silva, the former deputy prosecutor) continued to seek the arrest and extradition of Taylor. Court investigators tracked his movements even though he seemed safely ensconced in Nigeria. Unknown to Taylor, however, moves were afoot to bring him to justice.

Not long after her inauguration, I arranged a very discreet private meeting between the president and the prosecutor of the special court at the latter's request. To avoid any publicity (or leaks), the meeting was held at my residence in Monrovia early on a Sunday morning; UNMIL flew in Desmond from Freetown, avoiding the usual airport formalities. The aim of the meeting was to explore the president's willingness to ask President Obasanjo to extradite Taylor. Obasanjo had agreed to provide Taylor a place of exile to get him out of Liberia and stop the fighting. But he had done so saying that it would be up to the Liberian government to decide Taylor's ultimate fate. I imagine, however, that Taylor assumed that he was safe from prosecution; after all, in the past, former heads of state in Africa, irrespective of crimes that may have committed, were not prosecuted.

Several governments, notably the United States, pressed President Johnson Sirleaf to ask for Taylor's extradition. The human rights community argued that his prosecution would signal that impunity for appalling violations of human rights, in or out of office, would not be tolerated. The president was certainly anxious about the destabilizing impact of Taylor's presence in the region and the persistent rumors of his second coming. But she was aware too that handing Taylor over to the court would be an unpopular move among regional leaders, many of whom were opposed then (and now) to the idea that current or former heads of state could be charged and put on trial. There was the risk also that Taylor's acolytes might attempt to block an extradition through some kind of violence in Liberia.

We talked through the complexities involved in arresting and extraditing Taylor. The president was especially concerned about where the trial of Taylor might be held. She felt that holding the trial in Sierra Leone would be too close for comfort. Desmond reassured her that he would be able to move the trial to a location outside of the region.

I did not try to sway the president's final decision. It was a tough call and she would have to live with the consequences. I did reassure her, however, that if the extradition went ahead, the UN and UNMIL would fully support her decision based on the Security Council resolution[30] that authorized UNMIL to "apprehend and detain former President Charles Taylor in the event of a return to Liberia and to transfer him or facilitate his transfer to Sierra Leone for prosecution before the Special Court for Sierra Leone."

President Johnson Sirleaf decided, courageously in my view, to ask for Taylor's extradition to Liberia. President Obasanjo wasn't happy about the request as he too knew that this move would not be popular among his peers. He also worried (as he told me later) that a Taylor prosecution would make it harder to achieve peace agreements in the future, because leaders would be reluctant to cede power for fear of what might happen to them afterward. President Johnson Sirleaf's decision broke that taboo on prosecuting former heads of state for their misdeeds while in office.

The UN resolution on Taylor had been carefully crafted to ensure that UNMIL would not be cast in the role of international policeman. The phrasing made it clear that UNMIL could detain—not arrest—and transfer Taylor to the special court only if he returned to Liberia. This meant that the Nigerian government would have to physically transfer Taylor to Liberia so that he could be apprehended and then sent over to the court in Freetown.

President Obasanjo had agreed to the transfer on the condition that Taylor would not be formally detained and charged on Nigerian soil. Once he gave the green light, we began detailed planning to accommodate Obasanjo's demands and the Security Council's caveats. We worked closely with Nicolas

Michel, the astute and always helpful Swiss Under-Secretary-General and legal counsel at UN headquarters, as well with the SCSL team in Freetown. Nicolas developed a detailed guideline on how we should handle the transfer to avoid any claims that due process had not been respected. Somehow we managed to keep the whole exercise under wraps; there were no leaks.

The transfer scenario envisaged that Taylor would be brought back to Liberia on a Nigerian aircraft and then handed over to UNMIL. We would then transfer him to Freetown post-haste. Special security arrangements would be made at Robertsfield airport in the guise of a training exercise. President Johnson Sirleaf was insistent that we should keep Taylor's time on the ground in Liberia to an absolute minimum. She was extremely worried that an attempt might be made to liberate Taylor, possibly with collusion of military elements in UNMIL. That seemed farfetched to me, but I asked the force commander, General Obiakor, to take every precaution and to ensure that the circle of the need-to-know was kept very tight.

All was ready. I was in New York for a Security Council meeting and expected to return well in time for the operation. I intended to brief Secretary-General Annan in person but he was delayed on an overseas trip and I was only able to speak with him via a rather shaky mobile connection as I headed to JFK airport for my return trip. He was especially concerned that we had taken all the necessary precautions to ensure that due process was fully respected. I was able to reassure him (if not entirely myself) that we did indeed have matters in hand.

And then the game plan went astray. Taylor somehow got word of his imminent transfer (from whom was never clear) and bolted. Obasanjo was preparing to leave for the United States to meet with President George W. Bush. He was told that there would be no meeting if Taylor was not immediately apprehended. Taylor was caught but only just, as he was about to cross Nigeria's remote northeast Gamboru-Ngala border post into Chad. Press reports[31] at the time claimed that he was carrying a substantial amount of cash with him.

After the embarrassment of the escape, Taylor's transfer was immediately accelerated. As I headed back to Monrovia, a Nigerian air force executive jet was dispatched to Liberia with Taylor on board. Luiz da Costa as the officer-in-charge of the mission set in motion the reception and transfer arrangements on the basis of the protocol agreed with UN headquarters. Arriving at the airport, the Nigerian aircraft was quarantined next to an UNMIL helicopter stationed ready for an onward flight to Freetown. Three UNMIL staff boarded the plane: Nathalie Ndongo-Seh, UNMIL's legal officer, read Taylor his rights and confirmed that he understood them; Koka Rao, the mission's chief medical officer, conducted a medical examination to confirm that Taylor was fit to fly; and finally, Gery Brasselle, who usually worked as my close-protection officer, placed restraints on

Taylor's wrists and helped him off the aircraft. Taylor did not protest and did not attempt to resist his detention or transfer. Within an hour, he was on his way to Sierra Leone in an UNMIL helicopter under armed guard, escorted by a mission gunship flying cover.

We were careful not to humiliate Taylor. No pictures were taken at Robertsfield for public release, although we did video and record the transfer proceedings for future reference in case of claims of improper procedure. On landing in Freetown, he was directly taken into custody by the SCSL, which didn't have any qualms about publicity. In a picture that went around the world and ended up on the front page of the *New York Times,* Taylor was photographed descending from the UN helicopter in handcuffs with Gery towering over him.

Back in Liberia, we had prepared for possible repercussions. There were some demonstrations by Taylor sympathizers but hardly any violence. President Johnson Sirleaf was both criticized and praised—within and outside Liberia—for agreeing to send Taylor to the court. She made it clear, however, that she was not intending to send anyone else to Freetown. She also offered to meet Taylor's legal expenses and ensure that he had proper legal representation. Overall, I would say that public opinion, to the extent that it could be assessed, favored her action, especially in Sierra Leone, where Taylor ranked along with Sankoh as the author of the country's violent troubles.

True to his word, Prosecutor da Silva arranged for the Taylor trial to be shifted to The Hague, despite the protests of Taylor and his defense team. I certainly agreed that such a high-level and protracted trial held so close to home would have proved troublesome for both Liberia and Sierra Leone. Emotions in both countries were still quite raw and volatile.

After a trial and appeal that took ten years to complete, Taylor was sentenced to fifty years in jail. Justice was done and seen to be done. Will Taylor's fate serve as a deterrent to others? Has his trial and imprisonment helped to end impunity for grave crimes? Probably not; crimes against humanity and war crimes are still being committed in Africa and elsewhere. Nevertheless, I do believe that justice—restorative justice as the judicially literate call it— has its own intrinsic value that transcends its preventive or punitive value.

A Last Lap

As a signal of the progress made in Liberia, Kofi Annan announced that he would make a visit in July 2006 accompanied by his wife, Nane, as part of his last tour to West Africa as the UN Secretary-General. In one of those coincidences that mark (long) UN careers, I had presided over the UNDP's farewell party for Ellen Johnson Sirleaf when she left the UNDP to contest the Liberian election in 1997. Annan had spoken at the event. She lost that election, but now a decade later, in a stunning reversal of fortune, she was welcoming the Secretary-General as the elected president of Liberia.

When the Secretary-General visits, the UN goes into overdrive. In Liberia we possessed plenty of logistical capacity and did not have to depend on the government for much beyond the usual courtesies of protocol. But we had one headache that we had to manage: accommodation. Hotels in Monrovia were rather rudimentary. So I proposed to headquarters that Soheir and I would move out of our apartment at the UN building to make way for the Annans. There was space for security, and the telecommunications links were obviously better there than anywhere else in town. However, the answer came back from the Secretary-General's office that we should not trouble ourselves and that UNMIL could simply book the presidential suite at the leading hotel.

There was of course no leading hotel in Monrovia, much less a presidential suite. Luiz da Costa came up with the answer. He dispatched our mission photographer to the "leading hotel" to take some photos of what passed for a suite and sent them to New York along with some of our apartment. The response was swift; Soheir and I happily vacated the apartment knowing that the Secretary-General and his wife would greatly enjoy the sea air and spectacular view.

Remembering the Secretary-General's awkward arrival in Sierra Leone some years before (which led in part to my moving into peacekeeping), I made sure that this time he met a representative cross section of UN staff. This was not simply a public relations exercise; together with Luiz and Jordan, I had worked closely and productively with the UN team in Liberia and built a solid base of interagency cooperation, which ran counter to the narrative of the fragmented UN so often portrayed in the UN debates on field operations.

As in Sierra Leone, the UN Mission in Liberia had survived and persevered through some trying times. In that sense, the Secretary-General's visit was a celebration of a success in UN peacekeeping. Nevertheless, only when his plane took off did we relax—nothing had gone wrong. Leaving the airport, we clambered into the venerable armor-plated Volvo that the UNAMSIL mechanics had patched up for use by the Secretary-General. As Soheir and I headed back to town, feeling good about the visit, the car sputtered and gave up the ghost, stranding us by the roadside. I just thanked the Gods of Peacekeeping that they had not subjected the Annans to a similar fate.

Getting to Growth with Development

During two decades of war the Liberian economy fell apart. As I noted earlier in the chapter, the transitional government installed after Charles Taylor's departure proved totally incapable of turning the economy around. The fragile stability ushered in with Ellen Johnson Sirleaf's election offered renewed hope that the economic decline could be halted. But this required a fundamental reordering of national economic management and the restoration of some semblance of financial probity and fiscal discipline.

Changing the Paradigm

I have already mentioned GEMAP. Essentially, it was a crash program of economic reform. Candidate Johnson Sirleaf had opposed GEMAP but I (and others) worked to convince her that it would help enhance and not diminish sovereignty. I argued that for a country that could not pay its civil servants, educate its children, fund its security forces, or meet its financial obligations to regional institutions such as the AU and ECOWAS, sovereignty was an empty concept.

What really persuaded President Johnson Sirleaf to accept GEMAP, however, was her quest for debt relief. Liberia was one of only three countries that had not been allowed to join the HIPC Initiative, sponsored by the World Bank and the IMF; the others were Sudan and Somalia. The three countries were refused entry into the initiative because of their unpalatable political regimes. Ellen Johnson Sirleaf's election now opened up the opportunity for Liberia to get into the initiative.

On purely economic grounds, Liberia was clearly eligible for the initiative. During the early Doe years, Liberia had been able to access international borrowing including from the IMF (largely because of US support). However, as the economy went into freefall, debt reimbursement was suspended; no new loans were granted. But the debt did not disappear; the arrears continued to accrue even though any hope that Liberia might actually repay its debts evaporated.

The president and her tireless finance minister, Antoinette Sayeh, rightly wanted to get into HIPC as soon as possible in order to write off the debt mountain and to gain access to concessional credit. Even with a quantum leap in the quality of its national economic management, it was obvious that Liberia could never repay its debts in full. So the question was how to make the inevitable possible. HIPC was the answer. But even so, Liberia still needed to prove that it could manage its public finances and assets. GEMAP provided a measure of assurance that this would be the case.

Although criticized by some Liberians as neocolonialism, GEMAP proved its worth. The government was able to use GEMAP to get its financial house in order as well as to reverse dubious contracts and concessions awarded during the Taylor and NTGL years. The management committee, of which I was a member, was chaired by the president with the US ambassador as vice chair. This structure made GEMAP more palatable despite the intrusive character of the program. Pragmatism again prevailed. In June

2010, Liberia reached the so-called completion point and became eligible for debt relief. The inevitable had become possible.

Wolfowitz Visits

With GEMAP operational, new opportunities began to open up for Liberia, led by an unlikely champion, Paul Wolfowitz, president of the World Bank. He had met President Johnson Sirleaf in Washington, D.C. (where she enjoyed an open door with the Bush administration). He was greatly impressed by her and keen to extend World Bank support to Liberia.

Wolfowitz visited Liberia in July 2006 not long after Secretary-General Annan. I offered the Bank the use of what I had now dubbed the Annan suite for his visit. Wolfowitz's neocon reputation and his role in the Iraq war had of course preceded him, so I wondered what to expect.

I was especially keen to get Bank support for a joint UNMIL/UNDP program of road rehabilitation. Andrea Tamagnini, who had planned and supervised the repossession of the Guthrie plantation, developed a program to rehabilitate earth roads. He planned to use local ex-combatants with the technical and logistical support of UNMIL engineering units from China, Pakistan, and Bangladesh. Road rehabilitation not only employed people and put money into the local economy but also reconnected areas of the country that had been isolated for years.

With the help of our new and dynamic director of administration, Steve Lieberman (ex-US Navy), we persuaded DPKO that UNMIL should put up some cash, as the roads were needed by UNMIL for security purposes. Jean-Marie Guéhenno was a keen supporter of the initiative, which he saw as a practical way for the Bank and UN peacekeeping operations to cooperate on postconflict peacebuilding. Jordan ensured that the UNDP would also cofinance. We started the program in a small way but that still left a significant funding gap that I wanted the Bank to cover. Even though Mats Karlsson, the Banks's director for Liberia, was on board, the staff back in Washington, D.C., raised questions about sustainability. Wolfowitz's visit provided a golden opportunity to break through the logjam.

I thought that Wolfowitz, as a former deputy US secretary of defense, might still be interested in the military side of our work. So shortly after his arrival, we took him to see the joint Irish/Swedish quick-reaction force at its home base. They put on a good show and he inspected the troops while an Irish piper played the honors.

Afterward, the force commander, General Obiakor, and the military staff gave an overview of UNMIL's deployment and plans. The briefing included a fulsome reference to the strategic importance of roads, which opened the way for a discussion on the road program and its virtues. Wolfowitz immediately latched on to it; he wanted to show that the Bank could deliver tangible benefits for the people.

Later that evening over drinks, he freely admitted that when he was at the US Department of Defense, he had been skeptical about the UN operation in Liberia. He said that he was happy to be proved wrong. He was intrigued by the roads project and to my astonishment added that this was the kind of program that the United States should have launched in Iraq post-invasion. The upshot was that the World Bank committed support to the road rehabilitation program. It still took some weeks, but $5 million was approved.

Wolfowitz was obviously smitten by Liberia and its president. The following year in 2007, he took an energetic lead in organizing a major donor and investment conference in Washington, D.C., for Liberia. Although I remained quite skeptical about the lasting value of such mega-events, I felt that the UN could not absent itself, especially as President Wolfowitz had reached out to us.

There was an extraordinary turnout. For the opening of the conference, a stellar cast lined up on the podium, including Wolfowitz; the head of the IMF, Rodrigo de Rato; the US secretary of state, Condoleezza Rice; and Louis Michel, EU development commissioner. Ban Ki-moon was invited but at the last moment could not attend. I was designated as his replacement and had to deliver his statement in absentia. In doing so, I caused some confusion (and amusement) in the audience when I read out the statement, referring to my experience growing up as an IDP in war-torn Korea and then expressing my thanks to the UN for helping me to achieve my ambitions in life.

Actually, the conference was an affirmation of President Johnson Sirleaf's extraordinary reach. During my time in Liberia, a whole parade of the great and good visited—presidents, prime ministers, and philanthropists, including Chancellor Angela Merkel of Germany, President Hu Jintao of China, Queen Noor of Jordan, and George Soros, to name some of the more prominent. A few weeks after my departure, President George W. Bush also dropped in. It's hard to imagine any other small, impoverished African country attracting that kind of attention.

Although high-level visits do not always translate into ready resources, Liberia became a fashionable destination for aid. But it quickly became apparent that the country could not easily absorb and put to good use all the aid on offer, especially as most of it was offered in the form of projects rather than budgetary support, which would have been easier to digest. Despite the credibility of President Johnson Sirleaf (and the minister of finance), there wasn't much trust in the Liberian bureaucracy; the specter of corruption made for tight donor control, which the president, although a former aid official herself, found extremely irksome.

Despite these constraints, growth picked up substantially as agriculture and trade rebounded. Within a couple of years, growth was running at an annual average of about 8 percent; budget expenditures expanded in tandem. Investment in the social sectors, especially in health and education, grew rapidly. Private sector investment began to pick up too, with new investment in mining and in the rubber plantations.

Pulling Out

As I moved into my third year with UNMIL, I was reasonably confident that the new government and the mission were heading in the right direction. Public security had improved and the economy was recovering. Of course, President Johnson Sirleaf still faced significant political challenges in the legislature as well as the cross-border uncertainties generated by the crisis in neighboring Côte d'Ivoire. But our drawdown plan was in place even though the delays in standing up the new army and reforming the police meant that it was the more cautious variant of the plan that would be implemented.

When things go well, you are in demand; so once again, UN headquarters called, although I had not sought a new job. I was in no hurry to move. In fact, I was thinking that Liberia might be my last post, as I had passed the retirement mark for a career staff member. During a visit to headquarters, Jean-Marie Guéhenno had mentioned the possibility of a transfer to the Congo, where SRSG Bill Swing was due to leave later in the year. My name also surfaced in connection with Côte d'Ivoire following the departure of Pierre Schori.

I thought seriously about Abidjan because, as I mentioned before, I had left Côte d'Ivoire with a sentiment of unfinished business. On further reflection, however, I decided against doing so. While I believed that I could establish a workable relationship with President Gbagbo and Guillaume Soro, I knew that the baggage I carried from my earlier stint with ONUCI could weigh against me. The SRSG's job is always a tough one; if from the outset one or another of the protagonists has doubts about your impartiality, it becomes that much more difficult.

The DRC presented a very different perspective. I had previously served in Zaire as the UN resident coordinator during the Mobutu era. I also briefly visited Zaire during the final months of his regime, when I headed up a UN team sent (by Ellen Johnson Sirleaf, then head of UNDP's Africa Bureau) to review the security situation and assess the implications for the UN's development work.

I was tempted (flattered too) by the challenge of running the UN's biggest peacekeeping operation (at that time), but also wary of committing to several more years in a highly challenging position. Soheir and the family thought I should continue. Nevertheless, I hesitated; the scale of the challenge was enormous, and Liberia, although a generally successful assignment, had been a demanding one.

I was still mulling over what to do while attending a meeting of SRSGs in Switzerland, which Secretary-General Ban Ki-moon was due to attend.

As it turned out, he could not participate in person and did a live video conference instead. During his remarks he warmly praised the work of UNMIL and then, to my surprise, went on to announce that I would be taking over from Bill in the DRC. Everyone applauded; I was taken aback. No interviews were needed this time around. The die was already cast.

I returned to Liberia faced with the delicate task of telling President Johnson Sirleaf that I would be moving on. She asked that I stay at least until the end of the year to ensure a handover with my successor, Ellen Loj of Denmark. The latter already had some experience with Liberia, having chaired the Liberia Sanctions Committee during her stint as the Danish permanent representative to the UN. She also had a strong background in development cooperation, which I thought would be an asset for Liberia as the country moved forward with its postconflict transition.

Our departure from Liberia was an emotional one. The president, the government, and the legislature were fulsome in their appreciation. I was especially touched by the UNMIL military, which paid us a special compliment. The force commander, General Obiakor, arranged a "pulling out," a military ceremony that is organized, I was told, when a senior commander moves on. This involves manually pulling an open-top jeep past an honor guard. With some embarrassment, Soheir and I stood up in the vehicle, pulled along by soldiers from the various contingents while the guard (and staff) cheered us on.

The Alchemy of Peace

UNMIL completed its withdrawal at the end of March 2018. The mission drawdown was much slower than anticipated but undoubtedly UNMIL's continued presence contributed to the relative stability that the country has now enjoyed for a decade. Indeed, many Liberians would have liked the mission to remain, because they still have little confidence in the security forces.

After decades of terrible violence and several failed peace agreements, Liberia seems to have escaped—at least so far—the endless cycle of conflict. There is no single reason for that outcome. Like in Sierra Leone, peace came as the result of a fortuitous admixture of elements that produced, despite the odds, the right outcome.

The first element, Charles Taylor's departure from the scene, like Sankoh in Sierra Leone, was crucial to the success of the peace process. Both were incapable of leaving behind their warlord ways and adapting to peacetime leadership. Neither could accept peace except on their own, highly personalized terms.

Even though they could galvanize thousands of rebels, Taylor and Sankoh could not build political coalitions that would have made them less vulnerable to the opposition forces that were gathering to destroy them.

Once they were out of the game, their fighters and sympathizers were rud-derless, bereft of charismatic leadership.

A second element was that Taylor made a number of strategic mistakes. Most importantly, his use of the RUF as a proxy to fend off incursions from Guinea was a disaster both for him and the RUF. Similarly, his forays into Côte d'Ivoire weakened him and created a "second front" that left him even more exposed.

A third element was the Accra Comprehensive Peace Agreement. It succeeded where earlier agreements had failed. By imposing a time frame, mandating an interim administration that could not perpetuate itself, and calling for a robust UN peacekeeping operation, it created a strong political and security framework to underpin the transition from war to peace. Among all of the peace agreements in which I was involved during my peacekeeping days, the CPA was the most effective.

A fourth element was the unity of purpose of regional and international actors, even though at times they differed on details. The earlier support that Taylor received from Houphouët-Boigny and Blaise Compaoré evaporated, leaving only the mercurial Muammar Qaddafi as an ally. As the SRSG, I don't recall any paralyzing disagreements in the Security Council over strategy. In fact, the Council (strongly encouraged by the United States) authorized a dis-proportionately large UN peacekeeping force (at least judging by the ratio of UN troops to the local population). As a result, UNMIL avoided the "infirmity of incrementalism" that can leave missions undermanned when crisis strikes.

Although the mission buildup was slower than initially planned, by the time the elections were held in late 2005, we had sufficient forces to hold the ring. I could therefore say with confidence to all the contenders for power, including the placeholders of the former armed groups, that we had the means to prevent any effort to disrupt the elections. After the elections, there was no pressure from the Council for a rapid drawdown. This was vital because I was convinced that without the continuing presence of a strong UN force, one or another of the armed groups would have attempted to regain power by mobilizing ex-combatants and elements of the disbanded army.

A fifth element was the imposition of sanctions. The ban on dia-monds, although not completely watertight, cut into Taylor's war profits, as did the subsequent ban on timber exports. The Liberian economy had been destroyed and other sources of income (and patronage) had largely dried up. This made it increasingly hard for Taylor to keep his fighters in fighting condition.

The targeted sanctions against individuals also had an effect. As I know from my personal encounters with individuals on the lists, they were anxious to get off them and were willing to cooperate in order to do so. This was con-firmed to me by Lansana Gberie, who monitored the sanctions as coordinator of the UN Panel of Experts for three years. He told me that "the chief effect of the sanctions was psychological—those on the lists, who could well have been spoilers because they have the history and the resources, were aware that the whole world was watching them, and they could be subjected to prosecution like Taylor if they engaged in activities that could be destabilizing."[32]

The final, crucial element was that Ellen Johnson Sirleaf proved to be a highly effective postconflict leader. She gained legitimacy with her election victory and then credibility through her leadership of the peacebuilding agenda, aided by the close alignment between her postconflict priorities and those of the UN and the international community. While the violence had subsided by the time she took office, she still had to navigate a careful path among many competing demands. Liberia was bankrupt. So her standing with donors and creditors alike was critical to the debt relief and grant funding that Liberia needed to stay afloat and begin its reconstruction. But she showed personal courage in standing up to the litany of demands from a long list of disaffected groups and individuals who believed that the state owed them and that the president would give into their threats and demands. They underestimated her. The later years of her presidency were tarnished by allegations of nepotism and for the initial response to the Ebola epidemic, which hit Liberia very hard, but those criticisms cannot eclipse her extraordinary contribution to helping Liberia escape the legacy of merciless conflict.

The A-Team

My assignment as the SRSG in Liberia turned out to be a truly extraordinary experience, a highpoint in my years of UN service. All the elements of a successful mission came together: a clear mandate and the means to implement it; a government willing to engage and move forward; a committed and imaginative mission management team; and yes, some luck. Vainglorious no doubt, we were dubbed the "A-Team"—a mission that largely achieved its mandated purpose even though we recognized that the deep-rooted problems of the country would require many years of sustained commitment, above all from the government and people of Liberia.

I know that my successors worked hard to maintain the momentum of peace. My involvement was only one chapter in the story of UNMIL. But I left Monrovia with a sense of accomplishment and with the hope, naive perhaps, that I might achieve some measure of success in my next assignment as the SRSG in the Democratic Republic of the Congo.

Sadly, success and disaster often move in proximity. On January 12, 2010, a catastrophic earthquake hit Haiti. More than 300,000 people perished that day, including three members of our Liberia A-Team who had transferred to the UN's mission in Port au Prince from UNMIL: Luiz da Costa, Fred Wooldridge, and Jerome Yap, deeply valued friends and colleagues who passed too soon.

Part 2

Wars Without Winners: Peacekeeping in the Congo

The end of all political effort must be the well-being of the individual in a life of safety and freedom. In the case of the Congo, as elsewhere, the means to this end are, in the first place, the independence, peace, integrity and prosperity of the country.

—Dag Hammarskjöld

Not long before I was asked to head up MONUC, I read Adam Hochschild's acclaimed *King Leopold's Ghost,* an account of Belgian colonialism in the Congo.[1] Hochschild's book made a deep impression on me. It is a powerful story of both horror and heroes; a chronicle of rapacity, exploitation, and cruelty but also a testament to the courage and conviction displayed by those who fought against injustice.

I was inspired by Hochschild's book but I hesitated to accept another assignment in the DRC. Many years previously I had served as the UN resident coordinator in Zaire; it had been a fascinating and frustrating experience in equal measure. The bureaucracy was lethargic (even when paid) and corruption pervasive. Jean-Marie Guéhenno, the head of DPKO, insisted, however, that with my experience in Sierra Leone and Liberia, I could make a difference.

Peacekeeping operations in the DRC have a special resonance for the UN. This is where peacekeeping in its multidimensional form started back in 1960. It is also one of a handful of ill-starred countries where the UN peacekeepers have deployed, gone, and returned. Some lessons were learned and applied but peacekeeping operations in the Congo remain a recurring and tumultuous blend of hope and hubris. So too was my time as the SRSG in the DRC, which proved to be by far the most demanding job of my entire UN career. Not a lot went right and some things went badly wrong.

151

In my initial outline of this book, I had assigned one chapter for each country where I worked in a UN peacekeeping mission. However, as I wrote the Congo chapter, I found it increasingly difficult to keep to the planned length for the chapter. The Congo as a subject could fill a book by itself, such was the intensity and variety of challenges that my colleagues and I faced as would-be keepers of the peace.

Because of the volume of material, I have written four chapters on the Congo. First, I start with an introduction to the complex and tortured history of the Congo, followed by the early troubled years of the newly independent country when ONUC, the first peacekeeping mission in the Congo, was deployed.

A great deal of my time as the SRSG in the Congo was taken up by the crises in the Kivu provinces of eastern DRC, which is the focus of the second chapter on the Congo. It's the longest chapter, because the conflict in the Kivus was not a single conflict but rather a series of interlocking crises that erupted with depressing regularity.

In the third chapter, I write on what I call the "collage of conflict." The Kivu provinces were the epicenter of crisis but by no means the only theater of conflict in the DRC. Throughout my tenure, I had to deal with multiple crises, some of which were the consequence of events on the other side of the Congo's borders. They all had one thing in common—they invariably inflicted terrible harm on innocent people, which brought the protection of civilians to the top of MONUC's agenda, creating a "crisis of protection," which I discuss in the latter part of the chapter.

In the final chapter on the DRC, I look at the transition that marked the transformation of MONUC into the United Nations Organization Stabilization Mission in the Democratic Republic of Congo (MONUSCO) and reflect on our efforts to build as well as keep the peace in the DRC.

5

Into the Cauldron:
The Congo Past and Present

From the colonial era, the major legacy Europe left to Africa was not democracy as it is practiced today in countries like England, France, and Belgium; it was authoritarian rule and plunder. On the whole continent, perhaps no nation has had a harder time than the Congo in emerging from the shadow of its past.

—Adam Hochschild

Unbridled pursuit of wealth has shaped the polity of the Congo. This was a driving motivation for foreign incursions in the colonial era but also a depressing feature of postcolonial rule. I briefly review the colonial record in this chapter and provide an overview of the first UN peacekeeping mission launched just after the Congo became independent in 1960. I do so because these historical forces profoundly shaped the environment in which the second UN peacekeeping mission in the Congo was deployed.

African Kingdoms and European Incursions

As elsewhere along the long western littoral of Africa, Portuguese mariners were the first Europeans to arrive on the coast of the Congo. They came to a region that had an organized system of rule under the Kingdom of the Kongo. The Portuguese traded with the kingdom for slaves in return for a variety of European manufactures, including firearms.

The Kongo kingdom was one of several kingdoms that dominated a large part of what is today the DRC. In the southern savannah regions, other large and powerful polities emerged. These kingdoms were much more than chiefdoms or clans. There were organized systems of governance with elaborate cultural traditions and indigenous systems of belief. In some respects, they were proto-states in the sense they that had systems of governance and law that enabled the rulers to exercise authority over large groups of people spread out over sizable expanses of territory.

Western explorers and traders were not alone in their efforts to penetrate and profit from the interior of the vast Congo Basin. Incursions came from the eastern as well as the western coasts. Arab slave raiders and ivory hunters began pushing west from the coastal areas, eventually arriving in eastern Congo, where today Swahili—a linguistic legacy of the Arab incursions—is widely spoken.

The later colonization of the greater Congo Basin by Western powers essentially aborted the formation of indigenous nation-states. One cannot know how such states might have developed and whether the process would have been, like in Europe, a lengthy and bloody passage. The era of exploration and its colonial aftermath cut short any such "organic" process.

The Berlin Bargain

The European penetration of Central Africa in the latter part of the nineteenth century was at once a cause and a symptom of the growing rivalry between European powers in what came to be known as the "scramble for Africa." Africa beckoned as a potential source of wealth, imperial pride, and fertile ground for religious conversion. The European powers, no longer content with coastal enclaves and trading posts, rushed to establish colonies or protectorates throughout Africa.

In an attempt to referee these rivalries but also to advance Germany's own imperial ambition, the German chancellor, Count Otto von Bismarck, convened the Berlin Conference in 1884–1885. The outcome of the Berlin Conference was the division of Africa into spheres of influence; no Africans were present at the Berlin Conference.

The biggest winner in the Berlin bargain was Léopold, king of the Belgians. In 1876, the king established the African International Society, a supposedly humanitarian venture, and then two years later the International Association of the Congo, which was essentially a commercial venture. He had done so with the encouragement of Henry Morton Stanley, the legendary explorer who had traversed the Congo but subsequently failed to convince the British government to claim territorial hegemony over the region.

In the name of the African International Society, Léopold gained the uncontested right to run the Congo Free State (as it was now termed) as a personal fiefdom; the only proviso imposed on Léopold was that the Free State would be open to free trade and investment for all. The Berlin arrangement was a triumph for Léopold's shrewd lobbying of the major powers, playing one off against another. President Mobutu used the same tactic almost century later to maintain his hold on the Congo.

The Léopold Imperium and the Congo Free State

Adam Hochschild has trenchantly portrayed the shocking atrocities committed during Léopold's imperium.[1] Today, such acts would be denounced as crimes against humanity. The Congo Free State became an engine of exploitation designed to extract as much wealth as possible, principally for the benefit of Léopold and the companies that enjoyed royal favor and monopoly. A draconian system of forced labor was instituted. Traditional authority was either co-opted or repressed. Any sign of revolt or protest was crushed with exemplary brutality by the Force Publique, a Belgian-officered and African-manned force used to maintain public order. The Force Publique was the enforcer of the mandatory rubber quotas imposed on the Congolese with great ferocity.

Fortunately, the exploitation and repression in the Congo did not go unnoticed. Within a few years of the creation of the Congo Free State, a protest movement began to take shape. Presaging modern human rights advocacy campaigns, the movement grew to include activists and celebrities from the worlds of politics, faith, journalism, and the arts. Arthur Conan Doyle of *Sherlock Holmes* fame was one of them, as was Mark Twain. E. J. Morel, a crusading journalist in London, worked assiduously to keep the story alive, lobbying politicians and founding the Congo Reform Association.

Roger Casement, a British diplomat, was one of the people who joined Morel in supporting the work of the Reform Association. In 1903, the British government commissioned Casement, who had worked for Stanley on a project to build a railway around the unnavigable stretches of the lower Congo River, to investigate the situation in the Congo. His report, published in 1904, was a detailed and damning indictment of the Congo Free State.[2]

The British parliament reacted strongly to the report and called for the review of the 1885 Berlin agreement. Other countries, including the United States, followed suit. Urged on by socialist Emile Vandervelde, the Belgian parliament obliged Léopold to set up an independent commission of inquiry, which confirmed the essentials of Casement's report. On November 15, 1908, the Belgian parliament removed the Congo Free State from Léopold's personal control, making it a colony, the Belgian Congo.

Belgian Colonization and the Road to Independence

While the termination of Léopold's imperium ended the worst abuses in the Congo, the new colonial administration was a highly paternalistic one. There was no delegation of representational authority to the colony. The economic model remained one largely designed to exploit local resources, with Belgian and foreign companies investing heavily in mining and plantation agriculture. There was scant investment in social infrastructure; education and health were left in the hands of the churches.

After World War II the colonial administration began to consider the development needs of the country. Even so, as late as 1955, Anton Van Bilsen, a Belgian professor, proposed a thirty-year plan for political emancipation of Belgian Africa.[3] The generally conservative attitudes prevailing in Brussels and Léopoldville favored Van Bilsen's timetable, but the "winds of change" blowing across Africa did not bypass the Congo. The Belgian governor general in Léopoldville, Léon Pétillon, realized that some measure of emancipation was both right and inevitable. In 1957, a limited franchise allowed Congolese participation in municipal elections for the first time.

Local political movements began to emerge in the Congo, coalescing around two incompatible political groupings: the nationalists, who favored a strong and unitary national government; and the regionalists, led by political movements in Katanga and Bas Congo (the richest provinces), who viewed independence as an opportunity to assert their separatist ambitions.[4] The nationalist group was spearheaded by the Congolese National Movement (MNC), founded in 1959 and led by the charismatic Patrice Lumumba.

In January 1959, violent rioting broke out in Léopoldville. Later in the year, King Baudoin of Belgium was met with outright hostility during a visit to the Congo. Faced with growing disorder and fearful of an uprising, the Belgian government called the various Congolese political groups to Brussels for negotiations in January 1960. In an abrupt and extraordinary about-face, the Belgian government conceded that independence would be granted on June 30, 1960, following nationwide elections.

The Belgian government apparently believed that it could still control the situation by favoring moderate candidates in the elections and keeping Belgians in senior posts and advisers in key departments, including the Force Publique. The bet did not pay off.[5] Lumumba, who was viewed by the Belgian government as a radical inimical to its interests, won the largest number of seats in parliament and became prime minister.

A State Fails

The Congo gained its independence on June 30, 1960, equipped with only a handful of trained officials and deeply divided by regional rivalries (encouraged by outside powers) and an army already fragmenting along tribal lines. In retrospect, it seems hardly surprising that within a few days of becoming an independent state, the Republic of the Congo began to unravel.[6]

On July 12 the Congolese president, Joseph Kasa-Vubu, and the prime minister, Patrice Lumumba, cabled Dag Hammarskjöld, the UN's iconic Secretary-General, requesting the urgent dispatch of "military assistance" to protect "the national territory of the Congo against the present external aggression which is a threat to international peace."[7] The ostensible reasons for the request was twofold: first, clashes had erupted between Belgian troops still stationed in the DRC and Congolese soldiers who had mutinied against their Belgian officers (so much for Belgium's hope of retaining control of the military); and second, the secessionist declaration of Moïse Tshombe as the leader of the mineral rich-province of Katanga, the province in southern Congo that supplied much of the Congo's wealth.

Hammarskjöld,[8] already alarmed by the escalating breakdown of government authority, immediately referred the Congolese request, with his endorsement, to the Security Council. The Council responded quickly—amazingly so compared to the extended deliberations that have characterized the establishment of later peacekeeping missions—authorizing the deployment of ONUC the next day (but with abstentions by France, the UK, and China).[9]

The authorizing resolution was remarkably succinct—just three short operative paragraphs. There was no reference to Chapter VII of the UN Charter.[10] It simply called on the Belgian government to withdraw its troops from the Congo and authorized the Secretary-General "to provide the Government with such military assistance as may be necessary until, through the efforts of the Congolese Government with the technical assistance of the United Nations, the national security forces may be able, in the opinion of the Government, to meet fully their tasks."[11] Less than a week later, the Secretary-General was able to report that some 3,500 troops had been deployed.

To Katanga and Beyond

ONUC got off to a fast start. A comment from the second report of the Secretary-General to the Security Council exemplified that optimism: "Only about two weeks after the Security Council's final decision entrusting to me the task of carrying out its will, the United Nations troops will thus be in control of the security of the entire territory of a united Congo."[12] As so often happens in the Congo, disappointment followed as events took on an increasingly unpredictable and violent complexion.

Tshombe, encouraged by political and commercial interests in Belgium, France, the UK, and southern Africa, refused to accept the authority of the central government and the entry of UN forces into Katanga. Hammarskjöld dispatched Ralph Bunche, his representative in the Congo (and a Nobel Peace laureate), to Katanga to prepare the way for UN deployment. However, once in Katanga, Bunche advised against the deployment, fearing the risks of open conflict. As Brian Urquhart, a close UN associate of Bunche (and later the UN representative in Katanga), remarked, "we were neither authorized nor equipped to deal with the Katanga secession by force."[13] However, Conor Cruise O'Brien, the UN's man in Katanga at the time, provided a contrasting perspective, noting in his memoir of these events that "the definition and limitation of what UN 'military assistance' meant seems, when it was understood, to have come as a painful surprise to a Central Government which had supposed that the assistance in question would be entirely at its disposition."[14] As I was to experience personally, similar misperceptions of what UN peacekeepers could or could not do returned to haunt later UN peace operations in the Congo.

The political and security situation became increasingly unstable. In September 1960, Lumumba and his deputy, Antoine Gizenga, were dismissed by President Kasa-Vubu because of their nationalist and pro-Soviet policies. Their dismissal set in motion a train of events that led to Lumumba's brutal murder in Katanga in January 1961, allegedly with the complicity of the Belgian and US governments,[15] after he had been arrested and dispatched there by the young army chief of staff Colonel Joseph Mobutu.

Lumumba's death provoked outrage in Africa and beyond. In response to the outcry, the Security Council adopted a more assertive position. It called on the UN to "take immediately all appropriate measures to prevent the occurrence of civil war in the Congo, including arrangements for cease-fires, the halting of all military operations, the prevention of clashes, and the use of force, if necessary, in the last resort."[16]

The same resolution, however, spelled out a complementary doctrine that has been repeated in UN resolutions to this day: "the solution of the problem of the Congo lies in the hands of the Congolese people themselves without any interference from outside, and that there can be no solution without conciliation."[17] In reality, however, the affairs of the Congo have never been left entirely in the hands of the Congolese.

The situation in Katanga continued to deteriorate in the months that followed Lumumba's death. Hammarskjöld attempted to moderate the situation by setting up a face-to-face meeting with Tshombe to negotiate an end to hostilities. This was the ill-fated journey that led to Hammarskjöld's death on September 18, 1961, in a plane crash in northern Rhodesia (today Zambia).

Following the death of Hammarskjöld, stalemate set in. However, after more harassment and assaults on UN personnel, his successor—U Thant—authorized UN forces to remove the mercenaries and to rein in the gendarmerie (despite the opposition of the Belgian and UK governments). The UN operation that followed took on a life of its own as UN commanders on the ground advanced and to their surprise met no resistance. The secession ended two weeks later in January 2003.

The manner in which the Katanga secession ended left a legacy of expectation. Forty years later, the Congolese minister of defense, Chikez Diemu (a native of Katanga), berated me for what he perceived as the failure of UN troops to end a rebellion in North Kivu. He contrasted the inaction (in his view) of MONUC's Indian brigade with the earlier intervention of Indian troops (some of them the fearsome Ghurkhas) in Katanga. He clearly believed that MONUC's job was to do in Kivu what had been done in Katanga—to act, in effect, as the military surrogate of the Congolese government.

In June 1964, a year after the secession ended, ONUC closed down. Shortly afterward, in another demonstration of the infinite flexibility of Congolese politics, Moïse Tshombe was made the prime minister in a new coalition to be dismissed only a year by President Kasa-Vubu. A couple months later, in November 1965, Mobutu seized power, refusing to relinquish it until he was forced into exile in 1997.

The Emperor of Everything

Although my Congo chapters focus on my peacekeeping experience in the DRC, I cannot resist making a detour to write about Mobutu Sese Seko Kuku Ngbendu Wa Za Banga (also known as Joseph-Desiré Mobutu). Although Mobutu was no longer president when I was appointed as the SRSG to the DRC in late 2007, he was the president during my first sojourn in the Congo, from 1987 to 1990. He is very much a part of the larger story of the Congo and the events that led to the deployment of the second UN peacekeeping mission.

The Mobutu regime became known for its excess. He ran an elaborate system of patronage designed to keep his followers happy and the opposition quiescent, although he was not averse to using outright repression against individuals or entire ethnic groups.

I witnessed the excess firsthand. Mobutu's favorite folly was his palace in Gbadolité, in Equateur province, the region of his birth. I accompanied UN Secretary-General Perez de Cuellar on an official visit to Gbadolité in November 1987 when I was the UN resident coordinator in Zaire.

The visit was quite a show. Days before Perez de Cuellar's arrival, Mobutu's brother had died. So the president, we were informed, had to remain in Gbadolité. The presidential plane was sent to pick up the Secretary-General and his party. Greeted in Gbadolité with all the honors, we did a tour of the town, stopping at the family mausoleum to pay our respects, before proceeding to a luncheon hosted by the prime minister.

As the lunch was about to be served, the president and his wife, Mama Bobi Ladawa, appeared. The president, wearing his trademark leopard skin toque, courteously explained that mourning protocol prevented him from lunching with guests. He wished us *bon appétit* and looked forward to receiving the Secretary-General at the palace later in the day.

It was an excellent lunch accompanied by a fine selection of wines from the presidential cellar. As I was the designated note-taker, I had to keep my wits about me and watched with some regret as the offerings of Chateau Cheval Blanc passed me by.

After lunch we moved on to the presidential palace. Mobutu took great pride in giving the Secretary-General a guided tour of the palace, which was excess incarnate. The extravagance included marble floors flown in from Italy together with the Italian masons to install them. The runway of Gbadolité airport had been extended to accommodate the Boeing 747s chartered for the shipments (the airline station manager confided to me that it was a strictly cash-and-then-carry contract). The runway could even accommodate the Concorde aircraft that Mobutu chartered for long trips.

There was plenty of other *follies de grandeur.* These included the presidential yacht for river cruising as well as assorted palaces and residences scattered around the country and abroad. Conspicuous consumption was the order of the day. One particularly outrageous example was the event organized to celebrate Mobutu's tenth wedding anniversary. Soheir and I (along with a couple of hundred other guests) were invited to a lavish party given by the presidential couple at the Chinese-built Hall of the People (the people, of course, were outside gazing in through the railings). No expense was spared; French caterers were brought in from Paris; only the band was local.

As the evening progressed, I chatted to a member of parliament who surveyed the presidential largesse with dismay. He was from Haut Zaire (today Haut-Uele province) and told me rather dejectedly that there were times when he wondered if he and his constituents were still part of Zaire, so isolated were they. The transport and telecommunications infrastructure was crumbling and his only communication with Kinshasa was through a radio network maintained by the Catholic Church; the state had disappeared.

Over his three decades in office, Mobutu built a powerful personality cult, making all his public events (many of which I attended) a celebration of his own importance. They always started with a lengthy and noisy crowd-rouser that built into a crescendo of adulation as the great man arrived. He alone was the center of attention. When he addressed meetings and conferences, a gilded presidential chair was rolled out and deposited on an elevated plinth from which he could survey the adoring audience.

The Mobutu system of patronage and privilege characterized the whole of the Zaire administration. Ministers, provincial governors, and other senior officials took their cue from Mobutu and behaved in the same outrageous way (with a few commendable exceptions) and made the most of their time in office. Except for a handful of ultra-loyalists, ministerial tenure was usually short, a year or two, and then officeholders were off-loaded to allow for the patronage to be spread around. The privileges of power showed up in the contrast between the well-appointed private ministerial offices and the decrepit buildings in which the ministries were housed. Ministers traveled on a daily personal allowance of $1,000 but their waiting rooms were full of indigent people hanging around to plead for a favor.

Mobutu's self-aggrandizement was encouraged by the attention showered on him early on in his career. As a thirty-three-year-old army chief, he was invited by John Kennedy to the White House in 1963. As is well known,[18] he was the choice of the Central Intelligence Agency (CIA) for

Congolese strongman. And as late as 1989, despite Zaire's economic malaise and Mobutu's reluctance to commit to political reform, he was still welcomed at the White House as the first African head of state invited by the recently inaugurated President George H. W. Bush. In Bush's words, "he was one of our most valued friends."[19]

Geography and diplomacy created a platform for Mobutu to project himself onto the world stage. The United States and other Western interests employed him to deal with problems in countries from Sudan to South Africa. Mobutu adroitly parlayed the Congo's physical location at the heart of Africa to bolster his image as a regional power broker. When relations soured with one or other Western country (Belgium was a favorite target of Mobutu's ire), he would turn to another that needed his help. The conversations with the UN Secretary-General at Gbadolité in 1987 focused on regional disputes and conflicts and the role that Mobutu could play in helping to resolve them; as far as I can recall, domestic reform was not on the agenda.

Commercial interests played a part too. There were plenty of opportunities for companies (and individuals) willing to grease the wheels. Western governments turned a blind eye when their own national interests and nationals were involved. But Mobutu was not shy in confronting the international media on the issue. I remember that during a turbulent visit of Belgian prime minister Wilfried Martens in November 1988, Mobutu took on Belgian journalists who queried him about his reputed wealth and corruption. He was unapologetic, saying corruption takes two sides, and asked who taught Africans about corruption in the first place.

Given the history of Western exploitation in the Congo, especially by Belgium, Mobutu's retort was not without sympathizers, even among those who opposed him politically. He cleverly played the nationalist card against both his foreign critics and domestic rivals. Returning to the Congo more than a decade after the death of Mobutu, I was struck by how many Congolese freely acknowledged that he had helped to create a sense of national identity notwithstanding his well-publicized failings.

Mobutu's expansive lifestyle was paid for by his liberal use of state resources and corruption on a grand scale. The state mining company— Gécamines (the nationalized successor to Union Minière, the copper-mining giant that had supported the Katanga secession)—became a kind of presidential slush fund, tapped on demand to meet presidential needs and largesse. Copper prices peaked in the early 1970s as demand soared due to the Vietnam War; there was money to throw around.

In the name of promoting national ownership and *authenticité,* Mobutu also began expropriating large estates held by multinational companies and foreign-owned farms. "Zaireanization," as the expropriation was coined, was a turning point. It robbed the economy of much of its productive capacity (in the same way that Robert Mugabe's seizure of European-owned farms did in

Zimbabwe a couple decades later). The impact of Zaireanization was especially damaging in the more remote areas of the country, where the infrastructure was largely maintained by the estates so that they could get their produce to market.

The economic impact of the Zaireanization was compounded by the precipitous drop in copper prices as the Vietnam War began to wind down. As Michela Wrong recounts in her compelling story of the Mobutu years, the economy went into serial decline. Writing in 2000, she noted that "until Zaireanisation, the economy had grown by an average of 7 per cent per year. Look at a graph of just about any indicator and there, in 1974, is a sharp peak, followed by a long, slow, unstoppable swoop that continues to this day."[20]

Decline and Fall

By the time I arrived in Zaire in 1987, the economy was in freefall. The national currency, the zaire, dropped in value every hour as inflation exploded. The economic crisis coincided with the end of Cold War, and the demands for reform grew louder within and outside the country. Mobutu finally realized that he had to offer some concessions. On April 24, 1990, he announced to an assembly of national and foreign dignitaries the end of the political monopoly of the Popular Movement of the Revolution (MPR), the party that he had created and launched in 1967. Ever the showman, Mobutu stopped his peroration to wipe away a tear, asking the audience to *comprenez mes emotions* ("understand my emotions"). I was in the audience and sensed the incredulity: Was Mobutism really at an end?

Following Mobutu's declaration, a national conference was announced as the next step in a reform process that was intended to end in a new constitution and multiparty elections. As I expected, however, Mobutu dragged his feet. I was convinced that Mobutu would never give up the leadership. He had become the personification of Louis XIV's famous dictum: *l'État, c'est moi.*

The national conference, chaired by Monsignor Laurent Monsengwo, finally got under way in 1992. Étienne Tshisekedi—a long-standing political opponent of Mobutu (and father of the current Congolese president)—was appointed as prime minister but had no executive power and the government turned in circles. In 1994, yet another government was appointed, with Kengo wa Dondo as prime minister (Kengo was the go-to man when economic crises erupted). But the Kengo government could not prevent the progressive disintegration of the state. Violence broke out in several regions and Mobutu, by this time often absent abroad for cancer treatment, was not able to stop the rot; the 1994 genocide in Rwanda precipitated the final collapse of the regime.

Genocide to Genesis

The Rwandan genocide and its antecedents are well described and analyzed in several major works of scholarship. The 1994 genocide was the most deadly eruption in a recurring cycle of violence that had traumatized Rwanda, Burundi, and eastern Congo for decades.[21] This violence stemmed from the complex ethnographic makeup of the region,[22] exacerbated by colonial-era policies that emphasized communal identity, and compounded by demographic pressures and the competition for land and other resources.[23]

On April 6, 1994, the plane carrying Presidents Juvénal Habyarimana of Rwanda and Cyprien Ntaryamira of Burundi, who were returning from peace talks, was shot down on approach to Kigali airport. The assassination triggered a genocidal offensive by the Armed Forces of Rwanda (FAR) and the extremist Hutu militia, the Interahamwe, against the Tutsi population and moderate Hutus. As many as a million people were killed.[24]

Led by Paul Kagame, the Rwandan Patriotic Front (RPF), largely made up of exiled Tutsis living in neighboring Uganda, attacked and defeated the Rwanda army in a short but highly effective campaign. The fighting led to the massive flight of Hutu civilians fearing the wrath of the RPF; about 2.3 million Rwandans[25] crossed the borders into the DRC, Burundi, and Tanzania, of whom about 1.5 million fled into the DRC. Civilian refugees made up the great majority of the exodus but it also included FAR soldiers and Interahamwe militia. The government in Kinshasa did not disarm Rwandans crossing with weapons (unlike the Tanzanian government).

The Zairean government's failure to disarm the groups crossing the border reinforced the RPF's fears of a Hutu return. The response was draconian and devastating. In early 1996, the RPF attacked the border refugee camps, intent on destroying any threat from the *genocidaires* and inflicting massive casualties.[26]

As the RPF was attacking the refugee camps near Goma in North Kivu, a rebellion erupted in South Kivu in September 1996 led by the Banyamulege, a Tutsi community in South Kivu distinct from the Tutsi in North Kivu. Their rebellion received material aid from the RPF and the political support of Laurent-Desiré Kabila, a longtime opponent of Mobutu and occasional rebel leader (he was briefly associated with Che Guevara during the Cuban's ill-fated mission to the Congo in 1965; Che quickly gave up on Kabila and left after a few months). Proclaimed as the Alliance of Democratic Forces for the Liberation of Congo (ADFL), the rebellion's principal objective was to overthrow the Mobutu government. The first Congo war had begun.

The AFDL campaign, backed by Rwanda and Uganda, moved quickly. By March 1997, their forces were at the gates of Kisangani, halfway across the country. I was back in the DRC that month leading a UN team to assess the situation; Kisangani fell while I was in Kinshasa. The rebel forces then moved west without much opposition. Even the vaunted Presidential Division, trained by the Israelis, abandoned the fight. A last-minute mediation effort by Nelson Mandela failed and Mobutu left Kinshasa, never to return. On May 16, rebel forces entered Kinshasa and Laurent Kabila declared himself president and returned the country to its old name, the Democratic Republic of the Congo.

When long-ruling autocrats die or are overthrown, the odds that stability and progress will follow on seamlessly are not good. Congo post-Mobutu was no exception. Kabila quickly proved to be an intemperate ruler who hastened to jettison his erstwhile allies, Rwanda and Uganda. In August 1998, a new rebellion broke out in the Kivus, this one aimed at overthrowing Kabila. With the support of Rwanda and Uganda, the new rebel movement, named the Congolese Rally for Democracy (RCD), quickly overran large parts of eastern Congo. Kabila appealed for assistance; Angola, Chad, Namibia, Sudan, and Zimbabwe intervened with military support and mixed motives, igniting the second Congo war, sometimes labeled "Africa's World War," and with it the partition of the country.[27] The human impact of that war was colossal. Millions of people died, many of them as a result of the secondary effects of the conflict (hunger and disease).[28]

In April 1999, the UN Security Council called for a ceasefire and the withdrawal of foreign forces.[29] The resolution also called for an international conference on peace, security, and stability in the Great Lakes region, recognizing correctly that the crisis of eastern Congo could not be solved by the Congo alone; regional interests were inextricably bound up with the Congolese conflict.

Significantly, in its resolution the Council stated "its readiness to consider the active involvement of the United Nations, in coordination with the Organisation of African Unity [predecessor of the African Union], including through concrete sustainable and effective measures, to assist in the implementation of an effective ceasefire agreement and in an agreed process for political settlement of the conflict."[30]

This resolution clearly foreshadowed some form of operational UN engagement in the Congo, although the contours of that engagement were yet to be defined. I doubt the framers of that resolution ever thought that "active involvement" would lead to a UN peacekeeping engagement that has already lasted two decades and cost (as of the end of 2019) over $19 billion.

History Renewed

Three months after the April resolution was adopted, the principal contenders in the Congo conflict (the DRC, Angola, Rwanda, Uganda, Namibia, and Zimbabwe) signed a ceasefire agreement in the Zambian capital, Lusaka, on July 10, 1999. It called on the UN to "deploy an appropriate peacekeeping force in the DRC to ensure implementation of this Agreement."[31] Later in the year, the Security Council took the next step, formally authorizing the creation of MONUC[32] to monitor and support implementation of the Lusaka agreement. After almost half a century, UN peacekeepers returned to the Congo.

In fact, the initial UN commitment was limited to the deployment of 500 military observers. This cautious approach reflected the reluctance of some members of the Council to countenance yet another major UN peacekeeping commitment; as scholar Joshua Goldstein noted, the "US favoured a narrowly constructed peacekeeping mission in the Congo, notwithstanding the growing demands on the peacekeeping presence."[33] As I mention in a later chapter, the Council's penchant for "incrementalism" proved to be a crippling constraint for three of the four UN peacekeeping missions in which I served.

During its decade of operations, MONUC grew from a small mission of military observers into the largest UN peacekeeping operation in the world. My own part in the Congo drama played out during the latter phase of MONUC's operations after the 2006 national elections, which were expected to pave the way for the transition from war to peace. Alas, those elections did not end violent conflict in the DRC. Far from it; armed groups continued to proliferate and violence of varying intensity flared up in almost every part of the country, with consequent calls on MONUC for military and civilian assistance.

Throughout my time as SRSG in the Congo, armed violence was a constant and pervasive reality. But the DRC was not a single crisis nor a single conflict. An array of crises played out from one side of the country to the other. These crises involved a bewildering assortment of armed groups and acronyms. And just to complicate matters further, some of them disintegrated into factions while others integrated into the Armed Forces of the Democratic Republic of the Congo (FARDC)—the national army—only to reappear with another name when a new round of DDR was on offer.

All of these conflicts were characterized by brutal attacks on civilians and the massive displacement of local populations. However, the conflicts in the Kivu provinces, the subject of my next chapter, were the most dangerous of them all, requiring serial interventions by MONUC to protect civilians as well as intense diplomatic efforts to prevent open conflict between the DRC and its Great Lakes neighbors. Those were defining moments that brought the world to our doorstep.

6
Conflict Without End: The Kivu Wars

Military force—especially when wielded by an outside power—cannot bring order in a country that cannot govern itself.
　　　　　　　　　　　　　　　　　　　　—Robert McNamara

The first time I saw North Kivu, I was not in the Congo. I was on a trip to southwestern Uganda in 1967. I gazed across the border toward the green hills and the vast and mysterious country that lay behind them. On the other side of the border, all was not well. Further south, Jean "Black Jack" Schramme, a former Belgian commando, together with assorted mercenaries, was leading a rebellion against President Mobutu. Schramme succeeded in taking over Bukavu in July 1967, the stately (in its day) lakeside capital of South Kivu. The mercenaries held the town for several weeks but eventually succumbed to Mobutu's forces and fled across the border into neighboring Rwanda.

The violence of 1967 was a portent of the successive cycles of crisis and conflict that have periodically overwhelmed the Kivu provinces. The region is spectacular and yet it has become a place haunted by poverty, misery, and death. The Kivus should be prosperous. The provinces possess fertile soils and under them a wealth of minerals. They should be one of the great tourist destinations of the world, endowed as they are with unique natural treasures: mountains, forests, lakes, volcanoes, and the magnificent gorillas. And yet none of these wonders have really benefited the vast majority of the people in the Kivus who have struggled through one violent episode after another.

The recurring violence has bequeathed a lethal legacy of dispute and devastation perpetuated by a mosaic of armed groups and, it has to be said, the national army. As Séverine Autesserre has pointed out in her

167

insightful book *The Trouble with the Congo,*[1] there were multiple conflicts that pitted ethnic groups against each other in violent contests for
land, natural resources, and political primacy. Even within these groups
there were clashes as individual leaders and commanders competed for
patronage and power.

In this chapter, I look at the crises that beset the Kivus during my time
as the SRSG. In some ways this chapter is the heart of the book. I recount
the dilemmas that we faced as we endeavored to implement the multiple
facets of the mission's mandate, while striving to retain confidence—
locally and internationally—in the mission.

The crises in the Kivus severely tested MONUC's ability to fulfill a
central tenet of its mandate: civilian protection. They also tested the level
of trust between the Congolese government and MONUC, provoking in
turn unsettling questions about the purpose and impact of UN peacekeeping in the DRC.

Anatomy of a Crisis

The 2006 elections, which confirmed President Kabila in office, did not end
conflict in the Kivus. If anything, they intensified the discord, because the
Tutsi minority lost political power. Although by no means the only source
of conflict in the Kivus, the antipathy between the Tutsi and other ethnic
communities was the origin of much of the violence.

In early 2007, Laurent Nkunda, a Tutsi veteran of the earlier Congo
wars, launched an insurrection in North Kivu under the banner of the
National Congress for the Defense of the People (CNDP). The insurrection
was a rejection of the government's effort to integrate Nkunda's troops into
the FARDC and then reassign them to other parts of the country, depriving
him of his power base while also dismantling a line of defense for Rwanda
against any significant irredentist movement emerging from the Kivus.

The FARDC was unable to contain the insurrection. Not for the first
or last time, its frontline units fell apart due to poor tactics and a lack of
logistics. As the situation deteriorated, UN Secretary-General Ban Ki-
moon sounded the alarm, declaring that the crisis in the Kivus "has many
dimensions which call for a comprehensive solution" and adding that "a
purely military solution to this issue is neither desirable nor viable."[2] He
proposed that the "intertwined problems created by the activities of
Nkunda and his militia, the FDLR[3] [Democratic Forces for the Liberation
of Rwanda] and other foreign and Congolese armed groups must be
addressed simultaneously through an approach that involves all major
stakeholders both within the DRC and in the Great Lakes region."[4] This
was a significant policy development. For the first time the UN recognized that the Lusaka and Pretoria agreements—and the security and

institutional arrangements that resulted from them—had not solved the problems of eastern Congo even though there had been progress in stabilizing the Congo as a whole.

Ban Ki-moon's demarche led to a joint DRC-Rwanda communiqué, agreed in Nairobi in November 2007, aimed at "a common approach to end the threat posed to peace and stability in both countries and the Great Lakes Region."[5] Under the terms of the communiqué, both the FDLR and the CNDP were to be denied any form of support from either government. This was an implicit quid pro quo: the FDLR and the CNDP would both be dismantled or neutralized. The agreement committed the two governments to "eliminate the threat posed by illegal armed groups through peaceful and *military* means."[6] I have emphasized the word "military" because the use of military force became a central issue for MONUC as it responded to the crisis that was rapidly developing in the Kivus.

MONUC was requested to provide support to the planning and implementation of operations against armed groups but also to "protect civilians, in accordance with its mandate, against the negative impact of operations against the FDLR and monitor compliance with recognized standards of international humanitarian and human rights law."[7] This clause placed the mission, as I came to realize, in the paradoxical position of having to help plan military operations that could have serious repercussions for civilians while also protecting them from the consequences of those operations.

Giving Peace a Chance: The Goma Accords

The Nairobi communiqué provided only a temporary respite to the armed hostilities. In December 2007, the Congolese army launched an offensive against the CNDP north of Goma that failed. This episode prompted the government to call for a peace and reconciliation conference in the Kivus, which opened in Goma, the provincial capital of North Kivu, in January 2008. Its stated objective was "to create a space where representatives of the armed groups and community representatives to express grievances, share perceptions and fears and address the root causes of conflict in the region."[8] I arrived in the DRC as the peace conference was beginning and after brief introductions hurried off to Goma to join the talks.

Just about all the ethnic groups in the Kivus had been invited to the conference, including the Tutsi communities from North and South Kivu. The CNDP were present but not Nkunda, who feared for his safety. The government was there in force with a delegation led by General Denis Kalume, the interior minister, and Antipas Nyamwisi, the foreign minister, together with Vital Kamerhe, president of the National Assembly (today chief of staff of the president of the DRC, Félix Tshisekedi). The president arrived a few days later but did not attend the conference until the last day.

The conference was chaired by the abbot Apollinaire Malumalu, who hailed from Beni-Butembo in North Kivu. The abbot, quite diminutive physically, possessed great intellectual agility and an easy eloquence, having successfully led the national electoral commission during the 2006 elections. He had a delightful sense of irony and regaled me with stories of his days in the French Alps above Grenoble, where he had been posted by the Catholic Church as a missionary to minister to Alpine farmers, who had never met an African before. To his amusement, he found himself offering advice to the faithful about infidelity.

Actually, there were two conferences in Goma—the main one, presided over by the abbot, and a side meeting with the government and the CNDP, which I attended together with Roeland van de Geer, the EU special envoy for the Great Lakes, and Tim Shortly, who represented the US State Department. The aim of the side meeting was to convince the CNDP to sign on to the Goma peace agreements, which we wanted adopted by consensus in the hope of securing their rapid implementation (a forlorn ambition as later events proved).

It was a convoluted negotiation. Neither of the principals—Kabila and Nkunda—were present. So there were lots of interruptions as they were consulted. Kabila, present or not, obviously resented having to negotiate on equal footing with Nkunda. He told me that Nkunda had rebelled against the state of which he was the legitimately elected president; in his eyes, Nkunda was an outlaw. The unspoken implication, of course, was that MONUC should defend the state against the CNDP if the FARDC forces could not do so.

Nkunda was equally recalcitrant. He protested that he was protecting the Tutsi community from the *genocidaires* (the FDLR), which he claimed were in league with the government. Even though the likelihood of an all-out attack by the FDLR on Rwanda was improbable, the CNDP did constitute a defensive line for Rwanda (as well as access to cattle grazing in areas of North Kivu contiguous to Rwanda).

We held several rounds of negotiations and the CNDP walked out a couple of times. Finally, it came down to a phone call with Nkunda. He asked me if he should approve the agreement; I assured him that we were mediating in good faith and that the agreement would reduce tensions and set the stage for a more peaceful coexistence of the communities in the Kivus. He agreed to go along with the peace agreement.

Two peace deals (one for North Kivu and the other covering South Kivu) were signed on January 23, 2008, and included provisions for an immediate ceasefire, phased withdrawal of all rebel forces in North Kivu, reintegration of the CNDP into the national army, and resettlement of the displaced and the return of refugees. The accord also enjoined the FARDC and the United Nations to eliminate the threat of FDLR forces.

Peace Falters: The Shackles of the Past

The Goma conference adjourned leaving a number of tricky details on the disarmament and reintegration provisions of the accords to be decided later by a mixed technical commission composed of representatives of the signatories and the witnesses. After almost two weeks of intense negotiations, we were all tired. Ministers wanted to get back to Kinshasa and so did I. That was a mistake. In peace negotiations, trust and momentum are crucial ingredients; but so is proximity and we were soon far away in Kinshasa.

The Mixed Technical Commission on Peace and Security was set up under the umbrella of the Amani[9] program, which was established to guide and oversee the implementation of the Goma accords and to mobilize and channel funding for integration and stabilization. The ever versatile abbot Malumalu was appointed as the head of Amani. I asked my chief of staff, John Almstrom, to represent MONUC on the commission. Vice Admiral Didier Etumba (later to become General Etumba) was appointed as the government representative. The armed groups plus civil society were invited to designate members of the commission.

I also designated Alpha Sow from Mali, then head of MONUC's Bukavu office, as the MONUC eastern coordinator and member of the mixed commission. I wanted to ensure that all of our offices in the east of the DRC would be part of the program. Alpha had gone through the earlier troubles in Bukavu and knew Nkunda well. I believed that his calm, patient, and rather stoical temperament would help keep the negotiations on track.

The initial post-conference optimism began to dissipate during the two months of wrangling it took to get the mixed commission off the ground. Admiral Etumba insisted on a very narrow interpretation of the Goma accords tantamount to an unconditional disarmament by the CNDP. Even Alpha turned quite pessimistic, concluding that Etumba was there to impose rather than negotiate.

For its part, the CNDP was not willing to allow government officials back into areas under its control and began installing what looked like a parallel administration. The atmosphere soured with increasingly bellicose statements from both the government and the CNDP, which was threatening to walk out of the commission.

In a private meeting, the president told me that his patience with Nkunda was running out and that if there was no progress he would take action. He was quite agitated (although not impolite), telling me that if the process failed, MONUC would have to assume its responsibilities. That was code for MONUC taking on the CNDP. I responded that the Security Council wanted a peaceful outcome and would not countenance military action by MONUC if the government attacked the CNDP. Later on, I wondered if I had imparted an unintended message to the president: if you are attacked first, then MONUC can help even if the attack was provoked.

No Nkunda, No Jobs

By late June 2008 I was receiving reports from the government that the CNDP was preparing for an offensive even though MONUC military observers posted in areas close to CNDP positions could not confirm this information. But I could not discount that information either. I toyed with the idea of meeting Nkunda at his base in North Kivu. I decided not to do so, however, because Kabila (and his closest advisers) was already deeply wary of MONUC and resented the seeming deference accorded Nkunda by the international community and the mission.

The government's suspicion of MONUC intensified with the revelation in July of an unfortunate indiscretion by an outgoing Indian battalion commander. He had met with Nkunda in April immediately prior to his return to India. There was nothing wrong with such a meeting, as the battalion was responsible for the sector where Nkunda had his headquarters, so that they had to meet periodically to discuss security matters. However, the event turned into more of a party than a meeting; gifts and words of appreciation were exchanged. Unknown to the commander, the event was recorded and then leaked to the FARDC (and MONUC) by a CNDP defector. Despite the fact that the same commander had ordered his troops to fire on the CNDP during the December 2007 confrontation, his encounter with Nkunda was held up as proof that MONUC (and the Indian brigade in particular) was colluding with the CNDP.

As word got out, there were demonstrations in Goma and beyond against MONUC. A favorite slogan of the demonstrators was "no Nkunda, no jobs," which meant that MONUC wanted to protect the CNDP so that it could keep itself in business. This claim was absurd but it was spread by elements of the FARDC and local officials in North Kivu as way of exculpating themselves from their own failures and as a tactic to pressure MONUC to intervene on their behalf should hostilities resume.

Actually, at that moment, I was more alarmed by the increasingly belligerent allegations flying back and forth between Kinshasa and Kigali. The atmosphere was poisonous. I was convinced that until there was a stable relationship between the two countries, the peace in the Kivus would remain precarious. Throughout my assignment in the DRC, I sought ways to promote such a rapprochement. Although President Kagame always insisted that the troubles of the Kivus were the Congo's own responsibility, I had no doubt that given Rwanda's proximity and military prowess, peace in the Kivus was not possible without Rwanda's (and Uganda's) active acquiescence.

Peace Fails: Opening Shots

In late August 2008 there was an unexpected breakthrough. The CNDP agreed to rejoin the commission, which they had been boycotting, and accept the plan for the disengagement of forces that MONUC had been negotiating for several weeks.

My optimism was short-lived. Within a day, we began to receive messages that hostilities had again broken out in North Kivu. It was not clear who had started the fighting; both sides vigorously denied that they were responsible. Given the tense situation that had developed over the preceding weeks, the initial clash could have been unintended. Conspiracy theories flourished, of course. On the government side, it was claimed that the CNDP had intentionally misled the mixed commission in order to gain time to reinforce its positions. The CNDP countered that the government had provoked the conflict in order to cast the CNDP in the role of aggressor.

One of the cheerleaders of the "war party" on the government's side was Chikez Diemu, the defense minister. On Sunday, August 31, he called me to say that he had received information that the CNDP had blocked a critical road running from Goma to Rutshuru (a town that sits strategically at the junction of several roads in North Kivu, including the main road to Uganda). I immediately asked the MONUC force commander, Lieutenant-General Babacar Gaye from Senegal, to verify this information; he checked and advised me that the information was not correct.

I decided to break through the cycle of disinformation. I asked the minister if he would accompany me to Goma so that we could verify the information on-the-spot. One of the benefits of being the SRSG of MONUC was ready access to the mission's fleet of aircraft, which was a huge blessing in a crisis-prone country the size of the DRC. AIROPS and MOVCON, the unheralded heroes of UN peacekeeping operations, quickly got a flight ready and off we went to Goma.

On arrival we were met by Brigadier-General Bipin Rawat, commander of the Indian brigade in North Kivu. General Rawat (later the army chief in India) was to play a central role in the crisis that was developing. He arranged for us to overfly the length of the road in an Indian Lama helicopter, a flying bubble that affords an extraordinary wraparound view from the air. To take care of any unexpected trouble from the ground, two Indian helicopter gunships gave us an escort.

We flew over the length of the road (and some CNDP positions) and could easily confirm that it had not been cut. There were no CNDP manned roadblocks; commercial vehicles were moving along the road unimpeded. We headed back to Goma. On arrival, there were some journalists waiting on the landing strip, probably alerted by the minister's staff. I assumed he was now going to calm tensions by confirming that he had personally verified that the road was open and traffic was moving. I was quickly disabused. He launched into a tirade against the CNDP and their refusal to abide by the Goma accords. No mention of the road. I had to then intervene to confirm that we had not seen any obstruction of the road.

This incident was a forewarning of things to come. The minister was playing to the gallery (and the president), and MONUC was expected to play along. His remarks were not intended to calm the situation but inflame it, irrespective of the facts. By doing so, however, he forfeited the benefit of the doubt, and helped to create a deep rift between the government and the mission. Indeed, throughout the ensuing crisis, the breakdown of confidence between the government and MONUC made the planning and conduct of defensive operations far more difficult.

The clashes between the FARDC and CNDP continued for several days. MONUC units from the North Kivu brigade moved to block CNDP incursions into areas held by the FARDC and toward major population centers. As they attempted to do so, they (and MONUC civilians) ran into violent demonstrations orchestrated by elements of the FARDC and local officials accusing the UN of colluding with the CNDP.

I publicly rejected the claims of collusion, which I said were both baseless and ultimately self-defeating, since blocking UN troops allowed the CNDP greater freedom of movement. I suggested to President Kabila that we undertake a joint campaign to sensitize the population, which he agreed to. But he still insisted that Nkunda was intent on asphyxiating Goma and would not therefore countenance any further negotiations with him.

In calls with Nkunda (a tortuous exercise because he used multiple cell phones to avoid locational detection), I pressed him to begin disengagement. I also insisted that he should stop flying a CNDP flag and dismantle the parallel administration set up in zones controlled by the CNDP. Nkunda, however, relished the attention lavished on him by the media; he became ever more expansive, talking of liberating the country, which of course annoyed Kabila intensely (and possibly President Kagame as well).

We also attempted to engage the local populations in North Kivu in order to put a stop to the demonstrations against MONUC. But this was an uphill struggle given the fiercely anti-Tutsi feelings—stoked by government propaganda—that permeated society across the two provinces. The joint campaign of sensitization agreed to by the president never materialized.

As the crisis deepened, our meetings with the government's national security team in Kinshasa became ever more ill-tempered. I came away from those sessions disheartened. The ministers refused to allow the FARDC to withdraw from positions they had seized (even though they were hard to defend) so that we could separate forces and create buffer zones patrolled by MONUC. The heated discussions did not lead to a joint strategy but served to explain away the FARDC's failings and to serve as a pretext to justify MONUC's military intervention. We were warned that the "wrath of the population" would turn on MONUC should it fail to act decisively against the CNDP.

I have often found that when things go wrong, they do so in cascade. On September 2, a chartered flight carrying UN and NGO humanitarian staff crashed as it approached Bukavu airport. All on board perished. The site of the crash was high in the mountains of the Kahuzi-Biega national park in South Kivu and could be reached by troops from the Pakistani South Kivu brigade only by rappelling down from helicopters. The disaster was a terrible blow and reminded us how hazardous life could be for those who put their lives at the service of humanity.

In North Kivu, the military situation on the ground remained very fluid. DPKO authorized MONUC forces to deter the CNDP from taking additional territory and from seizing key roads. Both the Indian-led North Kivu brigade together with South African units and the South Kivu Pakistan brigade moved aggressively against CNDP forces that attempted to break out and gain new territory. Then, unexpectedly, on September 11, the CNDP declared a unilateral ceasefire. On September 19, the FARDC announced that it too would pull back to its pre–August 28 positions.

Whether the CNDP announcement was the consequence of MONUC's military interventions or other factors (particularly Rwandan pressure on the CNDP), I cannot say for sure. Anyway, I sought to capitalize on the moment. Working closely with Roeland van de Geer, the EU special envoy, and Tim Shortly from the US State Department, in a troika dubbed the International Facilitation, I proposed a disengagement plan in an effort to get the Amani program back on track.

In another conversation with the president at the time, I confirmed that MONUC would continue to monitor the CNDP movements closely and, as necessary, intervene to stop any generalized military offensive. Fatefully, I had declared that we would enforce a "red line," which meant that MONUC would not allow the CNDP to take over major population centers such as Rutshuru or Goma. That phrase eventually came back to haunt me (as it has haunted other far more prominent leaders since).

Convince or Compel

On September 15, 2008, President Kabila convened a meeting in Goma with his national security team plus the International Facilitation, the ambassadors of Security Council members, and MONUC. It was a thinly disguised attempt to put pressure on MONUC. General Etumba voiced strong doubts about the good faith of the CNDP, claiming that the FARDC was not responsible for the resumption of hostilities, a position echoed by the president. MONUC, Etumba claimed, was not responding effectively to the attacks from the CNDP, an affront that General Gaye and I adamantly refuted.

The following day, MONUC presented a comprehensive plan for the disengagement of forces. After some minor adjustments, the government accepted the plan and the minister of defense declared a ceasefire as a gesture of goodwill. The government then asked us to get CNDP concurrence to the disengagement plan. I knew that this would not be easy. The CNDP had not been defeated on the battlefield, so Nkunda was not going to readily accept a fait accompli dictated by either the government or MONUC. But once again ambitions moved ahead of reality. Vital Kamerhe publicly announced the plan, calling on MONUC to convince or compel the CNDP to conform, which was tantamount to an ultimatum. Predictably, the CNDP rejected the demand out-of-hand.

By late September, Christian Manahl, MONUC's chief of political affairs, was sending me increasingly gloomy reports from Goma. The FARDC was not sticking to its side of the bargain; notwithstanding assurances from Minister Diemu, the FARDC had moved into several positions vacated by the CNDP. This made it difficult for me to convince the CNDP that it should maintain the ceasefire (as Nkunda was quick to point out to me).

As if to make the point, the CNDP advanced around Sake (a few kilometers from Goma), leading to renewed clashes with the FARDC. They also launched attacks on FARDC positions along the Goma-Rutshuru axis and captured the military camp of Rumangabo. I negotiated another temporary ceasefire, involving the FARDC withdrawing from a strategic position it had captured from the CNDP while the CNDP withdrew from the Rumangabo camp.

The seizure of that camp once again illustrated the breakdown of trust between the Congolese authorities and MONUC. The North Kivu brigade had advised the FARDC that the camp was vulnerable and that its defenses should be strengthened, which the FARDC failed to do. Then as MONUC forces were moving to assist the Rumangabo garrison, they were blocked by violent protests stirred up by fictitious claims that MONUC was going to help the CNDP.

A General Retreats

In early October 2008, General Gaye was due to leave MONUC after four years of distinguished service. His nominated replacement was Lieutenant-General Vicente Diaz de Villegas from Spain. General Diaz had prior experience as a commander of special forces, which I thought would be a valuable asset given the nature of the warfare in eastern Congo.

I had asked DPKO to allow for a handover between the incoming and outgoing commanders and for General Diaz to then join me in Brussels for a meeting with the DRC Contact Group, a coordinating entity that brought together a number of governments and organizations in support of the Congolese peace process.

I met the general immediately on my arrival in Brussels and invited him to join me for dinner, along with Edmond Mulet, then assistant secretary-general in DPKO (Hedi Annabi's successor) so that we could go over my presentation to the contact group. However, the general insisted that we speak straightaway; we did and then, to my absolute astonishment, he told me that he was resigning from MONUC.

It took me a few moments to fully grasp exactly what he was saying. He added that he did not believe in the mandate that he would have to discharge as the MONUC force commander: MONUC could not compel the CNDP to enter the DDR process, while the FARDC was grossly incompetent and would be unable to handle the CNDP or indeed take on the FDLR. I responded that he was right to raise these concerns, which I shared. Nevertheless, I urged him to return to Kinshasa so that we could review the situation and decide on the best course of action. He refused to reconsider and told me that he had already submitted his resignation to the Spanish minister of defense and would not return to Kinshasa.

I persisted with the dinner invitation and in the evening we met with Edmond, whom I had briefed beforehand. I thought he, as a native-Spanish speaker and the number two in DPKO, might be more effective than me in convincing Diaz that his resignation was premature and that he should give us at least a few months before throwing in the towel. Edmond made a valiant effort at changing the general's mind but, like me, without success. After Brussels, I returned to Kinshasa to face a renewed crisis minus a force commander.

MONUC on the Line: The October Crisis

The Brussels discussions and General Diaz's defection had given me a pause to reflect on how we could better manage the crisis from both a military and a political perspective. On the military side, several problems emerged as the crisis deepened and persisted. First, we obviously could not count on the FARDC to mount an effective defense (Diaz was right on that score); the FARDC had become part of the problem and a threat to MONUC. Units retreated or even deserted, triggering havoc. The FARDC commanders were neither uniformly incompetent nor lacking in courage, but they received minimal logistical support and their troops often went unpaid.

Second, it was becoming clear that if we wanted to totally contain the CNDP, a different military strategy and configuration would be needed, especially if, as many MONUC colleagues and independent observers believed, the CNDP was receiving support from Rwanda. While MONUC was billed as the largest peacekeeping operation in the world, it was not set up as an expeditionary force. Moreover, it was spread out over a vast country; the Kivu provinces alone are approximately the size of California, with a population of 10 million.

The robust response led by the Indian North Kivu brigade under General Rawat had initially contained the CNDP. Other units, notably from

South Africa and Benin, as well as the Pakistani brigade in South Kivu, had not shied away from confronting the CNDP either. Nevertheless, these contingents were not set up for lengthy offensive operations. The Indian forward units, for example, were running low on ammunition, and resupply had been hindered by delays in east African ports and on the roads to eastern Congo.

Third, although General Rawat was willing to engage the CNDP robustly, the attacks on his units by the population and the incidents with the FARDC in Goma and Rutshuru, compounded by ill-judged remarks coming from government spokesmen (including the newly appointed foreign minister, Alexis Thambwe Mwamba), raised serious doubts in New Delhi (and New York) about the role of the mission. Like ONUC in its day, we asked: For what and for whom are we here? And if the FARDC is unwilling or unable to defend its own people, should MONUC act as its military surrogate?

A fourth dilemma arose from MONUC's dispersion of forces in small, forward-operating bases or mobile-operating bases. Prior to my arrival in the DRC, General Gaye and Deputy Special Representative Ross Mountain (serving also as the UN humanitarian coordinator) had pioneered this approach as a way of improving civilian protection through proximity. I certainly endorsed that deployment, but it had the unintended effect of reducing the mission's ability to quickly concentrate force to deal decisively with major challenges to its authority as the peace process collapsed.

Finally, the mission's ability to realign its forces in function of the evolving situation on the ground was inhibited by rigidities imposed by some of the troop-contributing countries. At the height of the North Kivu crisis, we should have deployed elements of the Pakistan South Kivu brigade north to add weight to the Indian brigade. But any such realignment was ruled out as politically impossible. Neither contingent would operate in the other contingent's sector.

On the political side we faced other dilemmas. The first was the perverse attitude of the Congolese government, which continued to fuel popular hostility to the mission. This resulted in aggressive demonstrations in Kinshasa and other cities. Although I remained in continuous contact with President Kabila (who took to calling me at sunrise to ask what MONUC was doing when there was news of a FARDC setback), it was plain that he expected much more from the mission: he wanted us to defeat the CNDP, which he considered as a personal affront to his presidency. So much so that he linked our fates, warning me at one point: "we are on the same ship, we will go down together."

The second was Rwanda's increasing antipathy to the mission. With MONUC forcefully confronting the CNDP, the Rwandan government claimed the mission had taken sides. Behind that concern, I assumed, was Kigali's apprehension at the prospect that the CNDP might be disarmed and dispersed, thereby removing a defensive asset in case of attacks on the Tutsi community on either side of the border. Personally, I doubted that the FDLR still posed an existential military threat; if anything, the FDLR was more of a danger to the citizens of the DRC than to those of Rwanda, but that was not the view in Kigali, at least not publicly.

A further worry arose from the humanitarian impact of the military operations. At that point there were over a million IDPs in North Kivu. The displacement crisis produced a crescendo of criticism by humanitarian organizations, who claimed that MONUC had forfeited the benefit of the UN's neutrality. Moreover, even though the Security Council had explicitly mandated MONUC to act against the armed groups, as the fighting persisted and spread some members of the Council became increasingly uneasy, stirred by the powerful messaging of the humanitarian lobby.

These competing perceptions of what the mission should or should not be doing began to erode the morale and cohesiveness of the mission staff, which was becoming ever more polarized as the conflict dragged on. The military was dismayed by the FARDC's dismal performance and by the attacks on military convoys by local militants; civilian staff members, however, were incensed by what they perceived as the arrogance of Nkunda and his CNDP cohorts, acting as proxies for Rwanda.

These concerns were summed up in a note I received from MONUC's North Kivu office. I was advised that the staff were finding it increasingly difficult to explain MONUC's actions and inactions to interlocutors due to "their lack of understanding of the leadership's strategy."[10]

I did have a strategy, based on four premises. First, I wanted to prevent any further territorial encroachments by the CNDP. Our credibility in the DRC and beyond would have been shattered if we had not responded forcefully to the CNDP or allowed Goma to suffer the same fate as Bukavu a few years before when Nkunda and company had captured and looted the town despite the MONUC presence. Second, we needed to keep open, with the help of the International Facilitation, the avenues for political engagement with the CNDP despite the military clashes. Third, as I mentioned earlier, I was convinced that a DRC-Rwanda rapprochement was a prerequisite for peace in the Kivus. And finally, we needed to mobilize international pressures on Rwanda to rein in Nkunda.

The staff memo meant that I had not done very well at explaining that strategy. It signaled that I needed to clarify and communicate MONUC's position and policy more effectively. Even though I could not speak openly about all aspects of the strategy (especially the relationship with Rwanda), I had to make sure that our intentions were better communicated inside and outside of the mission. I asked Kevin Kennedy from DPKO, who had lengthy experience with Congo operations, to join the mission as the communications director in an effort to strengthen our outreach. I also reinforced our communications team in Goma with an energetic spokeswoman,

Sylvie van den Wildenberg, who had good contacts in the local and international media.

Better communications, however, could not overcome a fundamental flaw inherent in the doctrine of convince or compel, which implied that MONUC would do what the FARDC was incapable of doing. Realistically, we did not have the means or motivation to force the CNDP into reintegration. Along with "red lines," this was a phrase too bold, which I should have publicly disowned even if it meant another rift with the government and a further loss of public support in Kinshasa and Goma.

With or without convince or compel, the mission was stretched too thinly. In a Security Council briefing at the time, I spoke of MONUC's constraints and appealed for a surge capacity. I wanted to bolster MONUC's frontline capacities with special forces and added air mobility so that we could root out irregular armed groups operating close to population centers. I argued that these capacities should be a backed up with better intelligence-gathering capacities, including drones, so that we could to monitor and interdict, if needed, groups that posed an imminent threat to civilians.

The Security Council subsequently approved a reinforcement package.[11] However, I knew that it would take many months to get all the elements in place and operational (actually it took almost a year). So I floated the idea of temporary support from a multinational task force. There was a DRC precedent for short-term support. The French-led Operation Artemis had helped during the worst of the violence in Ituri and then Operation EUFOR RD Congo, deployed during the 2006 elections, had provided a force multiplier at critical moments. I believed that even a modest deployment to Goma would have a stabilizing effect. The UN Secretary-General backed this idea and launched an appeal to the European Union, which unfortunately, as I mention further on, did not get any traction.

While I tried to boost MONUC's military capabilities, I was eager to defuse the dangerous confrontation building up between the DRC and Rwanda. In an effort to lower the temperature, I called for the reactivation of a joint verification mechanism as a confidence-building measure, but my initiative was soon stymied by a disruptive turn of events on the front lines.

The Fall of Rutshuru

On October 26, 2008, the CNDP broke the tenuous ceasefire and began a major new offensive, quickly recapturing the big FARDC camp at Rumangabo. Once again when MONUC units moved to reinforce FARDC positions, they were obstructed by violent crowds of demonstrators, causing some nasty casualties among the MONUC troops.

Worse was to follow. Units of the North Kivu brigade had deployed around the southern sector of the strategically situated town of Rutshuru, with FARDC troops deployed to guard other entrances to the town. But as soon as the CNDP attacked, the FARDC units fled, abandoning their heavy weapons and firing on MONUC troops who tried to deter them. I had declared publicly the inviolability of red lines, which included Rutshuru, and said the same to Nkunda. The failure to secure Rutshuru was a major setback and an embarrassing one for me personally. The mission was blamed in the local press for abandoning Rutshuru to concentrate forces to prevent the fall of Goma. Actually, the opposite was true; the fall of Rutshuru made Goma far more vulnerable.

The government forces were disintegrating all around MONUC positions. Some fled north but others retreated toward Goma, creating a new threat to the town: looting and mistreatment of the civilian population. We informed the governor of the province, Julien Paluku, and the minister of defense that we would engage "robustly" to protect civilians in Goma even if that meant using force against FARDC units. Fortunately, on this occasion, the government backed us up and authorized MONUC to apprehend "rogue" FARDC soldiers if need be (which we did).

Understandably, the morale of the civilian population in Goma began to crumble. Headquarters queried whether we should evacuate UN staff from the town. The head of the MONUC office in Goma at the time, Hiroute Guebre Sellassie, a plucky and passionate Ethiopian, strongly opposed any such move. She argued forcefully that if UN staff started to leave, there would be a general panic and the mission's credibility would be irreparably damaged.

I agreed with Hiroute and flew to Goma to help shore up confidence. I met with local journalists to publicly reaffirm that MONUC would defend the town. However, I tried to do so in a way that didn't convey the impression that I was throwing down the gauntlet to the CNDP in a "bring it on" type of gesture. We were still seeking a political response to the crisis. Annoyingly, the government called for MONUC to take sterner military action even though its own forces were in full retreat.

The CNDP advanced to within a few kilometers of Goma before declaring another ceasefire on October 29. Why did the CNDP break the ceasefire and then declare another one? Was it Nkunda's intent all along? Was it due to tensions within the CNDP, which Johan Peleman, the chief of our Joint Mission Analysis Centre (JMAC) was reporting? Or had Rwanda intervened out of concern that a multilateral task force might be deployed close to its border? We were not of one mind within the mission on the intentions of the CNDP (or Rwanda). But irrespective of the differences in our interpretations of the CNDP's motivation, we took the threat to Goma very earnestly. We could not afford a repetition of the Bukavu debacle.

The Defense of Goma

While we were endeavoring to contain the CNDP, the international political response began to take on a more urgent tone. The media had flooded
into Goma and the television footage of waves of people on the move in
great distress began to have an effect. But MONUC got a lot of disap-
proval. We were derided as ineffectual and the habitual bromides about
UN peacekeeping resurfaced. Human Rights Watch was reporting that
MONUC's "primary focus on deterring attacks on the provincial capital
Goma and its inability to respond promptly to new threats, has stopped it
from being able to prevent ongoing killings, forced recruitment, and new
displacements of civilians."[12]

However, the ground was shifting. Attitudes toward Rwanda, especially
in the United States and Western Europe, began to change. Articles critical
of Rwanda (and Kagame) appeared in the *New York Times*[13] and other media
that generally extolled the country's resurrection after the genocide. A
stream of high-level visitors arrived, including Jendayi Fraser, the US assistant secretary of state for Africa. Jean Ping, chair of the African Union, visited, as well as the South African foreign minister, Dlamini Zuma.

At the very end of October, Bernard Kouchner and David Miliband,
respectively foreign ministers of France and the UK, made a joint visit to
the DRC. I arranged to meet them in Goma. They arrived late from Kinshasa in a ferocious late-afternoon thunderstorm that almost aborted the
landing. Time was short, as they had to take off for Kigali before darkness.
Miliband insisted, however, that the team should go to the Kibati IDP camp
outside of Goma (and not too far from the CNDP's forward positions). So
we abandoned our planned in-house briefing and piled into a MONUC
SUV, with General Rawat providing commentary upfront. Wedged between
the two ministers as we bumped along the potholed road to the camp, I
made a strong pitch for the surge capacity.

They seemed convinced and, indeed, the Security Council approved a
reinforcement package a month later, but France turned down the request for
a temporary task force; President Nicolas Sarkozy claimed that MONUC
already had enough troops, but only 800 were actually operational (this was
not true). He seemed to have no idea of the multiple security challenges
that we faced in a country the size of Western Europe with a population
larger than that of France but with a military deployment not even the size
of the Paris police force.

The most important visitor from the operational perspective was Alain
Le Roy, who had succeeded Jean-Marie Guéhenno as head of DPKO. A
senior French diplomat, Le Roy had earlier in his career served in a peacekeeping mission (in Kosovo). Along with DPKO second-in-command,
Edmond Mulet, Le Roy was our main interlocutor at headquarters; both
proved to be steadfast colleagues at rough moments.

Soon after Le Roy's arrival we headed for Goma. The situation was extremely tense, with the threat of a CNDP attack hanging over the city. As a precaution, the Indian brigade moved its attack helicopters to more secure locations just in case the CNDP attempted to mortar Goma airport. With General Rawat and Colonel James Cunliffe, the UK-seconded chief of staff at MONUC's eastern force headquarters, we reviewed the plans for defending Goma. We were acutely conscious of what had happened in Rutshuru and agreed that the plan must take account of the strong possibility that the FARDC would not hold its positions on the outskirts of the city. The plan envisaged concentric circles of defense, with the FARDC stationed on the outside lines while MONUC would deploy its forces in fallback positions together with a mobile reserve (created by transferring units from elsewhere in North Kivu) that could be deployed if the FARDC lines gave way. Orders were issued to disarm any group (including wayward FARDC units) that tried to enter the city bearing arms.

Despite Nkunda's threats and bombast, the CNDP did not attack. I am not entirely sure why. Did he really want to engage in an all-out fight with MONUC? Was there dissent in the CNDP command as our JMAC team surmised? Did the Rwandan government lean on Nkunda? I cannot say what might have happened if the CNDP had attacked, but I do know that we were committed to defend the city.

The Killing Fields of Kiwanja

Though Goma was not attacked, the ceasefire broke down on November 4, 2008. It was broken this time by a militia group known as the Coalition of Congolese Patriotic Resistance (PARECO), which attacked the CNDP at Kiwanja, a village close to Rutshuru. The militia summarily executed villagers they accused of collaboration with the CNDP. Following intense fighting on November 4 and 5, the CNDP chased the coalition forces out of the village. Then during the night, CNDP soldiers went house to house and executed young men (probably about a hundred) whom they claimed were militia.

As soon as I learned of the massacre, I sent a team to Kiwanja led by Leila Zerrougui, the newly arrived deputy SRSG, who headed up the rule-of-law and human rights pillar of the mission. Despite the CNDP denials, she was quite categorical that the killings had taken place.

The Kiwanja killings illustrated the acute dilemma that a peacekeeping force confronts in the face of murderous violence. MONUC was harshly criticized by human rights groups[14] for not stopping the killings. But at the time of the assault, the only MONUC deployment in Kiwanja was an Indian company, which had been on full alert for several days and nights. It had already rescued NGO workers, staff of religious organizations, and some journalists. As the security situation worsened, however, several thousand people gathered outside the company base (which also guarded a helicopter landing site) in search of protection. The company focused on the protection of the IDPs against the threat of the CNDP, which was trying to disperse them. As a consequence, the company commander did not send his troops that night to patrol the village.

If he had done so, would that have halted the killings? Or would this have allowed the CNDP greater room to intimidate the IDPs sheltering at the base? It is hard to judge whether more or fewer lives would have been lost if the company had been sent into the village at night, leaving the IDPs exposed to the CNDP. But the perception spread that MONUC had stood by passively while civilians were killed, which certainly damaged the mission's reputation.

Diplomacy Takes Over

The purpose of Alain Le Roy's November 2008 visit was as much political as operational. We held a series of meetings with senior Congolese officials including the foreign minister, Alexis Thambwe Mwamba. He was quite blunt. He told Le Roy that the DRC had no armed forces and that the MONUC mandate should reflect this reality. Le Roy responded that the Security Council would not be willing to replace the FARDC with MONUC combat units. But he also reiterated that the CNDP would not be allowed to take over Goma and also stressed the importance of mobilizing regional actors to pressure Nkunda to rejoin the peace process.

Perhaps the most intriguing aspect of this meeting was Thambwe's briefing on his surprise visit to Kigali on October 28, which was followed by a return visit by a Rwandan delegation. The Rwanda government asked MONUC (through the head of MONUC's liaison office in Kigali, Joe Felli, a well-connected and well-informed former Ghanaian diplomat) to provide an aircraft for the delegation to make the trip. I was happy to oblige as a modest step toward rebuilding confidence between the two countries and between MONUC and the Rwandan government. The meetings went off reasonably well, we were told, and the prospect of a Kabila-Kagame summit was agreed to in principle. I thought Kabila had made a smart move by sending Thambwe Mwamba to Kigali. The timing was right. I sensed that the pressure on Kagame from friendly states was having an effect and may have forestalled a possible CNDP attack on Goma.

For his part, Alain Le Roy took the opportunity to announce that the Secretary-General was appointing former president of Nigeria, Olusegun Obasanjo, as his special envoy for the Great Lakes. Although some colleagues in the mission saw this appointment as a vote of no-confidence in the mission and my leadership, I was not upset. Knowing President Obasanjo from my days in West Africa, I was confident that I could work well with him. He had the prestige to engage with Rwanda (and Uganda) at the highest level in a way that I could not, given the shaky state of our relations with Kigali. Also our communication with the CNDP had suffered from the fighting. I was sure that Obasanjo could reopen communications without the DRC government firing off a new round of allegations that MONUC was surreptitiously aiding and abetting the CNDP.

Following our visit to Goma, Le Roy and I left for Kigali to meet the Rwandan government before heading to Nairobi for a hastily called meeting of the International Conference of the Great Lakes Region (ICGLR) and the African Union (AU), where heads of state, including Kabila and Kagame, and the UN Secretary-General would discuss the Congo crisis. We called on President Kagame to brief him on the situation from the UN's perspective. It was a prickly meeting. At one point, a senior Rwandan official present mentioned a report from MONUC that there had been firing from the Rwandan side of the border. Kagame hotly denied this report, which originated from an UN military observer; he angrily retorted that if the DRC or MONUC wanted to get into a fight with Rwanda, they had better watch out.

This was not a promising start, but as the meeting progressed, a calmer and more reflective Kagame emerged. Le Roy asked the president to exercise his influence on Nkunda. The president, rather disingenuously, denied any control over Nkunda and the CNDP and deplored what he saw as the tendency to always blame Rwanda for the troubles of eastern Congo. In his view, the root of the problem was a dearth of leadership in the DRC, but he did not refuse to help.

Another Nairobi Summit

The ICGL/AU summit brought together heads of state from the region to review the Kivu crisis. The UN Secretary-General attended along with President Obasanjo and Benjamin Mkapa (the former president of Tanzania, who had been designated as a special envoy by the African Union).

In a side meeting between Ban Ki-moon and President Kabila, the president calmly reiterated his views to the Secretary-General about Nkunda and the rebellion and called on the United Nations to support the DRC against the attack on its sovereignty.

By contrast, a separate session with President Kagame turned quite testy when the Secretary-General suggested that Rwanda's image was being muddied by the violence in the Kivus. Kagame took umbrage, retorting that mud washes off easier than blood. The Secretary-General handled the remark with equanimity and simply asked Kagame to exercise his "moral authority" over the CNDP. Moral authority was a polite way of getting around Kagame's blanket denial of support for the CNDP.

The president calmed down—he had made his point—and promised to cooperate with Obasanjo and Mkapa.

In a joint statement, adopted on November 7, 2008, participants in the summit called on all armed groups in North Kivu to observe an immediate ceasefire. They also decided to establish a mechanism to facilitate a comprehensive solution and help address the root causes of the crisis in eastern DRC. The "mechanism" was really a vehicle for Obasanjo and Mkapa to manage the regional dimensions of the crisis.

Following the conference, Obasanjo met with Laurent Nkunda (along with our stoical Alpha Sow, representing MONUC) and insisted on the importance of an immediate return to a durable ceasefire, backed by an effective monitoring mechanism. He secured Nkunda's recommitment to the principles of the Goma agreements and the Nairobi communiqué. On November 18 the CNDP announced it was withdrawing its forces from areas that it had recently overrun and requested that MONUC deploy in those areas.

This was a major breakthrough and I give full credit to President Obasanjo and his inimitable style of personal diplomacy, which included a jig with Nkunda. Their impromptu dance was filmed and earned him some criticism from Kinshasa. But as he said, he had to establish a rapport with Nkunda and the jig was one way of doing so.

From Nairobi, at the suggestion of my deputy Ross Mountain, we reached out to General Gaye with a request that he temporarily rejoin MONUC until we had a replacement lined up for the hastily departed Diaz. To my great relief, General Gaye accepted to return to the mission and he immediately flew to Nairobi for consultations. But other initiatives were also in motion.

The senior FARDC command in North Kivu was dismissed. John Numbi was brought in to stiffen the resolve of the FARDC. A policeman with a notorious reputation (his name comes up several times in the DRC story), Numbi told me that he would put the FARDC defensive lines back in place (which he did). However, through our well-informed JMAC, I learned that there was another reason that Kabila sent him to North Kivu. He had good connections to Rwanda and the CNDP. He had been involved in earlier negotiations with them and there were rumors of money changing hands. Numbi's arrival on the scene seemed to signal that a deal of some kind was in the offing.

Another rabbit came out of the hat on December 5. The DRC and Rwandan governments announced their agreement on a joint military plan to address the continued presence of the FDLR. They also pledged to take concrete steps toward the restoration of full-fledged diplomatic relations. With that announcement, I sensed that the immediate crisis in the Kivus was at an end. Both sides had found a workable compromise. But as ever in the Congo, further surprises were in store.

Nkunda, No More

A month later the CNDP imploded. Bosco Ntaganda, the CNDP chief of staff at the time, announced on January 5, 2009, that he had replaced Laurent Nkunda as leader of the group. JMAC had reported earlier on factional divisions within the CNDP hierarchy but I didn't expect such a dramatic turn of events. Why was Nkunda unseated? I can only speculate that he had acquired too high a profile for Kagame and was dispensable, especially as Kabila was adamant that Nkunda would have to leave before any settlement could be agreed.

Yet another surprise followed. On January 16, Ntaganda announced that the CNDP and the government had agreed to an immediate cessation of hostilities and that the CNDP would begin integrating its forces into the FARDC. The CNDP would then participate in the operation against the FDLR on the basis of the joint Congo and Rwanda plan. On the same day, most of the government-aligned militias in North Kivu announced a cessation of hostilities.

All of these dramatic and unexpected developments created renewed hope that the crisis in North Kivu might be winding down. But Nkunda's demise and Bosco's elevation created another dilemma for MONUC.

The International Criminal Court had issued an arrest warrant for Bosco back in August 2006 for alleged crimes committed in Ituri in 2002 and 2003. MONUC had interacted quite openly with Bosco's predecessor, Laurent Nkunda; despite his violent past, he had not been indicted by the ICC (although there were recurring calls for an ICC indictment). Bosco, already under ICC indictment, was in a different category.

Human rights groups and the DPKO immediately instructed us to avoid contact with Bosco even though he was now in the government camp. Although I understood the moral argument for keeping Bosco at arm's length, this prohibition of contact nevertheless created practical problems. As a part of the no-contact rule, I had to resort to sending an advance team to any public place I visited in Goma to make sure that Bosco wasn't there.

I didn't need to meet Bosco, but we still had to deal with him on security issues. However, New York insisted that there should be no contact at all. Paradoxically, while we were being told to keep our distance, our sister mission in Sudan was transporting in UN aircraft a Sudanese official indicted by the ICC. He was needed for a UN peace conference and a waiver was granted. And not long before, Jan Egeland, the UN's top humanitarian official, had met with Joseph Kony, leader of the Lord's Resistance Army (LRA). So the policy wasn't very consistent; whatever we thought about Bosco, he was a fact of life in North Kivu that we could not ignore.

The alternative was to arrest him. In fact, I discussed this prospect with the new defense minister, Charles Mwando Simba (a former deputy prime minister I had known in Mobutu's days), who had replaced the garrulous

Chikez Diemu. I offered MONUC support to carry out an arrest operation, but recalling the Taylor arrest saga in Liberia, I insisted that such an operation would have to be carefully planned with a high degree of confidentiality; if Bosco got wind of it, he would go back to the bush and raise another flag of rebellion. As it was, President Kabila decided he could live with Bosco if that was the price of ending the CNDP rebellion and getting rid of Nkunda. He did not authorize the operation.

Another problem created by Bosco's pro-government defection came from the supposed integration of the CNDP into the FARDC. I strongly advised Minister Mwando to take the time to do proper vetting; General Gaye said the same to General Etumba, by now the chief of the defense staff. We soon realized, however, that instructions had come from the top that integration would go forward posthaste. In fact, it wasn't integration, it was a form of rehatting; the CNDP units became FARDC units mostly under their former commanders.

A Deal Is Sealed: Umoja Wetu

On January 20, 2009, President Obasanjo and I met with President Kabila to review the CNDP situation in light of the latest dramatic events. The Congolese president was in a buoyant mood because that same morning approximately 1,500 Rwandan troops crossed the border into the DRC in a coordinated joint operation—Umoja Wetu[15]—to attack the FDLR. The president explained that relations with President Kagame had improved significantly and the time was now ripe to take action against the FDLR.

He informed us that the operation would last about two weeks. He added that the Nairobi communiqué had not worked and so tougher measures would be required, conveniently forgetting that he had made the decision to reduce the deployed forces in an earlier joint operation against the FDLR (code-named Kimia I).[16]

More surprises were in store. Two days later, Congolese and Rwandan military commanders announced that "ex-general Laurent Nkunda" had been arrested on January 22 "while he was fleeing on Rwandan territory after he had resisted our troops at Bunagana with three battalions."[17] The exact charges were not specified. As far as I know, Nkunda has never been seen in public again.

While MONUC had no input to the Umoja Wetu campaign, I informed the government that the mission would monitor the campaign from a protection perspective. We quickly learned where the Rwandans were headed. While there were some operations against the FDLR, there was no disguising that the Rwandans first moved into areas largely controlled by the CNDP. We concluded that the real intent of the operation was as much about getting the CNDP under control as rooting out the FDLR.

Rwandan units, along with elements of the now ex-CNDP forces, attacked the FDLR, and the number of surrenders and civilian demands for return to Rwanda increased significantly. Nevertheless, the FDLR did not suffer a comprehensive defeat. They moved out of some areas, retreating further into the bush. But that was enough for the two governments to declare victory, although some weeks later, when I was in Kigali, a senior national security official confided to me that the campaign was more a political gesture than an operational success. This meant, from the Rwandan perspective, that Umoja Wetu was unfinished business.

Irrespective of the real or supposed motivation for Umoja Wetu, MONUC had not been informed of a major game-changing decision of direct relevance to our mandate and presence in the DRC. It deepened the lack of trust between the mission and the DRC government and confirmed my growing conviction that the Security Council would need to reevaluate the raison d'être for MONUC's presence in Congo sooner or later.

The Secretary-General Visits

At the end of February 2009, Secretary-General Ban Ki-moon made his first visit to the DRC since taking office. By chance, President Kabila had been his first guest at his official residence in New York after he took office in January 2008. So the mood of the meeting between the two was relaxed and there were none of the, by now, customary broadsides against MONUC from Information Minister Lambert Mende Omalanga.

In the official press release issued after the visit, the Secretary-General noted that an opportunity had emerged in the wake of the DRC-Rwanda joint operation against the FDLR "to reassert State authority through a more robust presence of Congolese troops backed by United Nations peacekeepers. That opportunity could also improve United Nations humanitarian access to those in need."[18] A day later, the Secretary-General met President Kagame in Kigali and asked him to ensure that "the joint military operation in the eastern Congo not worsen an already difficult humanitarian situation or impede aid workers' access to people in need of assistance."[19]

These statements exemplified the uneasy ambiguity in the UN's attitude toward the use of force against the FDLR: we were endorsing military action to reassert state authority but equally wary about worsening the humanitarian situation. It seemed that we wanted military action, just not too much. On the ground, however, it was not easy to maintain such a tentative stance as we endeavored to mount credible operations against the FDLR.

There was subtext to Ban Ki-moon's visit. Following the Rutshuru debacle, the government turned on the Indian brigade in North Kivu. Foreign Minister Alexis Thambwe Mwamba called for their removal, blaming them for what had happened, conveniently ignoring the collapse of the FARDC. He put his demand in writing to the Secretary-General. The Indians were understandably incensed. Echoing their earlier reaction in Sierra Leone in 2000, they made it clear that they would not stay where they were not wanted. The withdrawal of the Indian contingent would have severely weakened MONUC at the worst of times. I intervened with Thambwe Mwamba and demarches were made, as they say, at the highest level. We were then advised that the Congolese government had reconsidered. I breathed easier until I learned that the Indian government was demanding the Congolese government withdraw its letter to the Secretary-General. I knew that the government would not publicly disavow its own communication. Fortunately, the answer came through my deputy chief of staff, Achi Atsain, a former academic from Côte d'Ivoire who discreetly helped the minister's office draft a text that did not formally withdraw the letter but said that in the light of changed circumstances the letter was no longer applicable.

Soon, Thambwe Mwamba visited India and fences were mended. The formal consecration of the renewed relationship came during Ban Ki-moon's visit. Thambwe Mwamba held a welcome dinner for the Secretary-General at the lakeside base of the Indian brigade in Goma. Toasts were drunk, complimentary words were exchanged, and face was saved all around. Another unnecessary crisis was defused, but the whole episode reinforced my misgivings about our relationship with the Congolese government.

Goma Revisited and a Crisis Postponed

With the integration of the CNDP into the FARDC and the launch of the joint DRC-Rwanda operation, the contours of the Obasanjo/Mkapa mediation changed. The government insisted that the negotiations return to the Congo from Nairobi; Goma was chosen as the venue for the talks, as the CNDP was still nervous about its security in Kinshasa. Second, the focus of the agenda shifted from the principle of integration to the practicalities involved—grades and titles for officers, areas of deployment, and the release of prisoners. A third issue was the registration of the CNDP as a political party and, pending elections, the inclusion of CNDP representatives in the government, and the dismantling of the quasi-administrative structures established in the areas under CNDP control. A final element covered the arrangements for the return of refugees (including Congolese Tutsis who had fled to Rwanda) and IDPs.

I was anxious to ensure that the mission was fully engaged in the Goma discussions, as I expected that MONUC would be called on to help with the implementation of the outcome. Actually, in yet another ironic reversal of political fortunes, the CNDP had taken to asking MONUC for support in the negotiations. I met with the CNDP delegates to urge them to stay the course and give Presidents Obasanjo and Mkapa time to find solutions.

Obasanjo and Mkapa were able to secure an agreement, which was signed on March 23, 2009, in Goma. I attended the signature ceremony, after which President Obasanjo—ever the pragmatist—quietly observed that he gave the agreement about a year.

The agreement was a temporary respite, not a definitive solution to the Tutsi insurgency. Once the immediate crisis was resolved, the government lost interest; despite several interventions on my part, the government only partially honored the commitments made in Goma. This is not to say that the ex-CNDP were faultless. They did not want to give up what they had gained through force of arms, including their control of lucrative road blocks.

As I wrote previously, trust is the key to successful negotiations. In the Kivus there wasn't much to begin with and, as had happened after the earlier Goma agreements signed in 2008, what little that was left slipped away as the months passed. In November 2011, as President Obasanjo foresaw, a new rebellion, led by ex-CNDP elements—dubbed the March 23 Movement (M23) after the date of the Goma accord—broke out.

Endgame: Kimia Redux

The quid pro quo for integration of the CNDP and Rwanda's support for the Goma negotiations conducted by President Obasanjo was a renewed commitment by the DRC to root out the FDLR. Politically, Kabila could not sanction an extension of the joint operation, which had already earned him public and parliamentary opprobrium. But it was evident to the Rwandans (and the Congolese government) that the FARDC could not take on the FDLR unaided. MONUC's star began to rise. Both the Congolese and Rwandan military leadership started to show a renewed interest in working with MONUC.

Obviously, any collaboration with the FARDC involved major risks. So why did I even consider renewing the campaign against the FDLR? An easy answer is that the Security Council had instructed us to do so (with caveats, of course). That is true but does not provide a full or satisfactory answer. There were several reasons why I decided to recommend that we restart the Kimia operation.

First, the FDLR was an armed and violent group that had imposed itself on the local population by force, although in some areas, notably in South Kivu, the FDLR had integrated with the local populace. Nevertheless, the FDLR operated outside any national or local authority and were often in conflict with the local population. They controlled swathes of the countryside and profited from criminal rackets ranging from mineral mining to charcoal trading.

The presence of the FDLR, irrespective of Rwanda's irredentist fears, was fundamentally inimical to the cohesion of the Congolese state and as such had to be dismantled—like any other armed group. Ideally that should have been by negotiation. We encouraged voluntary surrenders and return and even opened a camp for one FDLR faction that we mistakenly believed would surrender. But the hardliners kept control and only when force was threatened or applied did we see a significant increase in the defections. And as I have pointed out, Rwanda would not countenance any direct negotiations with the FDLR.

The second reason, as I noted before, was my conviction that there could be no end to the wars in the Kivus without a rapprochement between the DRC and Rwanda (and also Uganda). This meant that we had to work with both governments to build a better relationship based on mutual security assurances. Kimia II offered that prospect.

A third motive stemmed from MONUC's mandate to assist with security sector reform. From experience, I knew that the FARDC operations usually fell apart due to poor command and control and inadequate logistics. I believed that with MONUC's aid, we could show that at a tactical level reform was possible. Our military staff developed a plan that would provide limited logistical support as well as assistance for training and staff development. As part of the package, we stipulated that the mission's human rights staff would monitor operations closely.

General Gaye and I met with both the political and military leadership in the DRC and Rwanda to lay out our proposals for support. I distinctly recall telling General Etumba, the chief of defense staff, that MONUC's support for Kimia II was not a blank check. I insisted that we would keep a close eye on the operations and pull the plug if necessary.

The proposed support for Kimia II raised deep concern within and outside the mission. Some of my senior colleagues warned of the potential reputational damage of cooperating with the FARDC on operations that could have a harmful humanitarian impact, especially the deployment of former CNDP combatants into areas with Hutu populations. The Secretary-General also warned the Security Council that the "use of force is not without risk to peacekeepers or to civilians: it is critical to recognize the threat of retaliation against civilians by the FDLR and other armed groups despite the best efforts of MONUC."[20]

These were legitimate worries. But it was clear to me that the FARDC would be deployed against the FDLR with or without MONUC support. This was the price Kabila had to pay to end the CNDP rebellion. So a familiar dilemma reappeared: Should we try to achieve an outcome for which we had no certainty of success?

There was a balance of risk. But I recommended to headquarters that we go forward with Kimia II. I argued that we could we not stand idly by and let the FARDC flounder with the concomitant dangers to civilians who would then be at the mercy of the Congolese army as well as the FDLR.

The plan of operation for Kimia II aimed to exert pressure in three separate triangular zones (identified by the JMAC team) that were dominated by the FDLR. MONUC would then backfill the areas with civilian teams and facilitate the deployment of police and government officials as part of the stabilization program for eastern Congo.

The behavior of the FARDC, predictably, was a constant worry. We stipulated, therefore, that we would provide support only to those FARDC troops directly involved in the Kimia operations that we could monitor. In our negotiations with the government and the FARDC, both General Gaye and I insisted on the capital importance of protecting civilians. If the FARDC did not do that, we argued, the campaign was lost before it began.

A Shot in the Dark

The DRC lacked many things but not high-level visitors. In May 2009 a Security Council delegation led by Jean Maurice Ripert, the French permanent representative to the UN in New York, arrived in the DRC. The delegation included Susan Rice, later the US national security adviser, and John Sawers, subsequently the head of the UK's foreign intelligence service (MI6). The South African and Ugandan ambassadors to the UN were also on the delegation. So it was top-level delegation, indicative of the significance of the DRC and MONUC to the UN's peacekeeping agenda.

In its subsequent report on the visit, the Council delegation alluded to the contradiction inherent in MONUC's mandate. While reiterating its support for action against the FDLR, it observed that "at times competing imperatives of protecting civilians and supporting FARDC-led military operations . . . had inevitable humanitarian consequences."[21]

A more positive note, however, came with the president's announcement during the visit of the renewal of diplomatic ties with Rwanda (ruptured since 1994) and the accreditation of ambassadors. The Council delegation was quite fulsome in its praise of this improvement in regional relations, even though the price of that progress was the FDLR campaign.

Overall, the Council visit went well. If there wasn't exactly a meeting of minds, there was no rupture either. For a SRSG, the visit of a Security Council delegation can be an uncertain prospect. So I was reasonably pleased with the visit as we sat on a MONUC aircraft, ready to leave Goma on the way to the Council's next stop—Kigali. Then things literally backfired.

Just before takeoff, with all the delegation aboard, one of my close-protection team accidentally discharged his handgun—three feet from where I was sitting. The weapon should have been inspected and cleared outside of the aircraft but the procedure was not followed. No one was injured but the bullet did penetrate the floor of the aircraft and the crew rightly refused to take off until a full inspection was conducted. We all disembarked.

If you run a UN peacekeeping mission, the last thing you need is a planeload of Security Council ambassadors waiting impatiently on a hot runway. There was no substitute aircraft immediately available and the delegation was on a tight schedule with appointments lined up in Rwanda and beyond. The only solution at hand was to drive the delegation to Kigali in a bus, a tortuous four- or five-hour ride over mountain roads. This was the stuff of bureaucratic bad dreams. Late in evening the delegation finally left for Kigali in a remarkably cheerful frame of mind (someone on the bus had started singing). I stayed at the border post, mortified.

Madame Secretary

In August 2009 not long after the Security Council's visit, another high-level visitor came calling—the US secretary of state, Hillary Clinton. In the aftermath of the genocide, the United States had been a largely uncritical supporter of the Rwandan government. That stance began to change in October 2008, consequent on the CNDP offensive. The United States (and others like the UK and the Netherlands) pressed President Kagame to rein in Nkunda, by then perceived as an alarming threat to stability in the Great Lakes region. Nevertheless, the United States remained committed to dismantling the FDLR even though a number of US-based human rights and humanitarian organizations were becoming ever more critical of the Kimia operation.

US secretaries of state are not often seen in Africa. This visit occurred only eight months after President Obama's inauguration, which was an encouraging sign. Secretary Clinton was accompanied by a strong team that included the very experienced assistant secretary of state for Africa, Johnnie Carson, and the newly appointed US special envoy for the Great Lakes, former congressman Howard Wolpe.

Despite the brevity of her visit to the DRC, Secretary Clinton still wanted to visit Goma. There was only one problem: her US Air Force plane could not land safely on Goma's truncated runway. I offered a MONUC aircraft as an alternative. I was of course extremely anxious to ensure that there would be no repeat of our Goma fiasco with the Security Council delegation. The US security team, which included an explosive-sniffing dog, gave the aircraft a very thorough inspection.

Together with General Gaye and the head of the Conduct and Discipline Unit, Yewande Odia (I expected questions about sexual abuse), I accompanied the secretary to Goma. As we flew across the Congo (the flight from Kinshasa to Goma takes about two and a half hours) we conducted an onboard briefing. I reviewed the multiple security challenges that MONUC was facing. We outlined the numerous initiatives we were undertaking on protection. Clinton was well informed and realistic. She seemed to recognize better than most the constraints and competing demands that we had to handle.

During her day in Goma, she fitted in a stop at a MONUC base and met with military and civilian staff. It was a cordial encounter and she graciously thanked everyone for their work and commitment. After all the criticism that the mission had endured over the previous few months, the visit of the US secretary of state to a MONUC facility was taken—at least by me and the staff—as a sign of confidence.

Later in the day the secretary made a visit to the HEAL Africa hospital, where she met survivors of sexual assaults. She was visibly moved by her visit to the hospital. Like others who have listened to the stories of the women and girls who have suffered from horrendous cruelty and injury, she spoke with emotion, pledging US material and moral support to end the scourge of sexual violence.

After the visit, Clinton addressed a meeting of civil society organizations and NGOs; she asked the audience to share their thoughts or to ask any questions. I anticipated that the secretary would hear a litany of complaints about MONUC, including our apparent failure to stop the epidemic of sexual violence. I was not far off in my assumption. There was indeed severe criticism, including from one speaker who held MONUC responsible for, among other failings, spiraling rents and food prices in Goma.

I was sitting in the front row of the audience, so I was literally on-the-spot. However, I was relieved and somewhat surprised—politicians often like to grandstand on such occasions—when Secretary Clinton did not join in the MONUC bashing. Not only did she not join the chorus, but she also refuted the notion that somehow MONUC was responsible for all the ills besetting the Kivus. That responsibility, she said very plainly, lay first and foremost with the government and people of the DRC. For once, I thought, someone gets it.

A Crisis of Confidence: The Lukweti Massacres

The note of confidence in the mission sounded by Secretary Clinton did not last long. The operations against the FDLR continued to create dissension within and outside the mission. The Secretary-General's policy committee instructed us to develop a comprehensive strategy on the FDLR. The strategy recognized the weaknesses of the FARDC and the dangers for the mission in providing assistance to the army. We made proposals to improve the performance and discipline of the FARDC in forward areas and developed a policy conditioning MONUC's aid to the FARDC.

My chief of staff, Bert Coppens, who kept me quietly advised of internal frictions during times of crisis, alerted me that Kimia was putting me at odds with some senior MONUC colleagues as well as the UN's humanitarian and human rights offices. Indeed, I was told in so many words by one colleague from the mission human rights team that I was delusional if I thought that the FARDC could become a worthwhile partner. The strategic goal of building a better relationship between the DRC and Rwanda was not considered worth the humanitarian consequences of the campaign, notwithstanding the Security Council's endorsement of that strategy.

As the operations against the FDLR went forward, the criticism of MONUC grew louder. The UN special rapporteur on extrajudicial killings denounced Kimia in very strong terms, stating that it had produced "catastrophic results."[22] At one point, a press release from Human Rights Watch suggested that MONUC might be implicated in "grave abuses" because of its assistance to the FARDC.[23] There were renewed allegations that Bosco was running the FARDC side of the Kimia operations.

At the end of October 2009, Alain Le Roy returned to the DRC. He came to assess the Kimia operation and also to review the future of MONUC. Some grim news awaited his arrival. An investigation carried out by the mission had confirmed that elements of the FARDC's 213th Brigade had been implicated in killings in the area of Lukweti in North Kivu. This information was circulating among human rights groups, including Human Rights Watch, which we expected would soon publish a report on its findings.

We decided that MONUC should invoke the suspension of aid, as we had warned would be the case if units were involved in serious human rights violations. Pending further investigation, we agreed that the suspension would initially apply to the unit of the 213th Brigade directly implicated in the atrocity. The following morning Le Roy made a public announcement to that effect.

I knew that this news would not please the government, so I wanted the president to be informed before the announcement was made. Unfortunately, my messages did not get through to him (although we did speak to both the minister of defense and the chief of the defense staff) and perhaps I should have advised Le Roy to await confirmation before we went public.

While the announcement was welcomed in UN circles and the international community, the president was highly displeased. He complained that he should have been informed before the announcement was made, even though that courtesy had not always been extended to the mission before the government took actions of direct concern to MONUC. Le Roy was willing to accept responsibility and explain to the president why we had to make the announcement so precipitously. He never got the chance to do so; the president peremptorily canceled a planned meeting with him.

At a meeting of the Security Council in October, I had defended Kimia II and urged the Council to continue its support. However, after the Lukweti events, and in the absence of a dialogue with the president, Le Roy and I concluded that MONUC would not be able to sustain support for the operation without some changes. With General Gaye and his newly arrived deputy (former UNAMSIL colleague Adrian Foster), we agreed that Kimia

should be reshaped; the FARDC and MONUC should instead focus on reinforcing protection in the strategic areas that had been cleared of the FDLR.

Fallout: Kimia to Amani Leo

In mid-December 2009, I spoke again at the Security Council and informed
the Council that Kimia II would be completed at the end of the year. I then
announced a new operation, Amani Leo,[24] which would concentrate on
holding ground recovered from the FDLR during the Kimia operations and
preventing attacks on civilians in areas of vulnerability, while undertaking
targeted interventions against any centers of command and control where
the FDLR might have regrouped. But I added that the menace of the FDLR
could be ended only by a combination of measures, including, most importantly, improved FARDC performance, which would be monitored through
our conditionality policy.

My statement did not sit well with the government. In late December,
the DRC ambassador in New York, Atoki Ileka, made a strong statement
to the Council, referring to the "bitter criticism of the FARDC" and that
"instead of following these doomsayers, the United Nations should be
driven by a desire to succeed, if only this once, where it sadly failed
almost half a century ago, allowing the country to fall into unspeakable
chaos."[25] No doubt the ambassador echoed sentiments emanating from the
presidency in Kinshasa.

I left the DRC several months after Amani Leo was launched. During
that period the overall security situation in North Kivu began to slowly
improve, signaled by the return of a large number of IDPs, the start of an
economic revival, and the reopening of the Congolese and Rwandan
embassies in Kinshasa and Kigali. Nevertheless, MONUC's operations in
the Kivus remained highly controversial. During my tenure as the SRSG, I
struggled to manage the competing demands of the mandate, which
enjoined us to protect civilians, uphold human rights, dismantle armed
groups, pursue security sector reform, promote peace, and encourage political dialogue and reconciliation. It was a frustrating experience and, to be
frank, I was not able to build a solid consensus within and beyond the mission on how best to resolve those contradictions.

The conflicts in the Kivus sapped our military capacities and con-
sumed our political capital, caught as we were in the entangling contradictions of the mission's mandate. Regrettably, however, the Kivu provinces
were by no means the only place in the DRC where we became enmeshed
in such ambiguities. In the next chapter, I detail some other major episodes
of armed violence and the acute challenges MONUC faced in implementing its mandate of civilian protection in the conflicting cross-currents of
the Congolese polity.

7

The Contagion of Conflict: Other Places, Other Wars

For violent fires soon burn out themselves; Small show'rs last long, but sudden storms are short.
—William Shakespeare, *Richard II*

Smart phones came of age during my decade in peacekeeping. The FARDC even went to war using mobile phones (the CNDP tried to blow up cell towers to block the signals). I received military flash reports on serious incidents via my mobile, which was programmed to receive text messages with a special alert sound. I came to truly dread that sound. It always meant trouble—caused by humans or nature—and yet another crisis to which MONUC would be expected to respond. The conflicts in the Kivus presented the most important challenge to MONUC, but they were by no means the only ones. Other outbursts of violence from an assortment of armed groups strewn around the country created numerous demands for MONUC engagement, signaled by the ominous beep from my mobile phone.

I cannot cover all of these episodes; I recount instead three outbreaks of violence that were emblematic of the recurring crises that periodically exploded in the Congo: the Bundu dia Kongo revolt in Bas Congo; the depredations of the Lord's Resistance Army in Orientale province; and the Enyele uprising in Equateur province.

These conflicts were all different in their origins and yet they were all similar because they reflected the perennial failure of the state and its security institutions to anticipate, prevent, or resolve violent conflict. In that sense, conflict was contagious in the DRC. There was never enough time, resources, or political commitment to either head off or fully resolve these crises; instead they festered, sapping the strength of the state and making it vulnerable to new waves of violence that required MONUC's intervention.

199

Kingdom of the Kongo

The crisis in Bas Congo centered around the Bundu dia Kongo (BDK) (whose name literally translated means "union with the lord Akongo"),[1] a political-spiritual movement or sect preaching an irredentist agenda. Led by a charismatic figure named Ne Muanda Nsemi, the sect seeks the return of the Kingdom of the Kongo. In precolonial times, the kingdom extended north and south of the mouth of the Congo River into what today are Angola and Congo-Brazzaville. As Daron Acemoglu and James Robinson point out in their book *How Nations Fail*,[2] the Kingdom of the Kongo became a huge commercial partner of Western Europe (starting with Portugal), exporting slaves and importing firearms.

In 2007, violent confrontations erupted over the outcome of elections for the province's governorship, which the Bundu dia Kongo and others believed were rigged. Civilians and police were killed. JMAC alerted me to the possibility of more trouble in Bas Congo on the occasion of the first anniversary of the 2007 incidents. The BDK had a "record of threatening and attacking public officials, staging violent demonstrations and taking other provocative actions,"[3] including threats and attacks on Christian churches and priests.

I agreed that we should deploy some troops from MONUC's Western Brigade just in case there was violence. I informed the government that we planned to move troops down to Matadi, the provincial capital of Bas Congo. Almost immediately I got a call from the president's national security adviser, who told me that the president was not happy about the deployment, which implied that the government had lost control of the situation. I was actually about to leave for Goma for the peace conference and agreed that the troops could stay in Kinshasa if there was no need for them. That was a mistake.

Returning from Goma, I traveled to Bas Congo in February 2008 to meet with local officials and civil society. I urged the authorities and the BDK to exercise restraint and work toward a peaceful resolution of the situation. I was talking to the wind.

Late in February, the government launched operations to restore, it claimed, state authority. Violence exploded as cordon-and-search operations were carried out by a special police unit (the Rapid Intervention Police [PIR]), including the so-called Simba (Lion) Battalion. Several BDK "temples" in Matadi were burned down and BDK leaders were arrested. Reports reached us of police brutality. At the beginning of March, we dispatched a MONUC formed police unit together with an infantry company and several teams of military observers to assess the situation and to protect civilians. We also offered to carry out joint patrols with the police to ease tensions, but it was too late; the damage had been done.

Owing to the allegations of torture and summary executions, MONUC's human rights office insisted, and I agreed, that we should conduct an investigation, which began in mid-March. The report of the investigation was published in May and confirmed that the police, and in particular the Simba Battalion, had responded with disproportionate force, killing over a hundred BDK members and then dumping bodies in mass graves and in rivers. I sent the report to the government, demanding that a full judicial inquiry be authorized as a prelude to prosecution.

I was assured by the minister of the interior, Dennis Kalume, that action would follow. As far as I know, none did. The BDK was banned but survives to this day despite several government crackdowns and the arrest of BDK leaders; it remains a violent and disruptive element in Bas Congo that is unlikely to be dismantled or neutralized by force alone. But as I found out on other occasions, the first instinct of the government was to react with force rather than to seek a political solution. This reaction stemmed in part from the conviction that the Congo was threatened by secessionist ambitions that had to be crushed before they got out of hand, even though such heavy-handed interventions frequently made matters worse.

Thunder and Lightning: Resisting the Lord's Army

On the other side of the DRC, another violent group with mystical pretension posed an even more violent threat than the BDK. This threat, however, was the product of another country's wars. The Lord's Resistance Army originated in northwestern Uganda among the Acholi people in response to the violence that devastated that region during civil war in Uganda.

In a long and bloody campaign, Ugandan president Yoweri Museveni had gradually pushed the LRA out of the country, dispersing them into the undergoverned spaces of northeast Congo, neighboring South Sudan and eventually the Central African Republic. By the time I got to the DRC, the LRA had established a rear base in the remote Garamba national park in Orientale province.

The LRA, led by the infamous Joseph Kony, employed brutal tactics not unlike those used by the RUF in Sierra Leone. Like the RUF, the LRA was able to survive without the elaborate logistics of modern armies; fear was its most potent weapon. And again, like the RUF, the LRA received support from a neighboring country, in this case Sudan, which was fighting an insurgency in South Sudan aided by Uganda.[4]

Talks between Kony and the Ugandan government dragged on for several years. During the negotiations, the LRA received food aid with the aim of keeping Kony at the negotiating table and to forestall further atrocities by LRA combatants raiding for supplies. MONUC was instructed to keep its distance from the LRA to avoid upsetting the negotiations. I was even told not to encourage any defections for the same reason. Nevertheless, after several ceasefires and on-and-off negotiations, the talks finally collapsed in November 2008 when Kony refused to sign the final peace deal.

The number of LRA fighters in the DRC was quite small—estimated anywhere between 250 and 1,000.[5] However, they could move surprisingly fast by foot over long distances. In response to attacks on civilians, the FARDC launched a small defensive exercise code-named Operation Rudia.[6] The operation was headquartered in the town of Dungu, once a thriving commercial center with a Greek community that ran agricultural estates in the Haut Ulélé region before Zaireanization. Rudia, which involved about 3,000 Congolese troops, was meant to function like a protection force, but it suffered from all the usual logistical and disciplinary failings associated with FARDC operations.

Earlier in the year, I was in Washington D.C., and met with officials at the US National Security Council to confer on the situation in the DRC. The LRA was on the agenda and my interlocutors pressed me to go after the LRA and to target Kony. I explained that MONUC had only a very small detachment in the area and I doubted that we could easily find him in such a vast region. I was then informed that the United States had information on Kony's whereabouts. However, when I asked if I could see it, I was told that would not be possible, as the information was classified and could be shared only with governments with which the United States had security cooperation agreements. The UN did not qualify for that select company.

From that visit, I gathered that the demise of the LRA was a high US priority. But it was some weeks before I understood to what lengths the US government would go to dismantle the LRA during the waning days of the George W. Bush administration.

On my way back to Kinshasa from a meeting in Kigali in early December 2008, I planned to visit Dungu, the jumping-off point for operations against the LRA. A senior member of the US delegation attending the Kigali talks asked if he could join me, as he had never been to that area before. I agreed. We spent the day in Dungu talking to the MONUC battalion, the FARDC command, and local authorities before heading back to Kinshasa.

My traveling companion from the State Department thanked me for the opportunity to visit Dungu. Two days later I found out why he had been so keen to do so.

On December 14, I awoke to learn that at first light (in eastern Congo, one hour ahead of Kinshasa), Ugandan fighter bombers had hit the LRA camps in the Garamba. That action had been followed by helicopter attacks, and a joint DRC-Uganda task force was launched to track down the survivors of the aerial bombardment. There was only one problem—the bombers missed their targets. Alerted by the sound of the planes, the LRA combatants and civilians alike had fled the camps into the bush. The mission planners, I was told later, had not counted on the early-morning ground mist, and the pilots could not make proper visual identification of the targets.

I cannot be sure whether that account of the bombing mission is accurate. What was obviously true, however, was that MONUC had again not been informed of a major military operation by a government that had asked for UN assistance in dealing with the LRA. Later I learned that the operation—Lightning Thunder—had been planned by the US Africa Command in cooperation with the Ugandan and Congolese governments. The latter had given its assent to the operations even though its operational involvement in the strike was minimal. In light of what was to come, it was probably providential that MONUC had not been associated with the operations.

The DRC and Ugandan governments trumpeted the operation as a victory. But within days, intelligence sources as well as JMAC suggested that the raid was not as successful as initially claimed. There were causalities but the majority of the LRA fighters got away, dispersed into smaller groups, and fled west away from the Garamba.

In what came to be known as the Christmas Massacre, bands of the dispersed LRA inflicted a terrible toll on local people as they moved westward across Orientale province, abducting children and raiding villages as they foraged for food. Hundreds of people were killed or injured in a horrendous campaign of brutality. The FARDC could not stop these atrocities. Although there were skirmishes and some LRA losses, the Congolese army didn't possess the air or land mobility, command skills, and tactical intelligence to mount an effective campaign of interdiction.

Even though we were not consulted or involved in the planning or execution of Lightning Thunder, it did not take long before MONUC was taken to task. Humanitarian NGOs (notably Médecins Sans Frontières [Doctors Without Borders]) claimed that we had failed in our duty to protect civilians as MONUC's mandate stipulated. Other agencies (Human Rights Watch in particular) did recognize, however, that the mission was far too stretched to provide effective, large-scale protection against the LRA.

The campaign was carried out on Congolese territory by Ugandan special forces with support (and intelligence) from the United States. But it was not an open-ended commitment from the Congolese side. President Kabila was nervous about leaving Ugandan forces on Congolese territory for too long. Memories of Uganda's intervention in the Congolese war were still fresh.

The Ugandans scaled down their presence but left "intelligence squads" in place. In a rerun of the post–Umoja Wetu demarche, the government requested MONUC's support for a new operation—Rudia II—to help keep up the pressure on the LRA after the departure of the Ugandan forces. But as with Kimia II, we faced the familiar risks involved in working with the FARDC. But the LRA campaign showed that not all violence in the DRC elicited the same response from the international community.

First, unlike the campaign against the FDLR, there was no significant opposition in humanitarian circles to MONUC deploying with the FARDC against the LRA. If anything, we heard calls for a more active and robust MONUC intervention. There were (justified) complaints about the FARDC, but not to the point that MONUC was accused of risking complicity in war crimes.

Second, there were no calls for any political dialogue with the LRA. Following the collapse of the Juba talks and the Christmas Massacre, the LRA was considered beyond the pale and ineligible for dialogue.

Third, the LRA posed an operational challenge, which was essentially tactical rather than strategic. The number of LRA combatants was much smaller than the number of FDLR combatants, but the former were widely dispersed and engaged in hit-and-run operations (deadly ones) rather than trying to defend territorial gains. And unlike the FDLR, they were not embedded in the Congolese population, nor did LRA fighters run commercial rackets in connivance with local chiefs or military authorities. From my contacts with the Ugandan government and military, I gathered that as long as the LRA stayed well away from the border, they were not unduly fussed by its presence in the DRC. They seemed much more concerned by the Allied Democratic Forces–National Army for the Liberation of Uganda (ADF-NALU) group camped out in North Kivu close to the Ugandan border.

While I worried about a diversion of our scarce resources from the Kivus to an LRA campaign, I agreed that we should support Rudia II, essentially for humanitarian reasons. Unlike either the CNDP or the FDLR, the LRA did not pose a significant threat to the territorial integrity of the Congo. But the fear of the LRA was having a drastic effect on the population in Haut Uélé. The LRA attacks kept communities away from their fields and interrupted the usual flow of commerce. Moreover, once it was known that local communities were receiving food aid, they became more vulnerable to LRA attacks. So we needed not only to escort food aid convoys but also to assist with continuing protection.

Obviously, MONUC did not have the capacity to provide such a level of coverage. The FARDC was indispensable to this effort and we agreed to provide limited supplies and transportation to keep them in the field and to avert delinquency. Even this modest aid to the FARDC was a worry. Reports started to reach us of FARDC abuses. General Gaye and I had warned the FARDC command and the Ministry of Defense that we would repeat the sanctions we applied to the 213th Battalion after the Lukweti atrocity if similar incidents happened in Rudia. Upfront we decided to stop MONUC support for the battalion involved. Unlike the reaction when we suspended aid to the 213th Battalion, there was no pushback from the government side; the battalion was replaced.

Over the following months the LRA attacks declined. I am not sure whether this was the result of successful interdiction by the FARDC and

Ugandan forces or possibly the movement of the LRA to the Central African Republic. Either way, Uganda quietly maintained forces in the DRC. Nevertheless, a decade later the Secretary-General is still sending reports of LRA atrocities in the DRC to the Security Council. At the time of writing, the whereabouts of Joseph Kony still remain a mystery.

The Fishpond War

While we struggled to bring the long-running conflict in the Kivus to an end and contain the LRA, other flare-up crises seemed to come out of nowhere. One erupted in late October 2009 in a remote part of Equateur Province in northwestern Congo, triggered by a communal dispute over the control of fish ponds. The dispute between the two villages—Enyele and Monzaya—quickly escalated into a violent confrontation even though the villagers were all from the same ethnic group. By early November 2009 at least 16,000 civilians had fled across the Congo River to neighboring Congo-Brazzaville. Forty-seven police members of the notorious Police d'Intervention (the unit that had intervened against the BDK in Bas Congo) were massacred as they moved into the area.

The rebellion, led by yet another charismatic figure claiming spiritual powers, spread rapidly, threatening to engulf a good part of Equateur. This was a war fought by the poor against the poor. International attention and aid were largely focused on the east of the country, even though areas such as the one where the Enyele uprising broke out were just as deprived and desperate.

As the uprising mushroomed, there were fears that ex-combatants from the former Mobutu forces might join in (Equateur was the home province of Mobutu); in the 2006 elections, the province had voted overwhelming for Jean Pierre Bemba, the opposition leader, whose family also hailed from Equateur. It was the only province with a governor who was not a member of the presidential majority coalition.

As the situation worsened and the violence spread, John Numbi contacted me with an urgent request for assistance. He needed to move reinforcements quickly into the province and wanted MONUC air transport to do so. We responded that while we were very concerned about the growing impact of the uprising, we could not provide any support if it involved the Simba Battalion or any other units involved in the Bas Congo operations. I was mindful of Numbi's support for MONUC at a critical moment in November 2008, but I agreed with the DSRSG, Leila Zerrougui, and Todd Howland, head of the human rights team, that our support should be strictly conditioned and closely monitored by a MONUC human rights team. Numbi agreed.

MONUC airlifted additional FARDC reinforcements into the area, together with elements of the MONUC rapid-reaction force, which had been established as part of the MONUC reinforcement package approved in late 2008 in the wake of the CNDP crisis. This was not as straightforward as we had thought. The force commander had to strong-arm the Egyptian contingent, the mainstay of the newly created rapid-reaction force, to agree to the movement of forces; they had assumed (wrongly) that their area of responsibility was only in eastern DRC. In fact, due to earlier difficulties with the movement of troops between areas of responsibility, we had insisted that the agreement should specify that the rapid-reaction force could be deployed country-wide.

With this extra support, the crisis was brought under control. For once, the FARDC units (two battalions trained respectively by Belgium and South Africa) performed and behaved reasonably well. Later the Belgian ambassador, Dominique Struye de Swielande, admitted to me that it had been a nervous time for the Belgian embassy. If the Belgian-trained battalion had committed atrocities or crumbled, there would have been major political repercussions back home.

Our human rights team reported some violations but not on the scale of what we had seen in other FARDC operations (of course, that was of no comfort to those people who had suffered abuse). Both battalions had been deployed, for once, with proper logistics, including rations (supplied by Belgium and South Africa). By February 2009 the rebellion was receding. There were still some isolated incidents, but it looked as if we could begin to pull back some of the MONUC forces.

Barely a month later, at the beginning of April, there was a serious setback. A group of about a hundred armed Enyele attacked Mbandaka, the provincial capital, including the governor's residence and the airport. The group had come down the Congo River undetected by the Congolese riverine units that were supposedly guarding the waterways. This was an audacious attack, made possible by the insurgents' intimate knowledge of the river and its multiple meanderings. A United Nations peacekeeper and two civilian contractors associated with MONUC were killed during the attack. But the airport was retaken in a joint operation mounted by FARDC and MONUC units.

I flew up to Mbandaka to get a better idea of what had happened and to meet with MONUC and UN staff and troops. The civilian staff was pretty shaken up. Mbandaka, once a prosperous river town, had been decaying for decades as the river traffic declined due to insecurity and poor maintenance of the navigation channels. But apart from the day when Bemba had been arrested by the ICC, life in Mbandaka had been relatively secure (although rather monotonous).

Back in Kinshasa, the blame game began. The government spokesman, Lambert Mende Omalanga, always quick to disparage MONUC, accused the UN troops in Mbandaka of a dereliction of duty. I declared that we would conduct an investigation and publish the results, which we did. General Foster conducted the investigation and found that troops were on guard, including at the landing where the Enyele had come ashore. The soldiers on duty had sounded the alarm, but they had not fired on the insurgents, who were in the middle of a crowd of civilians, including children. But it was true that some of the MONUC troops were absent. It was Easter Sunday, and in the absence of a high alert level, the Christian soldiers had received permission to attend church services.

After the Mbandaka attack, the rebellion faded and the leaders fled across the river into Congo-Brazzaville and surrendered. The fatalities in Mbandaka were the only ones suffered by MONUC as a result of hostile action during my time in the mission. Illness and accidents were far more lethal. But there could have been many more during the Enyele uprising, save for an extraordinary display of courage and skill by a Russian helicopter crew.

The crew flew into Dongo (the main town in the area) to resupply UN military observers who were there reporting on the situation. On landing, the helicopter was attacked and members of the crew were hit by gunfire. They managed, nevertheless, to evacuate wounded MONUC soldiers guarding the helipad, together with the civilian and military personnel already on board. The rotors and fuel tank were damaged by the gunfire but somehow the pilots still took off and flew everybody to safety in Congo-Brazzaville some 130 kilometers away on the other side of the Congo River.

The helicopter crew was not from the military, so no medals could be conferred. But we arranged an award ceremony and I presented the crew members with special certificates of commendation. During that ceremony I was impressed by how self-effacing the crew looked and behaved, confirming that heroes are not necessarily the most demonstrative or assertive of people.

The Limits of Protection

The contagion of conflict in the Kivus and elsewhere took an immense toll on the Congolese population. As a result, the Security Council progressively strengthened MONUC's protection mandate, eventually making protection MONUC's top priority.[7] This proactive stance on civilian protection was also reflected in the rules of engagement for MONUC's forces, which gave them authority to intervene with force to protect civilians.

These stipulations created an expectation of protection that MONUC struggled to meet. However, we never presented to the Council—at least not during my time as the SRSG—a candid estimate of the troop numbers required to provide a satisfactory level of protection in the Congo. We focused instead on improving tactical interventions. If we had run the numbers, I suspect that we would have been dismissed as fantasists. I roughly estimate that to provide effective protection in the most vulnerable areas of the DRC, with reasonable ratios of troops to vulnerable population, and some mobile reserve capacity, we would have required about 60,000 troops, plus all the usual equipment and air support. This would have meant an annual budget of $4–5 billion. There was never any realistic hope of getting to a UN operation of that scale. But this did not alter the perception that MONUC was failing in its mandated duty to protect civilians, especially women and girls, who were the most at risk.

I came to realize, rather belatedly I admit, that MONUC was not well organized structurally to deal with the complex challenge of protection in the DRC. We needed a stronger focus on protection from a broader, whole-of-mission perspective that went beyond the military dimension. To rectify that failing, I put in place two institutional innovations.

The first was to create a senior staff group specifically dedicated to the management of protection. I invited UN agencies outside of the mission to join the group, including the UNHCR and OCHA. I encouraged the group to anticipate and plan for protection. JMAC was tasked to undertake conflict mapping to identify the zones where conflict was most likely to break out and where civilians would be most at risk. Interestingly, we found that the control of key roads (and the money that could be made from them) was often the source of violence among and between communities; so too, and more obviously, was access and control of mining sites and land for grazing cattle.

In areas that were identified as high risk from a protection perspective, we deployed joint protection teams made up of military and civilian staff, sometimes with UN agency participation. The purpose of these teams was to develop better intelligence and understanding of the threats posed by belligerent groups. I asked all mission staff members if they would like to join one or the other of these deployments. Many agreed to do so. I was especially encouraged by younger staff members, who not only joined the teams (which often worked in very remote and potentially dangerous areas) but also contributed many good ideas for how we could improve our protection work.

A number of other operational innovations were adopted. MONUC market patrols were set up to escort village women to local markets. As a way of encouraging more direct contact between peacekeepers and people, mobile patrols were told to dismount and walk through villages rather than to drive through them. Help lines were set up to improve communications with MONUC forward bases. Liaison officers who spoke the local language (and not only French or Swahili) were recruited to develop better interactions with communities.

The second initiative was an integrated protection strategy. An interagency committee chaired by the UNHCR developed the initial draft of the strategy. I agreed that MONUC should adopt this strategy but also adjust it so that the burden of protection was more evenly and realistically shared. I wanted to make the point that MONUC alone could not ensure the protection of civilians. A range of complementary measures had to be put in place to make protection a national and not just a UN priority. Above all, the judicial system urgently needed to be strengthened and expanded. Calls for ending impunity rang hollow in the absence of functioning courts, independent prosecutors, and a proper penal system.

Military justice in the DRC—or rather the lack of it—mirrored the weaknesses of civilian justice. I was pleased, therefore, that the mission's rule-of-law and human rights teams did not stop at simply reporting on the failings but also looked for solutions. These included assistance for the training and deployment of military prosecutors. I endorsed their request that MONUC provide fuel so that the prosecutors could get out in the field to investigate cases (another example of why, occasionally, we needed to bend UN rules in the broader interest of the mission's mandate). But with close to 50,000 FARDC soldiers stationed in eastern Congo, this was a colossal task, complicated by the absence of any military prisons where offenders could be held.

Looking back, I question whether I spent enough time and energy seeking out and pushing for political ideas and solutions to the protection crisis. It was the failure to protect that got all the attention. When I met with Security Council members, we would usually focus on the immediate symptoms of the protection crisis and what operational measures MONUC might take to prevent or respond more effectively to protection needs. This demand for more protection was amplified by the media and international campaign groups as well as local civil society organizations. Every critical article in a major newspaper or adverse comment produced a fresh round of soul-searching. But we did not act on the deeper roots of the protection crisis. To quote Mats Berdal, a perceptive and articulate academic observer of peacekeeping, "UN field operations have become increasingly divorced from the central enterprise of mediating and reaching political settlements to conflicts."[8]

Rape Capital: Battling Sexual Violence

While our duty of protection applied to the population at large, the epidemic of sexual violence attracted particular attention from the international media and human rights activists. Nicholas Kristof of the *New York Times* dubbed the DRC "the world capital of rape" (among other atrocities).[9]

Sexual violence in the Congo eclipsed even the horrors that had been inflicted on the women and girls of Sierra Leone and Liberia. So shortly after my arrival in the DRC, I went to Panzi hospital in Bukavu to meet with Denis Mukwege, the renowned Congolese surgeon who treats survivors of sexual violence who have suffered appalling injuries. He has since won the Nobel Peace Prize for his truly heroic work. He introduced me (with their permission) to some of his patients. The stories I heard from his patients mirrored those that I had heard in Sierra Leone and Liberia. The women I met recollected with quiet, dispassionate dignity what happened to them (and the social rejection they experienced as a result).

I always left such encounters feeling angry and also exasperated. Victims and activists alike frequently called on MONUC to help put an end to sexual violence, but we could not hope to do so without curtailing the depredations of the armed groups. And that was not feasible without engaging with the FARDC, even though that engagement carried enormous risks.

We had already been warned by Human Rights Watch of possible charges of complicity should the mission have advance knowledge that a FARDC unit would commit crimes under international humanitarian law or even that a unit was likely to commit such crimes. This stipulation worried me greatly. As I subsequently said to the Security Council in a closed session, the mission could not always be absolutely sure that a unit would behave properly, even if the commanders and troops had no previous record of misconduct. Short of stopping all assistance to the FARDC (which clearly some activists wanted), we could not guarantee FARDC's absolute compliance with the terms of the conditionality policy that we had developed (and already applied after the Lukweti massacre). All we could do was assess the preponderance of risk.

To ensure that the mission was not caught up in allegations of complicity, we progressively tightened up the policy. This included compiling a list of FARDC commanders with whom the mission would not work. Any unit commanded by one of the individuals on the list would not receive MONUC support. I personally handed the list to the minister of defense; General Gaye did the same with the chief of the defense staff.

To make the policy more palatable, however, we framed it as a support for the implementation of President Kabila's own publicly declared policy of zero tolerance for sexual abuse. Despite this proviso, the government accepted the policy grudgingly. In reality, the conditionality policy was a palliative of limited value; it protected MONUC not the population. That goal required the implementation of a coherent strategy to put the armed groups out of business and the FARDC in barracks. We had neither the mandate nor the means to achieve that goal.

Walking the Talk

Of course, MONUC needed to lead by its own example and demonstrate that it "walked the talk" on sexual violence and misconduct. For a peacekeeping operation, sexual exploitation and abuse is akin to a gangrenous wound—left to fester, it becomes fatal. So as I had done in Liberia, I set up a monitoring committee with the assistance of MONUC's conduct and discipline unit, headed by Yewande Odia, a no-nonsense British lawyer. We invited outside participation in the committee and decided to put case-load information in the public domain. I reasoned that the regular dissemination of information would help deflate claims that the mission was indifferent to or unaware of the scale of the problem. At the same time, I commissioned an independent assessment of the effectiveness of our efforts as a mission to prevent and deal with sexual exploitation and abuse and also posted the report online for public reference.

With military and civilian staff spread out over dozens of locations, many of them isolated, we had to find ways to ensure that we found out about cases quickly. To do so, we began to track the behavior of units that we thought posed a particular risk. We also pushed for more pre-deployment training so that incoming units knew that the UN had its own definitions and rules on sexual exploitation and abuse, which may not have applied in their home countries.

During my tenure as the SRSG, the number of reported cases of sexual exploitation and abuse involving MONUC personnel dropped year after year (although there was underreporting, I am sure). However, with the frequent rotation of contingents and civilian staff, we could not afford to be complacent. I knew that any case of sexual misconduct would seriously undermine confidence in the mission, which was already struggling to retain international support.

The widespread incidence of sexual exploitation and abuse, and more generally armed conflict, was in some respects symptomatic of the broader failures of governance in the DRC. MONUC was not mandated or equipped to deal with the roots of those failings, even though they impinged directly on the mission's ability to accomplish the goals set by the Security Council. As MONUC approached a decade of operational engagement with the DRC, the time seemed right to address these contradictions with a fundamental rethink of the mission's mandate and how the mission could better advance the goal of peace and the protection of civilians in Congo.

8

Pursuing Peace:
Stabilization, Peacebuilding,
and Transition

When building castles on the beach, we can ignore the waves but should watch the tide.
                                                            —Edsger Dijkstra

Dmitry Titov, a DPKO veteran, once termed peacekeeping the art of the impossible. I often recalled Dmitry's words as I wrestled with our demons in the DRC. The mission was permanently on alert. At times, I felt the mission had become a crisis response agency rather than a peacekeeping operation moving steadily toward peacebuilding and the exit after a decade of operations.

In 2009, MONUC marked its tenth anniversary. During those ten years, the mission had practiced the art of the impossible with mixed success. Nevertheless, the Security Council and the Secretary-General continued to harbor the hope of a mission drawdown calibrated on progress with the peacebuilding agenda, even though that seemed like a remote prospect as one crisis after another erupted around us. Our head of political affairs, Christian Manahl, suggested, and I agreed, that the ten-year milestone provided a timely starting point for a conversation on where the mission was heading.

I was keen to get that conversation started because I was increasingly doubtful about the viability of MONUC's mandate. There were too many incidents of DRC politicians and officials using MONUC as a scapegoat for their own failings or else acting unilaterally on the assumption of MONUC's unquestioning support. I began to wonder whether the mission itself was an impediment to peacebuilding in the DRC. Were we becoming an alibi, shielding the government from its responsibility to implement the reforms needed to prevent or at least manage the crises that frequently shook the DRC?

There were a number of critical questions that we needed to ask and answer. First, how could we get the government to fully assume and discharge its fundamental responsibility for both protection and peacebuilding? Second, how could we gradually shift the mission from an essentially reactive mode to a more forward-looking approach that focused on root causes and not just static protection? Third, how was the stabilization program in the eastern region of the country working? And finally, in light of the answers to those questions, was our mission's organizational model (including the deployment of our military resources) fit for purpose? If not, what kind of transition might be required to better position MONUC to face the challenges ahead?

In this concluding chapter on the DRC, I look back at how I endeavored to build a platform for peace. Then I review our stabilization initiative in eastern Congo and assess our (failed) efforts at security sector reform. I conclude with a commentary on how we attempted to rethink and reframe the mission's mandate after a decade of operational experience.

Building a Platform for Peace

Peacebuilding is about people. It cannot be done by sitting at a desk issuing memos (although I did plenty of that). A SRSG must be an agent for peace and not only a manager of a mission. So, as in my previous missions, I engaged with a wide array of institutions and individuals across the DRC. This added up to a marathon of meetings, conferences, and visits as mission colleagues and I attempted to stay in touch with people and events around the country. It added up to a lot of queasy air miles, crisscrossing the turbulent vastness of the Congo Basin, followed by nervous helicopter flights and tedious hours of travel along fractured roads and tracks to reach isolated communities and MONUC outposts.

Politicians and Prelates

I met regularly with President Kabila. Apart from the brief freeze after the November 2009 suspension of MONUC aid to the FARDC, I was received when I asked to see him. He was unfailing courteous and quietly spoken. There were no angry tirades. But I wasn't able to develop more than a polite relationship with him. I was not helped by the antipathy of the president's closest adviser, Augustin Mwanke Katumba; apparently, he held a grudge against the UN since he was subjected to sanctions following an investigation into his involvement in mineral trafficking.[1] Later, our response to the Lukweti atrocity compounded Kabila's earlier disenchantment over MONUC's unwillingness to obliterate the CNDP, which forced him into the deal with Rwanda.

Inevitably, most of my discussions with the president centered on security crises; we never seemed able to get beyond the urgent to deliberate on the broader issues relating to the future of the country. This may well have been due to the president's reluctance to accept any return to the International Committee to Support Transition (CIAT). This was a kind of Linas-Marcoussis-style monitoring committee, which my predecessor as SRSG, Bill Swing, chaired. Bill was an immensely experienced former US diplomat (which included a spell as the US ambassador to the DRC) who was greatly respected in the Congo (so much so that a popular song—"Coco Swing"—was written for him). Nevertheless, I am sure Kabila was determined to put CIAT, and the oversight that it implied, behind him.

My interaction with the political class did not stop at the presidential palace. I reached out to national and local political leaders, meeting them regularly in Kinshasa and in the provinces. However, my exchanges with parliamentary groups from regions affected by conflict were less cordial, as many parliamentarians blamed MONUC for not resolving or stopping the violence in their communities. I continually emphasized, however, that the United Nations was committed, as in the past, to the country's territorial integrity and would not countenance any attempt at secession or separation. But I also spoke out on the protection of civilians and the need for security sector reform.

I repeated these sentiments during my visits to the provinces. I usually met with the governor and the legislative assembly. Invariably, there would be a litany of complaints about the central government as well as some directed at MONUC. Moïse Katumbi, the popular governor of Katanga, was a notable exception; he saw MONUC as an ally, although, like other governors, he voiced complaints about the predatory behavior of the central government.

One of my first calls after I arrived in the DRC was on Monsignor Laurent Monsengwo, the archbishop of Kinshasa, who in earlier times had endeavored to secure a peaceful transition from Mobutu's monomaniacal rule. The Catholic Church exercises great influence in the DRC. I got to know a number of the clergy as I traveled around the country and I encouraged our staff—uniformed and civilian—to work with the religious communities, who commanded the respect and allegiance of the population. They lived day-in and day-out with their parishioners and had their finger on the pulse of society.

The archbishop (later cardinal) was not shy about criticizing the government. He was especially critical of its failure to meet its social responsibilities, leaving the church (and NGOs) to make up for that failing. This was a model of social welfare that had carried over from the colonial era, but times had changed and the archbishop complained loudly that the government was not shouldering its fair share of the financial burden.

Whenever I was in the east, I made a point of calling on one cleric in particular—Bishop (now Archbishop) Maroy Rusengo of Bukavu. He always greeted me with great civility, even when he was upset with something that MONUC had done (or not done). He understood and expressed well the fears and opinions of the people of Bukavu and indeed South Kivu. He occasionally shocked me with his comments, but I needed to hear them. Our meetings always ended with a prayer and a blessing. The bishop's gentle affirmation of faith was a welcome if temporary palliative to the troubles of Congo, which were never far away.

Partners and Protagonists

Like in my previous peacekeeping postings, I made a point of meeting regularly with the UN country team and chaired the weekly security coordination meetings. I also encouraged joint meetings between the MONUC heads of office and the UN country team representatives in the provinces. And on the occasion of the visits of the Secretary-General and the Security Council, the country team was always invited to present their views and ideas. I had not forgotten those early lessons from Sierra Leone.

Apart from the UN team, my other natural partners in building a platform for peace should have been civil society and the NGOs. In truth, however, my relationship with them in the DRC was strained. I was criticized for forfeiting, in their view, the UN's neutrality. In response, I always underlined the distinction between neutrality and impartiality. MONUC could not be neutral, I argued, because that would have implied a policy of nonintervention. What we could and tried to do was to apply common standards and act against violence whenever and wherever it was committed.

I was reproached especially for MONUC's relationship with the FARDC. The introduction of the MONUC conditionality policy helped to moderate but certainly didn't end the criticism. Any lapse by the FARDC (and not just the units receiving MONUC assistance) stirred up a storm of protest that washed over onto MONUC and its perceived "failure to protect."

On the other side of the divide, many Congolese, particularly in the Kivus, felt that MONUC did not support the FARDC sufficiently. I was accused of being too friendly with the NGOs, especially after the November 2009 suspension of aid to the FARDC. Eventually I accepted that I could not win this battle of incompatible expectations and focused instead on implementing whatever practical improvements in civilian protection that we could devise.

Stabilization or Building on Sand?

Following the success of the 2006 elections, the Security Council and the Secretary-General expressed some hopes that the peacekeeping mission in the DRC could gradually draw down. The Council recognized, however, that eastern DRC needed to be stabilized as a prelude to the ultimate departure of MONUC.

Work on a Kivu stabilization plan had begun under Ross Mountain and his program head, Lise Grande, before I got to the DRC. The plan was a comprehensive one and included the restoration of government services, capacity building, infrastructure development, and assistance for the return, resettlement, and reintegration of refugees and IDPs as well as demobilized combatants. Subsequently, the government adopted and expanded this plan, naming it the Stabilization and Reconstruction Plan for Eastern Democratic Republic of the Congo (STAREC).

The original UN plan was priced at an estimated $136 million. The revised government plan shot up to $1.2 billion. Like the Amani program before it, there was an indulgence of ambition that bore little resemblance to reality. While the government's plan was wildly optimistic, a modest level of donor funding was mobilized and work began. I was very keen to see the stabilization program move ahead. I recalled the work we had done in Sierra Leone and believed that we might achieve something similar in eastern DRC, even though the scale of the challenge was infinitely greater.

While STAREC nominally covered the eastern region, it was centered on the Kivus. With the end of the CNDP rebellion and the start of Kimia II operations, I believed that we could use the plan to backfill in the areas freed of CNDP and FDLR control and create a dynamic of confidence that would in turn help revitalize the rural economy. Indeed, there was some progress. The small STAREC team, led by two committed and innovative colleagues, Spyros Demetriou and Philip Winter, started getting roads repaired, administrative centers rebuilt, schools and courts reopened, barracks for soldiers constructed, and police posts refurbished.

But it was not enough. Administration offices remained empty for want of staff, and deployment of the police was extremely slow. There were delays due to bureaucratic hassles and budgetary problems on the governmental side. Both Ross Mountain and I spent much time urging officials in Kinshasa as well as in the east to resolve these difficulties, but with limited success.

In the east, genuine concerns about security delayed the deployment officials and the police. The FDLR had let loose its campaign of terror and the CNDP was still dominating some areas despite the agreement of March 23, 2009. In addition, a hodgepodge of militias controlled the countryside as well as mining sites (sometimes in collusion with elements of the FARDC and the FDLR). The restoration of state authority was not high on their agenda; they were happy to make money out of the anarchy. The illegal trade in conflict minerals continued unabated despite international campaigns to end the traffic.

I witnessed one startling demonstration of an illicit operation. I was flying to the Walikale district, an area where the FDLR had been inflicting reprisals against the civilian population. MONUC had deployed extra forces to protect the more exposed villages. I was on board one of the "flying bubbles" from the Indian North Kivu brigade. The endless equatorial forest stretched to the horizon but down below there were patches of open terrain and some settlements. As we approached one of these settlements, our pilot alerted us to a small cargo aircraft flying at a lower altitude. The plane was preparing to land on the one paved street in the settlement. We circled around to get a closer look.

The aircraft landed on a short strip of road that ran a few hundred meters through the settlement. Within seconds people were swarming around the plane, loading sacks into the hold. But we were quickly spotted and the crowd scattered. The plane, which had not shut down its engines after landing, revved up and quickly took off, heading east. The whole operation took only a few minutes. I was told that the cargo was most likely coltan—a high-value mineral that finds its lucrative way into our mobile phones and other electronic devices.

This episode illustrated two weaknesses in our stabilization initiative: the security deficit and the paucity of gainful employment. They were intimately linked. Without security, reputable companies would not invest in the mineral or other sectors in the Kivus. Agriculture suffered too due to the widespread insecurity in the rural areas. Most of the rural population was (and still is) desperately poor. In the absence of other viable options, the illegal trade (in minerals and logging mainly) and the militias provided the only sources of income.

The stabilization initiative was intended to help the people of the Kivus break out of the poverty and conflict trap. I can see now that we were too optimistic. Stabilization starts with security and we could not ensure an adequate and sustained level of security that would allow for the other elements of the stabilization (and peacebuilding) equation to play their part. Moreover, our ability to sway key political actors and traditional leaders was no match for the far greater and more perverse incentives offered by the illicit economy of eastern Congo.

Reforming the Security Services: A Fool's Errand?

The repeated failures of the security services to live up to their mandated responsibility of ensuring the protection of Congolese citizens and the territorial integrity of the country was a core dilemma for both the stabilization initiative and the broader agenda of peacebuilding in the DRC. For that reason, I focused much of my public advocacy on security sector reform. The reform of the Congolese security sector was, and remains, a monumental task. Of course, reform means change, but unfortunately those who were best placed to bring it about were those least willing to do so. Not long after I arrived in the DRC, the government organized a major a conference on security reform. The conference took a broad approach, encompassing the uniformed services and the judicial system. A range of proposals and initiatives for reform emerged from the conference. But the reforms that actually followed were piecemeal and hesitant. This was not for want of trying. The European Union, for example, put in a team to work on cleaning up and automating the payroll to get rid of "ghosts" and ensure that soldiers were paid regularly.

A good part of the problems arising with the FARDC could be traced back to the integration model adopted in the 2002 Pretoria agreement. That agreement allowed for the integration of troops of the factions that had fought in the Congolese wars; it was the price of peace. It was a high price. The army that emerged was an ill-disciplined, poorly trained, and impoverished amalgam of veterans held over from the Mobutu era, troops loyal to the political factions and demobilized militias. The problem was aggravated over the years by the policy and practice of integrating successive waves of ex-combatants from nominally demobilized militias (more than fifty of them).

As a result of these so-called integration exercises, the FARDC officer corps included ex-militia leaders whose rank was determined by the number of fighters they brought forward for integration. This created a pernicious incentive that encouraged the formation of militias as a revenue-generating and career enhancement opportunity inimical to a disciplined and professional force.

The force commander and I had attempted to develop a dialogue with the government on security sector reform. I set up a working group of ambassadors of donor countries and encouraged successive ministers of defense and justice to hold regular meetings with them to advance reform. There were a few desultory meetings and they never led to decisive action.

The reality was that the president was not willing to launch a substantial program of reform. He acknowledged the need for reform but in practice avoided it. This was partly because any reform would mean downsizing the armed forces to make them more manageable and affordable (as happened in postconflict Rwanda and Uganda), with the concomitant risk that he might lose his hold on them. While Kabila had served in the FARDC (appointed by his father), he did not build or lead a wartime army like Museveni and Kagame had done. Instead, he built up a praetorian guard loyal to him in parallel to the regular army (just as Mobutu did), awarding it privileges and perks.

In November 2009, the Security Council adopted a resolution that, among other things, requested "MONUC, in cooperation with the Congolese authorities, to coordinate the efforts of the international community, including all bilateral and multilateral actors working in this field, on security sector reform issues, and *calls upon* all Member States and international organizations to fully cooperate with MONUC in this regard."[2] That clause, I knew, was a dead letter.

The difficulties with the CNDP and FDLR campaigns and the conditionality policy made the government very leery of giving MONUC any kind of role in national security policy. Quite simply, the government did not trust us. Moreover, senior defense officials were allergic to any coordination that would weaken their hand with key military partners. Also, I doubted that all of those partners were keen on MONUC coordination; post facto information-sharing, yes, but nothing more. For some of them, military cooperation was the door-opener for commercial deals and resource concessions, which outweighed concerns about the effectiveness of the FARDC.

There are two prerequisites for effective coordination: a clear policy goal and the means to make it happen. As far as security sector reform in the DRC was concerned, MONUC had neither. We had, as they say, "no skin in the game." Given that reality, I set to thinking, rather fancifully, about how we might get more leverage to implement the coordination provision in the Security Council resolution. I compared what the government was nominally spending on the FARDC and what MONUC was costing. The cost of MONUC was several multiples higher, which was understandable given the higher costs involved in fielding an expatriate force. Nevertheless, I wondered whether MONUC might safely reduce its force strength and then invest the savings in a program of security sector reform.

This idea was partly inspired by my experiences with security sector reform in Sierra Leone and Liberia. Of course, these were small countries with small armies. In the case of the DRC, it was obviously too late to replicate those single-donor/partner models, but it was equally obvious that the patchwork approach to security sector reform wasn't working, despite the Council's calls for reform. So I thought that the answer might be a consortium approach under UN leadership using savings from a downsized MONUC.

In a somewhat elided form the idea made its way to the Security Council. In his report to the Council in December 2009, the Secretary-General declared that, assuming "major military operations against foreign armed groups can be concluded in 2010, MONUC could then begin a phased troop drawdown at a pace consonant with the security situation on the ground. Should the Council so wish, this would permit the United Nations to reallocate, within a declining overall budget, additional resources to an intensified program of security sector reform and, more broadly, to the strengthening of the rule of law as a prelude to the eventual departure of the United Nations peacekeeping presence."[3]

I was quickly disabused of any notion that we might be authorized to do anything so far-reaching. The FARDC was a pariah in the Council and there was zero enthusiasm for directing assessed contributions to the reform of the Congolese army. So we continued with the fruitless attempt to promote security sector reform while coping with the consequences of our inability to achieve that goal—the unremitting violence against civilians, which the FARDC did not prevent and often made worse.

Lost in Transition

In November 2007, the Secretary-General presented to the Security Council a set of benchmarks[4] to guide the hoped for passage to peace and with it the drawdown of UN forces. Over the next couple of years, the mission developed an assortment of strategies, plans, policies, and programs to achieve these benchmarks. This ensemble of good intentions was easier to concoct than to implement. Events often conspired to render the strategies unrealistic and the benchmarks redundant.

The Unified Field Theory

Despite these disappointments, in September 2009 the Secretary-General declared that "MONUC will work with the United Nations and other partners to develop a strategy by which MONUC could progressively transfer to them responsibilities for tasks of a long-term nature, such as justice reform, the strengthening of governance and decentralization, in order to ensure a smooth transition."[5] The Secretary-General's policy committee subsequently decided that an integrated strategic framework would be used as a contribution to the Council's review of MONUC's mandate and the possible reconfiguration of the mission's structure; it was expected to include options and scenarios for drawdown.

The integrated strategic framework was the UN equivalent of the unified field theory—the holy grail of theoretical physics. It was intended to bring an agreed concept, enhanced coherence, and unity of purpose to the operational presence of the UN in crisis countries. I favored the idea, believing that the integrated strategic framework concept would provide an opportunity.

In my remarks to the Council in October 2009, I said that the integrated strategic framework presented a unique chance to review and rationalize the multiplicity of goals and tasks that had been incrementally piled on and applied by the mission. By the end of 2009, MONUC's mandate extended to more than forty separate tasks, and many of those tasks embodied multiple subtasks.

I argued, however, the exercise should be more than a review of the mission's structure and division of labor. I wanted to confront the fundamental problem of accountability. Time and again, the DRC government made decisions without consultation—much less concurrence—that had profound consequences for MONUC. I had come to the disheartening conclusion that MONUC's presence was postponing the day when the government would be fully accountable for its decisions, especially those concerning the protection of its citizens. The mission was doing important work, helping to protect hundreds of thousands of people, but in doing so we were perpetuating a willed dependency that disassociated responsibility from authority.

I felt that the time had come not only to talk about drawdown but actually to begin that process. In fact, at a meeting during the visit of a Security Council delegation to the DRC in May 2009, President Kabila had "encouraged the Council to begin consideration of the eventual drawdown of MONUC, including an elaboration of prerequisites in that regard."[6] The formulation of the integrated strategic framework presented an opportunity to build on the president's remarks and begin a drawdown based on an agreed joint assessment of the security situation in eastern Congo and, with it, the government's willingness to assume its responsibilities.

In September 2009, we began the initial work of preparing the integrated strategic framework. Under the direction of the chief of staff, Bert Coppens, and Ola Almgren, from Ross Mountain's office covering the humanitarian and development aspects, we sent out joint MONUC and UN country teams to the provinces to make assessments of where and how we might envisage a secure drawdown and which functions might be transferred to the UN country team and to national partners.

This was a complex and time-consuming exercise involving a multitude of institutions, agencies, and individuals with varying interests and agendas. It was further complicated by the interventions of numerous departments, offices, and programs based in New York and elsewhere. Keeping the UN country team and the mission on the same page was the relatively simple part of the exercise. Other layers of authority within the UN intervened, however, making the process almost unmanageable. Fairly soon, I began to ask what I had got myself into.

I met with the president and outlined the process of the strategic framework. I referred to his remarks to the Security Council delegation and suggested that a limited drawdown based on security assessments could coincide with the fiftieth anniversary of independence in June 2010. I was confident that we could usefully reduce some of the contingents without taking unnecessary risks. I also hoped that the savings might then be used for support to security sector reform. The president appeared to agree with this idea. I should have been mindful of the old aphorism: be careful what you wish for.

After managing to reconcile the many varying (and competing) points of view expressed by UN colleagues locally and at their respective headquarters, we completed a first full draft of the integrated strategic framework at the beginning of February 2010. The draft identified four key strategic goals of the United Nations in the DRC: addressing ongoing conflicts; stabilizing the conflict-affected areas; consolidating peace across the country; and making development viable.

It included a timetable for MONUC's drawdown based on the progressive transfer of security responsibilities to the national authorities and selected civilian tasks to the UN country team. I submitted the draft integrated strategic framework to the government and the legislative leadership. Even though New York emphasized that the framework was essentially a UN planning document, I wanted to ensure as much national buy-in as possible. It made no sense to write a document in isolation from those who would need to take it forward. Above all, I wanted to convey to the Congolese political leadership that MONUC was planning and working toward a future without MONUC.

Theory Meets Reality

As we completed work on the integrated strategic framework in late 2009, the Security Council launched a parallel initiative, requesting the Secretary-General to conduct "a strategic review of the situation in the DRC and MONUC's progress toward achieving its mandate, taking into account the Integrated Strategic Framework for the United Nations presence in the country, to further develop the existing benchmarks for this purpose, and to determine . . . the modalities of a reconfiguration of the mandate of MONUC, in particular the critical tasks that need to be accomplished before MONUC can envisage its drawdown without triggering a relapse into instability, and to report to the Security Council with recommendations by 1 April 2010."[7]

In contrast to the integrated strategic framework, which was a field-based exercise, the strategic review was conducted by a multiagency technical assessment mission (TAM) from headquarters-based departments, which arrived in February 2010. The initial TAM meetings revealed, however, that a very different narrative was now emerging from the government. The government wanted a much quicker downsizing than we had envisaged in the integrated strategic framework. Moreover, the exchanges confirmed that the government did not want MONUC to play any role in security sector reform coordination, which did not surprise me.

Alain Le Roy returned to the DRC at the end of February to preside over the conclusion of the TAM's work. At the first meeting with the prime minister, the gulf in expectations was plain. Le Roy presented the overall findings of the TAM, which included (among many other recommendations) a measured and phased reduction of MONUC forces. In response, the prime minister informed Le Roy that the president wanted the downsizing and withdrawal of the mission completed by mid-2011.

I knew that the prime minister would not make such a statement without being instructed to do so by the president. This was confirmed when we met with the president. He thanked Le Roy for the UN's contribution but added that it was time for the DRC "to fly with its own wings." While he quietly rejected any UN role in coordinating security sector reform, which he said the government would manage directly with bilateral partners (no surprise there), he still asked for UN assistance for military justice and police training. He reiterated, however, that the military should start to leave by June 2010 and complete its withdrawal no later than mid-2011. Le Roy reiterated the position he had taken in the meeting with the prime minister, namely that such a drawdown was too hasty and risked renewed instability. He proposed, however, and the president agreed, that the UN and the government should continue the exchange at a technical level.

I was not shocked that the president had decided to take a "rejectionist" line on MONUC's role in security sector reform. The Lukweti incident and the conditionality policy had not endeared MONUC to either the president or the FARDC. But I did not expect him to push for a complete withdrawal over such a short period. I was convinced, however, that this was essentially a political ploy. He wanted to show that he was master in his own house and to shore up his political standing ahead of the fiftieth anniversary of independence, with an eye also on the general election scheduled for 2011.

I had learned the hard way that Kabila surmounted crises by postponing them. I advised that we do the same; in other words, not resist the notion of a quick drawdown but instead use the proposed drawdown as a means to advance our accountability agenda by finally making the government publicly responsible for the security and protection of its own citizens. Le Roy suggested that a joint group should be established to review options.

The technical group met immediately. Ray Zenenga, who had worked with me in Liberia and Sierra Leone and was then heading up the Central Africa section in DPKO, was designated to lead the UN side. Zenenga was groomed in the Hedi Annabi school of peacekeeping diplomacy, which meant that he was careful, attentive to detail, and asked the right questions without revealing his negotiating strategy. He was joined by Kevin Kennedy, my former communications director, by then back at DPKO in New York, who was well-versed in the frustrations the mission faced in dealing with the Kabila government.

The government team was set on ensuring that the president's intentions prevailed. However, after several days of intensive negotiation, Zenenga was able to secure an interim arrangement. The withdrawal date was pushed back to August 2011 (two months ahead of the scheduled presidential election), but conditional on joint security assessments. It was also agreed that there would be an immediate but modest drawdown of forces starting before and continuing after the June 30 celebrations. For the rest, we decided to leave the negotiation in a state of "constructive ambiguity."

I was criticized by some of the TAM members for not anticipating and forewarning the TAM and Alain Le Roy of the government's intentions. For them, this seemed to confirm that I was out of touch and that I had lost the government's confidence. It was true that I had not anticipated the president's demand for such a rapid drawdown. Although in my conversations with him and in his interaction with the Security Council mission he had telegraphed his intention to request some kind of drawdown, I had obviously misjudged the scale of his intentions. Nevertheless, I was sure that the drawdown would be much longer than he demanded and that once the fiftieth anniversary was past, we could resume the negotiation and agree on a more realistic timetable.

As the TAM report and the drawdown were debated, I was disappointed that it turned into something of a "test of wills" between the Congolese president and the Security Council. I understood the importance of preserving the Council's prerogatives on deciding the drawdown timetable. Nevertheless, this rationale obscured a more fundamental question: Could UN peacekeepers realistically achieve their mandated responsibilities for civilian protection in the absence of any direct influence over the Congo's national security policy and structure?

MONUC Becomes MONUSCO:
A New Day or Just a New Name?

The drama surrounding the military drawdown dominated the planning for the transition. Nevertheless, the assessment did consider what civilian responsibilities and tasks might be transferred to the government and the UN country team as part of the transition. A number of collateral measures were proposed, aimed at simplifying the mandate, shrinking the operational footprint of the mission, and shifting its civilian focus toward stabilization.

First, it was agreed that security responsibilities for the western provinces would be fully vested in government security forces. This was essentially recognition of the facts on the ground, as we had already transferred almost 95 percent of MONUC military forces to the east. But it was the formal recognition that the government wanted. However, as a precaution, we stipulated that the force reserve could operate anywhere in the DRC in case of urgent need.

Second, and equally significant, we agreed with the government that the reconfiguration of forces in the east should be based on joint assessments (along the lines that we had conducted in Sierra Leone and Liberia) that would precede the reduction of forces. I wanted to shift the debate from numbers to needs. In this I had the quiet but crucial support of Pierre Lumbi, who had been recently appointed national security adviser. I was reassured, therefore, when the Security Council later endorsed the idea of the joint assessments and decided that the "future reconfigurations of MONUSCO should be determined on the basis of the evolution of the situation on the ground."[8]

Third, we adopted a phased approach for the transfer of residual civilian tasks in the western provinces to joint MONUC and UN country teams that would be established where MONUC's military presence was no longer required. This was intended to pave the way to a drawdown of MONUC's civilian as well as military capacities. There was a catch, however. While the UN country team was keen to absorb many of MONUC's civilian responsibilities, it did not have the means to do so. MONUC provided logistical and staffing capacities (especially in human rights and civil affairs) that could not be easily replaced under voluntary funding. The idea that there could be a seamless transition from UN peacekeeping to peacebuilding was simply not feasible in the absence of substantial funding, which was not available outside of the assessed peacekeeping budget.

Finally, the Secretary-General proposed, and the Council agreed, to the internal restructuring of the mission's management. I argued for a clearer delineation of functions: a regrouping of all protection, rule-of-law, and human rights responsibilities under one DSRSG, with the other DSRSG assuming responsibility for stabilization, peacebuilding, and humanitarian support (along with UN development coordination responsibilities). There was some pushback from the humanitarian community, which was keen on keeping the humanitarian and protection responsibilities together. I disagreed, maintaining that civilian protection needed to be anchored in a framework of rights and the rule of law rather than as an adjunct of the humanitarian assistance portfolio.

On May 28, 2010, the Security Council approved Resolution 1925,[9] transforming MONUC into MONUSCO—the United Nations Organization Stabilization Mission in the Democratic Republic of the Congo. But did anything change besides the title of the mission? Did the creation of MONUSCO fundamentally alter the rationale of the mission? Or was this simply window-dressing? I certainly believed that the UN peacekeeping operation in the DRC should be reshaped to achieve a greater focus on stabilization and less on crisis response. An explicit elaboration of the mission's role in stabilization—as reflected in the revised name—was both an expression of intention and a statement of hope.

Nevertheless, the Council still made the reconfiguration of the military forces contingent on "an improved capacity of the Government of the Democratic Republic of the Congo to effectively protect the population through the establishment of sustainable security forces with a view to progressively take over MONUSCO's security role."[10] That stipulation locked the new mission into the old logic of dependence: it said, in effect, that MONUSCO would continue to be the guarantor of civilian protection pending the improvement of the effectiveness of the security forces, a goal over which it had little or no influence.

Many of the tasks stipulated in earlier resolutions on MONUC were simply rolled over into the tasking for the new mission: strengthening civilian protection, ending impunity, implementing security sector reform, and preventing and sanctioning sexual violence were all included. Unfortunately, the Council did not undertake a frank appraisal of the government's commitment to those laudable objectives or the new mission's ability to convince or compel the government to implement them.

I felt that a timely opportunity to revisit the assumptions on which the mandate of MONUC had been constructed was lost. Instead those assumptions were largely perpetuated, flaws and all.

Journey's End

On June 30, 2010, the DRC celebrated fifty years as an independent state. A grand military parade was organized by the government. MONUC, represented by a multinational UN contingent, took part in the parade alongside units from the national army and police. I was pleased (and relieved) that the UN contingent was greeted with applause by the crowd.

Secretary-General Ban Ki-moon attended the festivities along with a galaxy of prominent personalities. King Albert of Belgium and the Belgian prime minister Yves Leterme were there and were well received. There was none of the rancor that marred the independence ceremony fifty years before, when a very maladroit speech by King Baudoin had provoked an angry response from Patrice Lumumba.

Presidents Kagame and Museveni were among the African heads of state present. This was the first time in many years that Kabila, Kagame, and Museveni had met in Kinshasa. The mood was convivial and contrasted sharply with the poisonous atmosphere of the Great Lakes summit held in Nairobi at the height of the Kivu crisis in late 2008.

The Kinshasa celebration held out the prospect (a precarious one, true) that we had turned a corner. I knew that the armed violence that had disfigured the eastern regions of the country for so long would not simply dissipate and disappear. Nevertheless, I hoped that with the steadying of relations with Rwanda and Uganda, the Congolese government would use the window of opportunity to focus on the stabilization and peacebuilding agenda, creating the space for the UN mission to accomplish its transformation from MONUC to MONUSCO—not just in name but in practice too.

With the closure of MONUC and the inauguration of MONUSCO on July 1, 2010, my leadership of the Congo mission came to an end and with it my UN career, which stretched back over more than four decades. The Secretary-General attended the inauguration of MONUSCO along with my successor, Ambassador Roger Meece (also a former US ambassador to the DRC). In his remarks at the ceremony, the Secretary-General generously thanked me for my service. I then accompanied him to the airport for his departure from the DRC. I left an hour later, heading for retirement.

My assignment in MONUC finished on a relatively positive note with the independence celebration and the prospect of more peaceful times created by the rapprochement between Kinshasa, Kigali, and Kampala. Within a matter of weeks, as I expected, President Kabila quietly shelved his demand for a precipitous drawdown of MONUC forces, having already told a visiting Security Council delegation that he was not calling for a "hasty withdrawal."[11]

A Congo Epitaph

In April 2010, *The Economist* published an article on UN peacekeeping in the DRC. It was titled "Unloved for Trying to Keep the Peace."[12] The article made the point that the UN peacekeeping operation in the DRC was not greatly appreciated for its work. That didn't worry me too much. In each of the three preceding peacekeeping missions where I had served, we had experienced hard times. For me the essential question was: Did we get the job done?

The UN peacekeeping operation in the DRC has an annual price tag in excess of $1 billion. This does not include the massive expenditures on humanitarian aid and development assistance. This is a small amount compared with the price of the stability operations in Iraq and Afghanistan (whose population combined is less than that of the DRC), which are said to have cost upward of a couple of trillion dollars (admittedly for warfighting and not peacekeeping).[13] Nevertheless, we have to ask: Has peacekeeping in the DRC been a worthwhile investment?

On the plus side, one can point to the reunification of the country and the departure of foreign forces under the supervision of MONUC. UN intervention, political and military, helped secure the first democratic elections and transition since independence—imperfect but recognized by the international community. The UN presence has helped to prevent the fragmentation of the country and with it further foreign incursions into the DRC. And although it's difficult to quantify precisely the numbers, over the years, hundreds of thousands of people in Congo have been protected by UN peacekeepers.

On the negative side, there has been limited progress on protection. Despite many innovations in protection practice, MONUC could not fundamentally alter the protection equation. Within a month of my departure, there was a horrific militia attack on civilians in the area of Walikale in North Kivu marked by the mass rape of many dozens of villagers. Then, in 2012, elements of the former CNDP walked out of the integration exercise and launched the M23 rebellion, again causing massive civilian displacement. The fielding of an intervention brigade in 2013 (which I had originally suggested in 2008 during the CNDP crisis) as a part of MONUSCO helped put an end to the M23 rebellion, but it has not solved the underlying security and protection challenges.

The protection crisis persists to this day, periodically erupting with mortal ferocity. Millions of people are displaced[14] across the country. The LRA, although much diminished, is still inflicting violence on civilians in Orientale province; the Ituri militias remain active as does Bundu Dia Kongo in Bas Congo. Other armed groups like the ADF-NALU in North Kivu have gained strength, attacking civilians as well as UN troops; rebellions have broken out in the Kasai provinces. The misconduct and abuse by the FARDC remains largely unchecked.

This catalogue of misfortune is not the fault of the UN. The DRC is an independent and self-governing country; its own leaders must accept the burden of responsibility even though they inherited a doleful historical legacy. Nevertheless, I continue to reflect on missed opportunities. A couple of regrets play back in my mind.

First, I was slow to recognize the complexity of the protection challenge. MONUC developed several innovative protection policies and practices, but they were not enough: we were responding to and not resolving the underlying reasons for the protection crisis. We got caught up in the mechanics of protection and did not focus enough on the politics of protection.

At base the problem was not about the robustness, capability, or number of UN troops, important though those elements were (and still are); it was about a profound incompatibility of goals. The government's priorities were not the same as ours. The mission was caught between "the assertions of a government determined to slough off the international oversight imposed during the transition but still not able to ensure its own territorial security or protect its citizens."[15]

MONUC could not alter the equation of war and peace in Congo. To do that the mission would have had to mount a much bigger military operation and take over the management of the security sector. Neither of these prerequisites was remotely feasible. In my periodic presentations to the Security Council, I should have argued for a more strategic approach by the UN, recognizing the limits to intervention.

Second, I was not able to build a relationship of confidence with President Kabila. As I learned from my earlier peacekeeping assignments, personal relationships count for a lot and can help you get through the rough patches. Maybe that was impossible given the divergence between the mission's mandate and the president's expectations. He was clearly disenchanted by our seeming unwillingness to deal aggressively with the CNDP, as well as our highly caveated aid to the FARDC. From the outset, I probably should have been more candid in setting out the constraints on UN military engagement, unwelcome though that message would have been.

In Memoriam: Wars Without Winners

There are no real winners in the Congo wars even though a few individuals and their families have acquired vast if precarious wealth. But the wars have produced many losers, above all the people of the Congo—the refugees, the internally displaced, the poor, and those who have fought injustice and lost their lives in doing so.

Not long before I left the Congo, I received a stark reminder of that cruel reality. Floribert Chebeya, a courageous Congolese activist who ran a group called the Voice for the Voiceless, was killed in circumstances that have never been satisfactorily explained. The Voice documented and denounced human rights abuses and as a result Floribert often faced the wrath of the authorities. Not long before his death, Floribert met with and briefed the Security Council delegation during their May 2010 visit. In his frank remarks to the delegation, he didn't spare the Congolese government or MONUC.

Two weeks after that briefing, Chebeya was summoned to meet the chief of police, the notorious General Numbi. He arrived at the meeting and was never seen alive again. His body was found a day later in the backseat of his car (his driver's body was never recovered). I immediately offered UN assistance to set up an independent investigation. The government did not take up my offer.

Sometime later a Netherlands forensic pathologist established the cause of Floribert's death as a heart condition (which was known), but there were indications of restraints and bruising on his body. Subsequently, several policemen were arrested, tried, and sentenced for his murder.[16] General Numbi denied any knowledge of what happened and was not charged (although he lost his post). For the family and friends of Floribert, the case remains unresolved.

I went to see Floribert's young widow, Anne, to offer our condolences. She was very scared and terribly worried for the safety of her children. I tried to reassure her and indeed I arranged for a UN patrol to keep a close eye on her house. But I wasn't able to say in good conscience that the culprits would be apprehended and those responsible for Floribert's death would be held accountable.

Secretary-General Ban Ki-moon was due to arrive later in the month for the independence celebration. His office asked whether he should still make the visit in light of what happened to Chebeya. I advised that the visit should go ahead. At that point, we did not have all the facts of the case and I suggested that the Secretary-General could use his visit to press for a credible investigation (which he did). I worried that if Ban Ki-moon pulled out because of Chebeya's death, relations between the UN and the DRC government would plummet again, risking the possibility of a sensibly managed drawdown in eastern Congo.

The Congo subsumes just about all of the challenges one can expect to meet when UN peacekeepers intervene in other people's wars. Chief among those challenges was finding the right balance between principle and pragmatism. I wrestled with that ambiguity right to the very end of my time in the DRC. My advice to the Secretary-General on whether to make his visit after the murder of Floribert Chebeya was an acute illustration of that recurring dilemma.

Did I give the right advice to the Secretary-General? I am not sure. The killing of human rights defenders continues in the DRC and on May 16, 2017, President Kabila awarded John Numbi the title of "National Hero."

The presidential election of December 2018 in the DRC brought to an end President Kabila's eighteen years in office. However, the election that brought his successor to office—Félix Tshisekedi, the son of Etienne—has been faulted as lacking legitimacy.[17] The question now is whether the United Nations will again find itself in the ambiguous and frustrating position of having to cooperate with a regime that does not believe in the mandate of the peacekeeping mission—and whether the mission will remain in the name of civilian protection only to find itself protecting the regime from its own failings.

Part 3

Out of the Shadows:
The Promise of Peace

It is not enough to win a war; it is more important to organize the peace.
—Aristotle

At the end of my mission in the DRC, I wrote, as is required of all SRSGs, an end-of-mission report. It was a long (too long) paper. MONUC was a complex operation, struggling to cope with the misfortunes of a country and a society that was—and still is—grappling with the legacy of a troubled past and the prospect of an uncertain future. I received a generous note from Edmond Mulet thanking me for my report and service. Then silence.

Quite some time later, a former colleague to whom I mentioned this rather forlorn windup to my UN career tried to find out what had happened to the report. He discovered that the document had been classified as "confidential" and not for circulation. I was annoyed but then relented, reflecting that this was perhaps not such a bad thing. Time provides perspective. Now that I am far removed from UN peacekeeping, I can perhaps offer a more objective and reasoned assessment of what works (or does not) and why.

So in this third part of the book, I look at my peacekeeping experiences from a cross-mission, cumulative perspective. In doing so, I do not provide an overarching analytical framework, but furnish instead some illustrations of the impact but also the constraints that United Nations peacekeeping operations, and their handmaiden, peacebuilding, face in their quest for lasting peace.

I also ponder the role of national leadership in the transition from war to peace, since, for better or worse, it is probably the most crucial factor in the equation of peace. The international community often invests great

233

hope in the ability of postconflict leaders to build peace and secure the future. That hope is not always fulfilled. But is that due to the failures of leadership or to the lack of realism in our expectations of what such leaders can achieve in rebuilding and reconciling deeply fractured societies?

9

Great Expectations: Intervention and Its Conceits

The most extravagant idea that can be born in the head of a political thinker is to believe that it suffices for people to enter weapons in hand, among a foreign people and expect to have its laws and constitution embraced. No one loves armed missionaries.
—Maximilien Robespierre

Before taking up my post as the SRSG in the DRC, I stopped in Paris to meet with senior officials from the French government. At the meeting, the head of the UN department at the Quai d'Orsay asked me why MONUC, despite being the largest UN peacekeeping operation in the world, was not able to end sexual violence in eastern Congo. I did not have a ready answer. That question continued to trouble me throughout my Congo days. But in some respects it was emblematic of a predicament that all peacekeeping missions seem to face at one point or another: disappointed expectations.

The United Nations, it is habitually claimed, is risk-averse. Large public bureaucracies usually are. They get blamed more for their failings than praised for their achievements. This is certainly true of UN peace-keeping. The deployment of a peacekeeping operation, especially one with a Chapter VII mandate, generates a wave of expectation. When the UN arrives in a country devastated by violent conflict, the local population expects humanitarian relief, deliverance from insecurity, and the return of stability; the international community anticipates an end to the suffering, a halt to egregious violence, and the early return of the dispossessed to their homes.

What follows often does not live up to those expectations. In the four peacekeeping operations in which I participated, we could not accomplish what was expected of us, at least not within the timeframe and means initially deployed. Disappointment quickly displaced the early euphoria. Was this the result of flawed and unrealistic mandates? Was it poor planning? Did we misunderstand or misread the ambitions and intentions of the protagonists? Was the moment even right for a peacekeeping deployment? Or was the mission authorized in default of any better solution? Or did those disappointments stem from failings of the mission and its leadership?

In this chapter, I look at the key challenges we faced as we struggled to meet and reconcile the perceptions of what peacekeeping was expected to do and what it was actually able to do. I look, in particular, at three challenges that are critical to the ultimate success of a peacekeeping operation: sustaining confidence in the operation; understanding the limits to intervention; and fashioning a junction between peacekeeping and politics.

The Quantum of Confidence

Confidence is an intangible but indispensable asset for any peacekeeping mission. But it's an elusive asset; like trust, confidence is hard to define, difficult to acquire, and easy to lose. When there is confidence in a mission and its leadership, everything seems possible. But confidence is a fickle companion. It can abscond quickly, leaving the mission and its leadership vulnerable to contradictory pressures from the Security Council, the international community, national leaders, and local communities.

I witnessed firsthand—in Sierra Leone and Côte d'Ivoire—what happens to missions when confidence is lost: demoralization and disenchantment set in, at times accompanied by calls for the mission leadership to be replaced. All of the SRSGs with whom I worked faced, at one time or another, a crisis of confidence; some survived the crisis, and others did not. I faced that same fate in the DRC.

But what is confidence and how do we define and sustain it? In none of the four missions where I served did we define a barometer of confidence that would have enabled us to gauge objectively our progress. Confidence in the missions rose or fell in function of an assortment of variables, some of them quantifiable, others not. We did not have full or even partial control over many of the elements that made up this "matrix of momentum." They included the overall state of the peace process; the intensity and extent of armed violence (especially against civilians); the increase/decrease in the number of refugees, internally displaced, and returnees; the number of combatants enrolled and completing demobilization, disarmament, and reintegration; the incidence of human rights violations; and the incidence of sexual violence and abuse.

Metrics told only part of the story; reliable indicators, more often than not, were simply unavailable. Richard Caplan of Oxford University has adroitly summed up this predicament: "Peace may fail for a variety of reasons, but many efforts to build peace have been hampered in one important respect: by the lack of effective means of assessing progress towards the achievement of a consolidated peace."[1] There were surprises too—good and bad. We did not foresee our breakthrough in the Sierra Leone talks in 2001 coming so quickly. Nor did we anticipate the outbreak of armed hostilities in Côte d'Ivoire in November 2004.

I found that media reporting and the views of campaign organizations significantly influenced the perception of the mission's performance in the Security Council and in the international community, especially in Europe and the United States. The advocacy groups were very adroit in their lobbying of the Security Council and individual member states. Like clockwork, every time I was scheduled to speak to the Council, there would be a flurry of press releases or even major reports commenting on the performance of the mission, often in very negative tones.

Advocacy campaigners and Western journalists tended to be pretty skeptical in their assessments of progress. At the mission level (and in DPKO), we usually tried to moderate expectations, reiterating that we did not control the future trajectory of the peace process; this depended, we argued, on the political will and willingness of the protagonists to find solutions, which we could promote but not provide. Nevertheless, peacekeeping operations cannot disentangle themselves from the state of the peace process; when a peace process is not working, the rationale and prospects for the peacekeeping operation are called into question. This is the confidence challenge that I explore next.

Red Lines and Referees

The greatest risk to confidence lies in what I call the "expectations trap." This is the presumption of progress that is baked into peacekeeping mandates, which presumes that a peace agreement means peace. But as has been remarked many times, missions often find themselves in a situation where there is no peace to keep when peace agreements fail.

In each of the four countries that I write about here, peace agreements were signed as a precursor to the deployment of the UN peacekeeping missions; the mandates of those missions assumed the good faith implementation of the agreements by the protagonists. In fact, only in Liberia was a peace agreement actually implemented more or less as expected; even so, the Accra Comprehensive Agreement on Liberia came after seventeen previous agreements had failed to secure lasting peace.

When armed peacekeepers are on the ground, it is often assumed— erroneously—that they have both the means and the will to actually enforce the provisions of peace agreements. And when that does not happen, the mission risks a precipitous drop in confidence. After the RUF renounced the Lomé agreement in 2000 and attacked UNAMSIL, the RUF was condemned but the mission was also derided for its perceived pusillanimity.

In Chapter 3 on Côte d'Ivoire, I recalled a conversation with the French ambassador, who expressed the view that the international committee monitoring the peace agreement, backed up by ONUCI, should have acted like a referee in a soccer match and shown a red card for the failure to respect the agreement. Both the government and its opponents expected ONUCI to pull out red cards and to enforce on their behalf provisions of the Linas-Marcoussis agreement they favored and then expressed grave disappointment when we did not.

The DRC has proved to be a graveyard of expectations. During my stint as SRSG, I managed to disappoint just about all of our interlocutors. The government expected MONUC to eliminate the CNDP and to aid the FARDC unconditionally; the Security Council oscillated between demands for robust action and calls for accommodation and negotiation; the humanitarian community called on MONUC to simultaneously maintain the peace, rein in violence, sanction human rights violations, and restrain both the national security forces and rebel groups without resorting to military action that might provoke population displacement.

Is there an answer to the expectations gap? A realistic mandate that reflects the means at hand would help temper expectations, especially in the case of long-running missions that accumulate numerous tasks over time. The Security Council should periodically take pruning shears to those mandates and not simply roll them over. Above all, there has to be a realistic assessment of success; mandate writing should not become an exercise in wishful thinking, however desirable a particular goal may be.

Giving Peace Another Chance

The Security Council places its faith in peace agreements, which provide the legitimacy for UN intervention. However, peacekeeping missions, even when they are operating under a Chapter VII mandate, are expected to help implement rather than actually enforce agreements. The Council (and troop-contributing countries) are highly circumspect when it comes to enforcement actions that could lead to open warfare between the peacekeeping operation and the protagonists, especially if one of them is the government of the country—however discredited—where the mission is deployed.

Much of the day-to-day burden of managing the fallout of a failed or failing peace process inevitably falls on the SRSG and the mission team. SRSGs are routinely called on to help find solutions to the disputes and disagreements that crop up during the implementation of peace agreements. But they are not always well placed to handle that role if they have to also take action against one or another of the protagonists.

In Côte d'Ivoire, President Gbagbo and his cohorts came to see ONUCI as their adversary. So too at times in the DRC, President Kabila (or his surrogates) were quick to find fault if MONUC deviated from unconditional support for the government's position. Even in Sierra Leone, where President Kabbah was a firm supporter of UNAMSIL, his minister of defense, Hinga Norman, did not spare UNAMSIL from periodic rants about the mission's failure to aggressively take on the RUF. Government opponents are equally ready to denounce alleged partiality of the UN missions when it suits their political purpose.

Conflict mediators frequently encounter this kind of partisanship. For the SRSG running a peacekeeping operation, however, such antipathy, whether real or feigned, has direct operational consequences. Governments can make life difficult simply by throwing up bureaucratic obstacles, as Laurent Gbagbo did in Côte d'Ivoire, or calling for the mission to be removed, as President Kabila has done on several occasions in the Congo. Rebel groups can play the same card too by refusing access to areas under their control or by backing out of disarmament programs, as the Forces Nouvelles did on several occasions in Côte d'Ivoire.

Governments and their adversaries are not shy of manipulating the media to pressure peacekeeping missions. This manipulation (or worse, incitement) can have damaging consequences for peacekeepers. Mobs attacked or menaced UN staff and facilities in each of the countries where I worked with a peacekeeping operation. While I cannot draw a straight line between those incidents and hostile media coverage, the antipathy in the media (local radio stations are particularly dangerous) undoubtedly contributed to the tension and targeting of UN operations (including those of the humanitarian agencies). We pushed back through UN radio and other ways, but that was not always enough to deter irate demonstrators bent on venting their anger on the UN, a highly visible and accessible target.

Intimidation can take other forms besides media manipulation; bureaucratic obstructionism and outright refusal to cooperate are tactics that governments (and their opponents) can easily employ. Also, as I know from personal experience, unhappy governments can make their displeasure known to the Security Council and the office of the Secretary-General. Even institutions within the UN system resort to the same tactic when they believe the SRSG is not sufficiently responsive to their priorities.

I will come back to some of these job challenges in my chapter on leading peacekeeping missions. But here I want to make the point that because of these constraints, the SRSG is not always the person best placed to resuscitate or rescue a failing peace agreement. Institutional flexibility may be needed to save a peace process from breaking down.

One approach is to separate out particularly contentious issues and find alternative channels to deal with them. This is what we did in Côte d'Ivoire with the creation of a high representative for the elections. Similarly, in the DRC, the mediation of Presidents Obasanjo and Mkapa on the CNDP integration provided an alternative forum at a time when MONUC was essentially persona non grata with the CNDP and Rwanda; in Côte d'Ivoire, the Mbeki mediation opened up a channel to the Forces Nouvelles that was temporarily closed to ONUCI.

Appointing UN special envoys is a risk, however. For the SRSG and the mission, there is a possibility that they will be marginalized and asked to implement decisions on which they have not been consulted. Also, the attention of headquarters and the Security Council gravitates to the reporting of the envoy rather than the mission, potentially leaving it as an onlooker. Another risk is that every time governments or their opponents have a problem with mission leadership, they may call for a special envoy.

There is no shortage of candidates for mediation. Conflicts that run on and on draw in a revolving cast of mediators, who can be used to prolong or even thwart peace negotiations. Serial mediation (and mediators) can complicate the search for solutions as the protagonists seek out intermediaries they consider more favorable to their position. Governments and their opponents are quite adept at divining who might be more willing to fight in their corner. President Gbagbo and the Forces Nouvelles in Côte d'Ivoire were particularly skilled in that art.

The DRC is a textbook case of the risks incurred by serial mediation and "good offices." At the time I left the DRC, there were nine separate special envoys named by various governments and organizations; we had to resort to coordinating meetings among the envoys. Even so, it was difficult to arrive at a common and consistent message.

To the extent that a special envoy can bring a new perspective and fresh insight to a stalled peace process, that initiative should be welcomed. However, throwing special envoys (or "disposable dignitaries" as one former senior UN official called them) as a quick fix to crises with complex and deep-rooted pathologies can be counterproductive and may inadvertently send a signal of no-confidence in a resident mission.

My experience with special envoys was generally good. I worked well with General Abdulsalami Abubakar in Liberia and Presidents Obasanjo and Mkapa in the DRC. President Mbeki included me in his initial forays to Côte d'Ivoire and I was part of the team that sat down with the prime minister to draw up the implementation plans sketched out in the agreements he negotiated. Later, however, his team made key decisions without any consultation with ONUCI (or other leading stakeholders in the Ivorian peace process), which backfired. I am not saying that the problems would have been avoided or resolved if we had been consulted, but we could have alerted him to potential trouble.

The internal reporting lines can sometimes add another layer of complexity for a SRSG who has to navigate the shoals of interdepartmental rivalries. Literally within days of Obasanjo's appointment, I began to hear stories of friction and how MONUC was going to be marginalized (and myself too). So I made sure the MONUC staff knew that we would extend our full support to the special envoys and then took the added precaution of calling Lynn Pascoe, head of the UN Department of Political Affairs, to convey the same message, which he greatly welcomed. This perennial interdepartmental tension may now dissipate with the new organizational arrangements for peace operations recently decreed by Secretary-General António Guterres (I'll come back to this topic in the concluding chapter).

The Limits of Intervention

I have already emphasized the vital ingredient of confidence as part of the recipe for a successful peacekeeping mission. I do not have a special formula for confidence building. As I discovered when moving from Liberia to the DRC, success in one country does not readily translate into success in another. Confidence depends on a multitude of factors, not all of which can be controlled by the United Nations or its peacekeeping mission. Nevertheless, the way a mission is initially structured and equipped to meet the tasks set out in its mandate does have a significant impact on the prospect of success.

Size Does Matter: The Peril of Incrementalism

My peacekeeping assignments took me to four multidimensional operations in countries with vastly different population numbers and land masses, ranging from little Liberia to the immense DRC. Obviously, the peacekeeping operations deployed to those countries varied substantially in shape and size. Nevertheless, there were some common denominators that enhanced or detracted from the propensity for success or failure.

When peacekeeping operations are established on the premise of a good faith implementation of a peace agreement, the Security Council may be tempted to keep the mission relatively small. In Sierra Leone, Côte d'Ivoire, and the DRC, the troop deployments initially authorized by the Council were modest; they were built up only following a major crisis. Moreover, the buildup of forces in all three missions was slow, taking from three years (UNMIL and ONUCI) to a decade (MONUC) to reach the highest level of deployment,[2] creating what I call the "peril of incrementalism."

Only in Liberia was the initial authorized deployment pretty much on par with the total number of troops eventually deployed; the buildup also reached almost full deployment within a year.[3] In relation to the population and size of the country, UNMIL's authorized troop level was disproportionately much larger compared to the other missions.

Why this exception? The United States was keen to make a strong commitment to Liberia due to its historical links with the country (amplified by the Liberian diaspora in the United States) and also to avoid the deployment of its own troops to the country (some US Marines did land in Monrovia but remained only briefly before the ECOWAS force arrived). Moreover, the United Kingdom, France, and the regional power, Nigeria, all had an interest in seeing the situation in Liberia stabilized as quickly as possible to avoid spillover into Sierra Leone and Côte d'Ivoire.

In Côte d'Ivoire, the UN military presence was bolstered by the French rapid-reaction force Licorne. The United States was a cautious backer of ONUCI (apparently for budget reasons) and refused a larger force. France, however, was keen to have an effective force on the ground, hence its willingness to cover the shortfall through the parallel deployment of Licorne. In a way, the UK also provided a force "stiffener" for UNAMSIL with its implicit assurance of over-the-horizon assistance in case of dire need. MONUC also benefited from additional support in Ituri with the EU's Operation Artemis and then again during the elections of 2006 with Operation EUFOR RD Congo.

Despite these stiffeners, UNAMSIL, ONUCI, and MONUC all struggled to dominate their respective theaters of operation. They were awarded extra troops in response to, rather than in anticipation of, crisis. Force generation for UN peacekeeping operations is always something of an uncertain exercise. That becomes even more difficult when the mission is in crisis and engaged in "kinetic" operations. I still remember a conversation with the ambassador of a potential troop contributor to the MONUC rapid-reaction force during the 2008 Kivu crisis. He asked me if there was any possibility that the troops might be fired upon. I assured him that it was quite possible that they might come under fire. I noted an instant drop in his enthusiasm. It took more than a year to source and deploy the MONUC surge capacity, which arrived when the worst of the Kivu crisis had passed. Of course, that raises the question: Did we really need those reinforcements? We did, because a year later when the Enyele crisis erupted, the mission had some capacity available to redeploy without diluting MONUC's presence in the Kivus.

Of course, numbers are not everything. Force capabilities—mobility, training, logistics, and above all force and contingent leadership—play a key part. I have seen how a committed and flexibly minded commander can change the whole ethos of the units under his command compared to his predecessor (I use the male pronoun for a reason: in a decade of peacekeeping I never encountered a senior female military commander and only one example—from India—of a female police commander).

Despite that caveat, the sluggish buildup of troops or an inadequate troop-to-task ratio can slow or even reverse the momentum of peace by allowing space to armed spoilers to resist or stall a peace agreement. I have no doubt that UNMIL's strong and ubiquitous presence in Liberia immediately prior to and after the 2005 elections served as a powerful dissuasion to potential spoilers. I speculate that had those UN forces not been in place and ready for trouble, there may have been an armed uprising against the government led by a combination of disgruntled ex-soldiers, former rebels, and disaffected political elements left out by the post-electoral dispensation.

By contrast, because of its deployment in dispersed locations, UNAMSIL was too thinly spread to react effectively when the RUF walked out of the Lomé agreement in 2000 and attacked the DDR sites and UNAMSIL units. Of course, the fissures in the mission command structure and the woeful performance of some units made matters worse; nevertheless, the mission was probably underresourced for the tasks at hand and the concomitant risks involved in managing a large, multisite disarmament program in what remains a very uncertain and possibly hostile environment.

Not by Force Alone

In his autobiography *Interventions,* Kofi Annan writes that "peacekeepers cannot decisively change the balance of force in any conflict."[4] I would add one caveat to that assertion. The *presence* of UN force as opposed to the *use* of force did influence the outcome of the conflicts in Liberia and Sierra Leone. That presence provided a counterweight to armed groups, which otherwise might have threatened or seriously impeded implementation of the peace process, including, crucially, the DDR programs.

Notwithstanding that caveat, UN peacekeeping operations are not resourced politically or materially to carry out extended expeditionary campaigns like in Afghanistan or Iraq (although those campaigns have also clearly shown up the limitations of force) aimed at defeating an enemy or forcing protagonists to abide by the terms of a peace agreement. "Compulsion" is not normally a part of the UN peacekeeping vocabulary. In the case of the Congo, back in 1999 at the outset of the peacekeeping operation, Annan cautioned that a "Chapter VII mandate had raised expectations that the Mission will enforce peace throughout the country. However, there is a wide gap between such expectations and the Mission's capacity to fulfil them."[5]

Unfortunately, as I have already pointed out, if UN peacekeepers are unable or unwilling to use force to secure implementation of a peace agreement, they risk denigration by one side or the other and a consequential loss of confidence. That was the case in the Congo six decades ago when Patrice Lumumba railed at Ralph Bunche for not allowing UN forces to put down a series of rebellions across the country (not only in Katanga). It happened again during my time as SRSG in the DRC. Time and again, government ministers, the Congolese media, and elements of "civil society" accused us of failing to use our Chapter VII mandate, which in their view obliged MONUC to use force (usually at their demand). Actually, Chapter VII of the UN Charter[6] does not mention "peacekeeping"—it had yet to be coined; nor was that chapter used in the enabling resolution that created ONUC, the earlier mission with which the Congolese government compared—unfavorably—MONUC's performance. We did employ force on numerous occasions, but largely for tactical reasons, to defend positions or prevent a militia from taking them. During the Kivu crisis, I made a mistake by allowing the word "compel" to be used in juxtaposition to the word "convince." In truth, we didn't have the wherewithal to forcibly compel the CNDP to disarm or integrate the FARDC if we could not convince them to do so.

Only after the fall of Goma in 2012 was the Security Council ready to approve a force intervention brigade of 3,000 troops, which was authorized to carry out "targeted offensive operations." This was a tailor-made operation, a one-off coalition of the willing (South Africa, Tanzania, and Malawi). Even so, that force seems to be losing momentum[7] and in December 2017 suffered serious losses as a result of insurgent attacks.

The UN's ambivalence about the use of force was not only an issue in the DRC. The missions in Sierra Leone and Côte d'Ivoire ran into similar difficulties. The governments of each of these countries expected the UN to use more force against their opponents than we were prepared or able to deliver (although, as I mentioned earlier, in Sierra Leone and Liberia the presence of UN force did provide a deterrent to the resurgence of armed violence).

This was partly due to the reluctance of troop-contributing countries to see their troops used in aggressive forward operations as a substitute for national forces. As Thierry Tardy, a former colleague at the Geneva Centre for Security Policy, has noted,[8] the UN's use of force is a "marriage against nature." Even so, some of the African contingents that I saw operating in the field were pretty robust. Also, as I have mentioned previously, individual commanders could make a major difference to the robustness of forward operations.

Leaving aside the reticence of the troop-contributing countries, some members of the Security Council are also deeply averse to intervening actively on behalf of governments not considered legitimate, or whose armed forces are accused of human rights abuses. We could not, for example, really use the FARDC as a force multiplier in the DRC given the army's involvement in serious violations of human rights. Quite the opposite: the FARDC's operations in eastern Congo became a millstone for MONUC.

Enforcement-Lite: Robust Peacekeeping in Practice

As I mentioned before, UN peacekeeping forces are not mandated or resourced to fight wars. But the protection of civilians does sometimes require the use of force. However, the protection of civilians takes peacekeeping beyond the earlier notion that force could only be employed for self-defense or in "defense of the mandate,"[9] but not quite as far as full-on enforcement action. The UN's response to this dilemma has been "robust peacekeeping," which is a sort of peace enforcement–lite.

Robust peacekeeping is essentially tactical in nature—intended as a short and sharp intervention to deal with a specific, localized armed threat. In my experience, it worked best when the threat was confined to a limited geographical area and relatively accessible terrain. It has had its successes, notably in the Ituri district in eastern DRC under the command of General Patrick Cammaert. The Dutch general moved robustly against the armed groups (the short-term, European-led Operation Artemis did not end the problem of militias in Ituri); he also enjoyed some unique intelligence capabilities (thanks to his national military connections). The interventions of the Ituri brigade certainly made life much safer for the people of Ituri, but they did not end the depredations of the militias, which were still operating several years later when I was the SRSG; they are still there today.

And robust peacekeeping is not trouble-free. As I already mentioned, the Security Council authorized MONUC "to use all necessary means within its capacity and in the areas where it is deployed"[10] for civilian protection, but there was always the risk that a UN intervention—even a limited one—might spark a much larger outbreak of violence and with it the displacement of local populations. When MONUC launched a series of operations against the FDLR, those operations earned us a heavy dose of opprobrium from civil society groups and human rights advocates, who accused the mission of doing more harm than good due to the FDLR's retaliatory attacks on civilians.

It's worth noting that robust action by UN peacekeepers is rarely directed against errant government forces (although during the 2008 Goma crisis we were authorized to take action against rogue elements in the name of civilian protection). In many respects, those national forces were just as bad—and sometimes worse—than the rebel groups and ethnic militias that constantly threatened civilians in the DRC and elsewhere. But as Brian Urquhart once remarked about his time in Congo, the "UN could not disarm the national army of the country we had come to help."[11] Fortuitously, we did not face that problem in either Sierra Leone or Liberia, since their militaries had been either cantoned or disbanded with UK and US assistance.

UN peacekeepers are often derided for a lack of robustness. The international community's enthusiasm for such operations fluctuates, however, in function of the nastiness of the group subjected to military action (the

LRA and the RUF, for example, elicited no sympathy) and the humanitarian impact of those operations.

A lack of robustness is often attributed to national caveats, which prevent contingent commanders from acting in an aggressive manner without prior approval from their home countries. This is true, but I noticed that the interpretation of national caveats could change appreciably from one commander to the next. In fact, the impediments posed by national caveats are by no means unique to UN peacekeeping operations. I was struck by a remark that Robert Gates made as he was stepping down from his post as US secretary of defense. He grumbled about national caveats—troop-contributing countries setting limits on how their troops could be deployed that "tied the hands of allied commanders sometimes in infuriating ways,"[12] a criticism frequently leveled at UN peacekeeping units.[13] Such caveats are indeed a major irritant and constraint, particularly in times of crisis when a force commander needs maximum flexibility. But regrettably, national caveats will always be a fact of peacekeeping life and should be factored into operational planning for any use of force by UN peacekeeping operations.

Peacekeeping, Politics, and the Search for Solutions

Force alone rarely provides the definitive answer to deeply entrenched conflicts. The unfortunate reality, however, is that, at least in the countries where I worked as a peacekeeper, negotiated political solutions were routinely disavowed and renounced by one party or another. In the end, it was the preponderance of force allied to physical exhaustion that eventually pushed the protagonists in Sierra Leone and Liberia back to the negotiating table. In Côte d'Ivoire, Laurent Gbagbo never accepted the outcome of the presidential election that was supposed to provide the political answer to the crisis; he left office under military compulsion.

Security Council resolutions usually endorse specific peace agreements as *the* political solution and basis for a peacekeeping deployment. This makes it difficult to change or adjust course when those agreements falter or fail. Council resolutions are cumulative, building on previous resolutions. They tend to double down on approaches agreed in earlier resolutions, which obviates the need for new and possibly contentious negotiations. The Council rarely, if ever, says, "Go back to the drawing board."

A case in point is the peace, security, and cooperation framework for the DRC signed by the Great Lakes countries. The framework sets out a whole list of well-worn political prescriptions for solving the problems of the Congo, ranging from security sector reform to a call for reconciliation, tolerance, and democratization. However, the Security Council did not question—at least not publicly—the basic assumption on which the framework and indeed MONUSCO's mandate is based: wholehearted government commitment and action on reform. Almost two decades of experience must surely raise serious doubts about the Congolese government's willingness to meet those obligations, which are meant to set the stage for the eventual withdrawal of UN peacekeepers.

What I have written does not mean that political solutions to violent conflicts are not possible. However, when this mantra is advanced as the answer to protracted violent conflicts, we sometimes forget that political solutions require political compromises. Those compromises may be unpalatable and they risk being branded as appeasement when they involve deals with undesirables. Winston Churchill summed up this quandary neatly in his cogent maxim "square or squash." UN peacekeeping normally doesn't squash, but cannot it square?

The Art of What's Possible

Is there an answer to the dilemma that I have posited? I have four suggestions that together might help UN peacekeeping operations achieve greater coherence between expectations and results.

My first suggestion is to encourage peace operations to develop a mission-specific political-security policy. Such a policy would not of course replace the Council mandate, but it would drill down on that mandate and explicitly assess and address the constraints and contradictions arising from it.

I have consciously adopted the term "policy" rather than "strategy." I do so because, as I have noted earlier in this book, UN peacekeeping operations are awash with strategies that are prone to early obsolescence or are simply shelved and forgotten. Moreover, strategies, once adopted by consensus, are hard to adjust without engaging in the same lengthy bureaucratic process that created them, which can become an end in itself rather than a tool for addressing and managing complicated and unpredictable situations.

A mission-crafted political-security policy might serve as a helpful filter for unrealistic expectations. It would also aid the SRSG and the mission to distinguish between the urgent and the important. As I have noted elsewhere, peacekeeping operations can easily lose sight of their strategic objectives in the on-rush of crisis.

The humanitarian, human rights, and development actors should be an integral part of that policymaking process, not to coerce or co-opt them but rather to ensure that the policy is informed by all the dimension of the UN presence. Those actors may not agree with the outcome of that debate but they need to be a part of it.

My second suggestion concerns the role of UN headquarters in setting policy. During his first term of office, Secretary-General Ban Ki-moon established a committee of principals to ensure intramural cohesion on policy and operational matters. The committee brought together the leading players in the UN Secretariat plus closely associated operational entities like the UNDP and UNCHR and the UN special representatives appointed for specific issues. The DRC featured among the major crisis situations that demanded top-level attention, so I was asked to participate in the committee on several occasions.

What I noted from those meetings was an understandable desire to secure the best of all worlds. The meetings never really confronted the difficult, unavoidable tradeoffs that we faced on the ground. The committee's background papers and its decisions were framed as consensus documents where all points of view and positions were reflected and aligned but without a real debate on whether they were feasible. In the deliberations, participants had time only for a couple of comments. For what I call the "single issue" participants—those whose mandates related to a single issue—the policy committee presented an opportunity to advocate for their issue without getting into the complexities of how exactly we were going to achieve the goal they were advocating. The heads of the Department of Political Affairs and DPKO were only two voices among several, even though they carried the burden of responsibility of putting into practice whatever the policy committee decided.

I understand that the current Secretary-General, António Guterres, is moving away from the common-denominator approach encapsulated in the policy committee. He has appointed a new and smaller executive committee. I am told that this smaller configuration is expected to frame the options in a more actionable form, reflecting, I hope, that the UN frequently faces the choice of lesser evils. I know that this remark will not sit well with those who see right and wrong in absolute terms. Peace operations do not always present such a straightforward choice, however.

My third suggestion is to revisit the purpose of technical assessment missions. They tend to get sidetracked by the demands of institutional mandates of the organizations and entities that make up the assessment team instead of the strategic challenges and choices that peacekeeping operations encounter. I suggest that instead of in-house assessments, peacekeeping operations should be subjected to independent "reality checks."

Such a process of review and assessment should engage outside expertise that does not have an institutional stake in the outcome. The review/assessment should focus on the core objectives of the mandate and the likelihood of their being achieved within the means and timeframe established by the Security Council. Such an exercise could provide a valuable counterweight to the unrealistic assumptions and expectations that, with the best of intentions, creep into Security Council mandates, and which, with the passage of time and events, can become ever more divorced from local realities. This is a particular risk for long-running missions like MONUC/MONUSCO whose mandates include many stipulations that have been rolled over from one resolution to the next for close to two decades.

10

Pipe Dreams and Possibilities: Navigating Pathways to Peace

All wars end; even this war will someday end, and the ruins will be rebuilt and the field full of death will grow food, and all this frontier of trouble will be forgotten.

—John Masefield

One of the activities that I found especially uplifting during my time in peacekeeping was when I was asked to reopen schools that had been destroyed or badly damaged during the war years. It was a simple act, but I found it immensely heartening to see children back in those schools even though they were equipped with little more than a roof and a blackboard. For me, these reopened schools expressed the reality of peace and the hope for better times to come.

Of course, rebuilding public infrastructure was only a small part of a much a larger ambition. We aimed to start stabilization, promote state-building, and nurture peacebuilding with the dual objective of tackling the origins of conflict while rectifying its consequences. There is frequent debate in the international community about the delineation of these concepts. I do not have the space to expand on this debate except to remark, in passing, that these are not mutually exclusive ideas or activities; in association with local and other partners (particularly from the UN), peacekeepers worked on all three dimensions without too much concern about the delimitation of conceptual boundaries.

In this chapter, I look at the challenges countries devastated by violent conflict face as they struggle to get beyond the "frontiers of trouble." First, I ask what kind of peace promotes or limits the opportunities for postconflict peacebuilding—the "parameters of possibility." Second, I consider what I call the "pillars of peace"—the critical scaffolding that supports the edifice of peace. Third, and finally, I offer some thoughts about leaders and leadership and the impact they have on a country's postconflict prospects. I do so because I was able to witness what a difference leadership makes not only for the successful outcome of a peace process but also for what follows.

The Parameters of Possibility

Countries emerging from prolonged conflict do not enjoy a clean slate on which a flawless future can be inscribed. They face many hard realities that frame the opportunities (and limits) for peacebuilding and serve as a caution to what we can reasonably expect from them in the immediate future. I want to cite three parameters in particular that condition what may be possible: the way in which a conflict is ended; the relative strategic value of the country; and the inclinations of its neighbors.

The Opportunity of Power

How and why a conflict comes to an end has a profound impact on the shape of the postconflict dispensation. A conflict that ends with a clear military victory provides the winner with greater space to pursue a self-willed course of action. A victorious leader who also has unequivocal control of the security forces (Presidents Museveni of Uganda and Kagame of Rwanda) has the freedom to carry out reforms that an elected leader in a country emerging from conflict may hesitate to do. Of course, the danger is that leaders who acquire power by force come to believe in their "divine right" to perpetuate their hold on power, by force if needed.

By contrast, leaders who come to office following a negotiated peace or a deal among political contenders (an "elite bargain" as it is known in academia) are likely to enjoy much less room for maneuver. They will need to accommodate, or circumvent, demands from competing centers of power. That was clearly the case with President Kabila. He acquired office by "accident." This has led him to adopt a highly cautious approach to any military reform. He opted for a policy of accommodation, which is why we made no significant progress in that area despite numerous calls from the Security Council.

President Ouattara has had to cope with a not dissimilar dilemma in Côte d'Ivoire. His power base, at least in terms of military muscle, lay with the Forces Nouvelles, which helped to enforce the electoral verdict in 2010. The Forces Nouvelles have been integrated into the regular army and other security agencies but the habits acquired during the warlord days have not been easily discarded, making reform from within difficult.

This was equally true during the time of his predecessor. With the ONUCI force commander General Fall and UN police chief Yves Bouchard, I tried to quietly advance a dialogue on security reform but without success. President Gbagbo could not totally rely on his own security forces and so opted to indulge them rather than impose reforms that might have provoked trouble. Reform can be a dangerous proposition; over time, however, the failure to reform can become equally hazardous.

The most direct political challenges for Presidents Johnson Sirleaf and Kabbah did not come from the military but from elected legislatures in which the presidential parties had not gained outright majorities. In a way, this was a form of power-sharing, which would normally be welcomed as a positive facet of democratic practice except legislators were quick to demand financial perks in reward for legislative support. I spoke out in both Sierra Leone and Liberia about the need for budgetary restraint and tried to convince opposition leaders of their shared responsibility. But in truth, the governments caved to some of the demands as the price for getting their legislative program on the books.

The Power of the Purse

My second observation about context is that the leaders of deeply impoverished countries with few marketable assets—natural or geopolitical—have limited options for setting their own postconflict agenda. By contrast, those that do have such assets have been able to resist the so-called liberal peace and keep (mainly Western) donors at bay on governance and human rights issues.[1]

Sierra Leone, Liberia, and Côte d'Ivoire have few high-value natural resources. As I mentioned in my chapter on Sierra Leone, the country's diamond resources were attractive to local warlords but enjoyed little economic significance on global markets. Both Liberia and Sierra Leone have minerals such as rutile and iron ore, but the size of the deposits and global demand did not allow either country to forgo foreign aid or debt forgiveness. Côte d'Ivoire's greater wealth resulted from its earlier years of stability, agricultural investment, and role as a hub for regional trade. However, these advantages were greatly eroded during the years of turmoil that followed Houphouët-Boigny's death. So all three countries (and their leaders) have had to cooperate with the international community, and especially the major donors, to ensure a steady flow of funding and investment needed for postconflict recovery and reconstruction.

The DRC is in different category. Of the countries I describe, only the Congo enjoys enough natural wealth that could allow it to thumb its nose at the international community. However, the DRC's riches have been systematically looted or squandered, undermining the country's capacity to set its own agenda and leaving it vulnerable to international pressures. The political economy of much of the Congo revolves around the often illegal exploitation of natural resources. This will not change, and initiatives aimed at redressing this situation will not work, until there is genuine determination and commensurate action from Kinshasa to shift incentives from private enrichment to public advantage.

Neighbors Not Friends

A third critical element in the postconflict equation is the influence and interference of powerful neighbors. The stability of the DRC, for example, has been profoundly influenced by the security concerns of Rwanda, Uganda, and Angola. The efforts of those countries to secure defense-in-depth on the DRC side of their common borders has had a lasting impact on the security and governance of the Congo. During the time when I was the SRSG, I gained the impression that President Kabila was more concerned by reactions in Kigali, Kampala, and Luanda than the opinions expressed in New York, Brussels, and Washington, D.C. I suspect that the calculation has not changed much since I left the Congo (with the possible exception of China, which now has substantial investments and growing influence in the DRC).

Several of the armed groups marauding in eastern Congo were the consequence of internal troubles of Rwanda (the FDLR) or Uganda (the LRA and the ADFL-NALU). Both countries expected, however, the DRC and MONUC to take action against these groups. There was considerable skepticism within MONUC about the intentions and good faith of the Rwandan and Ugandan leadership; nevertheless, we had no alternative but to cooperate with both governments.

I was pressured to deploy MONUC forces against these cross-border armed groups but to stop short of any political engagement. After the negotiations with the LRA failed, there was no appetite in the Security Council (or in the wider international community) for further engagement; the LRA was beyond redemption. We did have contact with elements of the FDLR and the ADF-NALU, but I could not push for any formal engagement with either group. If I had, this would have made both Kigali and Kampala even more suspicious of MONUC than was already the case.

Rwanda and Uganda had the capacity to create trouble for the DRC, and by extension MONUC, by stirring up local tensions in the Kivus and Ituri. MONUC was already struggling with multiple security threats and crises and we did not need additional ones. Nevertheless, I thought that the ADF-NALU group might have been amenable to some kind of political overture, and I authorized Christian Manahl to take informal soundings. However, during an early visit to Kampala, I realized—to my surprise—that the Ugandan government considered the ADF-NALU a bigger threat than the LRA and wanted a military solution, not a political one. The Ugandans pressured the Congolese to take military action and our political initiative faded. The group has subsequently morphed into a much bigger source of instability and violence in North Kivu, which over time might have been avoided if we had persisted with a political overture despite the opposition from Kampala.

Fortunately, in Sierra Leone and Liberia we did not have to worry about the destabilizing influence of neighbors. Once Charles Taylor was gone, neighboring Guinea had every interest in ensuring the establishment of friendly and stable governments in both countries. Côte d'Ivoire was beset by its own troubles and was also not inclined to meddle in the affairs of Liberia after Taylor's demise. To reduce cross-border tensions and build confidence, UNAMSIL and UNMIL began joint operations with the national forces of Guinea. We were greatly aided in these efforts to stabilize the frontiers by ECOWAS and its cooperative executive secretive, Mohammed Ibn Chambas, an invaluable ally.

The Pillars of Peace

The parameters that I have just outlined set the context within which we pursued our interventions in support of stabilization, peace, and statebuilding. Those interventions were aimed at erecting the "pillars of peace" to enable a more peaceful state and stable society to emerge from the devestation of the recent past.

The security services constituted the first pillar. This was a top priority given the past failure of those services to protect the state and its citizens. The second pillar centered on justice, the rule of law, and reconciliation, in the belief that past failings in these areas had helped to create and then perpetuate violent conflict. The third pillar focused on elections, seen as the principal—if not perfect—way of establishing the formal legitimacy of postconflict governance. The fourth pillar is economic recovery and reconstruction, as both a contributing dimension to stabilization and a central element of statebuilding.

Security for All

In a conversation on peacebuilding some years ago, I recall President Obasanjo setting out a hierarchy of security needs based on three concentric circles: the security of the state, the security of the regime, and the security of the individual. He observed that in Africa, the security of the regime had come to predominate over the two others. Regimes looked after themselves rather than the state and its citizens. He argued that African governments needed to reverse the security order, putting the individual at the center of the security paradigm.

My own experiences confirmed the pertinence of the president's analysis. Too often, the security forces were misemployed as a means to defend and enrich whichever regime happened to have gained power. Civilian politicians bore a good share of the blame because of their misuse of the security forces for political intimidation when they sought to entrench their political authority. They encouraged factionalism and discord in the security forces by rampant partiality to their own ethnic group in recruitment and promotions. So it was not surprising, although not excusable, that the military turned to the same tactics when they seized power in the coups that periodically shook up West African states after independence.

Making matters worse, the regimes in power (military and civilian) often left the security services to subsist in squalor and operate in penury. I vividly recall visiting military camps in Sierra Leone where the conditions of the soldiers and their families were almost as bad as those in nearby camps for the internally displaced. The operational readiness of the troops was minimal; there was no fuel and rations were running out. Admittedly this was a particularly low point for the SLA before the IMATT reforms began to take full effect.

I saw much the same in other countries. On a visit to MONUC forward operations close by the Kahuzi-Biéga national park in South Kivu, I witnessed a brigade of FARDC troops camped out on the edge of the park in squalid conditions. There were no sanitary facilities or proper shelter. The soldiers had brought with them their wives, children, and even elderly parents; they simply had nowhere else to go. This was supposed to be a fighting unit (there to protect civilians and the park from the FDLR and Mai-Mai militias), but it was encamped in mud and filth.

The police were generally better off than the military, partly as they could live off the local population. Small bribes and other forms of petty corruption were commonplace and largely accepted by a fatalistic population who saw no alternatives but to get along by going along. In the worst cases, however, the police acted with brutality and impunity and in doing so undermined popular confidence not only in the police but also in the rule of law; for the poor and vulnerable, the rule of law became the rule of the rich and powerful.

Without reliable, well-performing security services, economic and social development are likely to be stymied. Fortunately, some aid agencies have been willing to invest substantial development money in security reform. Wherever I could, I encouraged UN agencies to support such reform initiatives; I thought it was a good investment and would hasten the day when UN peacekeepers would no longer be needed.

The broader conclusion I reached was that security sector reform has to be an integral part of the planning for a peacekeeping deployment. Deploying peacekeepers to protect people against their own security forces is not the answer. When peace agreements mandate security sector reform, there has to be an external partner or partners willing and empowered to lead that work with the funding to do so (such as the United Kingdom or the United States did in Sierra Leone and Liberia). If such a partner is not available, and the UN is asked to deploy a peacekeeping operation with a protection mandate, then it should also be authorized to take on the task with the concomitant funding from assessed contributions. Such an idea would probably run into budgetary objections. However, the de facto alternative, as we have seen in the DRC, is a very significant political and financial investment with no certainty of the outcome.

But reform is not a panacea; without persistent encouragement and oversight from the military high command and political authority, the impact of reform is likely to be short-lived. We had such a commitment in both Sierra Leone and Liberia; it was totally absent in DRC and was not a priority in Côte d'Ivoire during the Gbagbo administration.

Healing Communities: The Rule of Law, Justice, and Reconciliation

The deterioration and collapse of the rule of law is both a cause and a consequence of violent conflict, so it is not surprising that the UN and donors have focused on building (or rebuilding) rule-of-law institutions as an integral part of the peacebuilding agenda. I went a step further and persuaded DPKO that we should modify the mission's organizational structure in both UNMIL and MONUC to achieve greater internal coherence and impact in this area. I created a rule-of-law pillar within these missions headed by a DSRSG to coordinate the mission components that dealt with the rule of law, justice, rights, and reconciliation. This gave the missions a strong platform to pull together the UN and other non-UN organizations for a structured dialogue with the government and other state institutions on how to strengthen the rule of law and its institutions.

Our efforts enjoyed mixed fortunes. Where there was a real interest in reform, as in Sierra Leone and Liberia, we saw progress; in other countries, like the DRC and Côte d'Ivoire (at least during the time I was there), there was little or no progress. Even when there was support from the government, vested interests could still block change, as my dealings with the chief justice in Liberia illustrated.

Coming from a development agency like the UNDP, I was very aware that international cooperation, however well intended and designed, cannot transform institutions and effect policy changes quickly or easily. Peacekeeping operations, however, can be quite prescriptive in their approach to institution building. By contrast, development agencies tend to take a more incremental approach, recognizing that lasting change cannot be imposed; it can only be absorbed.

I do not want to imply that peacekeeping operations should not be involved in rule-of-law and justice initiatives. To the contrary, they bring to the table staff capacities and resources that development agencies find difficult to match during the early phase of postconflict recovery, when they are likely to be stretched thin on the ground. Moreover, the political weight of a mission (and the SRSG's access to the senior levels of government) can be put to good effect in support of all agencies (including bilateral and multilateral agencies) working to resurrect the rule of law and rebuild judicial institutions.

Although I believe peacekeeping operations can play a constructive and much-needed role in strengthening, or even resurrecting, the rule of law, what we attempted to do was build back what was there before. We didn't really question the model or suggest alternatives that may have better ensured the resilience of the state and made it less vulnerable to violence. I found that leaders like Presidents Kabbah and Johnson Sirleaf, who were certainly not repressive tyrants, nevertheless focused on restoring rather than replacing what they had known in their younger years before the conflicts began.

I am writing about the rule of law and the institutions of justice from the perspective of the formal state institutions. However, there was (and still is) another dimension of justice that exists outside of the state-imposed norms and structures of justice, namely the jurisdiction of traditional authorities. They adjudicate day-to-day disputes—family matters, property claims, and criminal acts—among people who may be far removed from the formal institutions of the law. People in the rural areas had more faith and confidence in the traditional practices than in the remote and unfamiliar judicial apparatus of the state. However, those traditional practices sometimes rubbed up against the formal systems that we were trying to revive or restore.

As peacekeepers we sometimes found ourselves in situations where our ethical responsibilities as UN officials clashed with traditional practices. As I mentioned in my chapter on Liberia (but it applies in the other three countries as well), cases of non-militia or army rape in the community were traditionally handled through negotiation between the families (or their clans), which resulted in some form of compensation but not necessarily the formal punishment of offenders that we would have advocated.

We also found ourselves dealing with violent disputes that involved practices—including trial by ordeal—that are completely unacceptable in modern judicial systems. In Liberia on several occasions, UNMIL troops and police units were called in to quell local riots that ensued from the ritual killing and dismemberment of children. When such horrors happened, the search for the culprits often turned—literally—into witch hunts that culminated in the denunciation and killing of suspects. We found too that such incidents could quickly degenerate into communal violence if the suspects were individuals from another ethnic group.

While the conflicts that I described in the country chapters gradually wound down and ended (except in the DRC), underlying communal tensions and grievances did not. In the four countries that I cover, truth and reconciliation commissions were established to deal with the legacy of a violent past.[2] The outcome of these commissions was decidedly mixed. The commissions were all based in the capitals and their influence did not reach a great deal farther even though they organized visits to provincial towns.

Although peacekeeping missions are commonly mandated to promote reconciliation, we did not have a structured approach for doing so. As I have already mentioned, we developed strategies to deal with a variety of concerns—national recovery, sexual abuse, armed groups, civilian protection, and so on. What we did not manage in our plethora of strategy-making was to develop a strategy for promoting reconciliation at the local level among communities, especially in those areas most vulnerable to violence, such as the Kivus in eastern Congo.

The civil affairs sections of the missions tried to sort out a palette of local disputes that threatened to disrupt the peace. Working closely with civil society organizations, they had good sense of what was happening locally and could spot the danger signals. But there were limits to what the civil affairs teams could achieve. Solutions proved elusive when ambitious (or disgruntled) political leaders got involved in community disputes. Even when communities had agreed on some kind of modus vivendi, politicians were not above complicating matters for their own political or material ends.

I can see now that we should have invested more in the reconciliation agenda. We focused our energies and resources on trying, understandably, to reestablish and strengthen the rule-of-law institutions. Those efforts should have been complemented by a more structured and systematic approach to reconciliation—not as a substitute for the rule of law but as a way to grapple with the communal tensions that so often degenerated into violence that state institutions could not prevent or manage. Organizations like Interpeace,[3] which I worked with in Liberia (and as a member of its board since leaving the UN), have developed concepts and methodologies for helping communities develop their own capacities to prevent or cope with violence that could be usefully adapted and applied by UN peacekeepers.

The Chain of Trust: Elections and Legitimacy

The international community generally considers elections as a touchstone of legitimacy and a vital step on the road to lasting peace. I was closely involved with the presidential elections that renewed the mandate of President Kabbah in Sierra Leone and brought Ellen Johnson Sirleaf to office in Liberia. As I explained in my chapters on the DRC and Côte d'Ivoire, I was also closely engaged on electoral issues but with no evident progress. Even though the UN was not formally in charge of those elections, we did have a strong interest in ensuring that they were conducted well enough to convey legitimacy on the winner.

We advocated for national ownership of the elections and for putting the national electoral authorities in the driver's seat. In reality, of course, the UN and the donor agencies were putting the petrol in the electoral tank, without which the electoral vehicle did not move forward. We were willing to take a back seat as long as the electoral process was moving in the right direction. However, by providing substantial technical assistance and policy guidance, the UN and the peacekeeping operation assumed a measure of de facto responsibility—and reputational risk—for those elections.

Security Council resolutions that authorize UN missions to provide support for elections can inadvertently create the expectation that a peacekeeping operation (or a peace support mission for that matter) is able to deliver a "clean" election. But the UN and its electoral staff cannot by themselves guarantee a level playing field if the government in power is determined to subvert the process, which was the obvious intent of the Gbagbo administration (and the Kabila government in the DRC).

Logistical support for elections that does not carry some measure of caution is risky. An election may meet the formal test of legality (usually decided by the constitutional authority put in place by the political power of the day), but this does not automatically confer on the winner legitimacy. Accepting electoral results in the name of stability does neither the country nor the UN any service; it postpones, not solves, the problem.

The Fortunes of War: The Political Economy of Conflict

War is ruinous. As many observers have pointed out, and the World Bank has rigorously documented,[4] the poorest states around the world tend to be those that are engulfed in violent conflict or recently emerging from a lengthy period of conflict; they are also more likely to relapse into armed struggle. Nevertheless, while war is generally disastrous for the population at large, someone profits—warlords, governing elites, and foreign interests.

The countries that I write about each suffered dramatic falls in their economic fortunes and growing impoverishment of their people as a result of violent conflict. But the economic decline actually started before the worst of the violence. This was due in part to factors beyond immediate government control (volatile commodity prices, for example) but more often as a result of mismanaged and rapacious economic governance, which hastened the descent into conflict. The most egregious case is the DRC, where Mobutu and his successors sustained a system of economic exploitation that benefited a few to the great detriment of the many.

UN peacekeeping operations are not habitually mandated to implement economic reform measures. The national recovery plan for Sierra Leone and then the economic governance program in Liberia (GEMAP) were important but essentially short-term operations aimed at enabling the two governments to get some "early wins" rather than as a corrective to the extractive model of governance that had materialized over many years. I believed that those wins would generate public support, help stabilize the political situation, and give the governments time to develop and implement the major institutional reforms so clearly needed.

The stabilization measures did not attempt to reshape the political economy. Peace interventions are often motivated by the onset of a massive humanitarian crisis, driving the international community to demand quick action, including the deployment of peacekeepers. It would be hard for any Secretary-General to resist such demands by arguing that the UN needs a fuller understanding of the intricacies of the country's political economy before it deploys peacekeepers. Nevertheless, as a mission builds, some capacity should be developed within the team to do this kind of fundamental analysis so that the UN—locally and at headquarters—is better advised on measures, including the incentives (or sanctions) that might be utilized to block or at least attenuate the economic drivers of conflict.

Game Changers:
Leaders and Leadership for Peacebuilding

Peacebuilding, in good measure, is about nurturing societies that are capable of grappling with their demons by lawful and peaceful means. As a country emerges from the trauma of violent armed conflict, the character of its leadership is likely to have a profound influence on a society's readiness and ability to do so. I outlined in the earlier part of this chapter some critical contextual elements that may limit what leaders can achieve after armed conflict ends. But those parameters of possibility are not predestined; they can be overcome, or at least tempered, by national leadership that has the requisite political will and skills to do so.

The qualities of political leadership are not a single set of definable traits that apply in all circumstances, at all times. The qualities that make for outstanding leadership in violent times do not necessarily translate into peacetime accomplishments. Charles Taylor in Liberia gained military ascendancy and then an election victory. And yet within five years he had lost power, and ended up tried and convicted for war crimes. So what kinds of leaders are best suited for peacebuilding? What skills and personal attributes do they need?

Authentic peacebuilding has to be shaped and directed by a country's own leaders. But the aptitudes evident in wartime leaders—single-minded determination, self-will, and ruthlessness—are not necessarily the ones that can consolidate peace.

Presidents Kabbah and Johnson Sirleaf were willing and able to reach beyond their immediate political base to engage with communities and individuals previously hostile to them. Both were relatively open and sensitive to public criticism; they did not resort to violent repression (although Kabbah did sign the death warrants for soldiers implicated in a violent coup attempt). They recognized the need for compromise before it was thrust upon them. Although neither leader has enjoyed universal admiration (few politicians do), they were able to create an initial reservoir of goodwill in support of their leadership.

The downfall of President Gbagbo was foretold almost from the outset of his presidency. As I mentioned in my Côte d'Ivoire chapter, the credibility of the president as someone who could be counted on to keep his word soon evaporated. Even when I was there several years before the denouement, the president's credibility was in tatters. No one in the opposition—and increasingly among his international partners and regional neighbors—trusted him.

Some time ago I wrote about President Kabila's cautious, somewhat diffident style of leadership;[5] I wondered if this might be a case where "leading from behind" was the way to build peace in a deeply divided country. However, I also asked if his caution would further erode confidence in government and simply delay change to the point where the state would again falter and widespread violence would return. Several years on, I have to say that he did not make headway in tackling the fundamental problems of governance in the DRC. Popular belief in the government largely vanished, making compromise hard to accept by those who had been disappointed by the failed promises of the past.

The international community can only reinforce or caution national leadership, not substitute for it. Partners and donors should be prudent when they try to favor leadership "winners." Peacebuilding is a laborious process of trial and error that has to be fashioned from local materials with local hands. The political context in postconflict countries is fragile, and leaders—even tough and determined ones—have to survive, making unpalatable choices and uncomfortable compromises. So the international community—including major powers—should not overestimate their ability to secure positive change.

Peacebuilding is about institutions as well as individuals. The institutions of the state—political, judicial, and economic—matter; they link the state and society and, if soundly constructed and diligently led, help to adjudicate peacefully the dissension and strife that all states encounter at successive stages of their formation and growth. In practice, however, strong institutions also require strong men and women capable of making a qualitative difference to the way those institutions function. Leadership in peacebuilding is essentially about making that difference.

Part 4
Moving Forward: Peacekeeping Today and Tomorrow

The past is not dead. In fact, it's not even past.
—William Faulkner

I am conscious that this book is very much about the past. The past has its value, even though it is not always a predictable guide to the future, as the unpredictable evolution of warfare surely shows us. The world and its conflicts have not stood still; neither should UN peace operations. So in concluding this book, I look not only at the peacekeeping of the recent past but also at what the future may hold for UN peacekeeping and peacekeepers.

As a bridge between today and tomorrow, I first explore the leadership role of the person who is entrusted by the Secretary-General to run peace operations on the ground—the special representative. I do so because whatever new policy narratives emerge to guide future peacekeeping operations (and several are already in process), they will have to be implemented on the ground by the UN team, led by the SRSG.

The mandates that SRSGs manage are typically more indicative than prescriptive. And the seeming authority that mission leaders wield is perhaps more apparent than real. But it is the mission leader who must turn concept into practice. This makes the job of the SRSG at once fascinating and frustrating, which is why I have called it "a job like no other."

That job is changing in form and content as UN peacekeeping evolves to meet emerging challenges in the international environment and the nature of violent conflict. In concluding this book, I explore some of those changes and the way that the UN is positioning itself to deal with them, notably through Secretary-General Guterres's "Actions for Peace."

261

11

A Job Like No Other: Leading Peacekeeping Missions

Management is doing things right; leadership is doing the right things.
—Peter Drucker

A large, integrated UN peacekeeping mission is a billion-dollar enterprise. The special representative of the Secretary-General who heads up this conglomerate is assigned a formidable range of responsibilities. They may encompass oversight of tens of thousands of soldiers, police, and civilians; the mediation of a peace process; the disarmament of militias and combatants; the reform of the security services; the support of national reconciliation; the promotion of human rights and the rule of law; and the coordination of UN activities in the country. And that list covers only the headline responsibilities.

But a SRSG is not the chief executive officer of that enterprise. As the SRSG, you can request, recommend, or object, but you can authorize very little—not even the purchase of a packet of pencils. I was not particularly bothered by my inability to buy pencils (or anything else for that matter); there were far more complex and critical management challenges that demanded my attention. This chapter is about how I grappled with those challenges, some of which were created by circumstance, others self-imposed by the United Nations, and some by my own shortcomings. I conclude the chapter with reflections on what I learned from those experiences, reflections that future SRSGs may find handy as they prepare for their "job like no other."

The People of Peacekeeping

A peacekeeping operation is a kaleidoscope of humanity enlisting people from a multitude of nations and a medley of cultures. Managing the diverse array of individuals that make up a peacekeeping operation is probably the SRSG's

263

most taxing and critical responsibility. Evidently, the SRSG cannot and should not take over the day-to-day management of mission personnel. Nevertheless, this is a mission-critical function that cannot be entirely delegated.

As a mission leader in the pursuit of peace, you are expected to weave that diversity into a functioning whole. It now seems to me almost miraculous that those missions achieved what they did. Yes, there was misconduct and incompetence; mistakes were made. Nonetheless, those cases were very much the exception and not the rule. The vast majority of peacekeepers—uniformed and civilian—were honest, competent, and committed. And some paid for their service with their lives.

The selection of the civilian staff was (and, I suspect, still is) an elaborate, time-consuming exercise that engaged multiple layers of consultation at headquarters and in the field. A SRSG can make proposals and can recommend or object to a particular candidate, but at the end of the day the decision rests with headquarters in New York. For the most senior positions that choice is made on the thirty-eighth floor (the executive office of the Secretary-General), which weighs regional and gender considerations as well as host-country sensitivities. On the whole, I was fortunate and came out of that lottery with some very fine senior colleagues. But that was not a given; politics played heavily in the balance of choice.

The selection process was equally complicated farther down the line. Every unit at UN headquarters had its own preferences for candidates. In principle, candidates were screened on professional qualifications and experience as well as previous performance. However, this seemingly thorough process did not always produce the best results. After we ended up with some unfortunate appointments, I encouraged supervisors to start doing their own due diligence, calling around to find out more about the candidates, which often proved more revealing than the candidates' official records. This was not strictly orthodox, I admit, but it was a worthwhile precaution.

Of course, personnel management is much more than selection of staff. Problems of performance, motivation, training, and conduct are all part of the personnel equation; they are common to all UN organizations, but they are magnified in peacekeeping operations by distance and isolation. Life could be uncertain for both international and national staff working with no assurance of job security; many of the staff lived and worked in remote places where sometimes they felt forgotten or ignored. Technology could help reduce that gap, but the UN has been notoriously slow to adopt and adapt systems that serve the needs of the field staff. Commercial businesses routinely offer clients instant access to Internet personal pages and respond to questions through telephone help lines and the like. That was not UN practice up to the time when I left the organization. Perhaps it is now. I hope so; it would make the organization seem less inaccessible to its field staff and, by doing so, boost staff morale and productivity.

Women in Peacekeeping: The Gender Gap

In all peacekeeping operations men greatly outnumber women. On arrival as the new SRSG in UNMIL, I wanted to try to change that metric. For the international civilian staff, I introduced a policy that gave women candidates the first refusal on all posts, assuming they met the basic criteria for the post (which they mostly did). I reasoned that this policy would help us even up, to some extent, the hugely lopsided staff profile. But I was disappointed in that ambition.

I did succeed in significantly increasing the number of women to whom we offered international positions in the mission. Unfortunately, this increase in offers was matched by a parallel increase in the decline of those offers. Although we doubled the acceptance rate for female candidates, the refusal rate was twice as high as it was among male candidates. We noticed too that even after we received acceptances, there was quite a high rate of withdrawal by female candidates. The net result was that there was no substantial increase in the number of internationally recruited women in the mission.

I was puzzled by this failure to improve our recruitment rate for women and I asked some of our female staff why that was the case. They pointed out that missions like UNMIL, with its masculine preponderance and culture, were not easy places for women to work. They explained as well why younger female staffers were disproportionately likely to leave missions for other UN assignments based in North America or Europe— they provided better prospects for balancing family and professional life. These factors worked to limit the number of women in the middle ranks of the staff, which in turn reduced the pool of female applicants who could be selected to move up the ranks.

It was difficult to change that male-centric environment. But I did encourage more internal promotions as one way to slightly lessen the gender imbalance. Both UNMIL and MONUC were large missions with several provincial offices, as well as substantial headquarters establishments in the capitals, and a high staff turnover. So this offered the possibility to rotate staff and provide opportunities for women at the more senior levels of the mission. In addition, both in UNMIL and in MONUC, the Secretary-General appointed female DSRSGs—Henrietta Mensa-Bonsu and Leila Zerrougui (the latter now the SRSG in the DRC and head of MONUSCO), the first appointments at that level in those missions.

The marked gender imbalance in the civilian staff was even more pronounced among the military and police. I don't recall even one female commander of a military contingent, and only a handful of women were appointed as staff officers or military observers, although we did have a few (very few) women who held senior police positions. When I asked why this was so, I was told that this reflected the gender imbalance within the troop- and police-contributing countries, which was not something we could rectify at the mission level.

Although very few female officers were posted in the contingents, there were female soldiers serving on the front lines. I still recall my encounter with one of those soldiers assigned to guard duty on the strategic and dangerous road from Sake to Masisi in North Kivu in the DRC. I was traveling along the road, which was under constant threat from armed groups, and stopped to meet the troops at some of the outposts. At one of them, I was introduced to a young South African soldier. I shook hands with her. She smiled and then remarked politely that I had nice, soft hands. That comment provoked barely suppressed mirth in my close-protection detail and ended any martial pretensions that I may have harbored.

Getting to Zero:
The Struggle Against Sexual Exploitation and Abuse

The theme of sexual exploitation and abuse is a recurring one. Starting with the scandal that erupted in Sierra Leone, I saw firsthand the hugely detrimental impact that such exploitation and abuse has on the public perception—locally and internationally—of UN peacekeeping. There was much less awareness, however, of the impact on victims.

Early on, I realized that simply sending out memos telling people to behave themselves was not the answer to sexual exploitation and abuse. I decided to practice more direct methods and to personally repeat, ad nauseam, to mission personnel—civilian, police, and military—that we had an absolute obligation to abide by the peacekeeping code of conduct for both ethical as well as reputational reasons. During town hall meetings with the civilian staff, at military and police medal parades, and at other events, I stressed that we must abide by our duty of care; I warned of the consequences for those who did not. It was a constant refrain, one that I instructed all our senior staff, whatever the component of the mission, to echo. There was some awkwardness when I spoke out explicitly to troops from religiously conservative countries about what sexual exploitation and abuse meant in the United Nations, but I asked the force commanders and contingent commanders to be equally blunt in their messages.

One of the hurdles that we had to overcome was the lack of understanding of what constituted sexual exploitation and abuse. Under the UN code of conduct, for example, prostitution is a serious infraction. This is not the case for most military forces, provided the soldiers involved are off-duty. It may be discouraged but it is not a punishable offense. Also, the age of consent for consensual sexual relationships varies from country to country; for the UN that age is eighteen. Moreover, we had to make it clear that any relationship that involved material advantage of any kind was strictly forbidden and punishable.

A constant frustration was that as the SRSG and head of mission, I exercised no direct disciplinary authority—even for relatively minor infractions. For the civilian staff of the mission, I could recommend to headquarters the suspension of the individual pending the review and adjudication of the case. However, even that modest step could take weeks to approve and the suspension—if agreed by New York—included full pay pending the outcome of disciplinary proceedings.

In cases involving the military, my disciplinary authority was even more tenuous (although I have to note that proportionately there were more cases of sexual exploitation and abuse among the civilians than the military). On several occasions, I asked for individuals to be withdrawn from the mission and disciplined by their national authorities for egregious misconduct. A couple of times I also proposed that commanding officers of contingents and even whole units be removed for serial infractions involving cases of sexual exploitation and abuse. This kind of demarche usually produced an immediate response from the country concerned, with promises of remedial action. But it was a constant struggle and improvements sometimes proved short-lived despite promises of corrective action.

In the gravest cases of sexual exploitation and abuse involving military personnel, our inability to go beyond a call for the offenders to be recalled and prosecuted—the UN has no prosecutorial authority over the troops or police deployed to peacekeeping operations—severely damaged mission credibility. It is very unlikely that this policy will change. The prospects of any government handing over prosecutorial power to the UN to sanction its own troops seem highly unlikely.

Despite this, there are actions that the troop-contributing countries can take that would show that they treat allegations of sexual exploitation and abuse seriously. In Liberia, for example, we discovered a case of soldiers abusing local women (paying them for improper photographs). To their credit the military authorities of the troop-contributing country concerned authorized the contingent commander to convene a court martial on-the-spot, which he did. The soldiers (and the unit officer, although he was not present at the incident) were charged and found guilty. The unit officer was stripped of his rank and the soldiers were dismissed from the military; all were sent home, with the cost of their travel deducted from their (modest) pay. This was the right thing to do, and it also allowed UNMIL to show that action could be taken when abuses occurred.

I wish I could say that this example became a standard practice. Unfortunately, military authorities are generally reluctant to wash their dirty linen in public. They prefer to handle such matters in-house, away from the media spotlight—damaging the UN's reputation, which is held responsible for the failure to do the right thing. It would help if troop-contributing countries at least reported regularly on the disciplinary action they have taken on pending cases before fielding new troops. However, given the intense pressure on the UN to find troops—often at short notice for missions in trouble—this requirement may not be as high on the agenda as it should be despite commitments made to that effect.

Zero tolerance for sexual exploitation and abuse should translate into zero cases. Even though I doubt that the UN will ever get to zero cases, that must be the goal; if you settle for less, you will get less. I was sometimes annoyed, however, by media reports and NGO statements that highlighted the incidence of cases of sexual exploitation and abuse to the exclusion of any positive dimension of UN peacekeeping operations. But it was difficult to make that case publicly without coming across as an apologist for grave and unacceptable misconduct.

Blue and Black: Building Team UN

A peacekeeping mission is part of a network of UN relationships. As I mentioned in my anecdote from Sierra Leone about the quarrel over the use of colors for UN insignia, the relationship between a peacekeeping mission and the other UN entities needs to be carefully and continuously cultivated to avoid intramural rivalries and tensions.

By and large, I enjoyed cordial and constructive relations with the UN country teams. My prior experience as a UN resident coordinator helped me understand and anticipate UN agency susceptibilities. I made it a practice to meet regularly with the country-based heads of UN agencies; I also encouraged joint retreats between the senior mission and UN agency staff around themes of common interest, such as the protection of civilians and national capacity building.

My first peacekeeping experience in Sierra Lone showed me the importance of building a strong relationship with UN staff at large, not only heads of agencies. UN staff wanted and needed to know what was happening and how we planned to go forward. This was especially important for our national staff who had to explain to their families and friends why the UN was or was not taking a particular course of action. The staff working at the vortex of crisis in places like eastern Congo could easily find themselves threatened or intimidated because of their association with a peacekeeping operation. I attended UN town hall meetings and other gatherings to keep up contact, even though I could only meet a small fraction of the mission personnel and UN agency staff in-country. It was time well invested.

While I always tried to maintain a rapport with the UN staff at large, the relationship with senior mission colleagues was obviously the most critical. In both UNAMSIL and ONUCI, I had witnessed how poor relations among the senior staff had imperiled those missions. In ONUCI, I tried to forestall that problem by encouraging the SRSG to establish a senior management group to review current events and concerns as well the overall implementation of the mandate. I had tried earlier to set up something similar in UNAMSIL but failed, as the SRSG preferred a looser format that was simply information-sharing.

Of course, at the proverbial end of the day, the SRSG has to make the decision (or recommendation). The question was how to get to those decisions and who would be included in the decisionmaking process. I set up senior management groups in UNMIL and then MONUC. They included the DSRSGs, the force commander and his deputy, the police commissioner, the chief of staff, and the directors of administration, political affairs, and human rights; other senior staff were co-opted as the agenda dictated.

I wanted the senior management group to be focused and action-oriented. That in itself was a challenge, with some colleagues favoring a more discursive approach. At times, our senior management group meetings in MONUC proved to be divisive as we grappled with some prickly dilemmas, such as how and under what conditions we could work with the Congolese army. Tempers frayed; voices were raised. I took the position that having heard everyone out, it was incumbent on me as the SRSG to take responsibility for whatever decision or recommendation emerged, especially if it proved to be the wrong one (although a visiting friend from headquarters once quietly cautioned me "not to take too much responsibility").

The senior management group mechanism that I established to bring the mission leadership together was not universally popular. It produced some umbrage among those colleagues who felt excluded from the inner circle. While I understood that reaction, I was wary of large, meandering meetings that would also multiply the risk of sensitive information leaking into the public domain. I attempted to partly compensate by holding round-table meetings of section chiefs at least once a week where everyone could speak and where we could debate issues of mission-wide concern. Unfortunately, I was not always very patient in those encounters, which tended toward passive exchanges of information. If anything, I was overloaded with information, but that was not the case for everyone and my impatience did not serve well the goal of mission coherence.

I have dwelt on the topic of internal communication and cohesion at some length because in large and diversified peacekeeping operations, this is a perennial and central challenge for SRSGs. There is not a simple or unique solution, or at least I didn't find one. Coordination mechanisms help, but much depends on individuals and how they interact, none more so than between the civilians and the military, which I explore next.

Working with Warriors: Civil-Military Relations

The great majority of people working in peacekeeping operations are wearing uniforms. The military (contingents, staff officers, and military observers) and the police (police advisers and the formed police units) report respectively to the force commander and police commissioner. The uniformed components of the mission are guided by written rules of engagement and by concepts of operation that are drawn up and agreed upon with the UN Department of Peacekeeping Operations. However, the SRSG has the overall responsibility for the mission and the implementation of its mandate. The relationship between the SRSG and military and police commanders (along with the DSRSGs) is therefore of paramount importance and sets the tone for the mission.

These are tricky relationships. They involve an untested amalgam of characters, which sometimes can go badly wrong. Both in Sierra Leone and in Liberia (before my time in those missions), there were serious differences that led to changes in the military command. In my own case, as I have related in my narrative on the DRC, I also ran into an unwanted difficulty that led to the premature departure of a newly arrived force commander. On the whole, however, I enjoyed very amiable and constructive relationships with the senior military and police commanders, both as DSRSG and SRSG. I needed, however, some on-the-job learning to get to that point.

At the start of my peacekeeping career I made a couple of faux pas when dealing with the senior ranks of the uniformed services. I learned that I could not simply apply the more informal approaches that prevailed among the civilian elements of the mission. A few times I made the mistake of going directly to lower-ranking officers for information or advice, as I knew that they were the most informed on the issue. In doing so, however, I ruffled feathers. I soon understood that I was causing irritation at the top of the chain of command and awkwardness lower down. I was putting junior officers on-the-spot. It was acceptable for civilian staff to directly approach uniformed officers of comparable rank, but as the DSRSG or SRSG, I was expected to abide by the hierarchical convention.

Once I had learned that lesson, I actually found it easier in some respects to work with the uniformed services than the civilian components. Our interactions were generally well-prepared (it helps, of course, to have a bevy of staff officers doing the homework) and we could reach decisions fairly quickly. We did not always agree, but once the decision was taken, the action would follow. By contrast, the civilians were more likely to drag their feet in an effort to delay or reopen decisions. Also, I sometimes found to my disappointment that civilian colleagues were more prone to leak information or brief diplomats and journalists against decisions they did not like.

The relationship between the SRSG and the force commander is pivotal. When crises erupt, as they frequently do in peacekeeping operations, those relationships can become tense. If there is a fundamental incompatibility between the SRSG and the force commander, the mission is likely to run into trouble. Mutual respect and trust is vital. I was fortunate in that regard. With the one short-lived exception in the DRC, I enjoyed very good relations with all of the force commanders and their deputies with whom I was associated.

Most of the force commanders I worked with were Africans. While they were not political generals (they had all gone through professional military schools at home and abroad and climbed through the ranks), they nevertheless understood the politics of working and navigating in African states, which gave them invaluable insights on how to get things done.

Relations between the force commander and his sector and contingent commanders are equally sensitive and sometimes contentious. On several occasions contingent commanders applied restrictive interpretations of their rules of engagement and displayed conspicuous reluctance to follow the operational directives issued by the force commander, citing national caveats. I always backed up the force commanders in these cases and asked the DPKO to intervene forcefully with the countries concerned.

I also met regularly with sector and contingent commanders. While I was careful to respect the chain of command and not interfere with operational decisions of the force commanders, I did want to see what was happening and hear firsthand of any major operational difficulties. When I traveled around to meet with the contingents, I took along with me senior colleagues from the civilian side of the mission. It is perhaps not widely known, but in UN peacekeeping operations the individual contingents depend heavily on civilian support staff for a large variety of services—supplies (food and fuel), air transport, and so on. Although missions have units whose job is to provide integrated support for the military, there is always the potential for misunderstandings and finger-pointing, so I strongly encouraged interaction between the uniformed and civilian components—not only on logistics but also on substantive issues such the protection of civilians, DDR, and intelligence-sharing.

As always, an individual can make a big difference. I recall a meeting with a sector commander in South Kivu in the DRC who put me through a PowerPoint presentation with 120 slides that essentially told me why his brigade could not deal with the FDLR. This came after an earlier, well-rehearsed medal parade that seemed to display lots of military might. I was irritated by his seeming reluctance to take any risks, and let my displeasure be known. A few months later, the officer left on rotation. His successor did not put on a PowerPoint presentation for me but he did start pushing his troops forward to squeeze the FDLR out of strategic positions.

Messages, Messengers: The Power of Perception

It is often said that you are what you communicate. I learned the value of that maxim the hard way through missteps. As a UN resident coordinator, I had dealt extensively with governments and the media, but the leadership of a peacekeeping mission takes you to another level of exposure (and criticism) that I had not fully anticipated. Perception is not about facts but how those facts are conveyed and understood; correct or erroneous, they influence policy and dictate action. They can be very dangerous once they take root; the nasty attacks on Indian soldiers by mobs near Goma in 2008 stemmed from a misperception of what they were doing to rein in CNDP rebels. So I spent much of my time as a SRSG, especially in the DRC, trying to manage perceptions of what a peacekeeping operation is expected to do as opposed to what it actually can do.

Where Have All the Warlords Gone?

Gibril Massaquoi was a savvy young man who acted as the spokesman for the RUF during the latter stages of the war in Sierra Leone. Present at the UNAMSIL-led negotiations that eventually resulted in the peace deal and the end of the war, Gibril somehow always managed get out the RUF side of the negotiations before we could. Later, I discovered that he had several journalists on speed-dial, including Mark Doyle, who covered West Africa for the BBC. Massaquoi had mastered the art of instant communication.

Warlords seem to have an uncanny knack for communication. During my peacekeeping assignments, I encountered an alphabet soup of political movements and armed groups, sometimes headed up by charismatic figures that made the most of their moment in the media spotlight. Sankoh, Taylor, and Nkunda, among others, were good at simplifying their messages and making them media-friendly. By contrast, we were sometimes rather flatfooted because we needed to clear statements and not say anything too provocative.

The international media were drawn to these warlords, some of whom were violent psychopaths; regrettably, in their outrageousness, they provided readable copy. Most of them have long since disappeared into well-deserved obscurity. Few people now remember the names of those who once held the power of life-or-death. And yet at the time they were courted. Their words and views were sought out by journalists, diplomats, and mediators alike. In our public pronouncements, the missions reverted to well-worn mantras that warned of dire consequences for violent misbehavior and then called for dialogue and political solutions. I certainly employed such phrases with the necessary degree of solemnity. But privately I wondered whether our interlocutors, especially the most violent ones, were paying any attention.

Face-Off

As the SRSG you are the public face of the mission. While most missions have spokesmen or spokeswomen and directors of communication, sooner or later the big headaches end up on the SRSG's desk. In times of crisis the spotlight intensifies. So handling public perceptions, and sometimes harsh criticism, is a critical and unavoidable task for SRSGs. It's a task of several dimensions.

First, the SRSG has to be not only visible but also accessible, especially when things are not going well. During the late-2008 crisis in the Kivus, MONUC came under enormous pressure from all sides, including from UN staff. I made a point of going as frequently as possible to the region and meeting with the media who were camped out in Goma, as well as civil society groups and of course MONUC and UN personnel. At some of these encounters I got a rough ride, especially from local groups who simply wanted MONUC to go out and crush the CNDP by force rather than negotiate. Conversely, some of the INGOs were rather irate because we had tried to constrain the CNDP and in their view made matters worse. Nevertheless, I continued to meet with all sectors of opinion, knowing that if I did not I would be accused of indifference or, worse, arrogance.

Whenever possible during trips abroad, I met with journalists, commentators, NGOs, think tanks, and governments interested in Africa and peacekeeping. Again, some of these encounters could turn harsh. Diaspora audiences could be especially virulent. I still recall one particularly raucous event that I attended at Westminster Hall in London where a vociferous group of Congolese students and exiles turned out to denounce me and MONUC for an assortment of sins of omission and commission.

Fluency counts in public communication. As an anglophone, I found it easier to work in Sierra Leone and Liberia than in Côte d'Ivoire and the DRC. While my spoken French is reasonable, I could not manage the same turn of phrase that came so easily when I was speaking in English. Subtlety and humor is harder to express in a foreign language. I found it especially hard to deliver written speeches in French. The structure and rhythm of the language is different. In fact, I gave up giving those speeches unless it was a very formal occasion. Whenever possible, I spoke from a few notes to stay on course. That worked better and I came across, I was told, as more authentic.

Access, Advocacy, and Moral Authority

As the SRSG you are expected to move the peace process forward. To do that you have to advance arguments and offer advice to interlocutors who often do not want to hear much less accept them. The challenge was how to disentangle the message from the messenger. I had to get the messages across without closing down my access and with it the opportunity to influence the decisionmakers. It meant convincing leaders and their coteries that we were not trying to engineer their downfall, even though we may have opposed their policies and actions.

Governments generally do not like to be seen responding publicly to external pressures. I found that one of the most effective ways to change a policy or course of action was to first quietly raise the issue or pass a message and then leave our interlocutors to declare the change of course—and take the credit—as their own initiative.

I was criticized, mainly during my Congo days, for not publicly denouncing the government and other protagonists sufficiently. But I had to make a choice about when outspokenness would serve a larger purpose rather than an instant headline. That was a question of judgment, not an act of moral weakness.

Statements from a variety of organizations and individuals who purported to speak for the UN often complicated our relationships with government and armed groups alike. At times, we agreed with UN headquarters (including the Office of the High Commissioner for Human Rights) on a calibrated approach to the release of a statement or report that was likely to be highly critical of either the government or a rebel leader. But there were other occasions when we were blindsided by a strong public statement delivered by a UN visitor who then got on a plane leaving us to deal with the fallout. Although I had no control over what was said or published by UN officials outside of the mission, the government and local media assumed that the mission had some hand in the authorship. Unfortunately, given the decentralized structure of the United Nations, it's impossible to prevent that kind of "freelancing," which sometimes seemed more attuned to the attention of an international audience rather than to achieving real change on the ground.

UN peacekeeping missions are surrounded by a plethora of commentators, analysts, and critics. I tried (not always with good grace) to retain my objectivity in the face of what on occasion (especially during my time in the DRC) became a barrage of adverse reports and reporting. Actually, I rather envied how adept the campaign organizations were at lobbying, including with members of the Security Council, and was impressed by their ready access to the most senior levels of the UN Secretariat.

Many of the reports from organizations like Human Rights Watch, the International Crisis Group, Amnesty, and Oxfam were well researched and pertinent. They included dozens of recommendations (some at cross purposes, however), many of them directed at the peacekeeping operation (governments always received the lion's share). However, given the sheer number of these recommendations, they tended to get lost in the mass of material that hits a peacekeeping mission from all sides. I didn't make the suggestion at the time but now I would recommend that individual missions organize a joint roundtable once or twice a year with all the interested campaign organizations in order to discuss, rationalize, and take advantage of the wealth of ideas and information that these reports collectively generate.

The Importance of Being Earnest

Peacekeeping missions are rarely at peace. Crises, accidents, and disasters are staples of peacekeeping operations. The mission leadership is inevitably called on to explain what has happened, how the mission has responded, and if it has not, why not. As a consequence, the mission's public information team plays a major role in fashioning public impressions of the mission. But over the course of my decade in peacekeeping, the demands on the information team changed as the new media age began to take shape with mobile communications, social media, and the twenty-four-hour news cycle. Smart phones became available even in the most isolated regions, making it possible for local communities, politicians, and warlords to connect with the wider world.

We were not really ready for the new age of instant communication. This was not so much an issue of technology as approach. We needed, for example, to be incisive and quick in our responses and not rely simply on formal press statements, particularly in times of crisis. I encouraged our communications staff to get the story out before it broke publicly, to express concern, and to tell the public what we were doing to solve the problem. I learned to avoid explicit attribution or denial of responsibility. You never know at the outset of a crisis where the story may lead; early reports often turn out to be wrong.

As a part of this rethink of public information, I created a post of director of communications in MONUC, a person who reported directly to me. We were failing in our struggle to get our messages heard; we needed to marshal and redirect our public information resources to meet the demands of the news cycle and changing media landscape. As I mentioned earlier, I brought in Kevin Kennedy from headquarters to handle the communications portfolio; he was very familiar with Congo, peacekeeping, and UN ways, but also willing and able to innovate. I also hired a former Australian journalist, Ian Steele, who had worked for the UNDP on its groundbreaking *Human Development Report* series to help improve the way that we told the MONUC story, including our frustrations and failings.

My energetic and imaginative special assistant in MONUC, Herbert Loret, came up with another idea. He had arranged interviews for me with *Jeune Afrique,* the influential weekly review on African affairs published in Paris. In preparing for the interviews, he had met a *Jeune Afrique* journalist who was interested in joining the mission for a spell to work in and write about MONUC. I was all for this idea; it would improve our French-language outreach and help us to make our information output more media-friendly. I proposed that we hire her as a consultant. But again I ran into the UN's rules and regulations. I was told that we would have to come up with three names and then submit them for review and consideration. I knew that the process would probably take several months and I gave up; I was simply too tired to go through a long, drawn-out recruitment process with an uncertain outcome.

Of course, even with the best communications team in the world, it's hard to change perceptions if the underlying facts speak otherwise ("alternative facts" had not yet been invented). I didn't want to simply spin every adverse event to our advantage when clearly we had got the policy wrong or made an operational mistake. But I also didn't want to be pilloried by the media for pursuing a policy that was strategically right but visually dreadful. This was the case with the operations in the Kivus when we sought to constrain the CNDP, which produced graphic pictures of terrified women and children fleeing the fighting. If we had allowed the CNDP the space to completely take over North Kivu (including Goma), I am sure that the consequences for local people would have been grave and the criticism of MONUC even worse (as happened subsequently to MONUSCO following the fall of Goma to the M23 rebel group in 2012).

Fortunately, peacekeeping missions do have a unique ace up their communications sleeve: UN radio. This was far and away the most effective means of communication with the local population. Given the low levels of literacy, the limited circulation of print media, and the few television stations reaching beyond the capital cities, the UN radio stations were literally worth their weight in gold. We could have easily sold them off with a substantial return (actually, we did get offers).

UN radio gave the mission access to the general public in a way that no print media could match (this of course was before the coming of age of Twitter and Instagram and the phenomenal impact of Facebook). I resorted frequently to the radio to get out key messages through interviews and talk shows. UN radio was widely respected and therefore regarded with suspicion by the authorities; in Côte d'Ivoire and the DRC the governments tried to take the stations off the air. Even in UN-friendly Sierra Leone and Liberia, the authorities occasionally took exception to stories that criticized the government; we always offered the right of reply but did not change the story.

The Voyeurs of Violence

When a conflict is on the front page it tends to draw a stream of prominent visitors—ministers, politicians, diplomats, journalists, and celebrities. The volume of visitors is a kind of perverse barometer, an indicator of the intensity and awfulness of the conflict.

Some come for the photo-op, others to validate their humanitarian credentials. The best go home and try to do something to stop the horrors—through political intervention, public action, or donations of their time and money. The visits typically last for a couple of days, with visits to IDP or refugee camps a mandatory stop on the visitor circuit (the amputee camp in Freetown was high on the list) as well as a must-do visit with the president or prime minister and possibly the leader of the rebels or insurgents (Laurent Nkunda was always keen to get a VIP visit to boost his respectability). These trips typically concluded with some well-meaning expressions of support to achieve a settlement or to provide humanitarian aid.

Peacekeeping mission are an early port of call for visitors. Over the years, I briefed dozens of VIPs. I always spoke candidly in those briefings, explaining our difficulties and recognizing our failings. I believe this paid off in the sense that most visitors left with a better understanding of the complex challenges that our missions faced—complexities that were not always captured or conveyed in the international headlines. This was not the outcome in every case, however. Some visitors were there to confirm a judgment they already held but wanted to make those judgments more credible through a visit ("when I recently visited . . .").

Most of the visitors sought UN assistance to get them around the country. The UN's cost-recovery policy meant that we were supposed to charge for flights and other transportation. This created some awkward moments, especially with visitors from governments that were making substantial contributions to peacekeeping or humanitarian operations. My instinct was to apply that policy flexibly. The administration staff was reluctant to follow suit (understandably—their job was to manage the budget, not to make exceptions), but as the SRSG I exercised my *droit de seigneur* in the interest of the mission and its mandate.

One of the most prominent celebrity visitors to the DRC was George Clooney. He visited in January 2008 as a UN Messenger for Peace and toured MONUC bases in the east. He was well informed about the situation and very gracious and attentive in his interactions with the mission staff.

At the end of his trip, George promised to return. He kept his word. As the 2008 crisis in the Kivus deepened, he contacted me through an aide, David Pressman (who subsequently became the US ambassador to the UN for political affairs) to say that he was willing to fly into Goma to support our efforts. My initial reaction was yes, please come. He reserved a private aircraft in order to do so. As the situation worsened on the ground, however, I was persuaded that bringing in such a well-known celebrity at a time when all our energies should be concentrated on keeping the city safe would not play well in the Security Council or indeed in the media, which were already pretty critical of MONUC. With misgivings, I advised David that the time was not right for the visit (and later learned that Clooney had canceled the aircraft reservation at considerable personal cost). Afterward I greatly regretted my decision; I realized belatedly that he could have been a powerful advocate for MONUC, especially in the United States, balancing out to some degree the torrent of adverse commentary that was undermining confidence in the mission.

George Clooney was not our only celebrity visitor; another was Ben Affleck. He too had done his homework and wanted to be helpful. When a well-known or well-connected personality speaks up for a UN mission, especially one under media siege, their comments will probably draw more attention and carry greater credibility than anything that the mission itself puts out. So at the risk of sounding rather cynical, I would encourage SRSGs to actually encourage such visits; they can be a welcome lifeline for a mission under fire.

First Among Many Equals

Peacekeeping operations are a vast collective effort with many moving parts. As I have illustrated in earlier chapters, the success or failure of a peacekeeping operation depends on a host of factors, not only the performance of the head of the mission. SRSGs should see themselves as one among many who make peacekeeping operations work, both in the mission area and at UN headquarters. However, the SRSG remains accountable for the implementation of the mandate conferred on the peacekeeping operation and so has a unique role and responsibility. In concluding this chapter, therefore, I want to focus on some personal dimensions of that role.

A Person for All Seasons

The job of the SRSG is a multifaceted one that requires a shifting mix of diplomatic, political, and managerial skills and aptitudes that ideally include organizational capability, adaptive thinking, easy eloquence, personal empathy, enduring patience, and robust stamina; a sense of humor also helps.

It's almost impossible to find a single individual who combines all of those qualities. Some of them have to be learned or developed on the job. Even then, I do not think anyone ever meets the mark in every area of competence; I certainly did not. What counts is that there is a reasonable alignment between the demands of the job at hand and the personality, skills, and capacities of the SRSG assigned to do it. Prior experience is not always a reliable guide to future challenges, as I found out moving from one peacekeeping operation to another.

So what did I learn about the personal qualities required for managing large and complex peacekeeping operations? There are three qualities that I found especially important, ones that are likely to trip you up if you don't take them on board.

The first quality is awareness. Most of us working in peacekeeping operations had little direct experience of the rough-and-tumble of practical politics. Diplomacy and politics are not the same. Diplomacy is about the alignment of interests; politics is about the pursuit of interests. When pushing for a seemingly rational course of action, we did not always fully take account of the constraints, interests, and dangers that political leaders would face to implement what we were recommending.

The need for awareness is of prime importance for the management of the mission as well. Personal relations are built on compatibility and confidence, which develop (or not) with time and collaboration. In a UN peacekeeping operation, however, the senior team is put together without much consideration for personal dynamics. Those are largely left to chance, sometimes with unhappy consequences.

This means that the SRSG has to build as well as lead the senior team. As I reflect on my experience, I have to say that my record was mixed. With some colleagues, I got it right; with others, I did not. Personal factors always intrude (you cannot be compatible with everyone), but objectively I can see that I should have invested more time on teambuilding, even though the daily round of crises distracts from that pursuit. Of course, this a two-way street—team members share the responsibility of collaboration—but the SRSG as the leader of the mission will always bear the primary responsibility for getting the team to work and needs to be continuously aware of that responsibility.

A second and related quality I would emphasize is adaptability. SRSGs should take heed of the law of diminishing influence. A government's enthusiasm for peacekeeping can quickly diminish when it realizes that the UN peacekeeping force is not there as a surrogate. A regime's willingness to heed advice starts to lessen, and access to the top leadership becomes more sporadic as the "seduction of sovereignty" exerts its pull and the national leadership feels more confident. Good personal relations with national leaders can make a difference—up to a point. As has been pointed out, the relationship between a "mission and the host government will likely change over time. The close political engagement, which is needed and sought after in the early days . . . may become resented as national ownership and pride re-asserts itself."[1] That observation certainly reflects my personal experience. The "body language" has to evolve as changing realities take hold.

The third quality I would highlight is patience. Before I joined peacekeeping, I worked for many years on development cooperation and humanitarian programs. Those programs were, and still are, largely project-based, built around timeframes, inputs, activities, outputs, budgets, results, and outcomes. When you are engaged in development cooperation, or humanitarian relief for that matter, you become accustomed to working toward "deliverables." If problems occur, you are expected to find solutions. The field staffs of the operational agencies enjoy considerable latitude to develop local responses, especially in times of crisis.

Peace processes are different. The rhythm of peace is not amenable to fixed timeframes. And there is not always a solution or a workaround at hand. I found it difficult, however, to accept that we could not find a solution or that the best course of action might be not to take any action. At times, political realities dictate more patience and less push.

The Ten Commandments: A Primer for Would-Be SRSGs

To end this reflection on the job of being a SRSG, I thought it could be worthwhile to conclude with a few tips for future SRSGs to bear in mind as they prepare for their mission.

1. Make sure headquarters hears the news first. In my pantheon of memorable moments from peacekeeping, I include the disappearance of Johnny Paul Koroma when I was the officer-in-charge of UNAMSIL. He escaped custody on a Sunday morning and I wanted to get as much information as possible before reporting back to headquarters on Monday. That, I quickly learned, was too late. On Sunday evening, I received an irate call from DPKO asking me what had happened and why I had not informed headquarters immediately. Apparently, in New York, an ambassador of one of the permanent members of the Security Council had already called the office of the Secretary-General to express concern; and, of course, the story had made the newswires. When I explained why I had not reported immediately—I was still trying to get all the facts—I was informed that in future, I should send a report whether or not I had all the facts.

The lesson was not lost on me. From then on I made sure to err on the side of early reporting, even though I regularly bracketed the reports with a caveat about still gathering all the facts. However, the Sierra Leone incident points in some ways to a wider lesson for leaders of peacekeeping operations: maintaining the confidence of the Secretary-General is paramount.

While most of the day-to-day reporting and communication is with DPKO (or its replacement), the SRSG is appointed by the Secretary-General. So I always asked to see the Secretary-General when I was in New York. Focused brevity is the soul of success of such meetings. Both Kofi Annan and Ban Ki-moon were well informed and I did not need to go over what they already knew. What they really wanted to hear were my recommendations on how to deal with problems, not simply a repetition of those problems.

2. Never get too far ahead of (or behind) the Security Council. I still remember with some embarrassment the first time I addressed the Security Council. Arriving to make my statement in the Council chamber, I was rather overawed to be where so many dramas of international politics had played out over the decades, so much so that I went and sat at the wrong seat and I was politely redirected to my proper place by the president of the Council. In my subsequent appearances, I got the seating right but not always the messaging.

In one capacity or another, I addressed the Council on behalf of all the peacekeeping operations in which I worked. Most of those appearances were for the purpose of presenting the reports of the Secretary-General, which covered operational activities, progress on implementation of the mandate (or not), and the country situation. Paradoxically, although the SRSG doesn't have the final word on the text of the Secretary-General's reports, he or she will nevertheless have to respond to comments or answer questions that may arise from what is in the report.

SRSG presentations to the Council are normally done in two parts: an open session in the Council chamber and then a closed session in an adjacent, smaller room where only the Council members, the UN Secretariat, and the SRSG (and accompanying mission staff) are present. For both briefings, it's good to be succinct and focus on a couple of critical issues. Members start to fidget when the briefing drags on.

The closed session is where the SRSG can expand on the open presentation and express thoughts that are not intended for public consumption. Council members in turn convey their views, almost always in the form of prepared remarks. I found these exchanges quite formalistic with little in the way of substantive debate. It was not unusual for the heads of delegations (normally at the ambassadorial level) to deliver their remarks and then depart, leaving behind a more junior colleague as a presence at the table.

Only on one occasion did I get direct feedback on what I was saying. That was during my last session at the Council when I was winding up as the SRSG in the DRC. US ambassador Susan Rice pushed back about the drawdown and we had an exchange of views in the Council chamber. That was exceptional. However, I am told that of late the closed sessions are much less scripted, which may provide the SRSGs with a better opportunity for dialogue.

This doesn't mean that the SRSG cannot influence the views of the Council. I found that the Council was amenable to ideas put forward from the field (provided they did not cross any red lines of the permanent members of the Council). In fact, the Council is not always sure which way to go and a strongly argued and well-grounded proposal from the SRSG can sway the outcome (if the UN Secretariat is also on board). Not always, however.

My efforts to refocus the DRC mission, including to put UN money into army reform and retraining, went too far and fell flat. The Council was not ready to grasp the nettle. But on civilian protection I was probably a step behind. The constant criticism from the campaign organizations had an impact with Council members, which I was slow to address.

In conclusion, the SRSG should not get too far ahead of—or too far behind—the Council. Getting that balance right is the challenge. The SRSG should be willing to speak up when it's clear that things are not going well—provided you have specific ideas on how to address the problem. The Council likes to hear a plan and not just a problem.

3. Render unto Caesar the things that are Caesar's. SRSGs are mandated to work with national governments even if those authorities are abusive, repressive, and unresponsive. At the same time, they are also expected to uphold the fundamental principles of the United Nations—the respect for national sovereignty, human rights, and the rule of law. Security Council mandates do not always provide clarity of direction and SRSGs can find themselves caught between competing visions of what a mission is expected to achieve.

My biblical allusion evokes that dilemma. The phrase I have excerpted concludes with the admonition to render "unto God the things that are God's."[2] Stated in less lofty terms, this means we have to recognize that a UN peacekeeping operation is not there to replace the government, however hopeless it may be. SRSGs can cajole, persuade, pressure, convince, and, when needed, criticize and condemn, but they cannot substitute for government. While SRSGs should uphold the moral authority of the United Nations, they cannot exercise that authority through the power of compulsion.

When SRSGs take a public stand on an issue of principle, they should do so knowing that the immediate consequences will likely fall on their shoulders. Governments can find ways to make life very difficult if they wish, including through veiled threats to your personal security or longevity in post. SRSGs will not be shielded by the conventions of state-to-state reciprocity; permanent representatives accredited to the UN are never declared persona non grata.

The Secretary-General will likely intervene to calm the waters. And states with influence and leverage may do so as well. Nevertheless, SRSGs are well advised to build their own coalition of diplomatic and political support, both to help move the implementation of the mandate forward but also as insurance for troubled times. But no SRSG should go into the job thinking that it's a long-term career prospect.

4. Put up a Big Top. As a SRSG, I sometimes mused that my job resembled that of a circus ringmaster. Like the ringmaster, I was charged with managing contiguous circles of activity and making sure that the several acts did not collide. Like in the circus, there is juggling and there are tightropes to walk. There were a few clowns too and occasionally one had to crack the whip.

A circus is perhaps not such a bad metaphor for a peacekeeping mission. A circus is housed under a "big top"—a large tent—that can accommodate many performers. A SRSG has to conjure up that metaphorical big tent and bring together a disparate set of ambitions and actors. This may sound like a frivolous comparison, but "keeping the show on the road" requires political dexterity to ensure that all the protagonists remain in the tent and committed to the common goal—peace.

5. Let the word go forth. Good intentions, I learned, are not good enough; you have to be seen and understood to be doing good. Occasional press conferences and statements do not suffice. SRSGs have to invest systematically in talking to a wide range of audiences and listening to a multitude of voices—especially the hostile ones.

This may all seem self-evident. But I have to say that I didn't always follow the advice that I am now so freely dispensing. To the contrary, at times I found myself slipping into a defensive mode, gradually pulling up the drawbridge. It's exasperating to be constantly explaining and not getting much recognition or understanding of the complexities that you may be facing. Nevertheless, no matter how unsympathetic the media and other interlocutors may prove, constant communication is a necessity, particularly when things go wrong.

Good communication is a function of presence. As the SRSG your time is heavily mortgaged by the daily grind of meetings (filling the big top is a people-intensive exercise) not to mention the unforeseen crises, big and small, that every peacekeeping operation encounters. So it's easy to overlook the need to be visible and vocal. That is why I recommend every SRSG running a large peacekeeping operation to appoint a senior staff member to plan, guide, and oversee the mission's outreach and to make sure that mission messaging is consistent and factual and avoids faux pas such as the civilian and military spokesmen offering differing versions of the same events.

6. Make friends in the region. I have already written about the role that regional neighbors play in peace processes. They are close by, often facing the risk of spillover should a crisis explode and refugees start pouring over the border. If the crisis has ethnic overtones, the neighboring government may well face domestic pressures to intervene. Neighbors are habitually well informed through their local intelligence networks. Naturally, they pursue their own interests but that makes it all the more important to bring them into the process along with the representatives of regional organizations like ECOWAS and the AU.

Working closely with neighbors and regional organizations can help to bolster the mission but it does carry risks. One has to be very careful not stir up mistrust, especially when neighbors are known to be hostile to the government where the peacekeeping mission is deployed. That is why, in some circumstances, an outside special envoy or the likes can be helpful; a SRSG may need a trusted "offshore" colleague to help manage the neighbors.

7. Build a team, gradually. This "commandment" may seem rather self-evident. However, as I pointed out at the start of this chapter, a SRSG does not have a free hand in the choice of the people with whom he or she will have to work. If you are joining a well-established mission, a team will already be in place. I did bring in a few people who had worked with me elsewhere whose competence and commitment I could count on. Nevertheless, a newly arrived SRSG should take the time to carefully assess the staff already on the ground and how they are performing and where there may be a need for change.

Change requires deft and discreet handling, especially when senior staff members are involved. This is never a pleasant or simple task and I would advise SRSGs to be cautious, at least initially, otherwise they will become quickly bogged down in endless personnel problems. For that reason, it is essential to have a seasoned and tactful chief of staff (as I did) who can spot the problems and recommend action before they get out of hand. That is not a job for UN beginners.

8. Bend, don't break the rules. Both as a DSRSG and SRSG, I was irritated at times by the administrative impediments that made it difficult to respond quickly to situations (or opportunities) that arose. Directors of administration like Steve Lieberman in Liberia were open to new ideas and new ways of doing business. But not all directors of administration were so flexible. There was a tendency to either say no to those ideas or refer the matter to UN headquarters. This culture of caution was inspired in part by a fear of audit criticism, which stymied innovation.

I have to admit that after several run-ins with mission administration, I realized that I was alienating colleagues who felt they were only doing their job. I started instead to look for ways to manage situations within the rules rather rejecting them. My cash-transfer scheme for the elections in Sierra Leone was a case in point. There were other loopholes that I used that did not put colleagues at risk or further deepen the bureaucratic divides within the mission. Years later, post-peacekeeping, I was rather pleased when a former colleague mentioned at a public event how she had used my "bend, don't break" approach as a way of circumventing institutional inflexibility.

9. Keep the issue of sexual exploitation and abuse at the top of your agenda. Large multidisciplinary peacekeeping operations have to deal with an array of misconduct. So it's important to empower a strong conduct and discipline unit within the mission. However, preventing and, when needed, sanctioning sexual exploitation and abuse is a top priority. It is the right thing to do that also requires doing things right. Allegations of sexual exploitation and abuse imprint a stain on a mission's reputation that is very hard to remove. As the SRSG, your personal accountability will be on the line. It was a recurring nightmare, especially in the DRC due to the sheer number of people that we had to "police" (and I use that word deliberately) and the immensity of a continent-sized country. I have outlined some of the defensive measures I took to tackle the problem. More than any other disciplinary failing, a perceived failure to energetically prevent and sanction sexual exploitation and abuse will weigh heavily on a SRSG; frankly it's a career stopper if not handled diligently.

10. Get some sleep and take a break. There are no weekends in peacekeeping; holidays get postponed or interrupted; birthdays and anniversaries are missed. Crises have a habit of cropping up at the most inconvenient times. The SRSG is always on duty. Inexorably your stamina is drained and your resilience diminished. As exhaustion sets in, your judgment suffers; small problems get magnified. I am not trying to evoke any sympathy with these remarks. The job of a SRSG is very demanding, but it is equally fulfilling even if there are times of great stress. You have to finds ways to manage the pressures.

Sleep does not always knit up the "raveled sleeve of care." But it does help to restore a degree of balance and equanimity. So take a few breaks outside the mission area, particularly with family, even though family reunions can sometimes end up as a race against the clock as you try to catch up on everything that needs to be done at home, from chasing plumbers to making medical appointments.

If you can manage it, local breaks can be helpful as a means to briefly put aside the daily cares. I remember some relaxing Sundays in Sierra Leone spent at a beachside house where a group of friends and colleagues would gather for fresh oysters (gathered locally) and cold Chablis (definitely not local). The setting was more South Pacific than Sierra Leone. Only a year before, that area had been attacked by the RUF as it tried to reach Freetown. The scars of the attack were still visible. Nevertheless, those quick trips allowed us to step away from the business of peacekeeping and then return to Freetown a little less stressed. Sitting at the beach is not most people's image of peacekeeping, but I am able (partially) to appease my conscience by recalling Kofi Annan's admonition to "have fun."

12

Facing the Future: Actions for Peace

We must not promise too much or raise expectations higher than are jus-
tified by the will of governments to act, but we must do whatever we can
to raise the standards of international behavior and responsibility. I
think we can only hope to succeed in that if we have a very clear idea of
what was wrong up to now.

—Kofi Annan

Not long after I left the UN, I participated in a reflection on the future of peacekeeping occasioned by a review on peace operations in 2010 published by the Center on International Cooperation of New York University.[1] One of the conclusions of that review was that "while conditions on the ground necessitate action, and sometimes additional reinforcements, the era of continued growth for multidimensional peacekeeping may be coming to a close."[2] This comment reflected a then-current opinion in UN circles that peacekeeping had grown too big, too expensive, and too unmanageable. The future lay, it was argued, in a much greater emphasis on conflict prevention and resolution through diplomacy and peacebuilding. Peacekeeping, if needed, should be the last resort and preferably in the form of "peacekeeping lite" with less emphasis on the military dimension.

Reality turned out differently. Within a couple of years of that report's publication, major new missions were authorized for South Sudan, Mali, and the Central African Republic. Many of the problems and dilemmas that I encountered during my time in peacekeeping cropped up again in these new operations, prompting renewed soul-searching and calls for change and reform.

So is the UN now prepared and equipped to tackle and surmount the challenges that have habitually beset its peacekeeping operations? And is it ready (or preparing) for new challenges that are emerging for UN peace operations such as terrorism and asymmetric warfare, technological advances, and, more generally, an international political environment that is challenging the basic tenets of multilateral cooperation?

As ever in the UN, it is very difficult to reach a consensus on change. Perhaps that is the unavoidable fate of an organization constructed around the precept and practice of multilateral cooperation and that operates on the basis of mutual consent. Nevertheless, the UN in its peacekeeping operations has not stood still; it has learned from mistakes, peered into the future, and endeavored to respond better to the complexities and constraints that those operations encounter. Secretaries-General Ban Ki-moon and António Guterres both commissioned major studies and reports that examine and respond to long-standing as well as new demands on peacekeeping operations. These include the landmark 2015 report of the High-Level Independent Panel on Peace Operations (HIPPO)[3] and, more recently, a study led by a former force commander in the DRC, Lieutenant-General Carlos Alberto dos Santos Cruz, on improving the security of peacekeepers.[4] Significantly, Secretary-General Guterres presented to the General Assembly in October 2017 a set of recommendations[5] on the restructuring of the United Nations peace and security pillar and the management of UN peace operations. These and other reports have been the subject of intense review and debate in the Security Council and General Assembly (and the Assembly's subsidiary bodies that deal with budgetary and peacekeeping issues).

Action for Peacekeeping

As the capstone of this process of reflection and reform, Secretary-General Guterres launched in early 2018 an initiative called Action for Peacekeeping (A4P). The stated purpose of A4P is "to renew mutual political commitment to peacekeeping operations"[6] by developing a set of mutually agreed principles and commitments to create peacekeeping operations fit for the future. This has been translated into a Declaration of Shared Commitments that are meant to "represent collective action to strengthen peacekeeping."[7] Presented to a high-level meeting of the General Assembly in September 2018, the declaration revolves around a set of eight priorities and commitments.

These priorities and commitments are not altogether new to the lexicon of peace operations. Essentially, they are an aspirational compilation and reiteration of previous resolutions, statements, and pronouncements from the General Assembly, Security Council, and Secretariat. They range from a restatement of the primacy of politics in peace operations to a reaffirmation of the commitment to strengthen the performance of peacekeeping operations and personnel. The declaration commits member states "to pursue clear, focused, sequenced, prioritized and achievable mandates by the Security Council."[8] However, the eight headline commitments include a raft of subsidiary promises, some of which may prove mutually incompatible. Well-meaning in its intent to bring UN member states together around an agreed set of aims, the A4P declaration does not propose novel solutions to the sharp contradictions and uncomfortable tradeoffs that so frequently confront peacekeeping operations and the people who run them.

This does not mean that A4P should be written off as a declaration of good if unrealistic intentions. Multilateral cooperation usually requires a navigational covenant to guide the stakeholders to their eventual destination, however distant that may be. Nevertheless, the lofty commitments of the declaration need to be calibrated against the more prosaic realities that were identified and prioritized in the HIPPO report. That report delineated four areas of focus: peace, politics, partnership, and people. I employ that nomenclature as the basis for some comments on the future of UN peace operations.

Peace and Prevention: Tilting at Windmills?

Secretary-General António Guterres, like his predecessor, Ban Ki-moon, has made a strong pitch for strengthening the UN's role in conflict prevention, calling in 2017 for a "whole new approach" and a shift from spending more time and resources on conflicts to preventing them. He added that "war is never inevitable" but peace is the result of "difficult decisions, hard work and compromise."[9] The Syrian catastrophe is a daily reminder of the terrible human cost that is incurred when prevention fails. But to prevent we have to understand why and how conflict develops, especially of the kind that the UN is often called on to help end.

In his fascinating book *Factfulness,*[10] the Swedish physician Hans Rosling includes a chart that plots out where countries lie on an income/life-expectancy axis. What is striking is that of the twenty-five countries in the lowest income and life-expectancy category, fourteen (or about 60 percent) have "hosted" significant UN peace operations, of which twelve were peacekeeping missions, plus a regionally led peacekeeping mission authorized by the UN (Solomon Islands); that number would be higher if multiple peacekeeping operations in the same country (e.g., Haiti and Central African Republic) were counted separately. If we move up the life-expectancy axis but remain within the lowest income parameter, the number of countries where UN peace operations have been deployed expands to thirty-four and includes an additional four others that have hosted major UN peacekeeping interventions.

Of course, these numbers do not prove that low income/life expectancy leads inexorably to violent conflict. The reverse is also possible: countries become poorer and life expectancy drops as a consequence of violent conflict (certainly the case in Liberia and the DRC). Moreover, over half of the countries in Rosling's lowest income category have not been torn apart by endemic violence. As Frances Stewart[11] and others[12] show, relative poverty attributed to identity, exclusion, and the absence of rights can be a dangerous driver of discontent. And of course there are also middle-income countries like Syria that have been decimated by self-induced violence (at least at the outset).

So I am not attempting to frame a general theory of conflict based purely on low GDP/life expectancy. There is another element that should be factored into the propensity for violent conflict within states: the inherent dangers of political transition. Add these elements together, however, and it appears that very poor countries going through political transitions seem especially vulnerable to violent disruption.

As I mentioned earlier, when a long-running authoritarian or patronage regime is forced out (either through the ballot box or violent upheaval), a seamless transition to a peaceful and stable society is far from ensured. To the contrary: in the four countries where I was involved in peacekeeping, the collapse of the regimes all ended up in bloody transitions, leading to armed intervention by regional, bilateral, and UN forces. So transitions are often a harbinger of trouble rather than heralds of peace.

More often than not, the UN has been unable to intervene early enough with diplomacy, mediation, or a peace operation to head off the descent into violence. Early warning is not a guarantee of early action. I recall that in the late 1990s, an interagency task force was set up at UN headquarters to monitor country situations likely to produce "complex humanitarian crises." I was a member of the group, which dutifully looked at a range of potential crisis countries. One of them was Côte d'Ivoire, which was put on the list as a country at serious risk as it struggled with the Félix Houphouët-Boigny succession. Shortly after, a permanent member of the Security Council let it be known to the office of the Secretary-General that there was no crisis in Côte d'Ivoire and the country should be dropped from the list (which it was).

The reality is that even failing states have friends. Ruling regimes game the system, sheltering behind the interests of one or another of the permanent members of the Council (or the lack of consensus within regional institutions such as the African Union), sometimes deploying specious arguments (the fight against terrorism is currently one such much-used pretext) to justify repression and to forestall calls for external intervention. As a consequence, UN and other diplomatic efforts at conflict prevention can be stymied or rebuffed, even in the direst cases such as Syria.

This is perhaps a gloomy commentary on the state of international relations and the constraints that limit the UN's ability to prevent violent conflict. It does not imply that the UN should abandon that ambition. After all, the UN Charter makes plain its determination "to save succeeding generations from the scourge of war,"[13] which is a call for conflict prevention. The question is what is the best route to prevention?

I fear that frequent calls for prevention that go unheeded, or are unsuccessful, are devaluing prevention as a viable tool to avoid or deter violent conflict. The assertive role—both in setting normative standards and authorizing operational interventions—that the UN and other international actors played in the years after the end of the Cold War has weakened. An example of this is the retreat from the "responsibility to protect," which was probably a conceptual high point of interventionism, with governments primarily held accountable to protect their own people. That responsibility is now infrequently evoked and indeed characterized as a regime change by another name.

In these circumstances, the UN may have to recalibrate its prevention role, concentrating on countries that are most vulnerable to violence—which tend to be those in the throes of transition—while also recognizing that UN engagement might, unhappily, prove more effective after rather than before the onset of large-scale violence, hard though it may be for the international community to accept this prescription.

The Primacy of Politics and the Paradox of Protection

Following the prevention logic, the A4P declaration stresses the primacy of politics and calls for political solutions to conflict, adding that "the pursuit of sustainable political solutions should guide the design and deployment of UN peacekeeping operations."[14] This point was made very forcefully in the HIPPO report too. I argued earlier that UN peacekeeping is neither politically nor materially resourced to impose definitive military solutions. Peacekeepers can help to contain violence and provide the space to allow political processes to gain ground. That was the case in Liberia and Sierra Leone and one ideally that would be the outcome in other cases.

Numerous commentators on peacekeeping operations have weighed in to underscore the premise that the use of force by UN peacekeepers,[15] however robust, cannot substitute for political solutions to conflict. I wholeheartedly subscribe to the soundness of that advice; the absence of such a workable political strategy explains well the frustrations and failures the UN has experienced in eastern Congo.

But regrettably, negotiated settlements do not always ensure durable political solutions. Over two decades, starting in the early 1990s, dozens of peace agreements were negotiated in West Africa[16] under international and regional auspices; few survived more than a few months. There was no peace to keep and the peacekeeping operations set up to help implement those agreements became hostages to the military fortunes of governments and rebels alike.

When peace agreements collapse, the political foundation of the UN peacekeeping presence can become fragile and tenuous. In such circumstances, should the peacekeeping force simply withdraw? That kind of binary choice is rarely—if ever—an option for the UN, even when there is no peace to keep. Occasionally, host governments like Eritrea and Chad have availed themselves of that option when they asked the UN to withdraw peacekeepers despite the Security Council's reluctance to do so. However, for the UN this choice is greatly inhibited by concerns for civilian protection, which is now a central dimension of major peacekeeping operations.

The Presumption of Protection

Since the Rwandan genocide and the Srebrenica massacres, peacekeeping operations perceived as failing to protect civilians have been intensely criticized and the UN's leadership has been faulted for allowing such failings to happen. In response to those (and other) tragedies, Kofi Annan published in 1999 his seminal report on the protection of civilians,[17] which became the principal raison d'être of the missions where I led operations. In the case of Côte d'Ivoire, it even became the ostensible casus belli, triggering the armed intervention by UN and French forces that effectively ended the Gbagbo regime.

The A4P declaration rightly recognizes that "host states bear the primary responsibility to protect citizens."[18] That is a crucial principal even though, as I have previously mentioned, failures in protection have often been quickly attributed to peacekeeping forces on the ground. There is a presumption that peacekeepers must afford civilian protection even if there is no political answer in sight and they do not have the capability to provide effective protection. In these circumstances, peacekeeping forces become de facto protection forces pending the return of some semblance of state protection. Protection is no longer an add-on to security responsibilities; it is *the* security responsibility. As a result, the protection of civilians is a common yardstick by which peacekeeping operations are judged. "Putting people at the center" has become a refrain of protection advocates who fault the UN for not doing a better job of protecting civilians.[19]

DPKO has invested in improving the protection performance of UN peacekeepers—uniformed and civilian—through policy changes, training protocols, and lessons learned. I personally spent a lot my time in the DRC (as have my successors, no doubt) trying to find better ways to ensure protection. But compared to the magnitude of the challenge, we could offer only a partial palliative. We could not overcome the huge obstacle posed by the government's own weak commitment to protection, which was sometimes amplified by the inadequacies of UN forces (some units had to be told bluntly to get out of their armored personnel carriers and actually meet the people they were supposed to be protecting). Too often, however, we were running against the tide, vulnerable to events beyond our control. Other peacekeeping missions, I know, have faced the same quandary.

While the peacekeepers' protection performance has to be constantly monitored and, if need be, improved, the UN still needs to spell out the limits to protection. When the Council establishes a UN peacekeeping operation with protection responsibility, the authorizing resolution normally contains a caveat stipulating that the mission is authorized "to use all necessary means, within the limits of its capacity and in the areas where its units are deployed"[20] (although in some resolutions this protection caveat has not been included). This is the peacekeeping equivalent of the fine print in credit card agreements; the language is noted but not fully understood. In reality, when a peacekeeping operation is deployed with a protection mandate, there is a common but unrealistic expectation that it will afford blanket protection to civilians irrespective of its areas of deployment and capabilities.

Protection and Politics

In the DRC and elsewhere, UN peacekeepers have saved many lives and protected many more. But UN peacekeeping forces are not, over time, the definitive answer to the challenge of mass protection of civilian populations. That answer lies with the government and people of the country concerned, whether it is the DRC or indeed any country that is suffering from a major protection crisis. It requires governments to place civilian protection at the center of their governance responsibilities and security policies.

Protection cannot be divorced, however, from the political resolve that is essential to protect citizens, year in and year out. That proposition takes us to the heart of the UN's protection conundrum: force is not an end in itself, but in the absence of the requisite political will, and the failure of nonforceful interventions such as mediation and reconciliation, force is the only protection alternative short of abandoning people to their fate. When the UN has not intervened forcefully to protect civilians, the subsequent outcry has severely damaged the organization's reputation.

Armed intervention creates its own dilemmas, however. When peacekeeping missions carry out military operations against armed groups that attack civilians, there is a commensurate risk that those operations will trigger worse violence, including reprisals against civilians. As I found out when we took action against the FDLR in eastern Congo, what followed was a call from the Security Council for political solutions, amplified (in that case) by activists claiming that the peacekeepers had forfeited their impartiality.

While I agree that robust operations in support of civilian protection should be the last option and undertaken with a full assessment and appreciation of the potential risks, if the military response is discounted in favor of political action, the question still remains as to how to generate the requisite political will required to ensure sustainable protection. Where are the entry points to engage with governments on issues that they customarily consider as the prerogatives of sovereign states? To cite the example of the DRC, the government did not want to engage on security sector reform, without which sustainable protection was a lost cause.

Of course, the search for effective tools for conflict prevention and resolution goes beyond civilian protection. Richard Gowan, a perceptive commentator on UN affairs, has proposed innovative ways to strengthen the UN's capacities for conflict prevention through the creation, for example, of "high-ambition coalitions"[21] of UN member states. From my experience in Liberia working with the International Contact Group on the Mano River Basin, I know that this approach can be very helpful. But the host government and other domestic actors must be willing to engage, which is not a given. The DRC government did not want to engage with any coordinated group and refused several demarches in that direction. Besides, such groups work well only if there are no "spoilers" inside or outside seeking to advance their interests to the detriment of the contact group's efforts. Nevertheless, the larger point is valid: the international community should be open to and willing to try out new ways of engaging politically with states beyond the traditional forms of state-to-state and multilateral diplomacy.

Nongovernmental interventions may be more effective in some circumstances, especially when governments are reluctant to internationalize their internal security problems (often the case). Bringing in the UN implies that the government cannot solve the problem alone, which may create doubts, at home and abroad, about the credibility and durability of the regime. Regimes with their backs to wall may be more open to more informal interventions that do not imply that they are under the tutelage of the international community. There are vibrant local and international civil society actors that can be brought into the process. In West Africa, for example, the Mano River Women's Peace Network has played an active and constructive role in pushing forward peace processes in that region.

As I mentioned in my chapter on Sierra Leone, in matters of war and peace, external actors (like myself), however well-meaning, are not always attuned to the historical legacies and cultural norms that can have a profound impact on the search for political solutions, especially in regions and among communities far from the capital city. So it makes sense to help local communities to build their own resilience and capacity for conflict resolution. This will require the UN, as one commentator has suggested, to "prioritize skills and profiles that are about understanding and influencing people."[22]

In any event, senior mission leaders should be better informed about the country and communities where the mission is operating. I would certainly support the idea of assigning, even on a temporary basis, anthropologists, economists, and historians to work with the senior leadership team. To cite the DRC once more, resource conflicts in the east over land, mineral mining, control of key roads, charcoal production, and even marijuana trafficking were a constant source of intercommunal tensions and violence. But our capacity to defuse these conflicts was limited by insufficient knowledge of the specific drivers of conflict as well as inadequate engagement with local communities.

When speaking of political solutions, Secretary-General Guterres used the word "compromise."[23] He urged warring groups (and states) to find compromises in the greater interest of peace. I have to say that this prescription needs to apply to the UN Secretariat itself. There is an undeclared but constant battle between the human rights and humanitarian organizations on one side and the political and operational entities on the other about the best way to achieve peaceful outcomes. At times, these quarrels have taken on an almost righteous overtone.

Again, from personal experience, I know that one can quickly run into hostile reactions from advocacy organizations and agencies (in and outside of the UN) if you are seen as being too close to unsavory governments or undesirable individuals. And yet compromises are an inescapable corollary of politics and political solutions, even though they may involve people who are not outstanding examples of enlightened humanity. As always, the dilemma is where to draw the line: When does compromise become appeasement?

The Dance Card: Partnerships and Peacekeeping

Partnership is a sensible recognition that the UN's capacities are limited (and likely to become ever more so as budgets are pared back) and that the organization needs a broad base of support to achieve its goals in an increasingly complex international environment. So not surprisingly, the A4P declaration stresses the importance of a two-dimensional "peacekeeping partnership": the first encompasses other institutions with political and security roles, and the second encompasses governments that host peacekeeping operations.

The HIPPO report states that a "stronger global-regional peace and security partnership is needed to respond to the more challenging crises of tomorrow."[24] The A4P declaration goes in the same direction and declares its readiness to "enhance collaboration and planning between the UN and relevant international, regional and sub-regional organizations and arrangements, including the African Union (AU) and the European Union (EU) . . . while recognizing the need for a clear delineation of roles between respective operations."[25]

When parameters are set and respected, security partnerships can indeed serve as both a political and a force multiplier. That was the case with the UK intervention in Sierra Leone and again with the deployment of an EU task force in Ituri in northeastern DRC. By contrast, uncoordinated interventions in the same theater of operations can be really counterproductive and potentially dangerous, as happened with the Ugandan-US operation against the LRA in eastern Congo, which left MONUC in the dark and inadvertently led to the massacre of civilians.

The events of November 2005 that I described in my chapter on Côte d'Ivoire are a good illustration of the strengths and limits to security partnerships. France's Operation Licorne was mandated by the Security Council to aid ONUCI as a kind of quick-reaction force. Coordination arrangements were set out before deployment, including reporting to the Council. On the ground, a mechanism was established that brought the ONUCI and Licorne force commanders together on a regular basis for consultation and planning. I joined several of those meetings and found them to be generally cordial and constructive even if there were differences of opinion on how to tackle some operational worries.

Those arrangements were put to the test when the violent crisis erupted following the Ivorian bombing of a French military encampment. Those arrangements both failed and worked. They failed in the sense that the French government authorized an armed retaliation against the Ivorian forces without informing the UN or ONUCI beforehand, even though the attack was bound to have major repercussions for the mission. They worked, however, when the crisis was under way, with ONUCI and Licorne coordinating their security movements and working together to protect the Forces Nouvelles ministers in Abidjan and coordinating joint patrols to shelter or evacuate people at risk in the city.

From these and other experiences, I believe that the success of an institutional partnership with security dimensions depends on two essential enabling elements that go beyond the "clear delineation of roles." The first element is clarity about the political goals of the partnership and not only its military objectives. The UN should not become a subcontractor to facilitate the political objectives of other organizations. If it does, there is a considerable risk that the UN may compromise its credibility and blur its own identity. The second element is having command and coordination responsibilities and mechanisms established in advance to minimize the potential for disruption and confusion, especially in time of crisis. Once troops are deployed, that becomes more difficult and subject to the interplay of personalities.

The second set of partners the A4P declaration speaks for are "host governments," which "commit to make all efforts to build and sustain peace and cooperate with peacekeeping operations in the pursuit of Security Council mandates, including facilitating access, and recognize national responsibilities related to the safety and security of peacekeepers."[26] This commitment makes two assumptions: first, that a government is in place and in control, and second, that it is willing to fully cooperate with the peacekeeping operation. If only it were that straightforward. In reality most peacekeeping missions (at least the four in which I worked) are deployed in situations where the government of the day was not fully in control of the country (hence the need for a peacekeeping mission) and, in two cases, not fully committed to the mission mandate as decided by the Security Council.

To the extent that the declaration is aspirational in intent, then the A4P commitment on partnerships with host governments is a reasonable statement. But the operating reality is often not as benign as the statement implies. So I would suggest that mandates need to be crafted and mission leaders prepared for a variety of scenarios, including those in which there is less than optimal cooperation from the host government.

The Heart of the Matter:
Peacekeeping, People, and Performance

In earlier chapters, I dwelt on a spectrum of personnel issues, including sexual exploitation and abuse, the gender gap, conduct and discipline, and the sometimes fraught relationship between UN headquarters and the field-based operations. The A4P declaration makes a number of commitments in these areas. Even though they largely reiterate previously declared ambitions, they bear repeating since they remain both valid and elusive.

As a headline commitment, the declaration speaks of "ensuring the highest level of peacekeeping performance, and to hold all civilian and uniformed peacekeepers, particularly leadership, accountable for effective performance under common parameters while addressing performance shortfalls."[27] On the surface, this is a reasonable proposition. Senior officials should be held accountable for the achievement of key goals and the proper management of the staff who report to them. The question is how to measure and assess "effective performance."

As I was leaving peacekeeping, UN headquarters announced that all SRSGs and other heads of missions would be required to sign performance compacts. Unfortunately, the compact set benchmarks such as gender targets and vacancy rates that depended on variables that were not under the direct control of the SRSG. So when it comes to defining the "common parameters" for effective performance, I hope that the framers will set realistic and achievable goals that are neither unattainable aspirations nor unduly detailed targets that amount to micro-management.

I believe that a structural change in senior mission leadership is needed to make large missions more manageable and goal-oriented. I suggest that the UN appoint chief operating officers responsible for mission management, planning, scenario development, and goal monitoring. The SRSG is simply too stretched to take on this role, and the deputies manage specific portfolios (humanitarian operations, rule of law, elections, etc.) that do not give them the necessary breadth of oversight.

Training is emphasized in the A4P declaration's commitment to support effective performance and accountability of the uniformed personnel. This responsibility lies with both the troop-contributing countries and the United Nations, which are expected to work together to deliver on the commitment. Having witnessed units that arrived in the mission area with only a vague notion of what lay in store for them, I can certainly applaud this commitment. But as I mentioned before, the pressure to get troops into the field, especially when there is a full-blown crisis under way, can be very detrimental to the judicious choice of contingents. Upfront pre-deployment training would help. But there are very few standby units available for UN peacekeeping and so I fear that the inadequacies of the past may well persist into the future.

There is another facet of training that is not really addressed in the A4P declaration: leadership. A recent paper[28] cowritten by one of my former colleagues, Kevin Kennedy, points out that leadership training is largely absent from the declaration. The authors write that "the UN Secretariat faces the challenge of finding and rapidly deploying leaders who possess the requisite mix of skills, knowledge of the operating environment, political judgment, and physical and mental stamina. Few, if any, mission leaders can be expected to be fully prepared upon being selected, no matter how rigorous the selection process." I wonder if this uncomfortable conclusion may have been inspired by Kevin's time working with me. Nevertheless, I agree with every word.

The paper goes on to say that "senior mission leaders therefore require continuous, institutionalized, and sustained training and learning support." Again, I fully agree and I hope that this recommendation will be taken forward by the Secretariat and the member states even though they have been rather stingy about spending on training, which is sometimes viewed as an expensive add-on. Indeed, I have heard diplomats argue that senior leaders should already possess the necessary capabilities *before* they are appointed; why else would they be appointed in the first place?

Peacekeeping is a "moveable feast," however. The challenges evolve, change, and mutate as the mission ages. Rarely, if ever, is the mission leader who was there at the start of the peacekeeping operation still there when it closes down. MONUC/MONUSCO, for example, has been led by eight SRSGs covering a span of two decades. While some problems remain constant, new demands and priorities inevitably emerge, as does the operating environment and the skills needed to manage that environment. So a continuing investment in the training (and retraining) of senior leadership—

current and prospective—is a good investment. Regrettably, as the paper makes clear, that is not happening; training tends to be an early victim of budget cutbacks, which are now the order of the day in peacekeeping operations. I hope this trend is reversed. I hope too that training is broadened and deepened at all levels, especially for younger staff. The training I received as a young staff member in the UNDP benefited me throughout a long UN career, including my stint in peacekeeping.

I want to add a final comment on a deeply troubling issue about which I have already written: sexual exploitation and abuse. The A4P declaration rightly recommits to the "UN zero-tolerance policy with its victim-centered approach on all forms of sexual exploitation and abuse."[29] Given the recurring scandals, this commitment was to be expected in a major, intergovernmental policy document on UN peacekeeping. But the reference to a "victim-centered approach" is rather overdue. I found that the UN legal and administrative services could be unduly cautious in providing restitution to victims until due process was fully completed. There is of course a legitimate concern about fraudulent cases (I encountered some), but nevertheless this presumption of UN blamelessness did not serve the organization well. So a more flexible response that provides early support to the victim where there is a prima facie case to answer would be morally as well politically right.

Fit for Purpose: The Push for Reform

Reform is a hardy perennial in the UN's institutional garden. The introduction to the A4P declaration includes a passing reference to the "Secretary-General's vision for reforming the peace and security pillar of the UN Secretariat and his commitment to improving the ability of the UN to deliver on its mandates through management reform, which will enhance the impact of peacekeeping."[30]

I was a (small) part of the reform program that Kofi Annan set in motion early in his first term as Secretary-General. Prior to the Annan reforms, Secretary-General Boutros Boutros-Ghali had created the Departments of Peacekeeping Operations and Political Affairs to provide greater focus and coherence to UN peacemaking and peacekeeping activities and operations. Annan's successor, Ban Ki-moon, hived off the management support for peace operations and created a separate Department of Field Operations to improve management support but also, it was rumored, to clip the wings of what had become the most prominent department in the UN Secretariat.

The latest round of reform, put in place on January 1, 2019, by Secretary-General Guterres, partially merges the previous Departments of Peacekeeping and Political Affairs into a new Department of Political and Peacebuilding Affairs, which inherits functions from both Political Affairs and DPKO while a new Department of Peace Operations takes over some of the functions earlier assigned to Political Affairs and DPKO. The reform also transforms Field Operations into a new Department of Operational Support that adds some responsibilities formerly handled by the Department of Management, which now becomes the Department of Management Strategy, Policy, and Compliance.

I should admit that it took me some time to get my head around this alphabet of acronyms, which have created reporting lines of some complexity. How will this all work out in practice? Will these changes encourage a more holistic approach to peace operations and a closer link between analysis and action? Or will the old frictions between Political Affairs and DPKO be replaced by new ones between Political and Peacebuilding Affairs, and Peace Operations?

Kofi Annan, when asked about his experience in managing UN reform, would recount an amusing but instructive anecdote. A few months after he took office, he was hosting a monthly luncheon meeting with the Security Council during which he was taken to task by one of the permanent members of the Council for what the ambassador perceived as the dilatory progress on the reform agenda. In response, Annan made the point that reform was a process not an event. The ambassador retorted that God had made the Heavens and the Earth in six days, so why was the reform process taking so long? To which the Secretary-General responded that God had worked alone but that he, Annan, had to work with fifteen members of the Council.

So in assessing the current round of reform, we should be mindful of Secretary-General Annan's advice: reform is a process. The merger of the former geographic desks in Political Affairs and DPKO should help to curtail the perpetual friction that marred interdepartmental cooperation on peace operations in the past. However, the new mega-structure—Political and Peacebuilding Affairs—carries its own risks. It is formed around a bifurcation of functions, with peacebuilding responsibilities grouped under one column and regional/country analysis and engagement under another, while the new Department of Peace Operations inherits a whole range of technical functions such as DDR, security sector reform, rule of law from DPKO, as well as some management functions from the Department of Management.

To be effective, these arrangements will require a form of matrix management that brings units and individuals together across organizational boundaries to devise and implement policy guidance and operational directives in a coherent manner. But getting people to work together harmoniously and constructively outside of a vertical hierarchy is not easy. Changing the organigram alone will not provide the impetus for change or break down the institutional silos that tend to afflict all large and complex organizations. This is why in my opinion issue-led rather than mandate-based coordination is a more effective way of tackling complicated, multifaceted problems of the kind that peace operations face.

The decentralization of personnel management functions to the field missions via the newly created Department of Operational Support will prove, I sense, to be particularly challenging. In principle, this reform, if achieved, would be a major and long-overdue development that will be welcomed by the field missions. For that to happen, however, UN headquarters will have to be ready and willing to "let go." The top management of the new structures will need to push forcefully for that decentralization. When we first experimented with the multiple-hats model in UNAMSIL, the strong support of management at UN headquarters led by Mark Malloch Brown was indispensable for making that innovation work; reform doesn't happen on autopilot.

Peacekeeping: Where Next?

Does peacekeeping have a future? I would like to say no, safe in the belief that conflicts of the kind in which the UN has intervened in recent decades will be prevented in the first place. But I fear that this will not be the case. Given the international community's mixed record on conflict prevention, I anticipate that UN peacekeepers will continue be called upon to intervene in other people's wars. The question then becomes: When and under what conditions will the UN intervene and with what prospects for success?

In 2010, the Security Council held a debate on exit strategies for peacekeeping missions. In his opening remarks, Secretary-General Ban Ki-moon suggested that "from the earliest planning stages of a peacekeeping operation, an end point must be envisaged at which the countries concerned could implement peace agreements and achieve at least the minimum level of sustainable stability, among other results."[31]

I don't think I made many friends around the Council table when I submitted that the problem was not so much exit as entry strategies. I added, however, that if mandates were obliged to encompass an exit strategy upfront, we would probably never field another peacekeeping operation, since it was impossible to determine with real certainty what the future would hold. To the extent that the success of a peacekeeping operation is intimately associated with the state of the state, it will always function in a zone of ambiguity. To manage that ambiguity, UN policymakers and mission managers need to look around corners, armed with flexibility and equipped with alternatives.

Over several decades the UN has built up an impressive capacity and experience in peace operations, a multilateral asset of unique value that should not be lightly discounted or quickly discarded. UN peacekeepers are not resourced to do war-fighting, but there is nevertheless room for UN peacekeeping even though the operations delegated to the UN are likely to be "second tier"—interventions that either are not of sufficient strategic interest to engage major powers directly (or through a security alliance such as NATO), or else left to a regional intervention like the AU mission in Somalia. This doesn't make UN interventions any less valuable, but it does mean that they will likely be "slow burn" affairs that drag on and do not lend themselves to easy resolution and withdrawal (of course, that observation could also be applied to some operations of the North Atlantic Treaty Organization [NATO], such as those in Afghanistan).

Unfortunately, money is often the driver when UN peacekeeping operations are being debated and framed. Even though UN peacekeeping expenditures represent the equivalent of less than half of 1 percent of world military expenditures,[32] these operations are often—at least at the beginning—underfunded and undermanned, making it difficult for them to exert meaningful pressure on the protagonists. It's a false and unwise economy, which becomes readily apparent when crisis strikes (often the case) and the UN scurries to get reinforcements or else has to rely on a bilateral intervention to help stave off disaster.

Of course, the enterprise of peacekeeping should always be cost-conscious, open to innovation, and ready to change its ways when that is patently required. The demands for and on peacekeeping will evolve and, one hopes, diminish. Nevertheless, if peacekeepers are asked to intervene in other people's wars, the United Nations has to ensure that the mission mandate is realistic, properly funded, and well grounded in the historical and contemporary realities of the country where it is deployed. As I have attempted to show, every war is different, and UN peacekeepers can make a difference only when they are politically and materially equipped to tackle the complexity of the conflicts in which they are asked to intervene.

The arc of conflict can be long. Once the threads of comity unravel, they cannot be easily or quickly stitched back together again. And while outsiders may try to prolong or shorten a conflict, they cannot ultimately define it. That is quintessentially a national duty and responsibility. What peacekeeping can do is create time and space for that national will to assert itself.

After decades of murderous violence and numerous failed peace agreements, that is what happened in three of the countries I have written about—Sierra Leone, Liberia, and Côte d'Ivoire. Sadly, large areas of the DRC remain enmeshed in extreme violence. Nevertheless, in each of those countries the struggle for power, privilege, and possession that precipitated the capture and collapse of state institutions, ushering in years of violent upheaval and the dispatch of peacekeepers, remains a present danger that calls for constant vigilance to prevent the past from again becoming a prelude to the future.

I look back now at my decade in peacekeeping with mixed emotions. Those years were at once exhilarating, frustrating, fulfilling, disappointing, uplifting, exhausting, and not without with moments of self-doubt and despair. There were intervals of exuberance, especially in Sierra Leone and Liberia, where I witnessed and participated in the return of peace; by contrast, during my time in Côte d'Ivoire and the Congo, violence continued with depressing frequency as the political process failed to address and resolve the issues that fueled that violence. But ultimately, my days in peacekeeping were immensely gratifying.

I was fortunate to work with many extraordinary people of all ranks and nationalities. That is sometimes forgotten in the welter of criticism that is never far from peacekeeping operations. The profession of peacekeeping is a demanding one and the United Nations has to find and field the best and demonstrate that the world is not indifferent to human suffering and misery. Yes, there have been glaring lapses in the behavior of some peacekeepers that have tarnished the reputation of many. Such failings need to be dealt with quickly and openly; the UN cannot afford to be less than candid. But the United Nations and its member states should also take pride in knowing that the vast majority of UN peacekeepers—civilian and uniformed—do a decent job, often in tough and hazardous conditions, and behave honorably.

Kofi Annan did indeed get it right when he said I would never have another job like peacekeeping. But it became much more than a job to me; in a way, other people's wars became my wars even though I never suffered the appalling fate of the millions of people caught up in those conflicts. I hope, nonetheless, that I played a part in finally bringing those cruel catastrophes to an end.

Notes

Chapter 1: A Journey in Peacekeeping

1. For a more detailed description of the evolution of UN peacekeeping operations, see "United Nations Peacekeeping," http://www.un.org/en/peacekeeping/operations/current.shtml.

Part 1: Things Fall Apart

1. Acemoglu and Robinson, *Why Nations Fail.*
2. Ibid.

Chapter 2: Sierra Leone

1. Personal correspondence.
2. Gberie, *A Dirty War in West Africa.*
3. See, for example, "Foday Sankoh," *The Economist.*
4. Designated as the Economic Community of West African States Monitoring Group (ECOMOG).
5. See US Institute of Peace, *Peace Agreement Between the Government of Sierra Leone and the Revolutionary United Front of Sierra Leone 1996.*
6. United Nations Peacemaker, *Peace Agreement Between the Government of Sierra Leone and the Revolutionary United Front 1999,* art. 9.
7. Ibid., art. 7.
8. Ibid.
9. Ibid., art. 6.
10. United Nations Security Council (UNSC) Res. 1181 (July 13, 1998).
11. Olonisakin, "UNOMSIL."
12. UNSC Res. 1270 (October 22, 1999).
13. UNSC Res. 1289 (February 7, 2000).
14. See Sheeran, "The Use of Force in United Nations Peacekeeping Operations."
15. UNSC Res. 1270.

16. UNSC, *Report of the Secretary-General to the Security Council on the Protection of Civilians in Armed Conflict.*

17. For the specifics of the May crisis, see Jennings, "UNOMIL."

18. See UNSC, *Report of the Independent Inquiry into the Actions of the United Nations During the 1994 Genocide in Rwanda,* p. 51; and United Nations General Assembly (UNGA) and UNSC, *Report of the Panel on Peacekeeping Operations.*

19. Olonisakin, "UNOMSIL."

20. Annan, "2 December 2000 UN Success in Sierra Leone."

21. United Nations, "Secretary-General Appoints Alan Doss As Deputy Special Representative in Sierra Leone."

22. Kaldor and Vincent, *Evaluation of UNDP Assistance to Conflict-Affected Countries.*

23. "Sierra Leone," *New Humanitarian.*

24. UNSC, *Eighth Report of the Secretary-General on the United Nations Mission to Liberia,* para. 76.

25. Residual Special Court for Sierra Leone, *Agreement Between the United Nations and the Government of Sierra Leone on the Establishment of a Residual Special Court for Sierra Leone.*

26. See Gberie, "The Special Court for Sierra Leone Rests."

27. Maguire, "Cambodia and the Pitfalls of Political Justice."

28. See Humphreys and Weinstein, "What the fighters Say."

29. See "Sierra Leone: National Recovery Strategy (2002–2003)," p. 5.

30. See Kaldor and Vincent, *Evaluation of UNDP Assistance to Conflict-Affected Countries.*

31. Personal communication.

Chapter 3: Côte d'Ivoire

1. See Mengisteab and Daddieh, *State Building and Democratization in Africa.*

2. See Philippe Hugon in Seelow, "Côte d'Ivoire."

3. For a summary and timeline of the various peace agreements aimed at ending the conflict in Côte d'Ivoire, see Sidibé, "Peace Processes in Côte d'Ivoire."

4. See UNSC, *Report of the Secretary-General on Côte d'Ivoire.*

5. See United Nations Peacemaker, *Linas-Marcoussis Agreement.*

6. Ibid.

7. See UNSC, *Report of the Secretary-General on Côte d'Ivoire,* para. 31.

8. Ibid., para. 88.

9. United Nations Peacekeeping, "Côte d'Ivoire-MINUCI-Mandate."

10. See UNSC, "Letter from the Permanent Representative of Côte d'Ivoire to the President of the Security Council of the United Nations."

11. See UNSC, *Report of the Secretary-General on the United Nations Mission in Côte d'Ivoire Submitted Pursuant to Security Council Resolution 1514 (2003) of 13 November 2003,* para. 14.

12. Ibid., para. 86.

13. See UNSC Res. 1528 (February 27, 2004).

14. See UNSC, "Statement by the President of the Security Council."

15. Numbers varied between 800,000 and 1.3 million; see Bouquet, "Le Mauvais Usage de la Démocratie en Côte d'Ivoire," p. 6.

16. See United Nations Peacemaker, *Linas-Marcoussis Agreement.*

17. UNSC Res. 1479 (May 13, 2003).

18. UNSC, *Second Report of the Secretary-General on the United Nations Operation in Côte d'Ivoire,* para. 62.

19. Ibid., para. 15.

20. Ibid., para. 20.

21. See Dunhelm, "Bombardement de Bouaké."

22. See UNSC Res. 1572 (November 15, 2004), para. 9.

23. See Novosseloff, "ONUCI."

24. UNSC, *Third Progress Report of the Secretary-General on the United Nations Operation in Côte d'Ivoire,* para. 17.

25. UNSC Res. 1528.

26. UNSC Res. 1603 (June 3, 2005), para. 7.

27. United Nations Peacemaker, *Pretoria Agreement on the Peace Process in the Côte d'Ivoire,* (Pretoria I).

28. Ibid., para. 14.

29. See Colombant, "South Africa Ends Mediation Role in Ivory Coast."

30. Thomson Reuters Foundation, "Peace Now up to Ivory Coast Leaders."

31. UNSC, *Sixth Progress Report of the Secretary-General on the United Nations Operation in Côte d'Ivoire,* para. 64.

32. UNSC Res. 1633 (October 21, 2005), para. 3.

33. Ibid., paras. 6–10.

34. See Novosseloff, "ONUCI."

35. Ibid.

36. UNSC Res. 1975 (March 30, 2011).

37. See Amnesty International, "Côte d'Ivoire."

38. See "Côte d'Ivoire," *Jeune Afrique.*

Chapter 4: Liberia

1. See Brenton, "American Colonization Society."

2. See Yarema, *American Colonization Society,* p. 47.

3. Ellis, *The Mask of Anarchy,* p. 196.

4. Ibid.

5. Ibid., chap. 5.

6. US Department of State, *Report of the International Commission of Inquiry into the Existence of Slavery and Forced Labor in the Republic of Liberia.*

7. See Global Security, "Liberia and the League of Nations."

8. US Department of State, *Report of the International Commission of Inquiry into the Existence of Slavery and Forced Labor in the Republic of Liberia.*

9. Ellis, *The Mask of Anarchy,* chap. 5.

10. Toe, "Liberia's GDP Paradox."

11. See "Liberia Country Profile," *BBC News.*

12. For a complete list of the Liberia agreements, see Conciliation Resources, "Accord Series."

13. UNSC Res. 866 (September 22, 1993).

14. See Jennings, "UNOMIL."

15. See United Nations Peacekeeping, "United Nations Mission in Liberia—Background."

16. See Romano and Nollkaemper, "The Arrest Warrant Against the Liberian President."

17. On evacuating the Philippines after the Japanese invasion in 1942, US general Douglas MacArthur declared: "I shall return." He did but Taylor did not.

18. See US Institute of Peace, *Comprehensive Peace Agreement Between the Government of Liberia and the Liberians United for Reconciliation and Democracy (LURD) and the Movement for Democracy in Liberia (MODEL) and Political Parties.*

19. United Nations Peacekeeping, "United Nations Mission in Liberia—Background."

20. UNSC Res. 1509 (September 19, 2003).

21. See Jennings, "UNOMIL," p. 697.

22. See US Institute of Peace, *Comprehensive Peace Agreement Between the Government of Liberia and the Liberians United for Reconciliation and Democracy (LURD) and the Movement for Democracy in Liberia (MODEL) and Political Parties,* art. 25.

23. International Monetary Fund, *Liberia.*

24. Dwan and Bailey, *Liberia's Governance and Economic Management Assistance Programme.*

25. Johnson, *The Rise and Fall of President Samuel K. Doe.*

26. US Department of State, "U.S.-Liberia Relationship."

27. UNSC, *Thirtieth Progress Report on the United Nations Mission in Liberia.*

28. United Nations Mission in Liberia (UNMIL), *Security Sector.*

29. See UNMIL and Office of the High Commissioner for Human Rights (OHCHR), "Addressing Impunity for Rape in Liberia."

30. UNSC Res. 1638 (November 11, 2005).

31. See, for example, "Charles Taylor Caught in Nigeria," *BBC News.*

32. Personal communication.

Part 2: Wars Without Winners

1. The name of the Congo has changed several times since independence in 1960. The "Republic of the Congo," the name used at independence, was subsequently changed to the "People's Republic of the Congo" in 1964, to the "Democratic Republic of the Congo" in 1966, and then to "Zaire" in 1971. In 1997, the country became the "Democratic Republic of the Congo." To add to the confusion, the "Republic of the Congo," known colloquially as "Congo Brazza" (after the name of its capital, Brazzaville), lies right across the Congo River from the DRC. Throughout the book when I use "Congo," I mean the "Democratic Republic of the Congo."

Chapter 5: Into the Cauldron

1. See Cawthorne, *The World's Worst Atrocities.*

2. Casement, "Correspondence and Report from His Majesty's Consul at Boma."

3. See Renton, Seddon, and Zeilig, *The Congo.*

4. See Meredith, *The Fortunes of Africa,* chap. 63.

5. Ibid.

6. This chapter uses material from two papers that I previously published: "In the Footsteps of Dr Bunche" and "United Nations Organization Mission in the Democratic Republic of the Congo."

7. UNSC Res. 4387 (July 14, 1960).

8. Brian Urquhart, a close aide of Hammarskjöld, provides a remarkable, first-hand account Hammarskjöld's concerns and actions in Congo and Katanga in his autobiography, *A Life in War and Peace.*

9. UNSC Res. 4387.

10. Chapter VII permits the UN Security Council to authorize peace enforcement actions.

11. UNSC Res. 4387.

12. UNSC, *Second Report on the Implementation of Security Council Resolution S/4387 of 14 July 1960 and S/4405 of 22 July 1960.*

13. Urquhart, *A Life in War and Peace,* p. 98.

14. O'Brien, *To Katanga and Back,* p. 88.

15. See, for example, Rich, "The Death of Dag Hammarskjöld," p. 360; and Lynch, "U.N. to Probe Whether Iconic Secretary-General Was Assassinated."

16. UNSC Res. 4741 (February 21, 1961).

17. Ibid., pt. B.

18. See Kalb, *The Congo Cables.*

19. See Peters and Woolley, "George Bush, Remarks."

20. Wrong, *In the Footsteps of Mr Kurtz,* p. 98.

21. For a detailed analysis of this violence, see Lemarchand, *The Dynamics of Violence in Central Africa.*

22. See also Lemarchand, *The Dynamics of Violence in Central Africa,* for an analysis of the ethnic dimensions of the conflicts in Rwanda and Burundi and the Kivus.

23. A superb study of these interlocking elements can be found in Prunier, *Africa's World War.*

24. See Malvern, "United Nations Observer Mission Uganda-Rwanda" and "United Nations Assistance Mission for Rwanda I."

25. See UNMIL and OHCHR, *Report of the Mapping Exercise Documenting the Most Serious Violations of Human Rights and International Humanitarian Law Committed Within the Territory of the Democratic Republic of the Congo Between March 1993 and June 2003.*

26. Prunier, *Africa's World War.*

27. Ibid.

28. See especially Benjamin Coghlan et al., "Mortality in the Democratic Republic of Congo."

29. UNSC Res. 1234 (April 9, 1999).

30. Ibid.

31. UNSC Res. 815 (July 25, 1999).

32. UNSC Res. 1279 (November 30, 1999).

33. Goldstein, *Winning the War on War,* p. 660.

Chapter 6: Conflict Without End

1. Autesserre, *The Trouble with the Congo.*

2. UNSC, *Twenty-fourth Report of the Secretary-General on the United Nations Organization Mission in the Democratic Republic of the Congo.*

3. The name given to the remnants of the Hutu militias and Rwandese army that had fled to Congo to escape the advancing army of the Rwandan Patriotic Front, led by Paul Kagame.

4. UNSC, *Twenty-fourth Report of the Secretary-General on the United Nations Organization Mission in the Democratic Republic of the Congo.*

5. Government of the Democratic Republic of Congo and Government of the Republic of Rwanda, "Joint Communiqué on a Common Approach to End the Threat."

6. Ibid.

7. Ibid.

8. UNSC, *Twenty-fifth Report of the Secretary General on the United Nations Organization Mission in the Democratic Republic of the Congo.*

9. A Swahili word meaning "peace."

10. Internal communication to the SRSG.

11. UNSC Res. 1843 (November 20, 2008).

12. Human Rights Watch, "Killings in Kiwanja."

13. See, for example, Cohen, "Can Africa Trade Its Way to Peace?" referring to Nkunda's force being "well armed and financed by the Rwandan government."

14. Human Rights Watch, *Killings in Kiwanja;* and OHCHR and United Nations Organization Mission in the Democratic Republic of Congo (MONUC), *Consolidated Report on Investigations conducted by the United Nations Joint Human Rights Office (UNJHRO) into Grave Human Rights Abuses Committed in Kiwanja, North Kivu, in November 2008.*

15. A Swahili phrase meaning "our unity."

16. A Swahili word meaning "a net."

17. Kanyunyu and Bavier, "Congo Rebel Leader Nkunda Arrested in Rwanda."

18. UNSG, "Activities of Secretary-General in Democratic Republic of Congo, Rwanda, 28 February–1 March."

19. Ibid.

20. UNSC, *Twenty-sixth Report of the Secretary-General on the United Nations Organization Mission in the Democratic Republic of the Congo.*

21. UNSC, *Report of the Security Council Mission to the African Union; Rwanda and the Democratic Republic of the Congo; and Liberia.*

22. UNSC, *Thirtieth Report of the Secretary-General on the United Nations Organization Mission in the Democratic Republic of the Congo,* para. 41.

23. Human Rights Watch, "UN: Act to End Atrocities in Eastern Congo."

24. Swahili words meaning "peace today."

25. UNSC, *6253rd Meeting of the Security Council.*

Chapter 7: The Contagion of Conflict

1. Global Security, "Bundu dia Kongo."

2. Acemoglu and Robinson, *Why Nations Fail.*

3. UNSC, *Twenty-fifth Report of the Secretary-General on the United Nations Organization Mission in the Democratic Republic of the Congo.*

4. See Lawrence, *The Lord's Resistance Army.*

5. See Institute for War and Peace Reporting, "Uganda: LRA Accused of Selling Food Aid."

6. A Swahili word meaning "return."

7. UNSC Res. 1843.

8. Berdal, "The State of UN Peacekeeping."

9. See Kristof, "The World Capital of Killing."

Chapter 8: Pursuing Peace

1. See UNSC, "Letter Dated 15 October 2002 from the Secretary-General Addressed to the President of the Security Council."

2. UN Res. 1906 (December 23, 2009) (emphasis in original).

3. See UNSC, *Thirtieth Report of the Secretary-General on the United Nations Organization Mission in the Democratic Republic of the Congo.*

4. UNSC, *Twenty-fourth Report of the Secretary-General on the United Nations Organization Mission in the Democratic Republic of the Congo.*

5. UNSC, *Twenty-ninth Report of the Secretary-General on the United Nations Organization Mission in the Democratic Republic of the Congo.*

6. UNSC, *Report of the Security Council Mission to the African Union; Rwanda and the Democratic Republic of the Congo; and Liberia.*

7. UN Res. 1906, emphasis added.

8. UN Res. 1925 (May 28, 2010).

9. Ibid.

10. Ibid.

11. UNSC, *Report of the Security Council Mission to the Democratic Republic of the Congo (13 to 16 May 2010).*

12. "Unloved for Trying to Keep the Peace," *The Economist.*

13. See, for example, Belasco, "The Cost of Iraq, Afghanistan, and Other Global War on Terror Operations Since 9/11."

14. United Nations High Commissioner for Refugees (UNHCR), "UNHCR DR Congo Factsheet—April 2017."

15. See Doss, "The United Nations Mission in the Congo," p. 668

16. "DR Congo: Floribert Chebeya Killers Sentenced to Death," *BBC News.*

17. See Ibrahim and Doss, "A Defeat for Democracy, a Disaster for the People."

Chapter 9: Great Expectations

1. See Caplan, *Measuring Peace,* p. 2.

2. See Doss, "Great Expectations."

3. Ibid.

4. Annan, *Interventions,* p. 77.

5. UNSC, *Third Special Report of the Secretary-General on the United Nations Organization Mission in the Democratic Republic of the Congo.*

6. For a more scholarly interpretation of what Chapter VII means, see Novosseloff, "Chapitre VII et Maintien de la Paix."

7. Berdal, "The State of UN Peacekeeping."

8. Tardy, "The UN and the Use of Force."

9. For a definition of this term and its operational implications, see the so-called Capstone Doctrine at https://peacekeeping.un.org/sites/default/files/capstone_eng_0.pdf.

10. UNSC Res. 1565 (October 1, 2004).

11. Urquhart, *A Life in Peace and War,* p. 155.

12. See Robert Gates in Shanker, "Defense Secretary Warns NATO of 'Dim' Future."

13. For a longer discussion of this issue in the UN context, see Novosseloff, "No Caveats, Please?"

Chapter 10: Pipe Dreams and Possibilities

1. See Soares de Oliveira, *Magnificent and Beggar Land,* on how Angola used its oil wealth to resist the neoliberal model.

2. For a structured analysis of the impact of postconflict truth-telling and reconciliation, see Kofi Annan Foundation and International Center for Transitional Justice, *Challenging the Conventional: Can Truth Commissions Strengthen Peace Processes?;* and Kofi Annan Foundation and Interpeace, *Challenging the Conventional: Making Post-Violence Reconciliation Succeed.*

3. Interpeace is a Geneva-based international organization that supports locally led initiatives for peacebuilding around the world. See Interpeace, "About Us," https://www.interpeace.org/who-we-are/about-us.

4. See, for example, World Bank, *World Development Report 2011—Overview.*

5. Geneva Centre for Security Policy, *After the Fall.*

Chapter 11: A Job Like No Other

1. International Forum for the Challenges of Peace Operations, *Considerations for Mission Leadership in United Nations Peacekeeping Operations,* p. 18.

2. Matthew 22:21.

Chapter 12: Facing the Future

1. Centre on International Cooperation, *Annual Review of Global Peace Operations 2010.*

2. Centre on International Cooperation, *Annual Review of Global Peace Operations 2011.*

3. UNGA and UNSC, *Report of the High-Level Panel on Peace Operations on Uniting Our Strengths for Peace, Politics, Partnership, and People* (HIPPO Report).

4. United Nations, "Improving Security of United Nations Peacekeepers."

5. UNGA, *Restructuring of the United Nations Peace and Security Pillar: Report of the Secretary-General.*

6. See United Nations Peacekeeping, "Action for Peacekeeping."

7. Ibid.

8. Ibid.

9. Leone, "Conflict Prevention Is 'The Priority.'"

10. Rosling, Rosling Rönnlund, and Rosling, *Factfulness: Ten Reasons We're Wrong About the World.*

11. See Stewart, "Lecture on Inequalities and Conflict."

12. See also World Bank and United Nations, *Pathways for Peace.*

13. Preamble to the Charter of the United Nations, signed on June 26, 1945, in San Francisco.

14. See United Nations Peacekeeping, "Action for Peacekeeping."

15. See, for example, Berdal, "What Are the Limits to the Use of Force in UN Peacekeeping?" pp. 112–113.

16. For a comprehensive listing of these agreements, see Language of Peace, https://www.languageofpeace.org.

17. UNSC, *Report of the Secretary-General to the Security Council on the Protection of Civilians in Armed Conflict.*

18. See United Nations Peacekeeping, "Action for Peacekeeping," para. 9.

19. See, for example, Di Razza, "Making Peace Operations About People."

20. In the case of MONUC, see UNSC Res. 1565; successive resolutions renewed this provision.

21. Gowan, "Political Gap in Reform Agenda Leaves Questions on A4P Mechanisms."

22. See, for example, Di Razza, "Making Peace Operations About People."

23. Leone, "Conflict Prevention Is 'The Priority.'"

24. UNGA and UNSC, *Report of the High-Level Panel on Peace Operations on Uniting Our Strengths for Peace, Politics, Partnership, and People.*

25. See United Nations Peacekeeping, "Action for Peacekeeping," para. 18, https://peacekeeping.un.org/en/action-for-peacekeeping-a4p.

26. Ibid., para. 19.

27. Ibid., para. 13.

28. Kennedy and Powers, "Senior Leadership Training in UN Peace Operations."

29. See United Nations Peacekeeping, "Action for Peacekeeping," para. 21.

30. Ibid., para. 2.

31. UNSC, "Security Council Commits Itself to Improving Transition, Exit Strategies for United Nations Peacekeeping Operations."

32. United Nations Peacekeeping, "How We Are Funded."

Bibliography

Acemoglu, Daron, and James A. Robinson. *Why Nations Fail: The Origins of Power, Prosperity, and Poverty.* New York: Random House, 2012.

Agreement Between the United Nations and the Government of Sierra Leone on the Establishment of a Residual Special Court for Sierra Leone. January 16, 2002. http://www.rscsl.org/Documents/RSCSL%20Agreement% 20and%20Statute.pdf.

Amnesty International. "Côte d'Ivoire: UN Mission Closes Amidst Fragile Human Rights Situation." June 29, 2017. https://www.amnesty.org/en/documents/ior40/6630/2017/en.

Annan, Kofi A. "2 December 2000 UN Success in Sierra Leone Will Depend on Teamwork." In *The Collected Papers of Kofi Annan, UN Secretary-General 2000–2001,* vol. 2, edited by Jean E. Krasno. Boulder: Lynne Rienner, 2012.

Annan, Kofi A., and Nader Mouzavizadeh. *Interventions: A Life in War and Peace.* New York: Penguin, September 2012.

Autesserre, Séverine. *The Trouble with the Congo: Local Violence and the Failure or International Peacebuilding.* Cambridge Studies in International Relations. New York: Cambridge University Press, 2010.

Belasco, Amy. "The Cost of Iraq, Afghanistan, and Other Global War on Terror Operations Since 9/11." Congressional Research Service, December 8, 2014. https://timedotcom.files.wordpress.com/2015/01/rl33110.pdf.

Berdal, Mats. "The State of UN Peacekeeping: Lessons from Congo." *Journal of Strategic Studies,* August 30, 2016. https://tandfonline.com/doi/abs/10.1080/01402390.2016.1215307?src=recsys&journalCode=fjss20.

———. "What Are the Limits to the Use of Force in UN Peacekeeping?" In *United Nations Peace Operations in a Changing Global Order,* edited by Cedric de Coning and Mateja Peter. London: Palgrave Macmillan, 2018. https://doi.org/10.1007/978-3-319-99106-1_6.

Bouquet, Christian. "Le Mauvais Usage de la Démocratie en Côte d'Ivoire." *L'Espace Politique* vol. 3 (2007). https://journals.openedition.org/espacepolitique/894.

Brenton, Felix. "American Colonization Society (1816–1964)." *Black Past,* December 30, 2008. http://www.blackpast.org/aah/american-colonization-society-1816-1964.

Caplan, Richard. *Measuring Peace: Principles, Practices, and Politics.* Oxford: Oxford University Press, 2019.

Casement, Roger. "Correspondence and Report from His Majesty's Consul at Boma Respecting the Administration of the Independent State of the Congo." *Foreign Office Blue Books* no. 1, Cd. 1933, 1904. https://archive.org/details/CasementReport/page/n1.

Cawthorne, Nigel. *The World's Worst Atrocities.* London: Octopus, 1999.

315

Centre on International Cooperation. *Annual Review of Global Peace Operations 2010.* Boulder: Lynne Rienner, 2010. https://cic.nyu.edu/content/annual-review-global-peace-operations-2010.

———. *Annual Review of Global Peace Operations 2011.* Boulder: Lynne Rienner, 2011. https://peaceoperationsreview.org/wp-content/uploads/2015/06/GPO_2011.pdf.

"Charles Taylor Caught in Nigeria." *BBC News,* March 29, 2006. http://news.bbc.co.uk/2/hi/africa/4856120.stm.

Coghlan, Benjamin, Richard J. Brennan, Pascal Ngoy, David Dofara, Brad Otto, Mark Clements, and Tony Stewart. "Mortality in the Democratic Republic of Congo: A Nationwide Survey." *The Lancet,* January 7, 2006. http://thelancet.com/journals/lancet/article/PIIS0140-6736(06)67923-3/fulltext.

Cohen, Herman J. "Can Africa Trade Its Way to Peace?" *New York Times,* December 15, 2008. https://www.nytimes.com/2008/12/16/opinion/16cohen.html.

Colombant, Nico. "South Africa Ends Mediation Role in Ivory Coast." *51VOA,* August 30, 2005. http://www.51voa.com/VOA_Standard_English/VOA_Standard_2430.html.

Conciliation Resources. "Accord Series." http://www.c-r.org/downloads/Accord.

"Côte d'Ivoire: Henri Konan Bédié Maintient ses Propos Controversés sur les Étrangers." *Jeune Afrique,* June 28, 2019. https://www.jeuneafrique.com/795189/politique/cote-divoire-henri-konan-bedie-maintient-ses-propos-controverses-sur-les-etrangers.

Di Razza, Namie. "Making Peace Operations About People: A Needed Shift for the Protection of Civilians." IPI Global Observatory, June 26, 2018. https://theglobalobservatory.org/2018/06/making-peace-operations-about-people-neededshift-protection-civilians.

———. *Reframing the Protection of Civilians Paradigm for UN Peace Operations.* New York: International Peace Institute, 2017. https://www.ipinst.org/2017/11/poc-paradigm-un-peace-ops.

Doss, Alan. "Great Expectations: UN Peacekeeping, Civilian Protection, and the Use of Force." Geneva Centre for Security Policy, Geneva Papers: Research Series no. 4, December 2011. https://www.files.ethz.ch/isn/135708/Geneva%20Paper%20Research%20Series%204.pdf.

———. "In the Footsteps of Dr Bunche: The Congo, UN Peacekeeping, and the Use of Force." *Journal of Strategic Studies* 37, no. 5 (July 2014).

———. "United Nations Organization Mission in the Democratic Republic of the Congo (MONUC)." In *The Oxford Handbook of United Nations Peacekeeping Operations,* edited by Joachim A. Koops, Thierry Tardy, Norrie MacQueen, and Paul D. Williams. Oxford: Oxford University Press, 2015.

"DR Congo: Floribert Chebeya Killers Sentenced to Death." *BBC News,* June 23, 2011. https://www.bbc.com/news/world-africa-13895771.

Dunhelm, Vincent. "Bombardement de Bouaké: Au Coeur d'Une Affaire d'État." *Jeune Afrique,* August 4, 2017.

Dwan, Renata, and Laura Bailey. *Liberia's Governance and Economic Management Assistance Programme (GEMAP): A Joint Review by the Department of Peacekeeping Operations.* Washington, D.C.: World Bank, 2006. http://siteresources.worldbank.org/INTLICUS/Resources/DPKOWBGEMAPFINAL.pdf.

Ellis, Stephen. *The Mask of Anarchy: The Destruction of Liberia and the Religious Dimension of an African Civil War.* London: Hurst, 2007.

"Foday Sankoh." *The Economist,* August 7, 2003. https://www.economist.com/obituary/2003/08/07/foday-sankoh.

Gberie, Lansana. *A Dirty War in West Africa: The RUF and the Destruction of Sierra Leone.* Bloomington: Indiana University Press, 2005.

———. "The Special Court for Sierra Leone Rests—for Good." *Africa Renewal* 28, no. 1 (April 2014). https://www.un.org/africarenewal/magazine/april-2014/special-court-sierra-leone-rests-%E2%80%93-good.

Geneva Centre for Security Policy. *After the Fall: Leaders, Leadership, and the Challenges of Post-Conflict Peacebuilding.* Policy Paper no. 17. Geneva, 2011.

Global and Inclusive Agreement on Transition in the Democratic Republic of Congo (Pretoria Agreement). December 16, 2002. https://peacemaker.un.org/drc-agreementontransition2002.

Global Security. "Bundu dia Kongo (Kingdom of Kongo) (BDK)." https://www.globalsecurity
.org/military/world/para/bundu-dia-kongo.htm.

———. "Liberia and the League of Nations." http://www.globalsecurity.org/military
/library/report/1985/liberia_1_liberia_leagueofn.htm.

Goldstein, Joshua S. *Winning the War on War: The Decline of Armed Conflict Worldwide.* New York: Plume Penguin, 2012.

Government of the Democratic Republic of Congo and Government of the Republic of Rwanda. "Joint Communiqué on a Common Approach to End the Threat Posed to Peace and Stability in Both Countries and the Great Lakes Region." November 9, 2007. https://2001-2009.state.gov/documents/organization/112826.pdf.

Gowan, Richard. "Political Gap in Reform Agenda Leaves Questions on A4P Mechanisms." IPI Global Observatory, July 19, 2018. https://theglobalobservatory.org/2018/07/political-gap-reform-agenda-questions-a4p-mechanisms.

History Daily. "'I Shall Return': General MacArthur's Promise." *History Daily,* March 9, 2019. https://historydaily.org/i-shall-return-general-macarthurs-promise.

Hochschild, Adam. *King Leopold's Ghost: A Story of Greed, Terror, and Heroism in Colonial Africa.* New York: Mariner, 1998.

Human Rights Watch. *Killings in Kiwanja: The UN's Inability to Protect Civilians.* New York, 2008. https://www.hrw.org/report/2008/12/11/killings-kiwanja/uns-inability-protect-civilians.

———. "Problem in the Disarmament Programs in Sierra Leone and Liberia (1998–2005)." In *Youth, Poverty, and Blood: The Lethal Legacy of West Africa's Regional Warriors.* New York, 2005. https://www.hrw.org/report/2005/04/13/youth-poverty-and-blood/lethal-legacy-west-africas-regional-warriors.

———. "UN: Act to End Atrocities in Eastern Congo." December 13, 2009. https://www.hrw.org/news/2009/12/13/un-act-end-atrocities-eastern-congo.

Humphreys, Marcatan, and Jeremy Weinstein. "What the Fighters Say: A Survey of Ex-Combatants in Sierra Leone, June–August 2003." *Pride,* July 2004. http://www.columbia.edu/~mh2245/Report1_BW.pdf.

Ibrahim, Mo, and Alan Doss. "Congo's Election: A Defeat for Democracy, a Disaster for the People." *The Guardian,* February 9, 2019. https://www.theguardian.com/global-development/2019/feb/09/democratic-republic-of-the-congo-election-a-defeat-for-democracy-disaster-for-people-mo-ibrahim.

Institute for War and Peace Reporting. "Uganda: LRA Accused of Selling Food Aid." October 25, 2007. https://reliefweb.int/report/uganda/uganda-lra-accused-selling-food-aid.

International Forum for the Challenges of Peace Operations. *Considerations for Mission Leadership in United Nations Peacekeeping Operations.* Stockholm: International Forum for the Challenges of Peace Operations, 2010.

International Monetary Fund. *Liberia: Selected Issues and Statistical Appendix.* Country Report no. 05/167. Washington, D.C., 2005. https://www.imf.org/external/pubs/ft/scr/2005/cr05167.pdf.

Interpeace. "About Us." https://www.interpeace.org/who-we-are/about-us.

Jennings, Kathleen. "UNOMIL." In *The Oxford Handbook of United Nations Peacekeeping Operations,* edited by Joachim A. Koops, Thierry Tardy, Norrie MacQueen, and Paul D. Williams. Oxford: Oxford University Press, 2015.

Johnson, Yomi. *The Rise and Fall of President Samuel K. Doe: A Time to Heal and Rebuild Liberia.* Lagos: Soma, 2003.

Kalb, Madeleine. *The Congo Cables: The Cold War in Africa—From Eisenhower to Kennedy.* London: Macmillan, 1982.

Kaldor, Mary, and James Vincent. *Evaluation of UNDP Assistance to Conflict-Affected Countries—Case Study: Sierra Leone.* New York: United Nations Development Programme, 2006. http://web.undp.org/evaluation/documents/thematic/conflict/SierraLeone.pdf.

Kanyunyu, John, and Joe Bavier. "Congo Rebel Leader Nkunda Arrested in Rwanda." *Reuters,* January 23, 2009. https://www.reuters.com/article/us-congo-democratic-nkunda-idUSTRE50M14N20090123.

Kennedy, Kevin S., and Laura Powers. "Senior Leadership Training in UN Peace Operations." International Peace Institute, February 2019. https://www.ipinst.org/wp-content/uploads/2019/02/1902_Senior-Leadership-Training.pdf.

Kofi Annan Foundation and International Center for Transitional Justice. *Challenging the Conventional: Can Truth Commissions Strengthen Peace Processes?* Geneva, 2014.

Kofi Annan Foundation and Interpeace. *Challenging the Conventional: Making Post-Violence Reconciliation Succeed.* Geneva, 2018.

Kristof, Nicholas. "The World Capital of Killing." *New York Times,* February 6, 2010. https://www.nytimes.com/2010/02/07/opinion/07kristof.html.

Lawrence, Cline E. *The Lord's Resistance Army.* Santa Barbara: Praeger Security International, 2013.

Lemarchand, René. *The Dynamics of Violence in Central Africa.* Philadelphia: University of Pennsylvania Press, 2009.

Leone, Faye. "Conflict Prevention Is 'The Priority,' Says UN Secretary-General." International Institute for Sustainable Development, January 12, 2017. http://sdg.iisd.org/news/conflict-prevention-is-the-priority-says-un-secretary-general.

"Liberia Country Profile." *BBC News,* January 22, 2018. https://www.bbc.com/news/world-africa-13729504.

Lynch, Colum. "U.N. to Probe Whether Iconic Secretary-General Was Assassinated." *Foreign Affairs,* August 1, 2016. https://foreignpolicy.com/2016/08/01/u-n-to-probe-whether-iconic-secretary-general-was-assassinated.

Maguire, Peter. "Cambodia and the Pitfalls of Political Justice." *International Herald Tribune,* June 20, 2011. https://www.nytimes.com/2011/06/21/opinion/21iht-edmaguire21.html.

Malvern, Linda. "United Nations Observer Mission Uganda-Rwanda (UNOMUR)" and "United Nations Assistance Mission for Rwanda I (UNAMIR I)." In *The Oxford Handbook of United Nations Peacekeeping Operations,* edited by Joachim A. Koops, Thierry Tardy, Norrie MacQueen, and Paul D. Williams. Oxford: Oxford University Press, 2015.

Mamiya, Ralph. *Protection of Civilians and Political Strategies.* New York: International Peace Institute, 2018. https://www.ipinst.org/2018/05/protection-of-civilians-and-political-strategies.

Mengisteab, Kidane, and Cyril Daddieh. *State Building and Democratization in Africa: Faith, Hope, and Realities.* Westport: Praeger, 1999.

Meredith, Martin. *The Fortunes of Africa: A 5000-Year History of Wealth, Greed, and Endeavor.* New York: Simon and Schuster, 2014.

The New Oxford Annotated Bible. Edited by Michael D. Coogan, Marc Z. Brettler, and Carol A. Newsom. Oxford: Oxford University Press, 2007.

Novosseloff, Alexandra. "Chapitre VII et Maintien de la Paix: Une Ambiguïté à Déconstruire." *Bulletin du Mantien de la Paix* no. 100 (October 2010). http://www.operationspaix.net/DATA/BULLETINPAIX/5.pdf.

———. "No Caveats, Please? Breaking a Myth in UN Peace Operations." *Global Peace Operations Review,* September 12, 2016. https://peaceoperationsreview.org/thematic-essays/no-caveats-please-breaking-a-myth-in-un-peace-operations.

———. "ONUCI." In *The Oxford Handbook of United Nations Peacekeeping Operations,* edited by Joachim A. Koops, Thierry Tardy, Norrie MacQueen, and Paul D. Williams. Oxford: Oxford University Press, 2015.

O'Brien, Conor Cruise. *To Katanga and Back: A UN Case History.* New York: Simon and Schuster, 1962.

Office of the High Commissioner for Human Rights and United Nations Organization Mission in the Democratic Republic of the Congo. *Consolidated Report on Investigations Conducted by the United Nations Joint Human Rights Office (UNJHRO) into Grave Human Rights Abuses Committed in Kiwanja, North Kivu, in November 2008.* New York, 2009.

Olonisakin, Funmi. "United Nations Observer Mission in Sierra Leone (UNOMSIL)." In *The Oxford Handbook of the Use of Force in International Law,* edited by Marc Weiler. Oxford: Oxford University Press, 2015.

Peace, Security, and Cooperation Framework for the Democratic Republic of the Congo and the Region. February 24, 2013. https://peacemaker.un.org/drc-framework-agreement2013.

Peters, Gerhard, and John T. Woolley. "George Bush, Remarks Following Discussions with President Mobutu Sese Seko of Zaire." American Presidency Project, June 29, 1989. https://www.presidency.ucsb.edu/node/263537.

Prunier, Gérard. *Africa's World War: Congo, the Rwandan Genocide, and the Making of Continental Catastrophe.* Oxford: Oxford University Press 2009.

Renton, David, David Seddon, and Leo Zeilig. *The Congo: Plunder and Resistance.* London: Zed, 2006.

Rich, Paul B. "The Death of Dag Hammarskjöld, the Congolese Civil War, and Decolonisation in Africa, 1960–5." *Small Wars & Insurgencies* 23, no. 2 (2012).

Romano, Cesare P. R., and André Nollkaemper. "The Arrest Warrant Against the Liberian President, Charles Taylor." *American Society of International Law* 8, no. 16 (June 2003). http://www.asil.org/insights/volume/8/issue/16/arrest-warrant-against-liberian -president-charles-taylor.

Rosling, Hans, Anna Rosling Rönnlund, and Ola Rosling. *Factfulness: Ten Reasons We're Wrong About the World—and Why Things Are Better Than You Think.* New York: Flatiron, 2018.

Seelow, Soren. "Côte d'Ivoire: Les Ingrédients de la Crise." *Le Monde Afrique,* December 3, 2010. https://www.lemonde.fr/afrique/article/2010/12/03/cote-d-ivoire-les -ingredients-de-la-crise_1448699_3212.html.

Shanker, Thom. "Defense Secretary Warns NATO of 'Dim' Future." *International Herald Tribune,* June 10, 2011. https://www.nytimes.com/2011/06/11/world/europe/11gates.html.

Sheeran, Scott. "The Use of Force in United Nations Peacekeeping Operations." In *The Oxford Handbook of the Use of Force in International Law,* edited by Marc Weiler. Oxford: Oxford University Press, 2015.

Sidibé, Doudou. "Peace Processes in Côte d'Ivoire: Democracy and Challenges of Consolidating Peace After the Post-Electoral Crisis." Accord Conference, Paper Issue no. 1, 2013. https://www.accord.org.za/publication/peace-processes-cote-divoire.

"Sierra Leone: Disarmament and Rehabilitation Completed After Five Years." *New Humanitarian,* February 4, 2004. http://www.irinnews.org/news/2004/02/04/disarmament -and-rehabilation-completed-after-five-years.

"Sierra Leone: National Recovery Strategy (2002–2003)." October 2002. https://www .refworld.org/docid/5b430d154.html.

Soares de Oliveira, Ricardo. *Magnificent and Beggar Land: Angola Since the Civil War.* London: Hurst, 2015.

Stewart, Frances. "Lecture on Inequalities and Conflict." Lecture, Bradford University, England, October 20, 2009. https://www.academia.edu/28567701/Horizontal_Inequalities _and_Conflict.

Tardy, Thierry. "The UN and the Use of Force: A Marriage Against Nature." *Security Dialogue* 38, no. 1 (March 2007).

Thomson Reuters Foundation. "Peace Now up to Ivory Coast Leaders—Mediator." August 31, 2005. https://reliefweb.int/report/c%C3%B4te-divoire/peace-now-ivory -coast-leaders-mediator.

Toe, Aloysius J. "Liberia's GDP Paradox: Looking Beyond the 'Fastest Growing Economy' Public Relations." *The Perspective,* May 2, 2013. https://www.theperspective .org/2013/0430201301.html.

United Nations. "Activities of Secretary-General in Democratic Republic of Congo, Rwanda, 28 February–1 March." Press release. SG/T/2658. March 10, 2009. https:// www.un.org/press/en/2009/sgt2658.doc.htm.

———. *Ceasefire Agreement* (Lusaka Agreement). S/1999/815. July 23, 1999. New York: UN Security Council. https://www.securitycouncilreport.org/un-documents /document/rol-s1999-815.php.

———. *Charter of the United Nations.* October 24, 1945. San Francisco. https://www .refworld.org/docid/3ae6b3930.html.

————. *Eighth Report of the Secretary-General on the United Nations Mission to Liberia.* S/2000/1199. December 15, 2000. New York: UN Security Council. https:// undocs.org/S/2000/1199.

————. *Identical Letters Dated 21 August 2000 from the Secretary-General to the President of the General Assembly and the President of the Security Council: Report of the Panel on United Nations Peace Operations.* A/55/305-S/2000/809. August 21, 2000. New York: UN General Assembly. https://undocs.org/A/55/305.

————. "Improving Security of United Nations Peacekeepers." New York, 2017. https://peacekeeping.un.org/sites/default/files/improving_security_of_united_nations _peacekeepers_report.pdf.

————. "Letter Dated 15 October 2002 from the Secretary-General Addressed to the President of the Security Council." S/2002/1146. October 16, 2002. New York: UN Secretary-General. http://www.pcr.uu.se/digitalAssets/96/a_96819-f_congo_20021031.pdf.

————. "Letter from the Permanent Representative of Côte d'Ivoire to the President of the Security Council of the United Nations." S/2003/1081. November 12, 2003. New York: UN Security Council. https://reliefweb.int/report/c%C3%B4te-divoire/report -secretary-general-united-nations-mission-c%C3%B4te-divoire-s20043.

————. *Report by the Secretary-General Concerning the Credentials of the Alternate Representative of Costa Rica on the Security Council.* S/2009/223. April 29, 2009. New York: UN Security Council. https://undocs.org/S/2009/223.

————. *Report of the High-Level Independent Panel on Peace Operations on Uniting Our Strengths for Peace, Politics, Partnership, and People* (HIPPO Report). A/70/95 -S/2015/446. June 17, 2015. New York: UN General Assembly and UN Security Council. https://reliefweb.int/sites/reliefweb.int/files/resources/N1518145.pdf.

————. *Report of the Independent Inquiry into the Actions of the United Nations During the 1994 Genocide in Rwanda.* S/1999/1257. December 16, 1999. New York: UN Security Council. https://peacekeeping.un.org/en/report-of-independent-inquiry -actions-of-united-nations-during-1994-genocide-rwanda-s19991257.

————. *Report of the Secretary-General on Côte d'Ivoire.* S/2003/374. March 26, 2003. New York: UN Security Council. https://documents-dds-ny.un.org/doc/UNDOC /GEN/N03/294/63/IMG/N0329463.pdf?OpenElement.

————. *Report of the Secretary-General on the Implementation of Security Council Resolution 1625 (2005) on Conflict Prevention, Particularly in Africa.* S/2008/18. January 14, 2008. New York: UN Security Council. https://undocs.org/S/2008/18.

————. *Report of the Secretary-General on the United Nations Mission in Côte d'Ivoire Submitted Pursuant to Security Council Resolution 1514 (2003) of 13 November 2003.* S/2004/3. January 6, 2004. New York: UN Security Council. https://undocs.org/S/2004/3.

————. *Report of the Secretary-General to the Security Council on the Protection of Civilians in Armed Conflict.* S/1999/957. September 8, 1999. New York: UN Security Council. https://www.securitycouncilreport.org/un-documents/document/civilians-s1999957.php.

————. *Report of the Security Council Mission to the African Union; Rwanda and the Democratic Republic of the Congo; and Liberia.* S/2009/303. June 11, 2009. New York: UN Security Council. https://www.securitycouncilreport.org/un-documents /document/liberia-s-2009-303.php.

————. *Report of the Security Council Mission to the Democratic Republic of the Congo (13 to 16 May 2010).* S/2010/288. June 30, 2010. New York: UN Security Council. https://undocs.org/S/2010/288.

————. Resolution 1181. *The Situation in Sierra Leone.* S/RES/1181. July 13, 1998. New York: UN Security Council. https://undocs.org/S/RES/1181(1998).

————. Resolution 1234. *The Situation Concerning the Democratic Republic of the Congo.* S/RES/1234. April 9, 1999. New York: UN Security Council. http://unscr .com/en/resolutions/1234.

————. Resolution 1270. *Establishment of the United Nations Mission in Sierra Leone (UNAMSIL).* S/RES/1270. October 22, 1999. New York: UN Security Council. https://www.securitycouncilreport.org/un-documents/document/sl-sres1270.php.

————. Resolution 1279. *Establishment of the UN Mission in the Democratic Republic of the Congo (MONUC)*. S/RES/1279. November 30, 1999. New York: UN Security Council. https://www.securitycouncilreport.org/un-documents/document/drc-sres1279.php.

————. Resolution 1289. *The Situation in Sierra Leone*. S/RES/1289. February 7, 2000. New York: UN Security Council. http://unscr.com/en/resolutions/1289.

————. Resolution 1479. *Establishment of the United Nations Mission in Côte d'Ivoire (MINUCI)*. S/RES/1479. May 13, 2003. New York: UN Security Council. https://www.securitycouncilreport.org/un-documents/document/cote-divoire-sres1479.php.

————. Resolution 1509. *The Situation in Liberia*. S/RES/1509. September 19, 2003. New York: UN Security Council. http://unscr.com/en/resolutions/1509.

————. Resolution 1528. *Establishment of the United Nations Operation in Côte d'Ivoire (UNOCI) for an Initial Period of Twelve Months*. S/RES/1528. February 7, 2004. New York: UN Security Council. https://www.securitycouncilreport.org/un-documents/document/chap-vii-sres-1528.php.

————. Resolution 1565. *The Situation Concerning the Democratic Republic of the Congo*. S/RES/1565. October 1, 2004. New York: UN Security Council. http://unscr.com/en/resolutions/1565.

————. Resolution 1572. *The Situation in Côte d'Ivoire*. S/RES/1572. November 15, 2004. New York: UN Security Council. http://unscr.com/en/resolutions/1572.

————. Resolution 1603. *The Situation in Côte d'Ivoire*. S/RES/1603. June 3, 2005. New York: UN Security Council. http://unscr.com/en/resolutions/1603.

————. Resolution 1633. *The Situation in Côte d'Ivoire*. S/RES/1633. October 21, 2005. New York: UN Security Council. http://unscr.com/en/resolutions/1633.

————. Resolution 1638. *The Situation in Liberia*. S/RES/1638. November 11, 2005. New York: UN Security Council. https://www.securitycouncilreport.org/un-documents/document/Liberia-SRes1638.php.

————. Resolution 1843. *The Situation Concerning the Democratic Republic of the Congo*. S/RES/1843. November 20, 2008. New York: UN Security Council. https://www.securitycouncilreport.org/un-documents/document/drc-sres-1843.php.

————. Resolution 1906. *The Situation Concerning the Democratic Republic of the Congo*. S/RES/1906. December 23, 2009. New York: UN Security Council. http://unscr.com/en/resolutions/1906.

————. Resolution 1925. *The Situation Concerning the Democratic Republic of the Congo*. S/RES/1925. May 28, 2010. New York: UN Security Council. http://unscr.com/en/resolutions/1925.

————. Resolution 1975. *The Situation in Côte d'Ivoire*. S/RES/1975. March 30, 2011. New York: UN Security Council. http://unscr.com/en/resolutions/1633.

————. Resolution 4387. *Resolution Adopted by the Security Council at Its 873rd Meeting on 13 July 1960* (calling on Belgium to withdraw its troops from Congo). S/4387. July 14, 1960. New York: UN Security Council. https://digitallibrary.un.org/record/619961.

————. Resolution 4741. *Resolution Adopted by the Security Council at Its 942nd Meeting on 20–21 February 1961*. S/4741. February 21, 1961. New York: UN Security Council. https://undocs.org/S/4741.

————. Resolution 866. *Liberia (22 Sept)*. S/RES/866. September 22, 1993. New York: UN Security Council. http://unscr.com/en/resolutions/866.

————. *Restructuring of the United Nations Peace and Security Pillar: Report of the Secretary-General*. A/75/525. October 13, 2017. New York: UN General Assembly. https://peacekeeping.un.org/sites/default/files/improving_security_of_united_nations_peacekeepers_report.pdf.

————. *Second Report of the Secretary-General on the United Nations Operation in Côte d'Ivoire*. S/2004/697. August 27, 2004. New York: UN Security Council. https://undocs.org/S/2004/697.

————. *Second Report on the Implementation of Security Council Resolution S/4387 of 14 July 1960 and S/4405 of 22 July 1960*. S/4417. August 6, 1960. New York: UN Security Council. https://digitallibrary.un.org/record/620799.

————. "Secretary-General Appoints Alan Doss As Deputy Special Representative in Sierra Leone." SG/A/765. January 30, 2001. New York: UN Secretary-General. https://www.un.org/press/en/2001/sga765.doc.htm.

————. "Security Council Commits Itself to Improving Transition, Exit Strategies for United Nations Peacekeeping Operations." SC/9860. February 12, 2010. New York: UN Security Council. https://www.un.org/press/en/2010/sc9860.doc.htm.

————. *6253rd Meeting of the Security Council.* S/PV.6253. December 23, 2009. New York: UN Security Council. https://www.securitycouncilreport.org/un-documents/document /drc-spv-6253.php.

————. *Sixth Progress Report of the Secretary-General on the United Nations Operation in Côte d'Ivoire.* S/2005/604. September 26, 2005. New York: UN Security Council. https:// www.securitycouncilreport.org/un-documents/document/cote-divoire-s2005604.php.

————. "Statement by the President of the Security Council." S/PRST/2004/17. May 25, 2004. New York: UN Security Council. https://undocs.org/S/PRST/2004/17.

————. *Third Progress Report of the Secretary-General on the United Nations Operation in Côte d'Ivoire.* S/2004/962. December 9, 2004. New York: UN Security Council. https://undocs.org/S/2004/962.

————. *Third Special Report of the Secretary-General on the United Nations Organization Mission in the Democratic Republic of the Congo.* S/2004/650. August 16, 2004. New York: UN Security Council. https://www.securitycouncilreport.org/un -documents/document/rol-s2004-650.php.

————. *Thirtieth Progress Report of the Secretary-General on the United Nations Mission in Liberia.* S/2015/620. August 13, 2015. New York: UN Security Council. https://www.securitycouncilreport.org/un-documents/document/s2015620.php.

————. *Thirtieth Report of the Secretary-General on the United Nations Organization Mission in the Democratic Republic of the Congo.* S/2009/623. December 4, 2009. New York: UN Security Council. https://www.securitycouncilreport.org/un-documents /document/drc-s2009623.php.

————. *Twenty-fourth Report of the Secretary-General on the United Nations Organiza-tion Mission in the Democratic Republic of the Congo.* S/2007/671. November 14, 2007. New York: UN Security Council. https://www.un.org/ga/search/viewm_doc .asp?symbol=S/2007/671.

————. *Twenty-fifth Report of the Secretary-General on the United Nations Organization Mission in the Democratic Republic of the Congo.* S/2008/218. April 2, 2008. New York: UN Security Council. https://www.securitycouncilreport.org/un-documents /document/DRC-S-2008–218.php.

————. *Twenty-sixth Report of the Secretary-General on the United Nations Organization Mission in the Democratic Republic of the Congo.* S/2008/433. July 3, 2008. New York: UN Security Council. https://www.securitycouncilreport.org/un-documents /document/drc-s2008433.php.

————. *Twenty-ninth Report of the Secretary-General on the United Nations Organization Mission in the Democratic Republic of the Congo.* S/2009/472. September 18, 2009. New York: UN Security Council. https://www.securitycouncilreport.org/atf/cf/%7B65BFCF9B -6D27-4E9C-8CD3-CF6E4FF96FF9%7D/DRC%20S%202009%20472.pdf.

United Nations Department of Peacekeeping Operations. *United Nations Peacekeeping Operations Principles and Guidelines.* New York, 2008. https://peacekeeping.un .org/sites/default/files/capstone_eng_0.pdf.

United Nations High Commissioner for Refugees. "UNHCR DR Congo Factsheet— April 2017." April 30, 2017. http://reliefweb.int/report/democratic-republic-congo /democratic-republic-congo-internally-displaced-persons-and-0.

United Nations Mission in Liberia. *Security Sector: An UNMIL Perspective.* Monrovia, 2006.

United Nations Mission in Liberia and Office of the High Commissioner for Human Rights. *Report of the Mapping Exercise Documenting the Most Serious Violations of Human Rights and International Humanitarian Law Committed Within the Territory of the Democratic Republic of the Congo Between March 1993 and June 2003.*

Geneva, 2010. https://www.ohchr.org/Documents/Countries/CD/DRC_MAPPING
_REPORT_FINAL_EN.pdf.
———. "Addressing Impunity for Rape in Liberia." Geneva, 2016. https://unmil.unmissions
.org/sites/default/files/impunity_report_-_binding.pdf.
United Nations Mission in Sierra Leone. "Fact Sheet 1: Disarmament, Demobilization, and
Reintegration." DPI/2412B. December 2005. New York: UN Department of Public
Information. https://peacekeeping.un.org/mission/past/unamsil/factsheet1_DDR.pdf.
United Nations Peacekeeping. "Action for Peacekeeping: Declaration of Shared Commit-
ments on UN Peacekeeping Operations." https://peacekeeping.un.org/en/action-for
-peacekeeping-a4p.
———. "Côte d'Ivoire-MINUCI-Mandate." https://peacekeeping.un.org/en/mission/past
/minuci/mandate.html.
———. "How We Are Funded." https://peacekeeping.un.org/en/how-we-are-funded.
———. "United Nations Mission in Liberia—Background." https://unmil.unmissions
.org/background.
———. "Where We Operate." http://www.un.org/en/peacekeeping/operations/current.shtml.
United Nations Peacemaker. *Linas-Marcoussis Agreement.* January 27, 2003. https://
peacemaker.un.org/cotedivoire-linasmarcousis2003.
———. *Peace Agreement Between the Government of Sierra Leone and the Revolutionary
United Front 1999* (Lomé Peace Agreement). July 7, 1999. https://peacemaker.un.org
/sites/peacemaker.un.org/files/SL_990707_LomePeaceAgreement.pdf.
———. *Pretoria Agreement on the Peace Process in Côte d'Ivoire* (Pretoria I). April 6,
2005. https://peacemaker.un.org/cotedivoire-pretoria I2005.
"Unloved for Trying to Keep the Peace." *The Economist,* April 15, 2010. http://www
.economist.com/node/15912838.
Urquhart, Brian. *A Life in War and Peace.* New York: Norton, 1991.
US Department of State. *Report of the International Commission of Inquiry into the
Existence of Slavery and Forced Labor in the Republic of Liberia.* Washington,
D.C.: Government Printing Office, 1931. https://babel.hathitrust.org/cgi/pt?id=uiug
.30112059732252&view=1up&seq=6.
———. "U.S.-Liberia Relationship." Press release. February 27, 2015. http://wanabidiiplace
.blogspot.com/2015/02/wanabidii-press-releases-us-liberia.html.
US Institute of Peace. *Comprehensive Peace Agreement Between the Government of
Liberia and the Liberians United for Reconciliation and Democracy (LURD) and
the Movement for Democracy in Liberia (MODEL) and Political Parties.* August
18, 2003. https://www.usip.org/sites/default/files/file/resources/collections/peace
_agreements/liberia_08182003.pdf.
———. *Peace Agreement Between the Government of Sierra Leone and the Revolutionary United Front of Sierra Leone 1996.* November 1, 1996. https://www.usip.org/sites
/default/files/file/resources/collections/peace_agreements/sierra_leone_11301996.pdf.
World Bank. "Sierra Leone: Disarmament, Demobilization, and Reintegration (DDR)."
Findings no. 81 (October 2002). http://documents.worldbank.org/curated/en
/955321468102883526/pdf/298850ENGLISH0Infob81.pdf.
———. *World Development Report 2011: Conflict, Security, and Development—
Overview.* Washington, D.C., 2011. http://documents.worldbank.org/curated/en
/806531468161369474/World-development-report-2011-conflict-security-and
-development-overview.
World Bank and United Nations. *Pathways for Peace: Inclusive Approaches to Prevent-
ing Violent Conflict.* Washington, D.C., 2018. https://www.pathwaysforpeace.org.
Wrong, Michela. *In the Footsteps of Mr Kurtz: Living on the Brink of Disaster in
Mobutu's Congo.* New York: HarperCollins, 2001.
Yarema, Allen E. *American Colonization Society: An Avenue to Freedom?* Lanham: University Press of America, 2006.

Index

325

About the Book

ALAN DOSS OFFERS A RARE WINDOW INTO THE REAL WORLD of UN peacekeeping missions in Côte d'Ivoire, Liberia, Sierra Leone, and the Democratic Republic of Congo.

Doss's story is one of presidents and prelates, warlords and warriors, heroes and villains, achievements and disappointments—and innocent people caught in the midst of deadly violence. As he shares his front-line experiences, he reflects on the reasons for successes and failures and on the qualities that leaders need to successfully guide efforts to rebuild peace and prosperity in devastated societies. Not least, he also considers the UN's future role in conflict prevention and peacekeeping in a climate of increasing resistance to intervention in "other people's wars."

Alan Doss served, among other peacekeeping posts in Africa, as special representative of the UN Secretary General in the DRC and Liberia and head of the UN peacekeeping missions in those countries. He is now president of the Kofi Annan Foundation.